WORLD WAR HULK
FRONT LINE

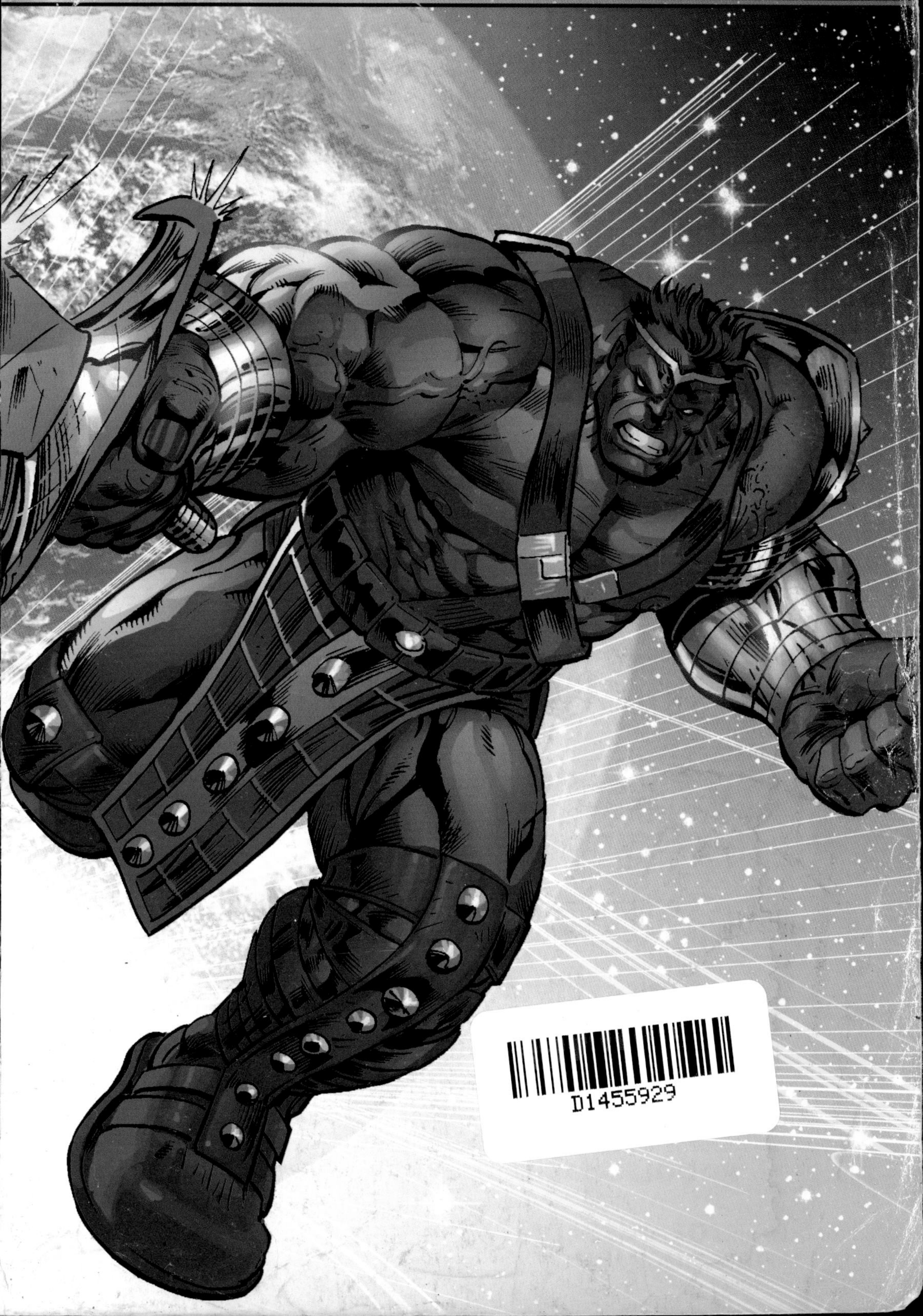

WORLD WAR HULK
FRONT LINE

WORLD WAR HULK PROLOGUE: WORLD BREAKER

Writer: **PETER DAVID**
Pencilers: **AL RIO, LEE WEEKS** & **SEAN PHILLIPS**
Inkers: **SCOTT HANNA, LEE WEEKS** & **TOM PALMER**
Colorist: **WILLIAM MURAI**
Letterer: **VC'S JOE CARAMAGNA**
Cover Artists: **JOHN ROMITA JR.,**
KLAUS JANSON & **CHRISTINA STRAIN**

Assistant Editor: **NATHAN COSBY**
Editor: **MARK PANICCIA**

WORLD WAR HULK: FRONT LINE

Writer: **PAUL JENKINS**
Artists: **RAMON BACHS** ("Embedded: Behind Enemy Lines"),
SHAWN MARTINBROUGH ("Costume Division: Death of an Android")
& **CHRIS MORENO** ("War Is Heck")
Colorists: **MATT MILLA** with **CHRIS MORENO** ("War Is Heck")
Letterer: **DAVE SHARPE**
Cover Artist: **JOHN WATSON**

Assistant Editors: **TOM BRENNAN** & **ALEJANDRO ARBONA**
Editor: **STEPHEN WACKER** & **BILL ROSEMANN**

Collection Editor: **CORY LEVINE**
Editorial Assistant: **JODY LEHEUP**
Assistant Editor: **JOHN DENNING**
Editors, Special Projects: **JENNIFER GRÜNWALD** & **MARK D. BEAZLEY**
Senior Editor, Special Projects: **JEFF YOUNGQUIST**
Senior Vice President of Sales: **DAVID GABRIEL**
Book Design: **RODOLFO MURAGUCHI**

Editor in Chief: **JOE QUESADA**
Publisher: **DAN BUCKLEY**

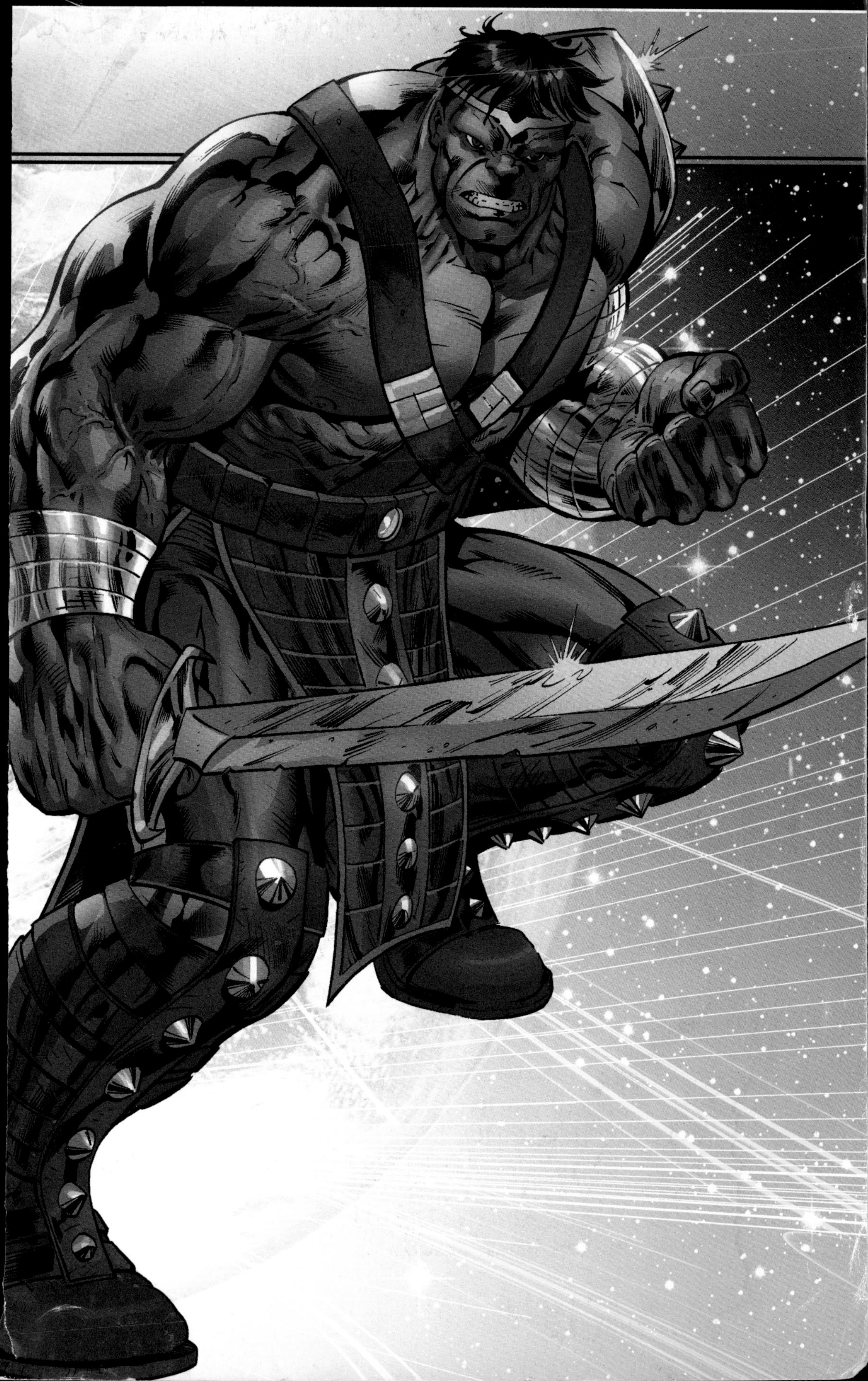

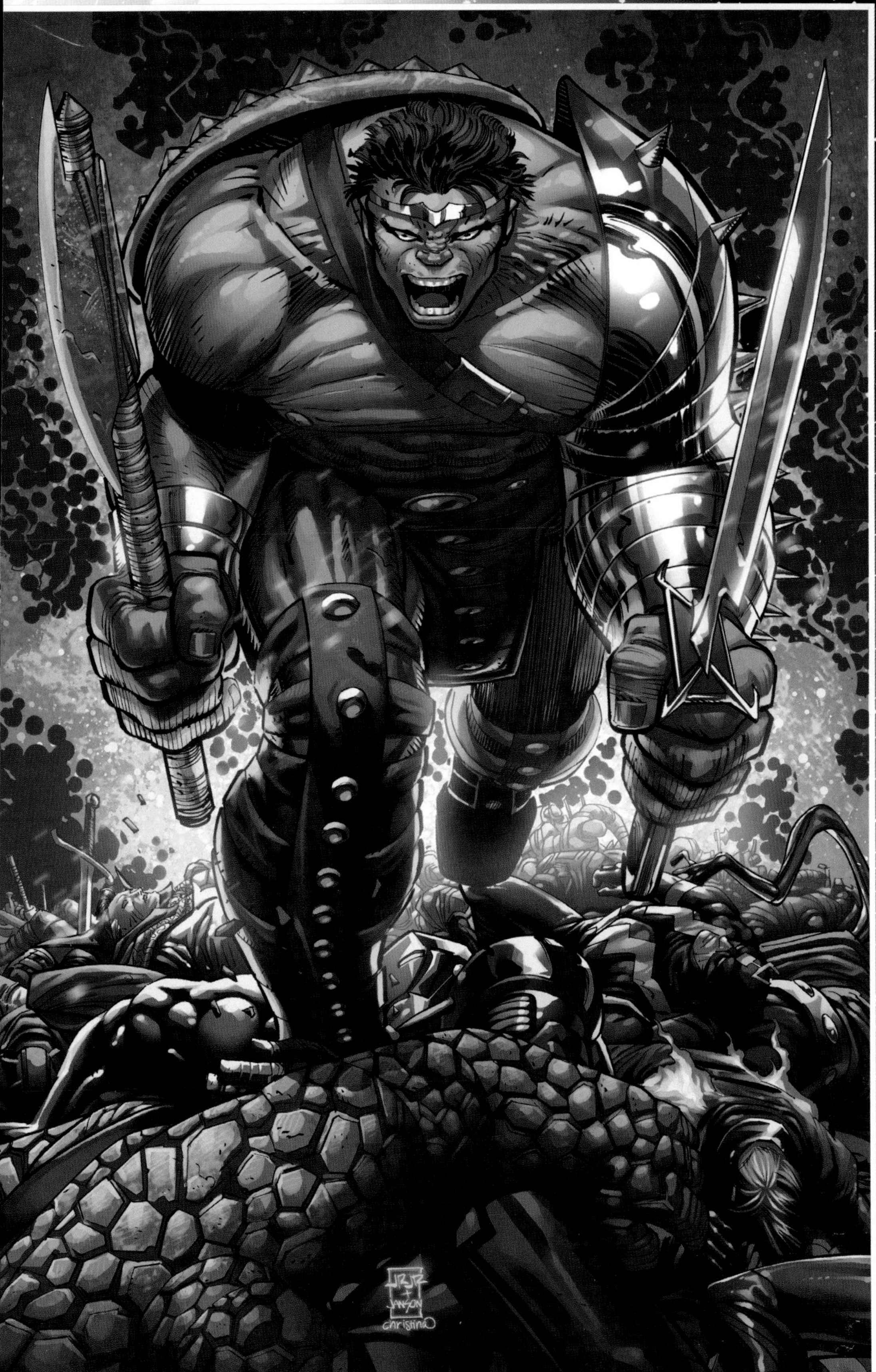

WORLD WAR HULK PROLOGUE: WORLD BREAKER

While trying to save the life of an innocent, Doctor Bruce Banner was caught in the blast of a gamma bomb and became

THE INCREDIBLE
HULK

...a rampaging monster with near-limitless power.

Fearing the threat he posed to humanity, Earth's most powerful heroes shot Hulk into space.

Landing on a faraway planet, Hulk became an Emperor and fell in love.

But the shuttle that sent Hulk away from Earth exploded, killing millions of people, including Hulk's queen and the baby growing inside of her.

Filled with rage, Hulk and his Warbound warriors have set course for Earth, to bring revenge upon those he holds responsible for destroying his world…

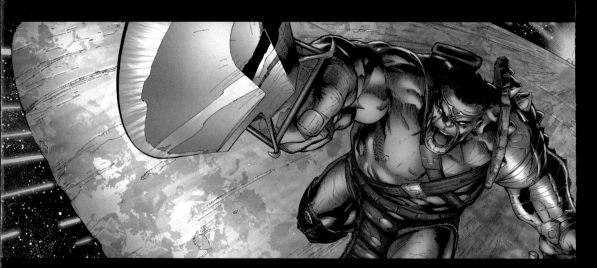

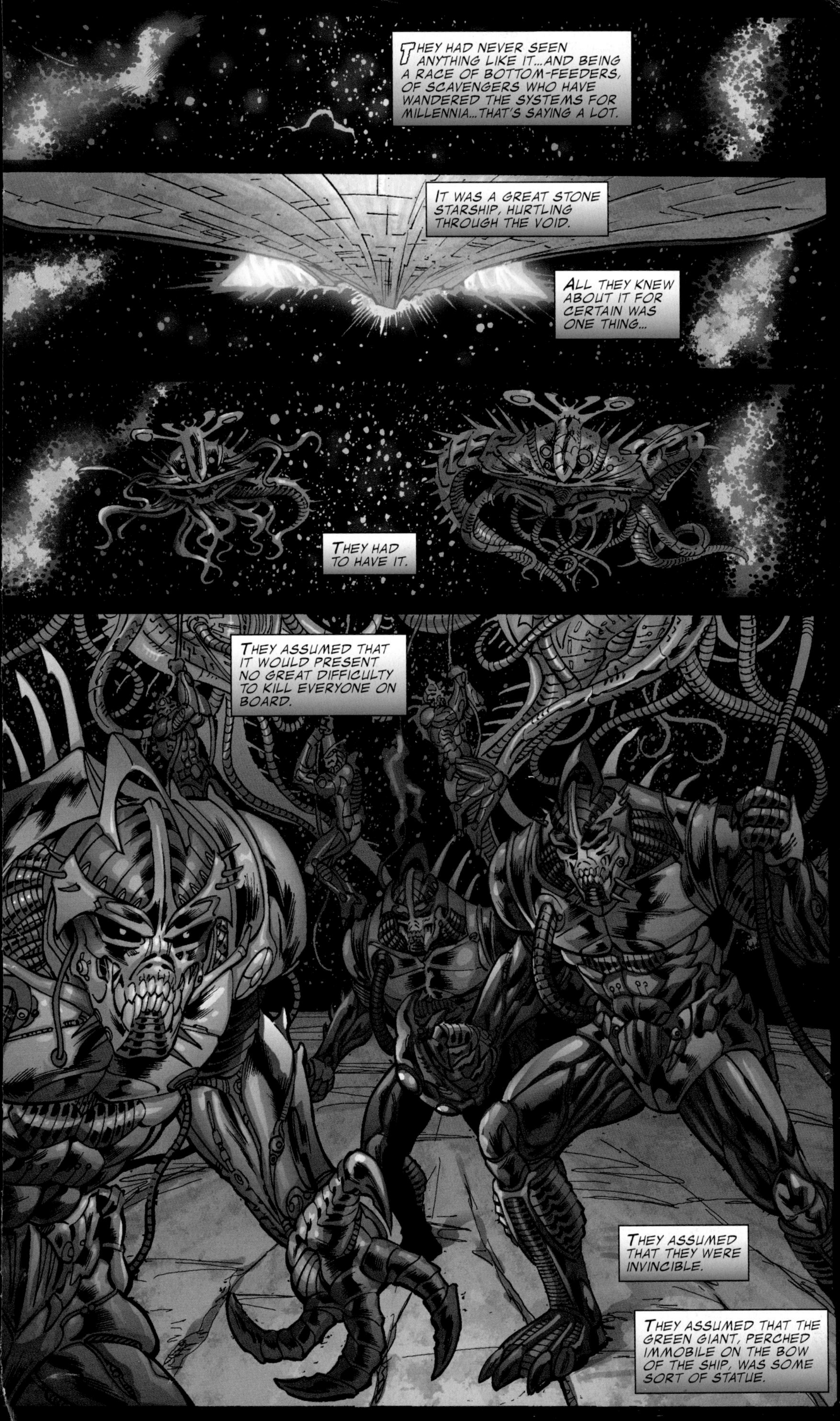
THEY HAD NEVER SEEN ANYTHING LIKE IT...AND BEING A RACE OF BOTTOM-FEEDERS, OF SCAVENGERS WHO HAVE WANDERED THE SYSTEMS FOR MILLENNIA...THAT'S SAYING A LOT.
IT WAS A GREAT STONE STARSHIP, HURTLING THROUGH THE VOID.
ALL THEY KNEW ABOUT IT FOR CERTAIN WAS ONE THING...
THEY HAD TO HAVE IT.
THEY ASSUMED THAT IT WOULD PRESENT NO GREAT DIFFICULTY TO KILL EVERYONE ON BOARD.
THEY ASSUMED THAT THEY WERE INVINCIBLE.
THEY ASSUMED THAT THE GREEN GIANT, PERCHED IMMOBILE ON THE BOW OF THE SHIP, WAS SOME SORT OF STATUE.

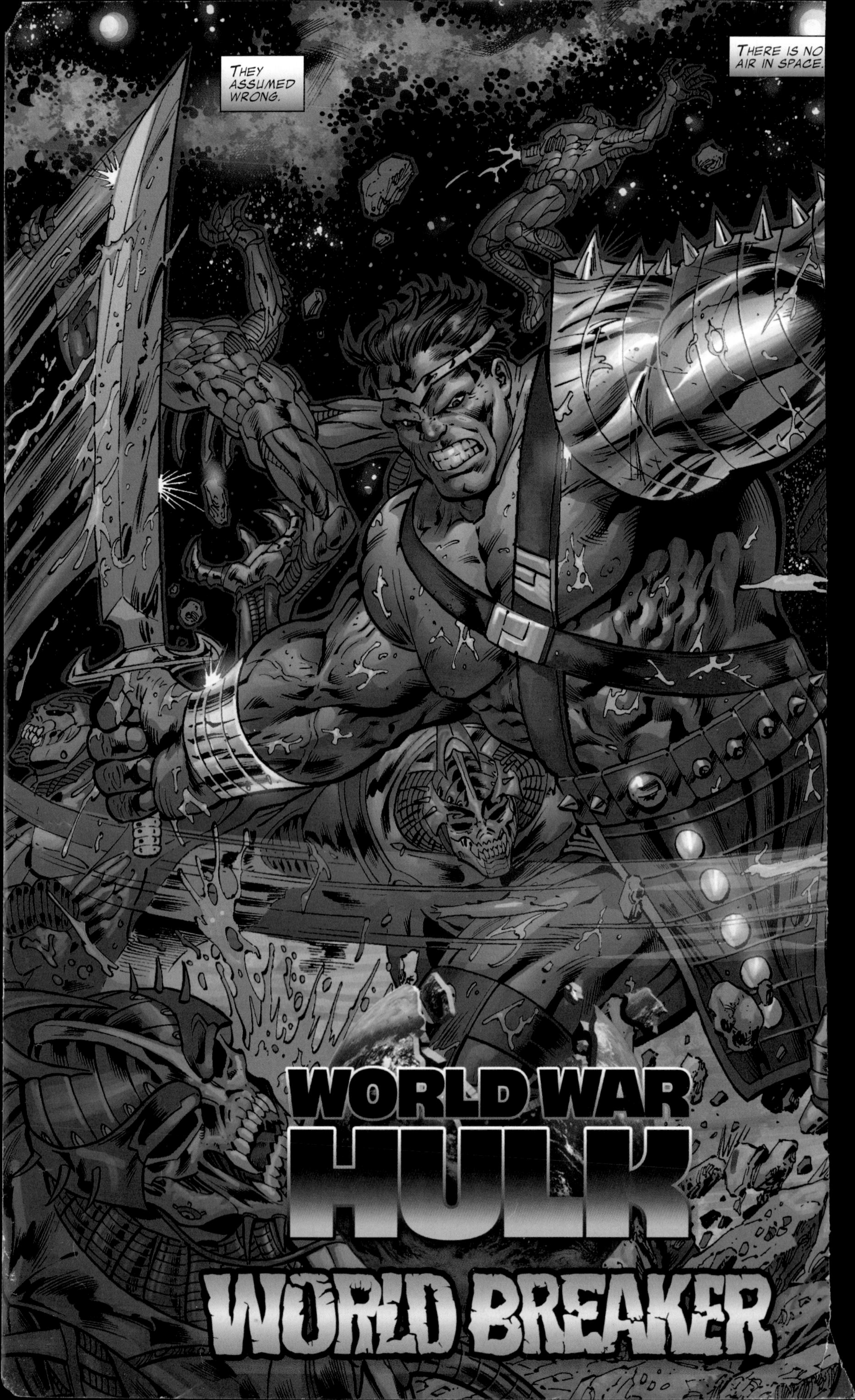
THEY ASSUMED WRONG.
THERE IS NO AIR IN SPACE.
WORLD WAR HULK
WORLD BREAKER

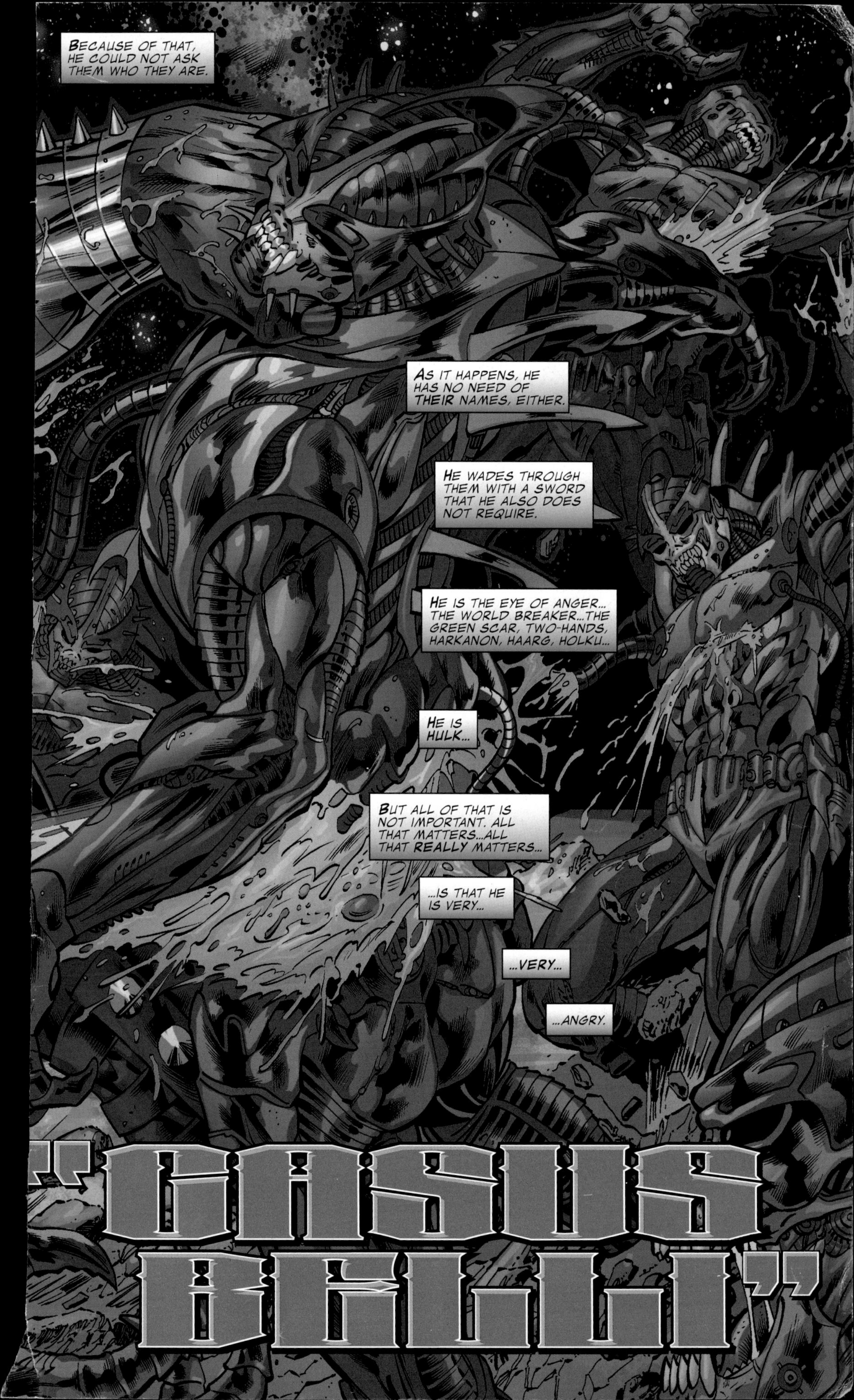
BECAUSE OF THAT, HE COULD NOT ASK THEM WHO THEY ARE.
AS IT HAPPENS, HE HAS NO NEED OF THEIR NAMES, EITHER.
HE WADES THROUGH THEM WITH A SWORD THAT HE ALSO DOES NOT REQUIRE.
HE IS THE EYE OF ANGER... THE WORLD BREAKER...THE GREEN SCAR, TWO-HANDS, HARKANON, HAARG, HOLKU...
HE IS HULK...
BUT ALL OF THAT IS NOT IMPORTANT. ALL THAT MATTERS...ALL THAT REALLY MATTERS...
...IS THAT HE IS VERY...
...VERY...
...ANGRY.
"CASUS BELLI"

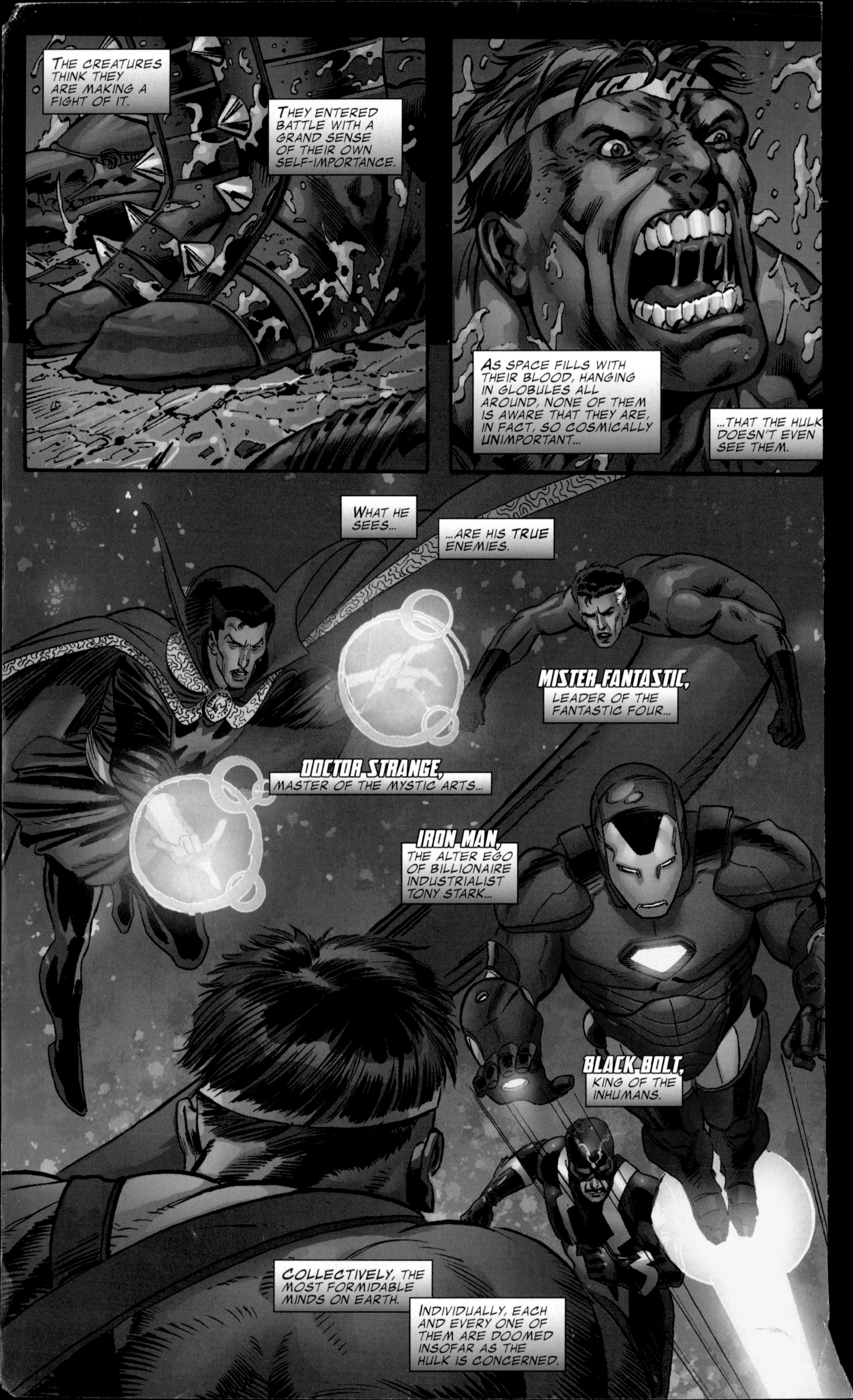
THE CREATURES THINK THEY ARE MAKING A FIGHT OF IT.
THEY ENTERED BATTLE WITH A GRAND SENSE OF THEIR OWN SELF-IMPORTANCE.
AS SPACE FILLS WITH THEIR BLOOD, HANGING IN GLOBULES ALL AROUND, NONE OF THEM IS AWARE THAT THEY ARE, IN FACT, SO COSMICALLY UNIMPORTANT...
...THAT THE HULK DOESN'T EVEN SEE THEM.
WHAT HE SEES...
...ARE HIS TRUE ENEMIES.
MISTER FANTASTIC, LEADER OF THE FANTASTIC FOUR...
DOCTOR STRANGE, MASTER OF THE MYSTIC ARTS...
IRON MAN, THE ALTER EGO OF BILLIONAIRE INDUSTRIALIST TONY STARK...
BLACK BOLT, KING OF THE INHUMANS.
COLLECTIVELY, THE MOST FORMIDABLE MINDS ON EARTH.
INDIVIDUALLY, EACH AND EVERY ONE OF THEM ARE DOOMED INSOFAR AS THE HULK IS CONCERNED.

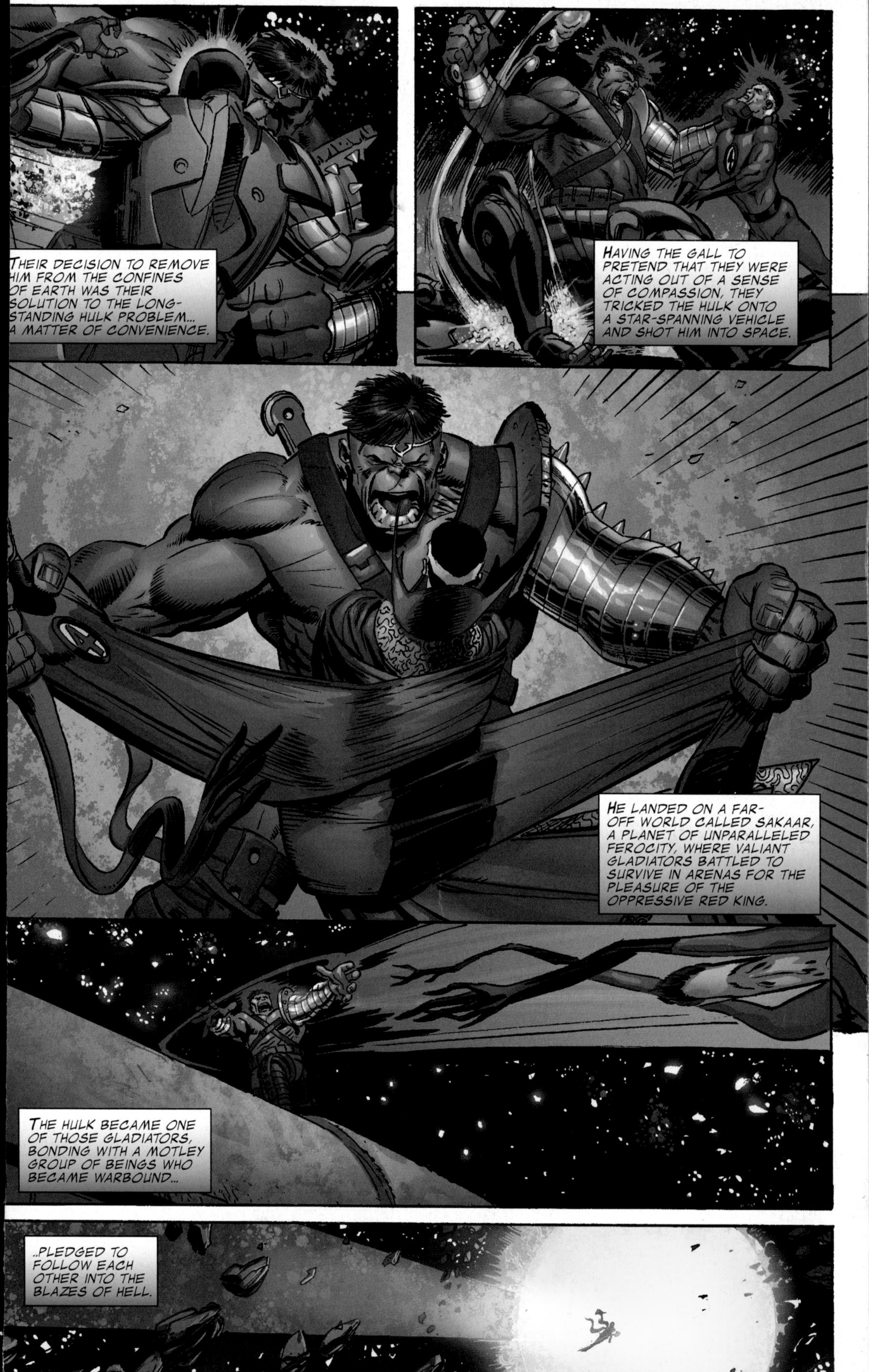
THEIR DECISION TO REMOVE HIM FROM THE CONFINES OF EARTH WAS THEIR SOLUTION TO THE LONG-STANDING HULK PROBLEM... A MATTER OF CONVENIENCE.
HAVING THE GALL TO PRETEND THAT THEY WERE ACTING OUT OF A SENSE OF COMPASSION, THEY TRICKED THE HULK ONTO A STAR-SPANNING VEHICLE AND SHOT HIM INTO SPACE.
HE LANDED ON A FAR-OFF WORLD CALLED SAKAAR, A PLANET OF UNPARALLELED FEROCITY, WHERE VALIANT GLADIATORS BATTLED TO SURVIVE IN ARENAS FOR THE PLEASURE OF THE OPPRESSIVE RED KING.
THE HULK BECAME ONE OF THOSE GLADIATORS, BONDING WITH A MOTLEY GROUP OF BEINGS WHO BECAME WARBOUND...
..PLEDGED TO FOLLOW EACH OTHER INTO THE BLAZES OF HELL.

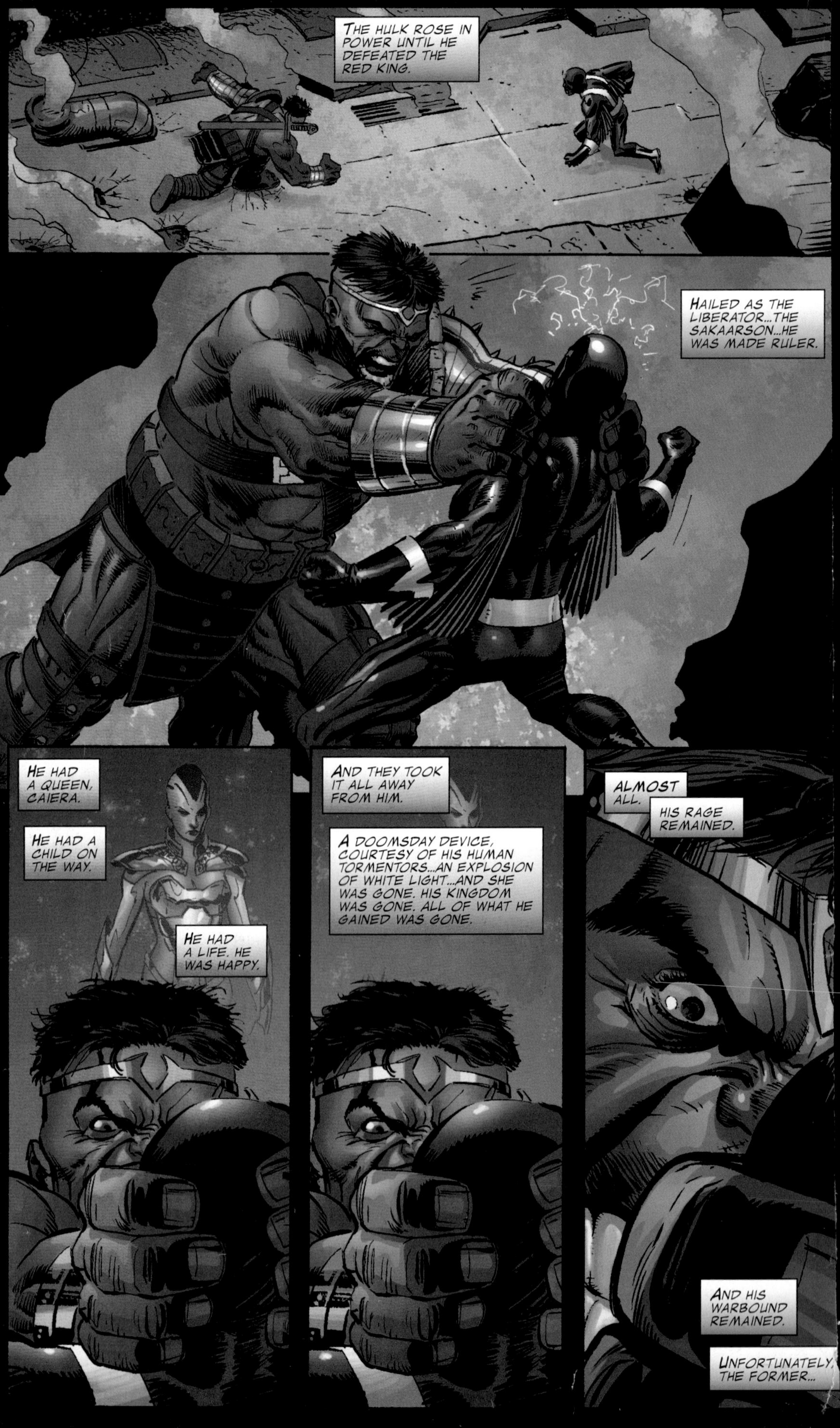
THE HULK ROSE IN POWER UNTIL HE DEFEATED THE RED KING.
HAILED AS THE LIBERATOR...THE SAKAARSON...HE WAS MADE RULER.
HE HAD A QUEEN, CAIERA.
HE HAD A CHILD ON THE WAY.
HE HAD A LIFE. HE WAS HAPPY.
AND THEY TOOK IT ALL AWAY FROM HIM.
A DOOMSDAY DEVICE, COURTESY OF HIS HUMAN TORMENTORS...AN EXPLOSION OF WHITE LIGHT...AND SHE WAS GONE. HIS KINGDOM WAS GONE. ALL OF WHAT HE GAINED WAS GONE.
ALMOST ALL.
HIS RAGE REMAINED.
AND HIS WARBOUND REMAINED.
UNFORTUNATELY, THE FORMER...

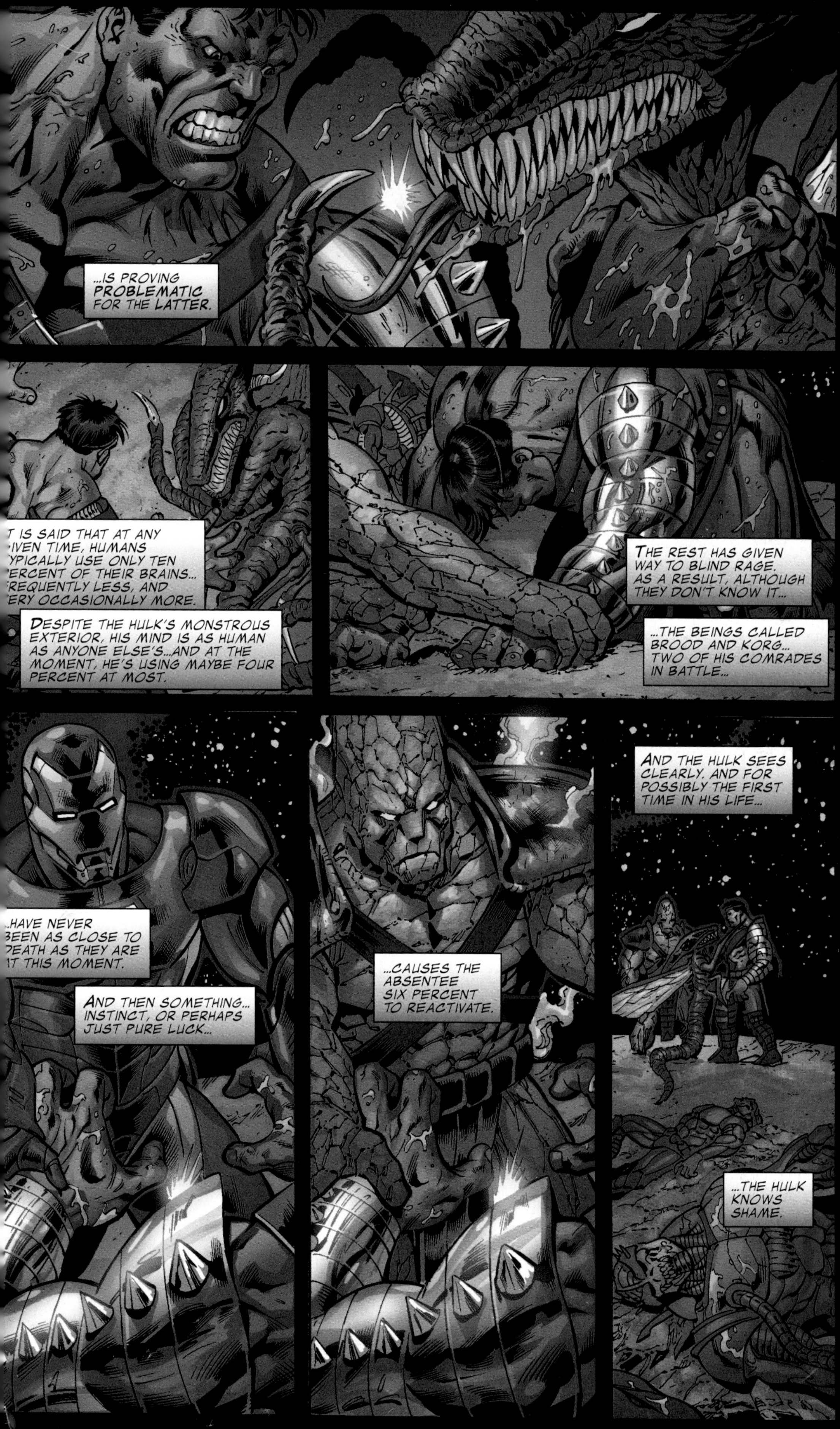
...IS PROVING PROBLEMATIC FOR THE LATTER.
T IS SAID THAT AT ANY IVEN TIME, HUMANS YPICALLY USE ONLY TEN ERCENT OF THEIR BRAINS... REQUENTLY LESS, AND ERY OCCASIONALLY MORE.
DESPITE THE HULK'S MONSTROUS EXTERIOR, HIS MIND IS AS HUMAN AS ANYONE ELSE'S...AND AT THE MOMENT, HE'S USING MAYBE FOUR PERCENT AT MOST.
THE REST HAS GIVEN WAY TO BLIND RAGE. AS A RESULT, ALTHOUGH THEY DON'T KNOW IT...
...THE BEINGS CALLED BROOD AND KORG... TWO OF HIS COMRADES IN BATTLE...
..HAVE NEVER BEEN AS CLOSE TO DEATH AS THEY ARE AT THIS MOMENT.
AND THEN SOMETHING... INSTINCT, OR PERHAPS JUST PURE LUCK...
...CAUSES THE ABSENTEE SIX PERCENT TO REACTIVATE.
AND THE HULK SEES CLEARLY. AND FOR POSSIBLY THE FIRST TIME IN HIS LIFE...
...THE HULK KNOWS SHAME.

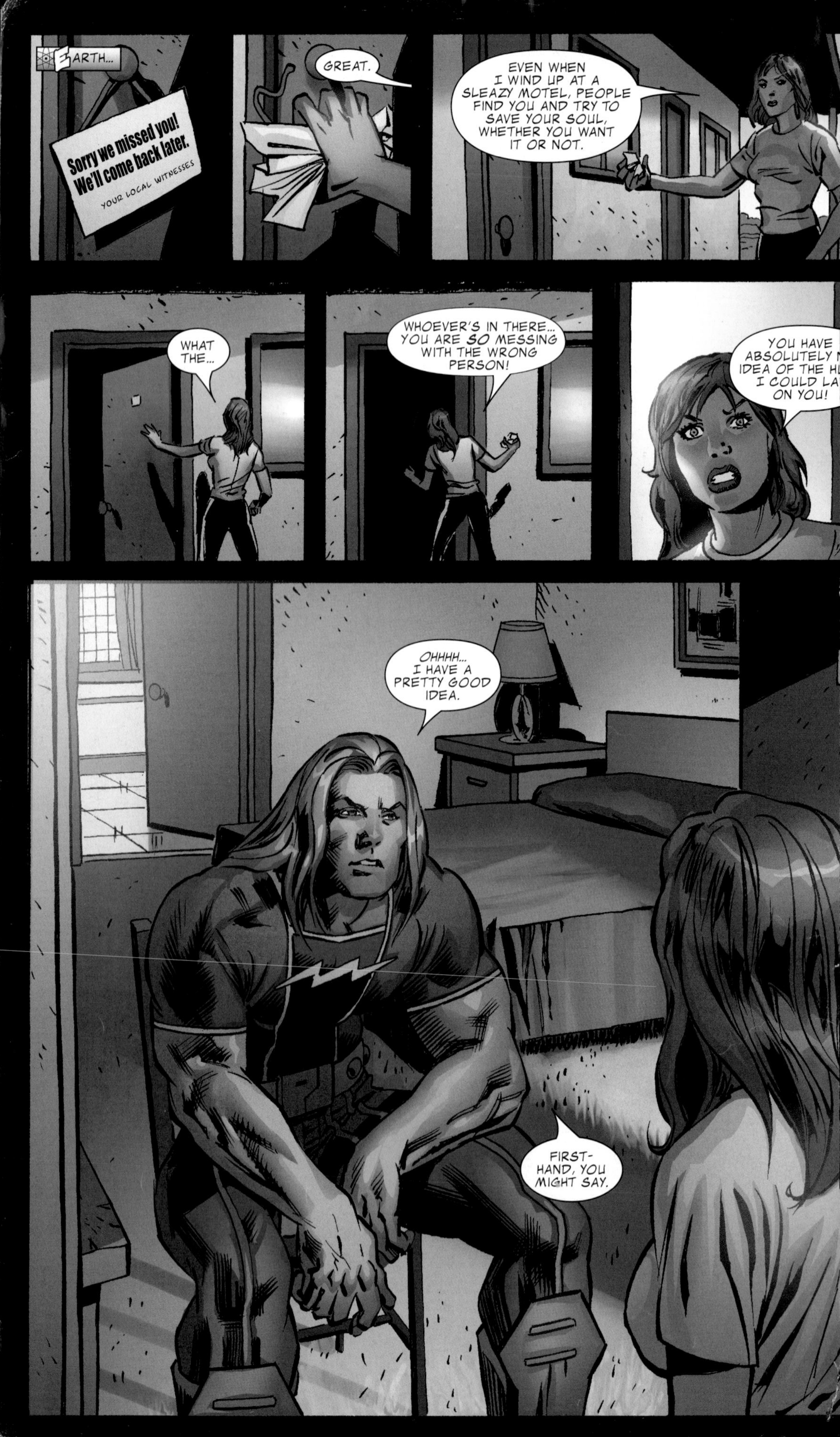
EARTH...
Sorry we missed you! We'll come back later.
YOUR LOCAL WITNESSES
GREAT.
EVEN WHEN I WIND UP AT A SLEAZY MOTEL, PEOPLE FIND YOU AND TRY TO SAVE YOUR SOUL, WHETHER YOU WANT IT OR NOT.
WHAT THE...
WHOEVER'S IN THERE... YOU ARE SO MESSING WITH THE WRONG PERSON!
YOU HAVE ABSOLUTELY N
IDEA OF THE H
I COULD LA
ON YOU!
OHHHH... I HAVE A PRETTY GOOD IDEA.
FIRST-HAND, YOU MIGHT SAY.

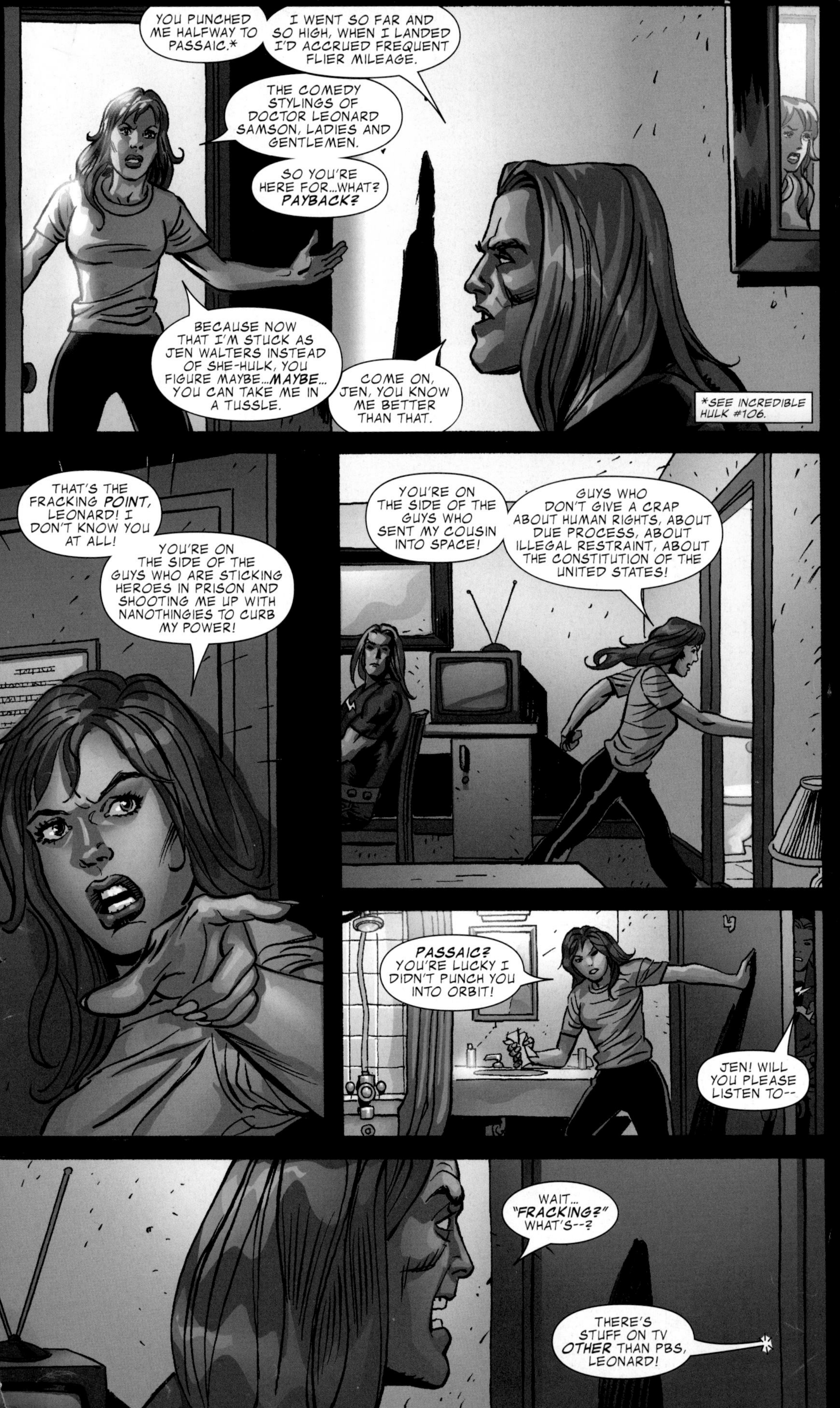
YOU PUNCHED ME HALFWAY TO PASSAIC.*
I WENT SO FAR AND SO HIGH, WHEN I LANDED I'D ACCRUED FREQUENT FLIER MILEAGE.
THE COMEDY STYLINGS OF DOCTOR LEONARD SAMSON, LADIES AND GENTLEMEN.
SO YOU'RE HERE FOR...WHAT? PAYBACK?
BECAUSE NOW THAT I'M STUCK AS JEN WALTERS INSTEAD OF SHE-HULK, YOU FIGURE MAYBE...MAYBE... YOU CAN TAKE ME IN A TUSSLE.
COME ON, JEN, YOU KNOW ME BETTER THAN THAT.
*SEE INCREDIBLE HULK #106.
THAT'S THE FRACKING POINT, LEONARD! I DON'T KNOW YOU AT ALL!
YOU'RE ON THE SIDE OF THE GUYS WHO ARE STICKING HEROES IN PRISON AND SHOOTING ME UP WITH NANOTHINGIES TO CURB MY POWER!
YOU'RE ON THE SIDE OF THE GUYS WHO SENT MY COUSIN INTO SPACE!
GUYS WHO DON'T GIVE A CRAP ABOUT HUMAN RIGHTS, ABOUT DUE PROCESS, ABOUT ILLEGAL RESTRAINT, ABOUT THE CONSTITUTION OF THE UNITED STATES!
PASSAIC? YOU'RE LUCKY I DIDN'T PUNCH YOU INTO ORBIT!
JEN! WILL YOU PLEASE LISTEN TO--
WAIT... "FRACKING?" WHAT'S--?
THERE'S STUFF ON TV OTHER THAN PBS, LEONARD!

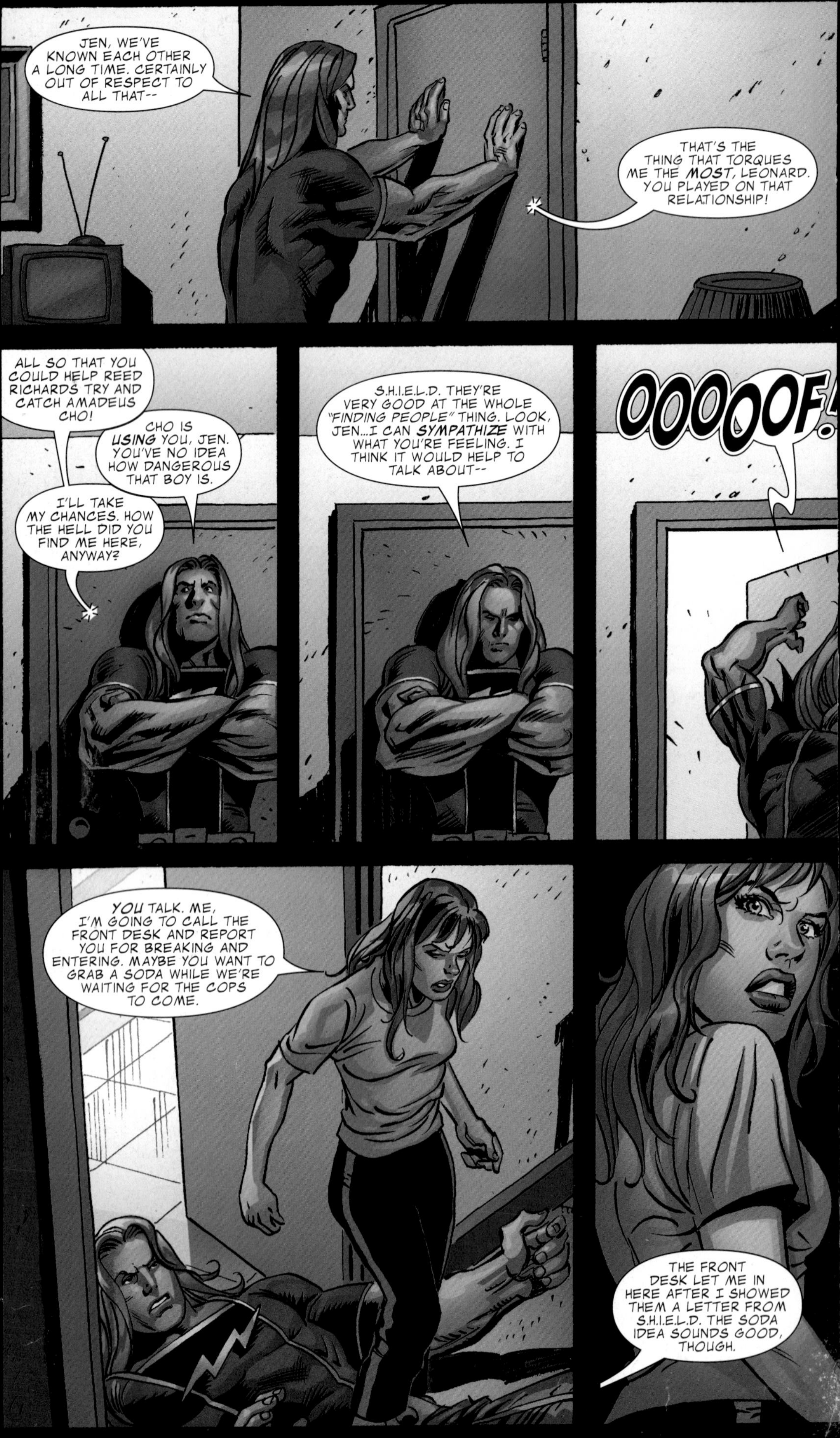

JEN, WE'VE KNOWN EACH OTHER A LONG TIME. CERTAINLY OUT OF RESPECT TO ALL THAT--
THAT'S THE THING THAT TORQUES ME THE *MOST*, LEONARD. YOU PLAYED ON THAT RELATIONSHIP!
ALL SO THAT YOU COULD HELP REED RICHARDS TRY AND CATCH AMADEUS CHO!
CHO IS *USING* YOU, JEN. YOU'VE NO IDEA HOW DANGEROUS THAT BOY IS.
I'LL TAKE MY CHANCES. HOW THE HELL DID YOU FIND ME HERE, ANYWAY?
S.H.I.E.L.D. THEY'RE VERY GOOD AT THE WHOLE *"FINDING PEOPLE"* THING. LOOK, JEN...I CAN *SYMPATHIZE* WITH WHAT YOU'RE FEELING. I THINK IT WOULD HELP TO TALK ABOUT--
OOOOOF!
YOU TALK. ME, I'M GOING TO CALL THE FRONT DESK AND REPORT YOU FOR BREAKING AND ENTERING. MAYBE YOU WANT TO GRAB A SODA WHILE WE'RE WAITING FOR THE COPS TO COME.
THE FRONT DESK LET ME IN HERE AFTER I SHOWED THEM A LETTER FROM S.H.I.E.L.D. THE SODA IDEA SOUNDS GOOD, THOUGH.

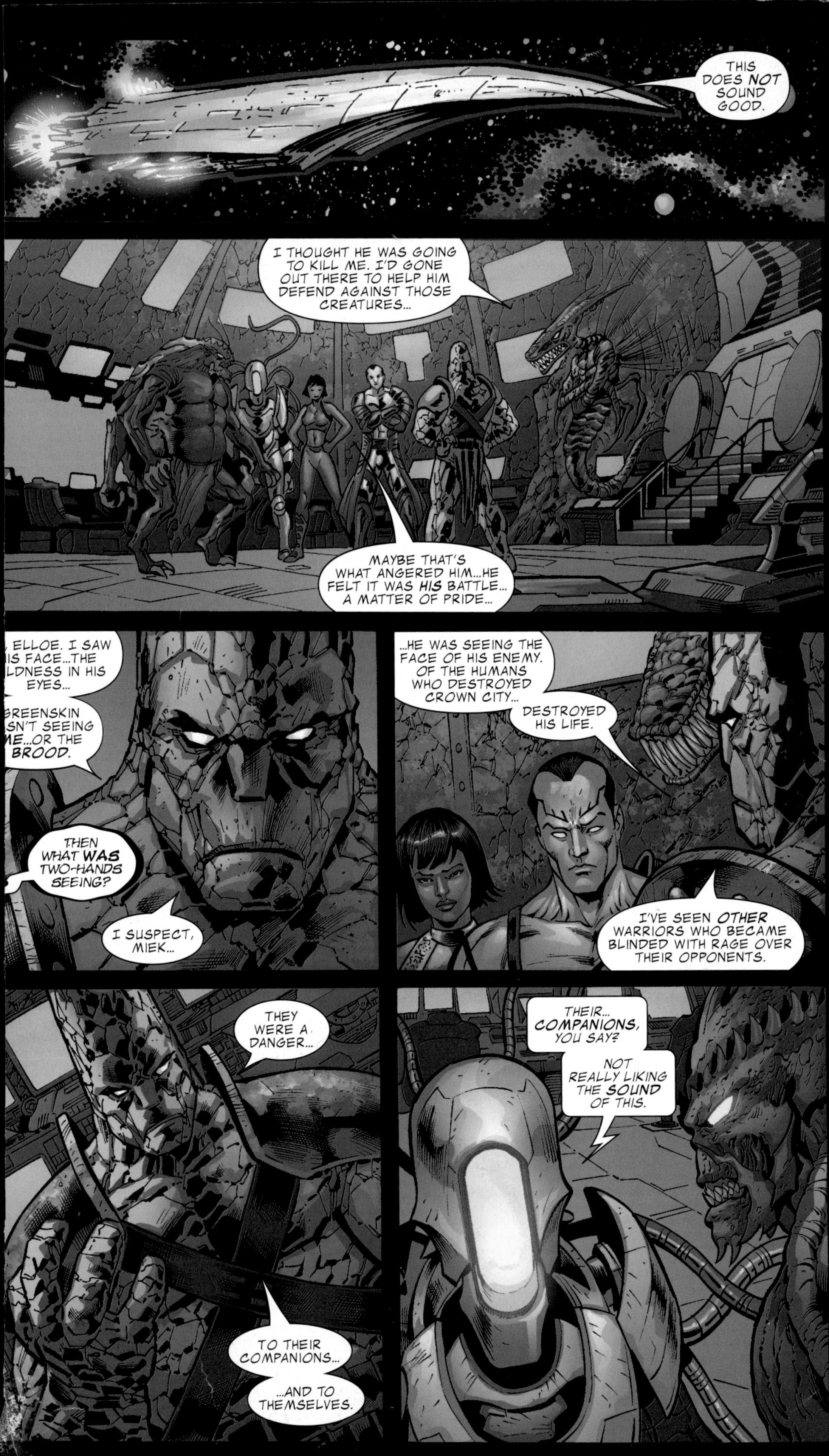
THIS DOES NOT SOUND GOOD.
I THOUGHT HE WAS GOING TO KILL ME. I'D GONE OUT THERE TO HELP HIM DEFEND AGAINST THOSE CREATURES...
MAYBE THAT'S WHAT ANGERED HIM...HE FELT IT WAS HIS BATTLE... A MATTER OF PRIDE...
, ELLOE. I SAW IS FACE...THE LDNESS IN HIS EYES...
GREENSKIN SN'T SEEING ME...OR THE BROOD.
THEN WHAT WAS TWO-HANDS SEEING?
I SUSPECT, MIEK...
...HE WAS SEEING THE FACE OF HIS ENEMY. OF THE HUMANS WHO DESTROYED CROWN CITY...
DESTROYED HIS LIFE.
I'VE SEEN OTHER WARRIORS WHO BECAME BLINDED WITH RAGE OVER THEIR OPPONENTS.
THEY WERE A DANGER...
TO THEIR COMPANIONS...
...AND TO THEMSELVES.
THEIR... COMPANIONS, YOU SAY?
NOT REALLY LIKING THE SOUND OF THIS.

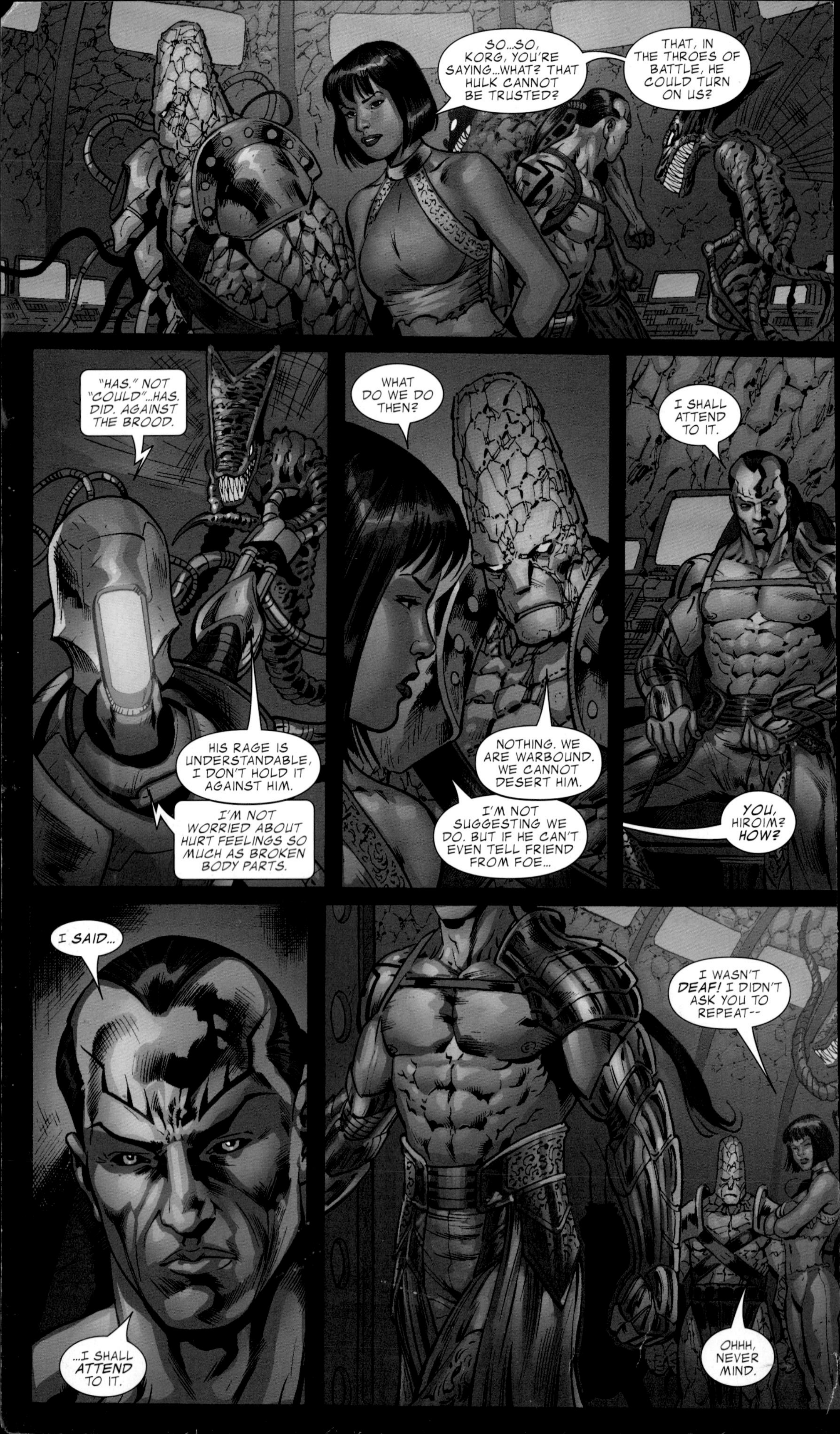
SO...SO, KORG, YOU'RE SAYING...WHAT? THAT HULK CANNOT BE TRUSTED?
THAT, IN THE THROES OF BATTLE, HE COULD TURN ON US?
"HAS." NOT "COULD"...HAS. DID. AGAINST THE BROOD.
HIS RAGE IS UNDERSTANDABLE, I DON'T HOLD IT AGAINST HIM.
I'M NOT WORRIED ABOUT HURT FEELINGS SO MUCH AS BROKEN BODY PARTS.
WHAT DO WE DO THEN?
NOTHING. WE ARE WARBOUND. WE CANNOT DESERT HIM.
I'M NOT SUGGESTING WE DO. BUT IF HE CAN'T EVEN TELL FRIEND FROM FOE...
I SHALL ATTEND TO IT.
YOU, HIROIM? HOW?
I SAID...
...I SHALL ATTEND TO IT.
I WASN'T DEAF! I DIDN'T ASK YOU TO REPEAT--
OHHH, NEVER MIND.

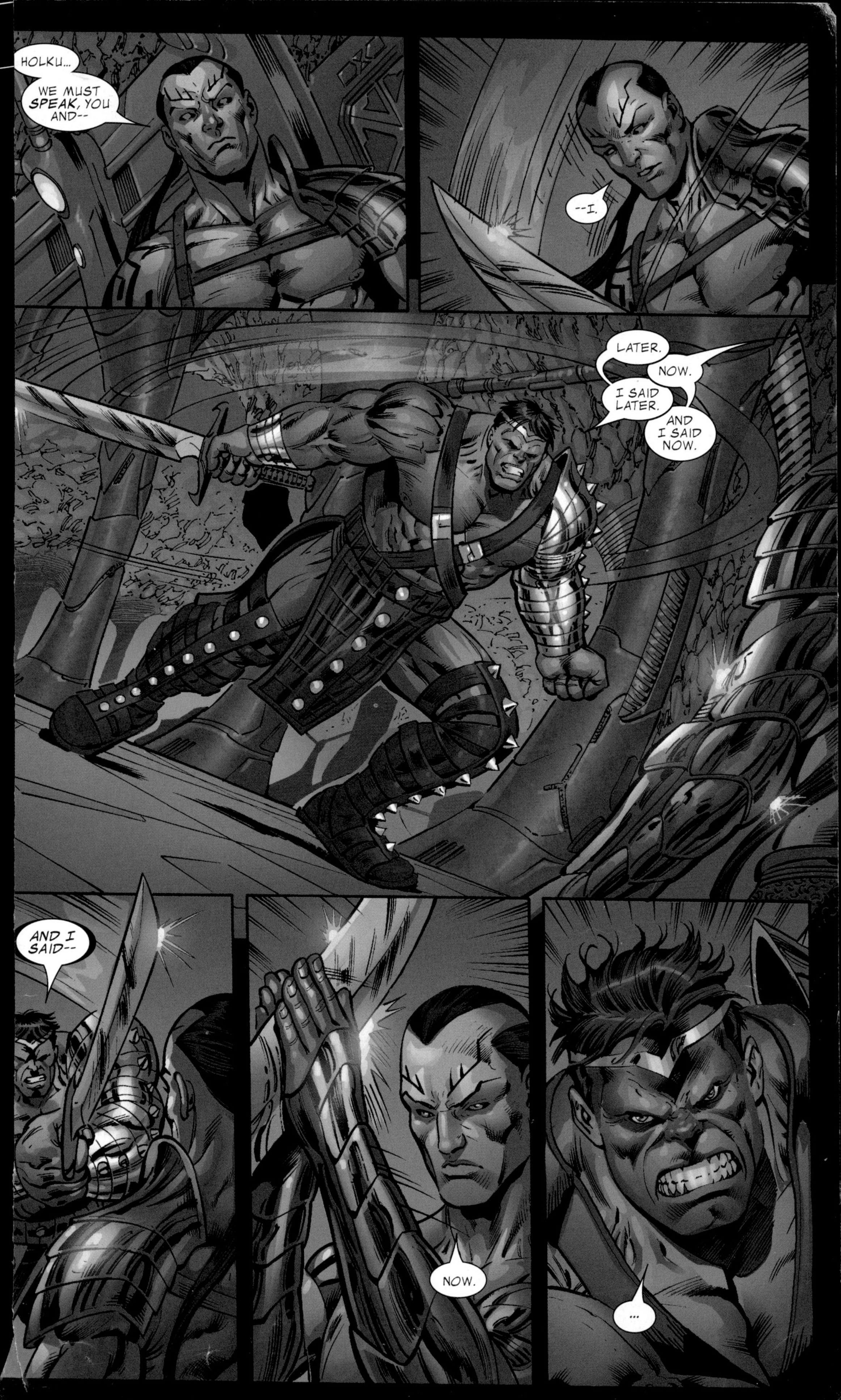
HOLKU...
WE MUST SPEAK, YOU AND--
--I.
LATER.
NOW.
I SAID LATER.
AND I SAID NOW.
AND I SAID--
NOW.
...

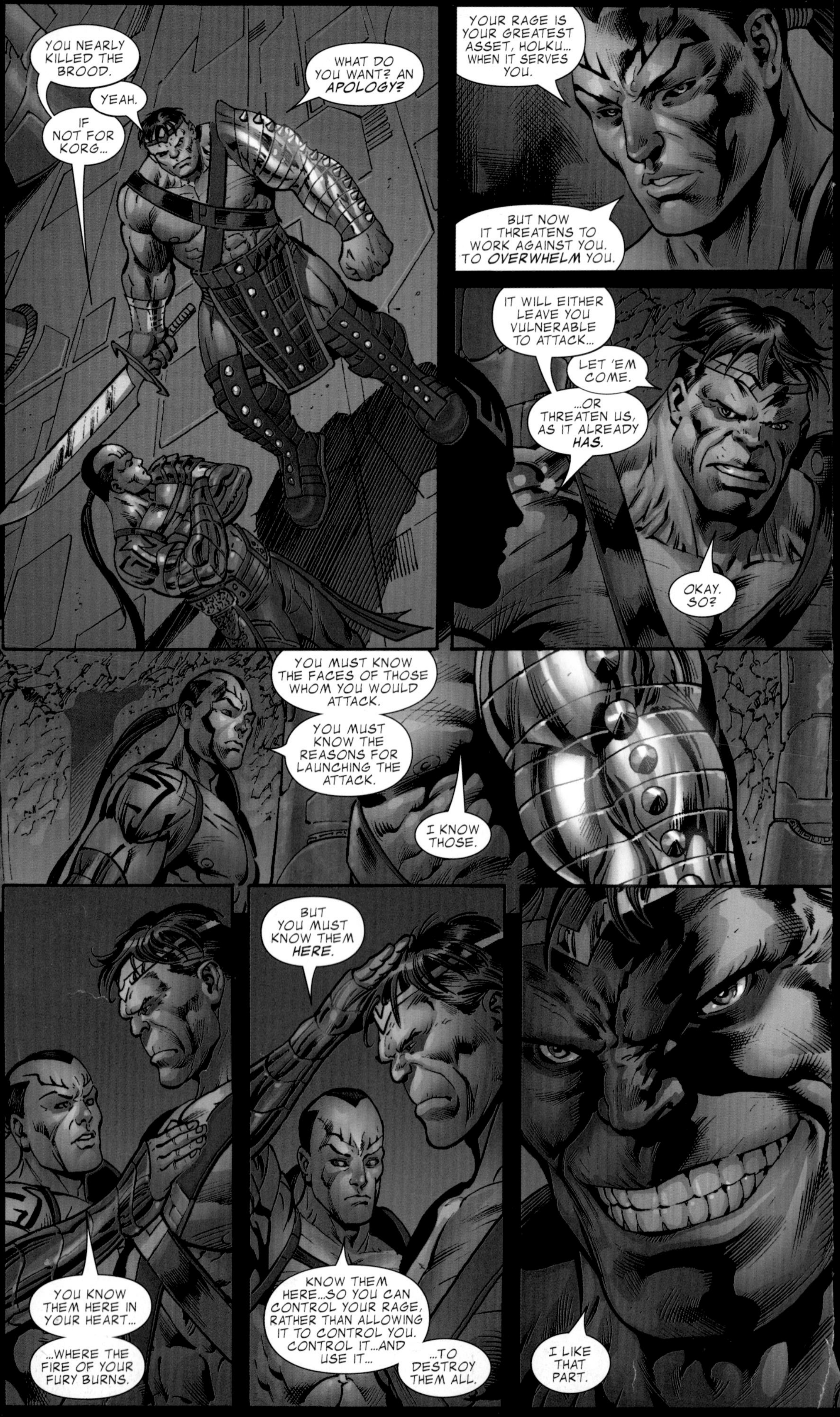

YOU NEARLY KILLED THE BROOD.
YEAH.
IF NOT FOR KORG...
WHAT DO YOU WANT? AN *APOLOGY?*
YOUR RAGE IS YOUR GREATEST ASSET, HOLKU... WHEN IT SERVES YOU.
BUT NOW IT THREATENS TO WORK AGAINST YOU. TO *OVERWHELM* YOU.
IT WILL EITHER LEAVE YOU VULNERABLE TO ATTACK...
LET 'EM COME.
...OR THREATEN US, AS IT ALREADY *HAS*.
OKAY. SO?
YOU MUST KNOW THE FACES OF THOSE WHOM YOU WOULD ATTACK.
YOU MUST KNOW THE REASONS FOR LAUNCHING THE ATTACK.
I KNOW THOSE.
YOU KNOW THEM HERE IN YOUR HEART...
...WHERE THE FIRE OF YOUR FURY BURNS.
BUT YOU MUST KNOW THEM *HERE*.
KNOW THEM HERE...SO YOU CAN CONTROL YOUR RAGE, RATHER THAN ALLOWING IT TO CONTROL YOU. CONTROL IT...AND USE IT...
...TO DESTROY THEM ALL.
I LIKE THAT PART.

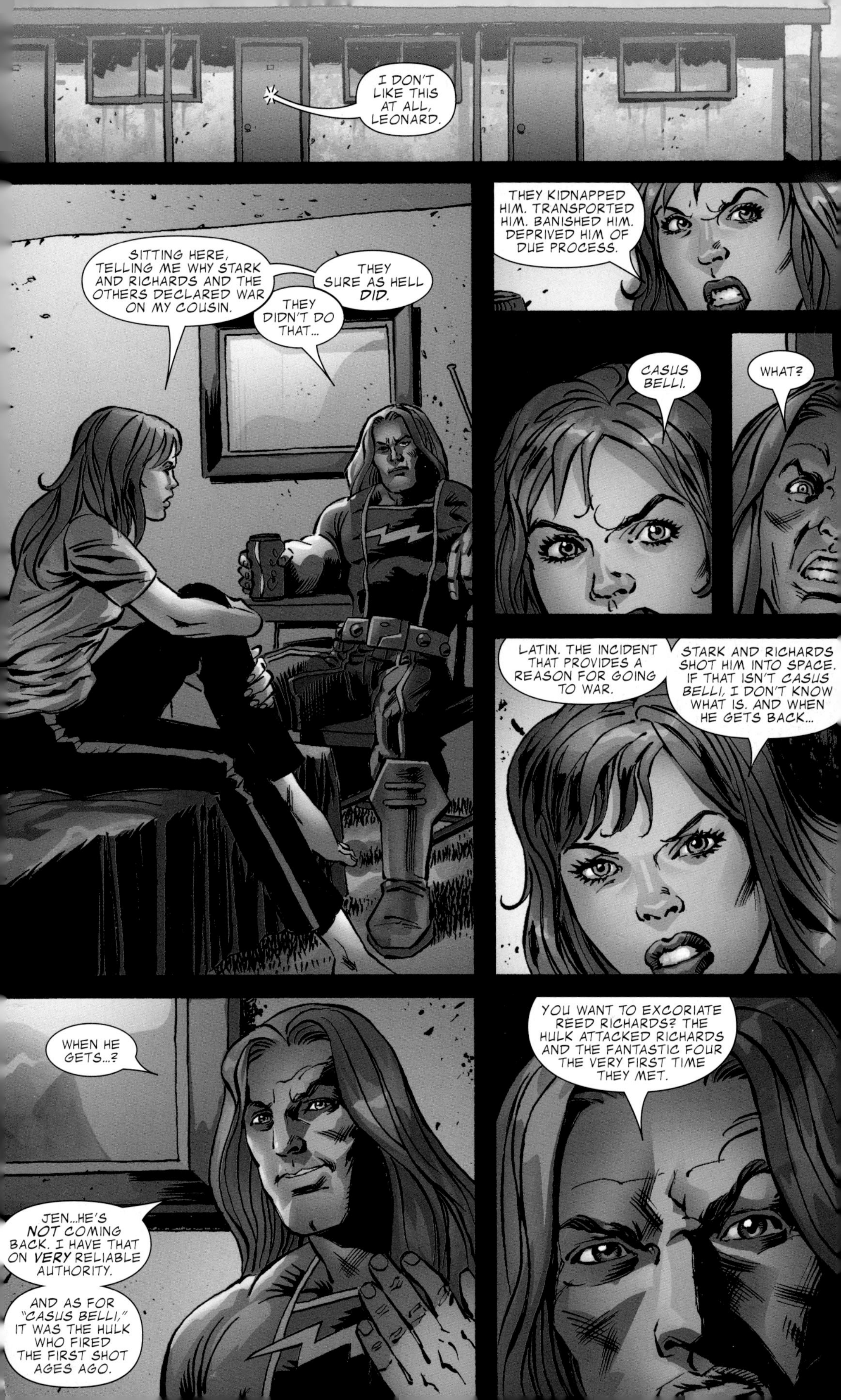

I DON'T LIKE THIS AT ALL, LEONARD.
SITTING HERE, TELLING ME WHY STARK AND RICHARDS AND THE OTHERS DECLARED WAR ON MY COUSIN.
THEY DIDN'T DO THAT...
THEY SURE AS HELL *DID*.
THEY KIDNAPPED HIM. TRANSPORTED HIM. BANISHED HIM. DEPRIVED HIM OF DUE PROCESS.
CASUS BELLI.
WHAT?
LATIN. THE INCIDENT THAT PROVIDES A REASON FOR GOING TO WAR.
STARK AND RICHARDS SHOT HIM INTO SPACE. IF THAT ISN'T *CASUS BELLI*, I DON'T KNOW WHAT IS. AND WHEN HE GETS BACK...
WHEN HE GETS...?
JEN...HE'S *NOT* COMING BACK. I HAVE THAT ON *VERY* RELIABLE AUTHORITY.
AND AS FOR "*CASUS BELLI*," IT WAS THE HULK WHO FIRED THE FIRST SHOT AGES AGO.
YOU WANT TO EXCORIATE REED RICHARDS? THE HULK ATTACKED RICHARDS AND THE FANTASTIC FOUR THE VERY FIRST TIME THEY MET.

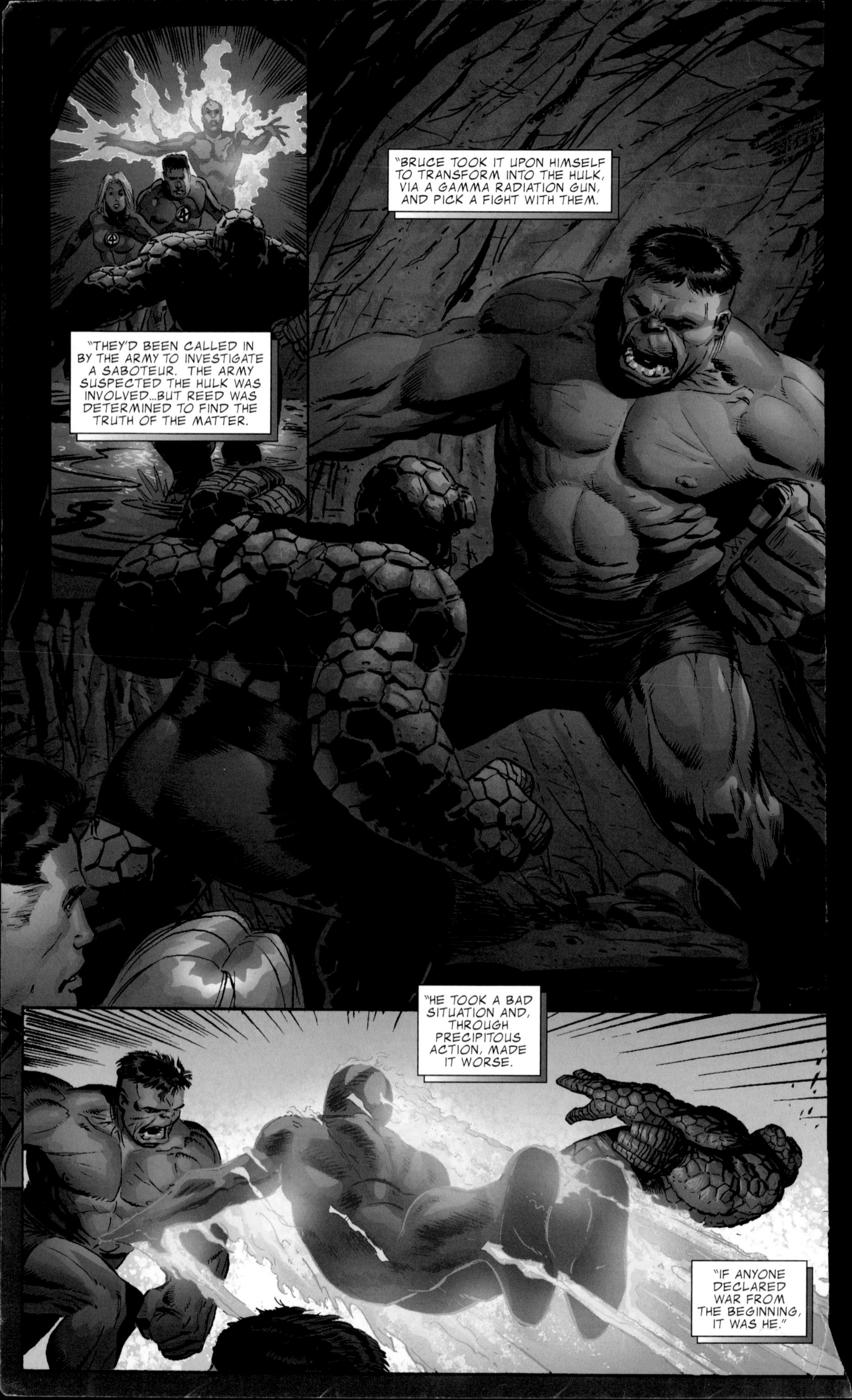
"THEY'D BEEN CALLED IN BY THE ARMY TO INVESTIGATE A SABOTEUR. THE ARMY SUSPECTED THE HULK WAS INVOLVED...BUT REED WAS DETERMINED TO FIND THE TRUTH OF THE MATTER.
"BRUCE TOOK IT UPON HIMSELF TO TRANSFORM INTO THE HULK, VIA A GAMMA RADIATION GUN, AND PICK A FIGHT WITH THEM.
"HE TOOK A BAD SITUATION AND, THROUGH PRECIPITOUS ACTION, MADE IT WORSE.
"IF ANYONE DECLARED WAR FROM THE BEGINNING, IT WAS HE."

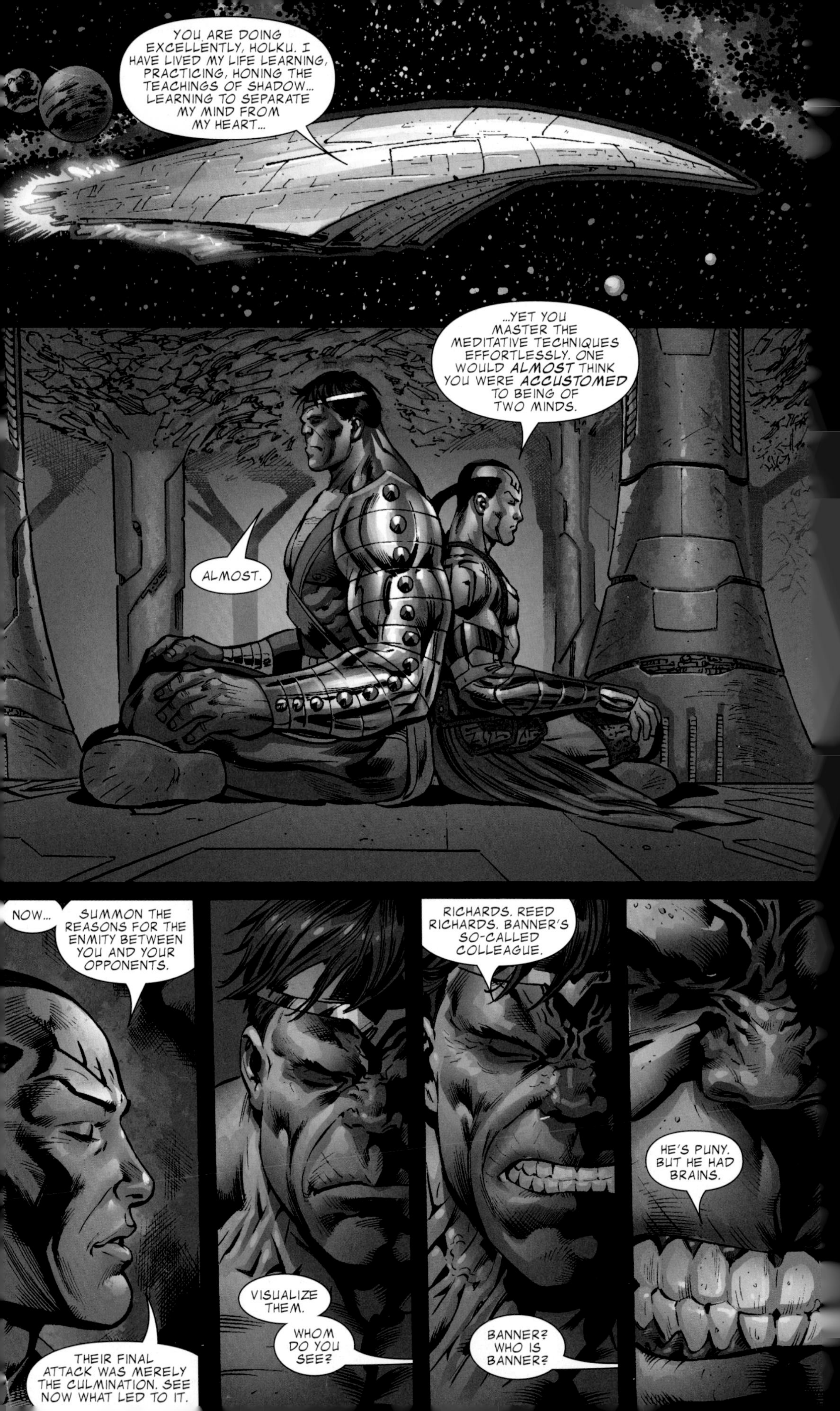

YOU ARE DOING EXCELLENTLY, HOLKU. I HAVE LIVED MY LIFE LEARNING, PRACTICING, HONING THE TEACHINGS OF SHADOW... LEARNING TO SEPARATE MY MIND FROM MY HEART...
...YET YOU MASTER THE MEDITATIVE TECHNIQUES EFFORTLESSLY. ONE WOULD ALMOST THINK YOU WERE ACCUSTOMED TO BEING OF TWO MINDS.
ALMOST.
NOW...
SUMMON THE REASONS FOR THE ENMITY BETWEEN YOU AND YOUR OPPONENTS.
THEIR FINAL ATTACK WAS MERELY THE CULMINATION. SEE NOW WHAT LED TO IT.
VISUALIZE THEM.
WHOM DO YOU SEE?
RICHARDS. REED RICHARDS. BANNER'S SO-CALLED COLLEAGUE.
BANNER? WHO IS BANNER?
HE'S PUNY. BUT HE HAD BRAINS.

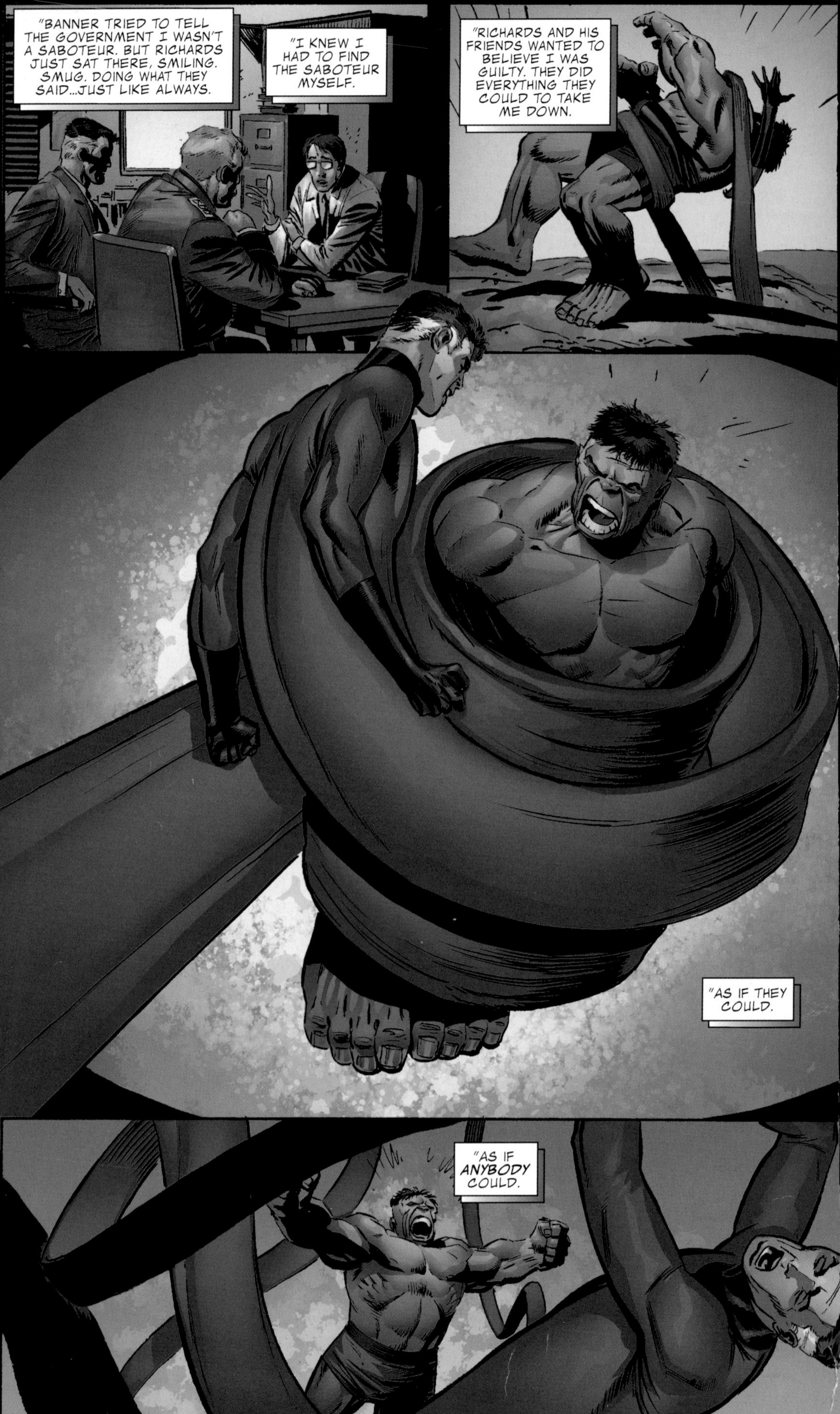
"BANNER TRIED TO TELL THE GOVERNMENT I WASN'T A SABOTEUR. BUT RICHARDS JUST SAT THERE, SMILING. SMUG. DOING WHAT THEY SAID...JUST LIKE ALWAYS.
"I KNEW I HAD TO FIND THE SABOTEUR MYSELF.
"RICHARDS AND HIS FRIENDS WANTED TO BELIEVE I WAS GUILTY. THEY DID EVERYTHING THEY COULD TO TAKE ME DOWN.
"AS IF THEY COULD.
"AS IF ANYBODY COULD.

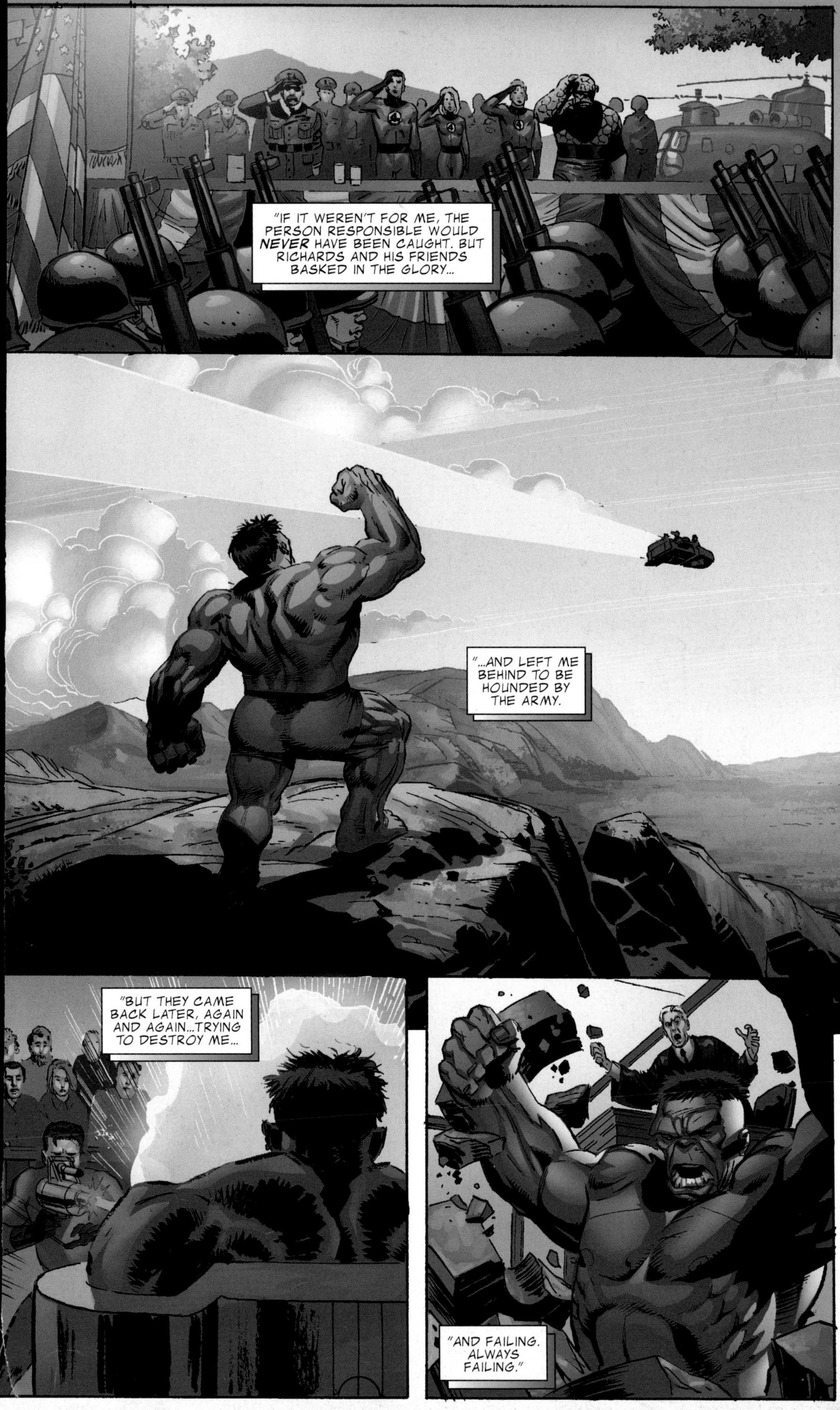
"IF IT WEREN'T FOR ME, THE PERSON RESPONSIBLE WOULD NEVER HAVE BEEN CAUGHT. BUT RICHARDS AND HIS FRIENDS BASKED IN THE GLORY...
"...AND LEFT ME BEHIND TO BE HOUNDED BY THE ARMY.
"BUT THEY CAME BACK LATER, AGAIN AND AGAIN...TRYING TO DESTROY ME...
"AND FAILING. ALWAYS FAILING."

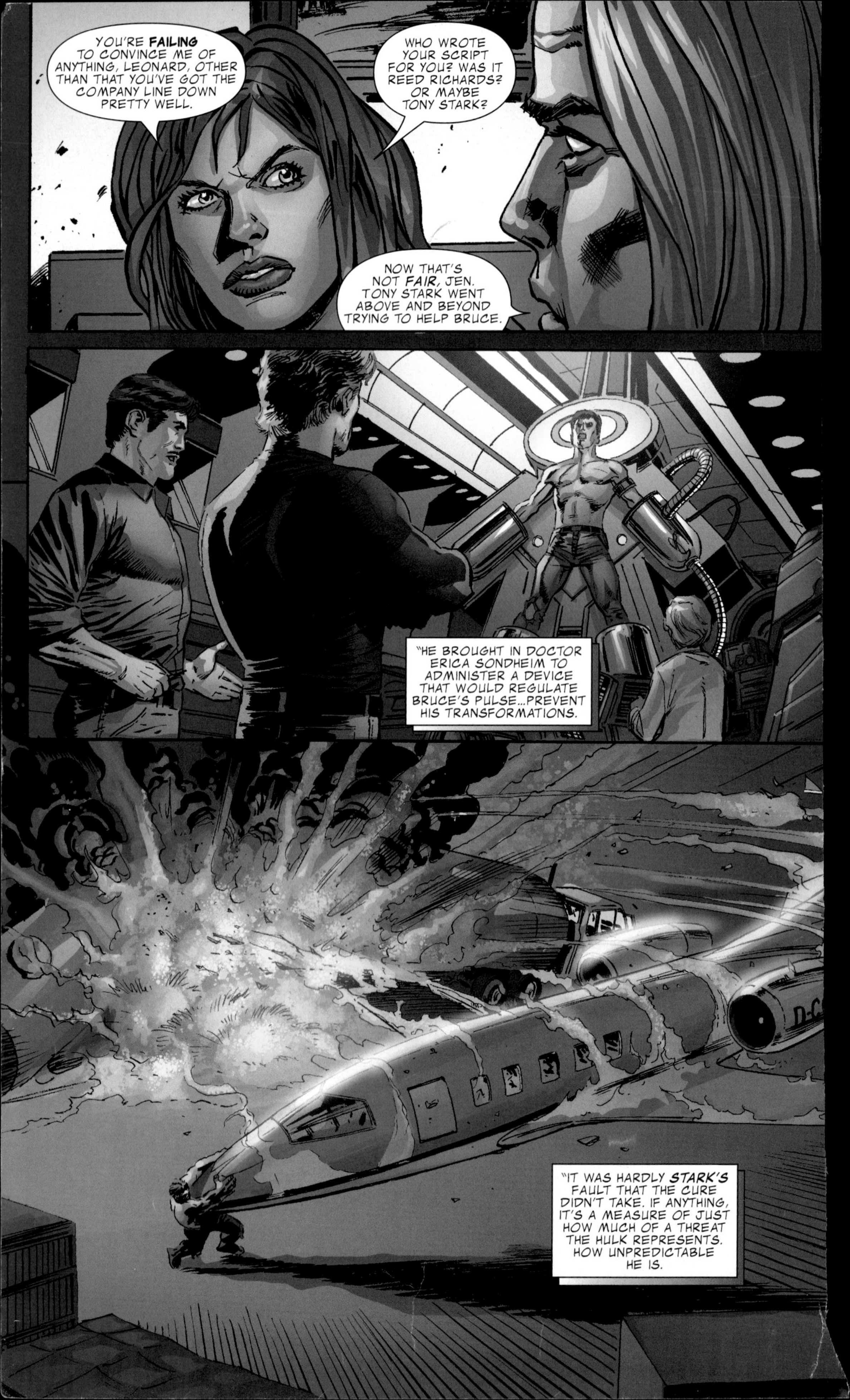
YOU'RE FAILING TO CONVINCE ME OF ANYTHING, LEONARD, OTHER THAN THAT YOU'VE GOT THE COMPANY LINE DOWN PRETTY WELL.
WHO WROTE YOUR SCRIPT FOR YOU? WAS IT REED RICHARDS? OR MAYBE TONY STARK?
NOW THAT'S NOT FAIR, JEN. TONY STARK WENT ABOVE AND BEYOND TRYING TO HELP BRUCE.
"HE BROUGHT IN DOCTOR ERICA SONDHEIM TO ADMINISTER A DEVICE THAT WOULD REGULATE BRUCE'S PULSE...PREVENT HIS TRANSFORMATIONS.
"IT WAS HARDLY STARK'S FAULT THAT THE CURE DIDN'T TAKE. IF ANYTHING, IT'S A MEASURE OF JUST HOW MUCH OF A THREAT THE HULK REPRESENTS. HOW UNPREDICTABLE HE IS.

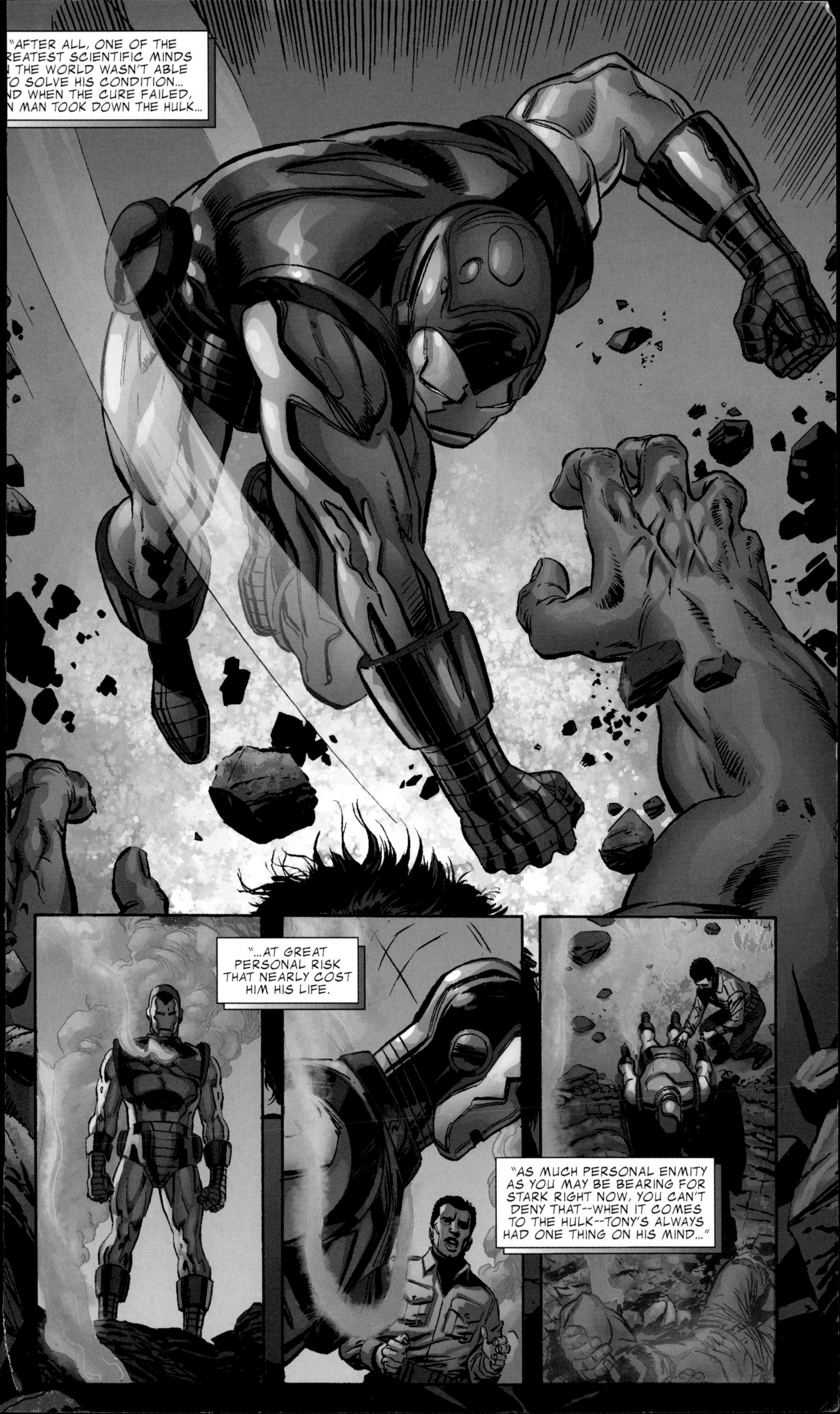
"AFTER ALL, ONE OF THE REATEST SCIENTIFIC MINDS N THE WORLD WASN'T ABLE TO SOLVE HIS CONDITION... ND WHEN THE CURE FAILED, N MAN TOOK DOWN THE HULK...
"...AT GREAT PERSONAL RISK THAT NEARLY COST HIM HIS LIFE.
"AS MUCH PERSONAL ENMITY AS YOU MAY BE BEARING FOR STARK RIGHT NOW, YOU CAN'T DENY THAT--WHEN IT COMES TO THE HULK--TONY'S ALWAYS HAD ONE THING ON HIS MIND..."

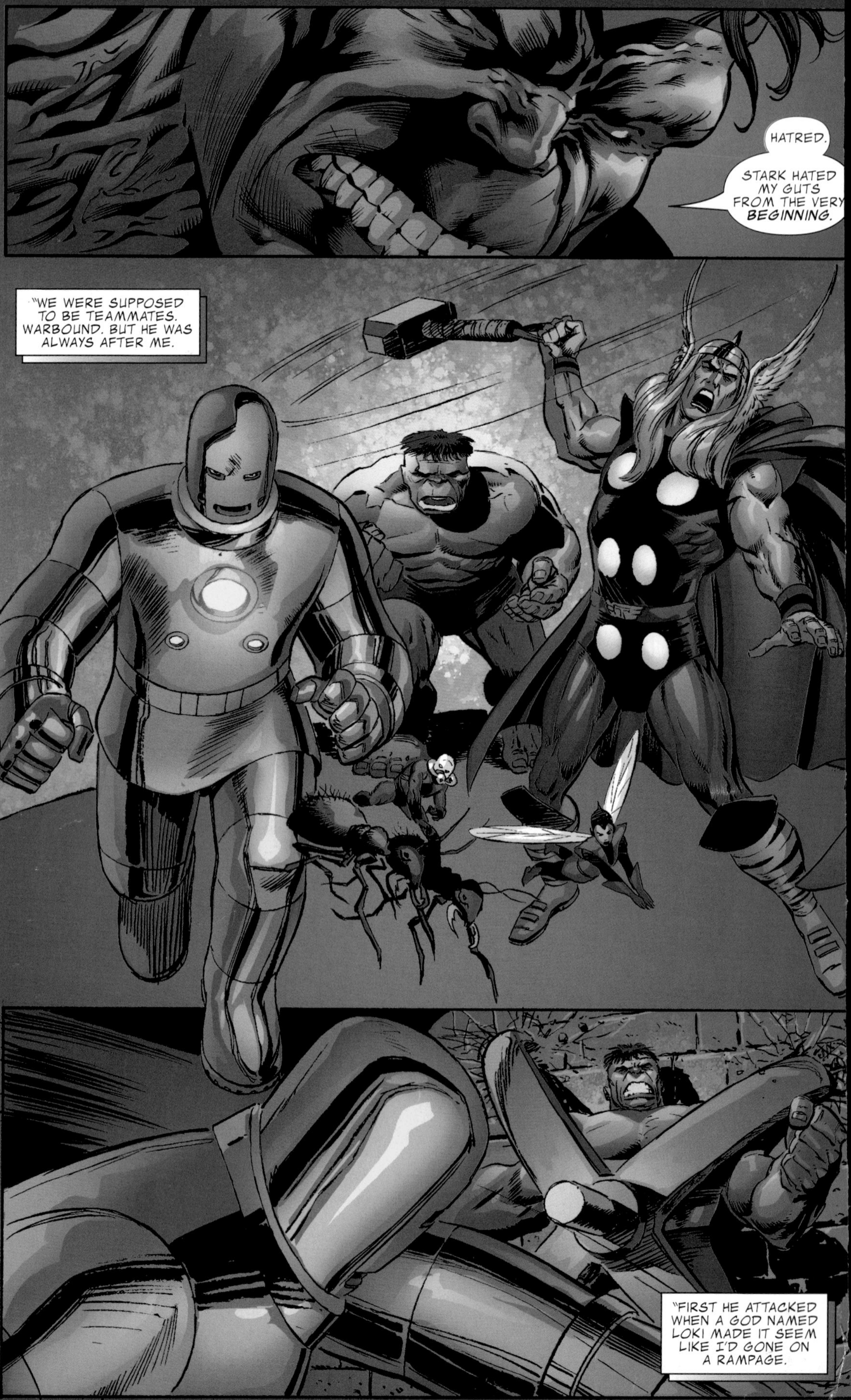
HATRED.
STARK HATED MY GUTS FROM THE VERY BEGINNING.
"WE WERE SUPPOSED TO BE TEAMMATES. WARBOUND. BUT HE WAS ALWAYS AFTER ME.
"FIRST HE ATTACKED WHEN A GOD NAMED LOKI MADE IT SEEM LIKE I'D GONE ON A RAMPAGE.

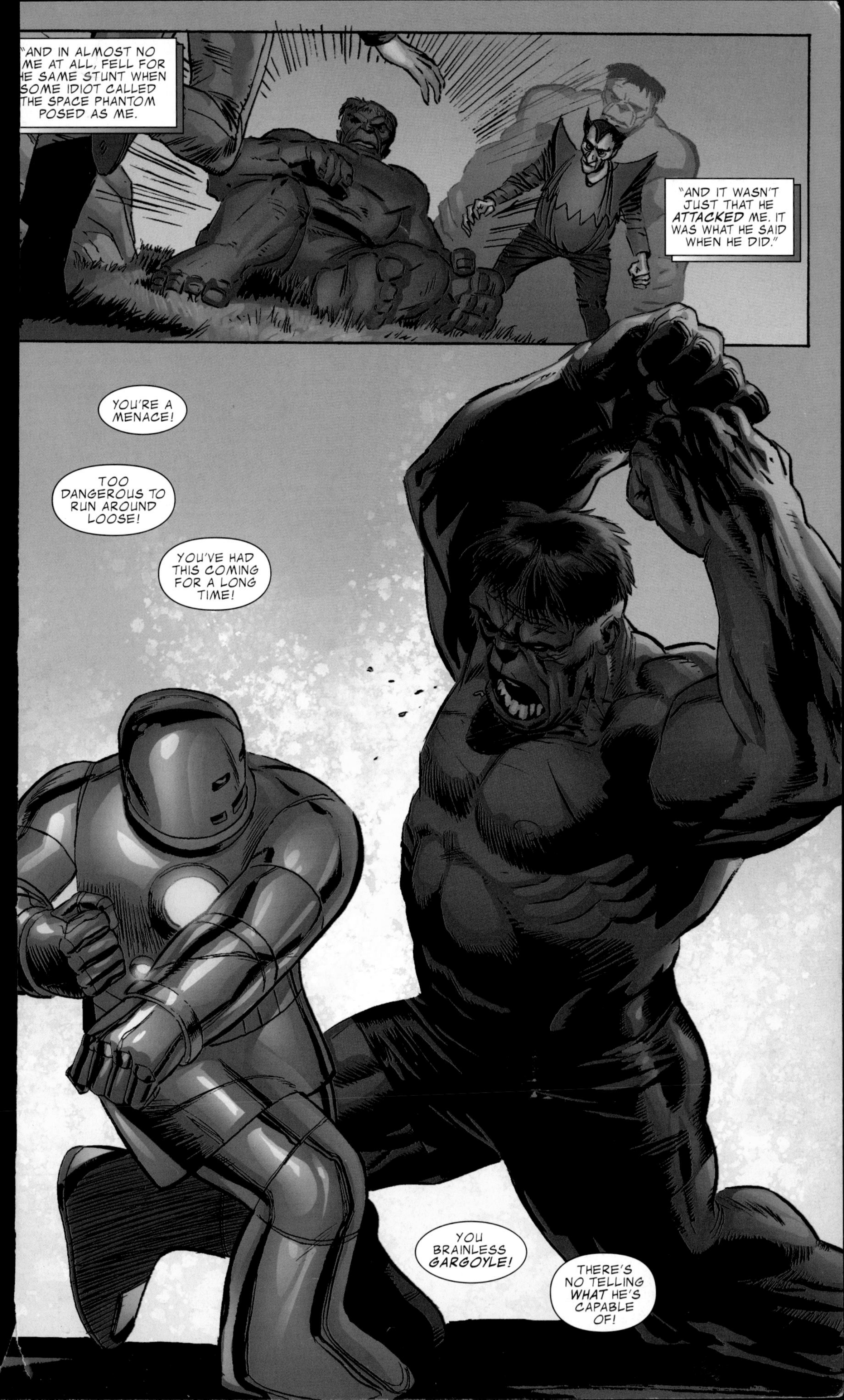
"AND IN ALMOST NO ME AT ALL, FELL FOR HE SAME STUNT WHEN SOME IDIOT CALLED THE SPACE PHANTOM POSED AS ME.
"AND IT WASN'T JUST THAT HE ATTACKED ME. IT WAS WHAT HE SAID WHEN HE DID."
YOU'RE A MENACE!
TOO DANGEROUS TO RUN AROUND LOOSE!
YOU'VE HAD THIS COMING FOR A LONG TIME!
YOU BRAINLESS GARGOYLE!
THERE'S NO TELLING WHAT HE'S CAPABLE OF!

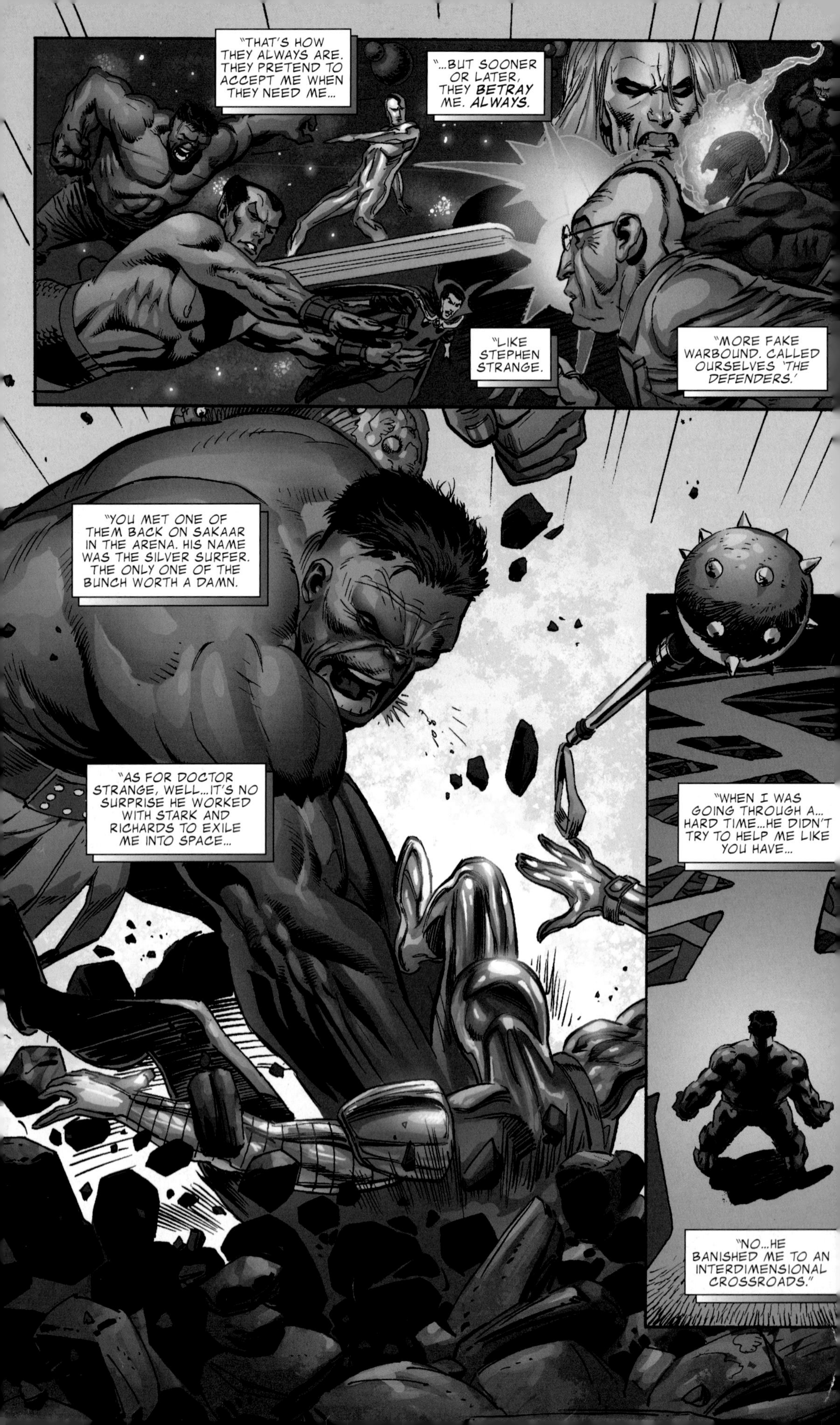
"THAT'S HOW THEY ALWAYS ARE. THEY PRETEND TO ACCEPT ME WHEN THEY NEED ME...
"...BUT SOONER OR LATER, THEY BETRAY ME. ALWAYS.
"LIKE STEPHEN STRANGE.
"MORE FAKE WARBOUND. CALLED OURSELVES 'THE DEFENDERS.'
"YOU MET ONE OF THEM BACK ON SAKAAR IN THE ARENA. HIS NAME WAS THE SILVER SURFER. THE ONLY ONE OF THE BUNCH WORTH A DAMN.
"AS FOR DOCTOR STRANGE, WELL...IT'S NO SURPRISE HE WORKED WITH STARK AND RICHARDS TO EXILE ME INTO SPACE...
"WHEN I WAS GOING THROUGH A... HARD TIME...HE DIDN'T TRY TO HELP ME LIKE YOU HAVE...
"NO...HE BANISHED ME TO AN INTERDIMENSIONAL CROSSROADS."

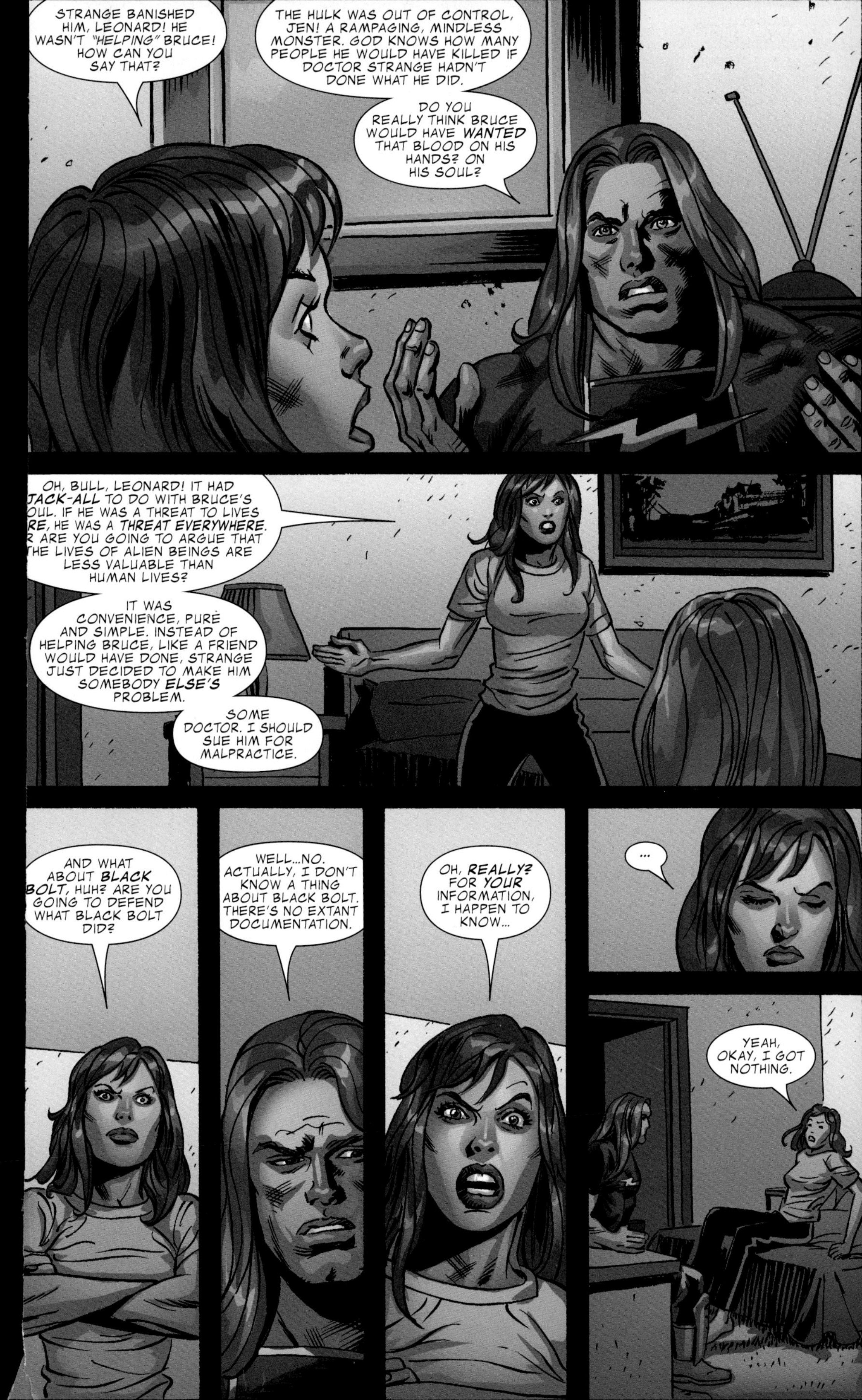
STRANGE BANISHED HIM, LEONARD! HE WASN'T "HELPING" BRUCE! HOW CAN YOU SAY THAT?
THE HULK WAS OUT OF CONTROL, JEN! A RAMPAGING, MINDLESS MONSTER. GOD KNOWS HOW MANY PEOPLE HE WOULD HAVE KILLED IF DOCTOR STRANGE HADN'T DONE WHAT HE DID.
DO YOU REALLY THINK BRUCE WOULD HAVE WANTED THAT BLOOD ON HIS HANDS? ON HIS SOUL?
OH, BULL, LEONARD! IT HAD JACK-ALL TO DO WITH BRUCE'S OUL. IF HE WAS A THREAT TO LIVES RE, HE WAS A THREAT EVERYWHERE. R ARE YOU GOING TO ARGUE THAT THE LIVES OF ALIEN BEINGS ARE LESS VALUABLE THAN HUMAN LIVES?
IT WAS CONVENIENCE, PURE AND SIMPLE. INSTEAD OF HELPING BRUCE, LIKE A FRIEND WOULD HAVE DONE, STRANGE JUST DECIDED TO MAKE HIM SOMEBODY ELSE'S PROBLEM.
SOME DOCTOR. I SHOULD SUE HIM FOR MALPRACTICE.
AND WHAT ABOUT BLACK BOLT, HUH? ARE YOU GOING TO DEFEND WHAT BLACK BOLT DID?
WELL...NO. ACTUALLY, I DON'T KNOW A THING ABOUT BLACK BOLT. THERE'S NO EXTANT DOCUMENTATION.
OH, REALLY? FOR YOUR INFORMATION, I HAPPEN TO KNOW...
...
YEAH, OKAY, I GOT NOTHING.

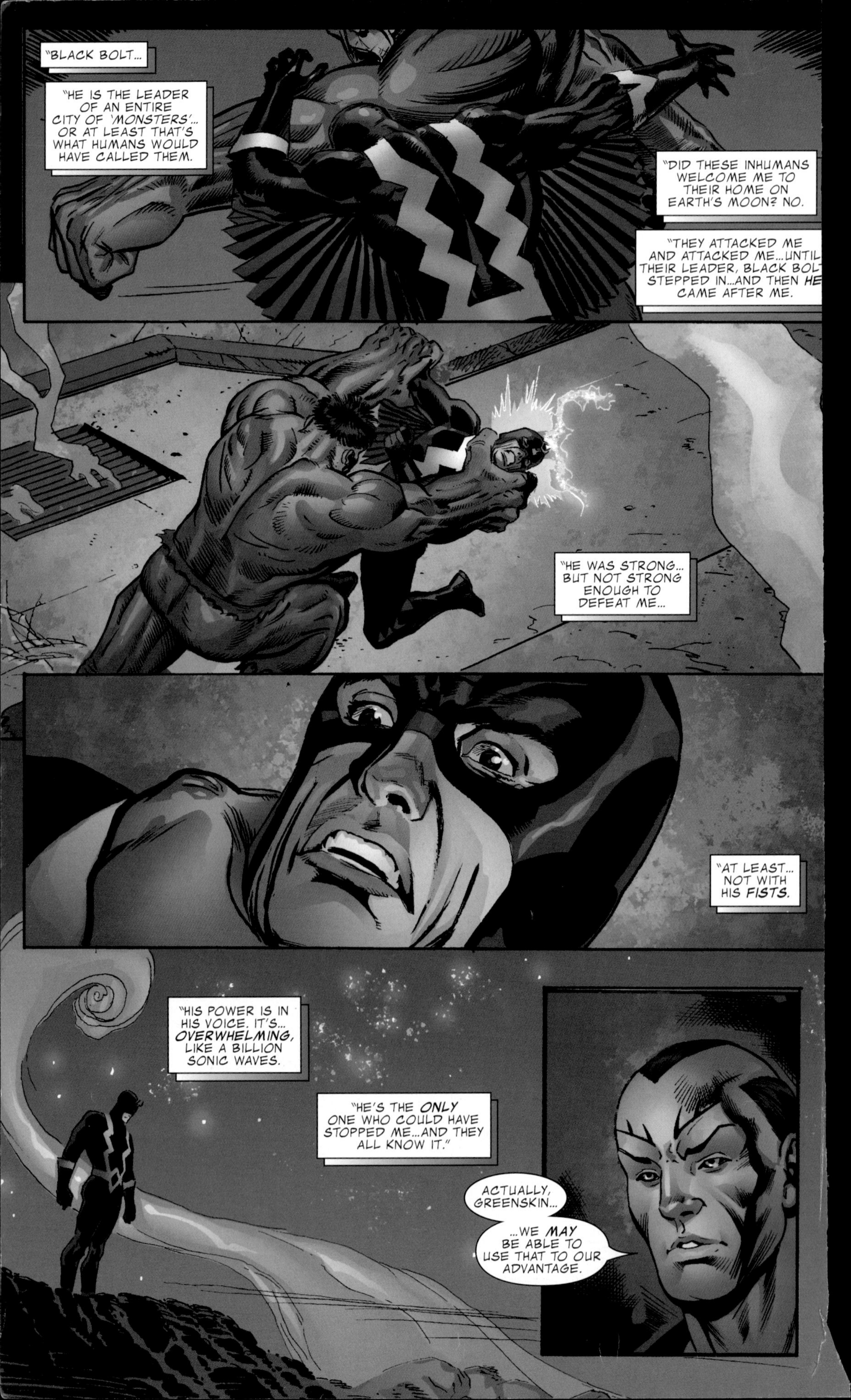
"BLACK BOLT...
"HE IS THE LEADER OF AN ENTIRE CITY OF 'MONSTERS'... OR AT LEAST THAT'S WHAT HUMANS WOULD HAVE CALLED THEM.
"DID THESE INHUMANS WELCOME ME TO THEIR HOME ON EARTH'S MOON? NO.
"THEY ATTACKED ME AND ATTACKED ME...UNTIL THEIR LEADER, BLACK BOLT STEPPED IN...AND THEN HE CAME AFTER ME.
"HE WAS STRONG... BUT NOT STRONG ENOUGH TO DEFEAT ME...
"AT LEAST... NOT WITH HIS FISTS.
"HIS POWER IS IN HIS VOICE. IT'S... OVERWHELMING, LIKE A BILLION SONIC WAVES.
"HE'S THE ONLY ONE WHO COULD HAVE STOPPED ME...AND THEY ALL KNOW IT."
ACTUALLY, GREENSKIN...
...WE MAY BE ABLE TO USE THAT TO OUR ADVANTAGE.

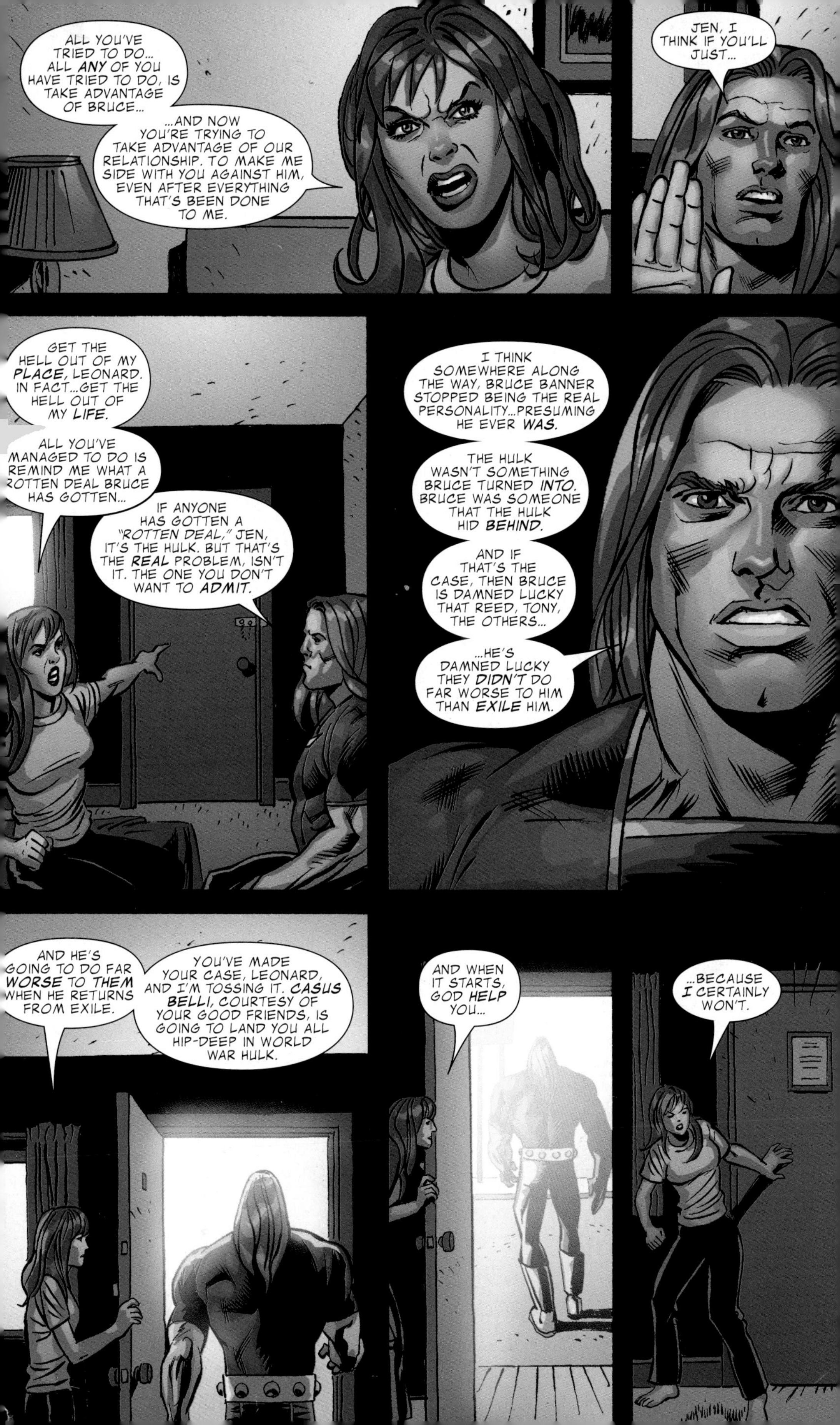
ALL YOU'VE TRIED TO DO... ALL ANY OF YOU HAVE TRIED TO DO, IS TAKE ADVANTAGE OF BRUCE...
...AND NOW YOU'RE TRYING TO TAKE ADVANTAGE OF OUR RELATIONSHIP. TO MAKE ME SIDE WITH YOU AGAINST HIM, EVEN AFTER EVERYTHING THAT'S BEEN DONE TO ME.
JEN, I THINK IF YOU'LL JUST...
GET THE HELL OUT OF MY PLACE, LEONARD. IN FACT...GET THE HELL OUT OF MY LIFE.
ALL YOU'VE MANAGED TO DO IS REMIND ME WHAT A ROTTEN DEAL BRUCE HAS GOTTEN...
IF ANYONE HAS GOTTEN A "ROTTEN DEAL," JEN, IT'S THE HULK. BUT THAT'S THE REAL PROBLEM, ISN'T IT. THE ONE YOU DON'T WANT TO ADMIT.
I THINK SOMEWHERE ALONG THE WAY, BRUCE BANNER STOPPED BEING THE REAL PERSONALITY...PRESUMING HE EVER WAS.
THE HULK WASN'T SOMETHING BRUCE TURNED INTO. BRUCE WAS SOMEONE THAT THE HULK HID BEHIND.
AND IF THAT'S THE CASE, THEN BRUCE IS DAMNED LUCKY THAT REED, TONY, THE OTHERS...
...HE'S DAMNED LUCKY THEY DIDN'T DO FAR WORSE TO HIM THAN EXILE HIM.
AND HE'S GOING TO DO FAR WORSE TO THEM WHEN HE RETURNS FROM EXILE.
YOU'VE MADE YOUR CASE, LEONARD, AND I'M TOSSING IT. CASUS BELLI, COURTESY OF YOUR GOOD FRIENDS, IS GOING TO LAND YOU ALL HIP-DEEP IN WORLD WAR HULK.
AND WHEN IT STARTS, GOD HELP YOU...
...BECAUSE I CERTAINLY WON'T.

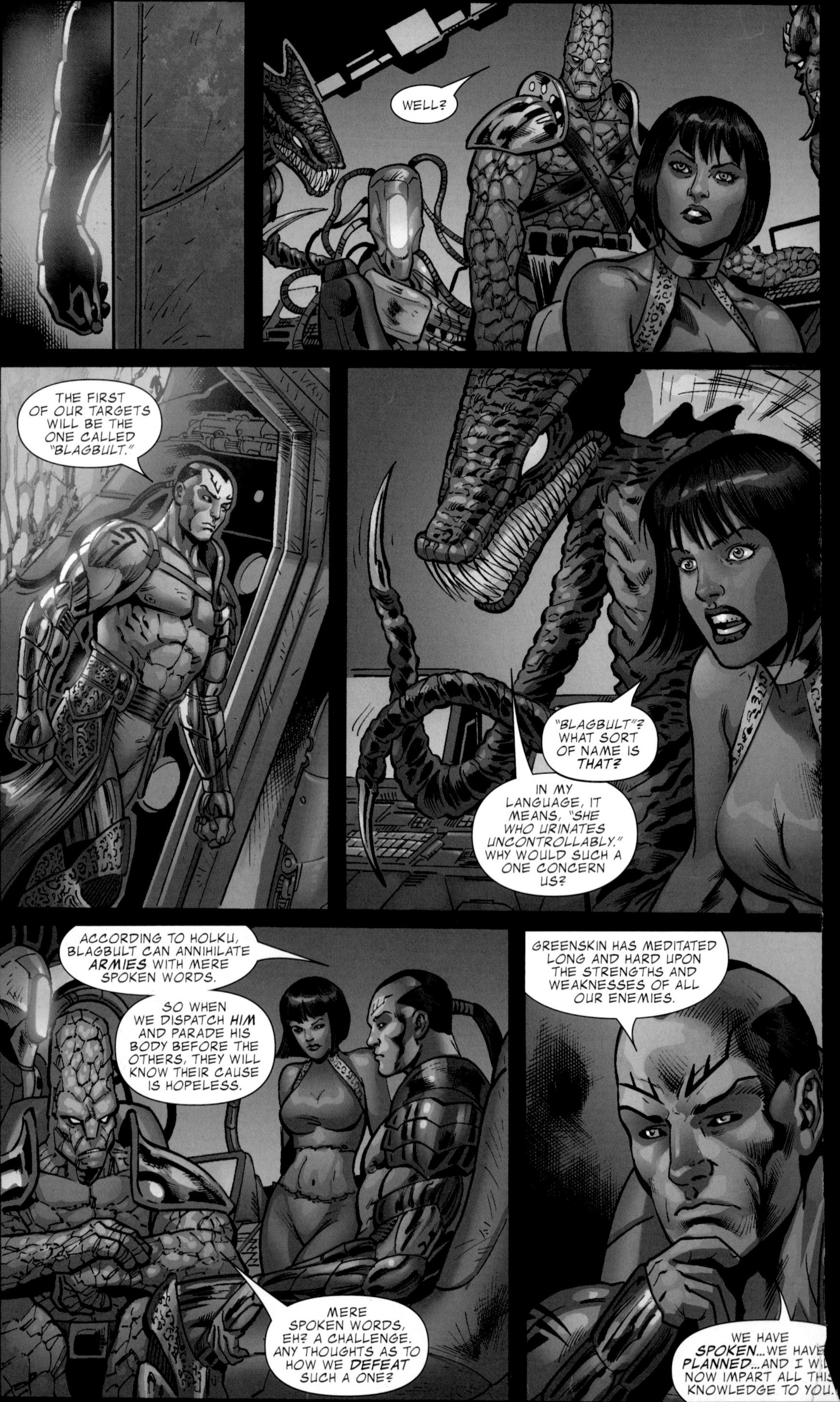
WELL?
THE FIRST OF OUR TARGETS WILL BE THE ONE CALLED "BLAGBULT."
"BLAGBULT"? WHAT SORT OF NAME IS *THAT?*
IN MY LANGUAGE, IT MEANS, "SHE WHO URINATES UNCONTROLLABLY." WHY WOULD SUCH A ONE CONCERN US?
ACCORDING TO HOLKU, BLAGBULT CAN ANNIHILATE ***ARMIES*** WITH MERE SPOKEN WORDS.
SO WHEN WE DISPATCH ***HIM*** AND PARADE HIS BODY BEFORE THE OTHERS, THEY WILL KNOW THEIR CAUSE IS HOPELESS.
MERE SPOKEN WORDS, EH? A CHALLENGE. ANY THOUGHTS AS TO HOW WE ***DEFEAT*** SUCH A ONE?
GREENSKIN HAS MEDITATED LONG AND HARD UPON THE STRENGTHS AND WEAKNESSES OF ALL OUR ENEMIES.
WE HAVE ***SPOKEN***...WE HAVE ***PLANNED***...AND I WI NOW IMPART ALL THIS KNOWLEDGE TO YOU.

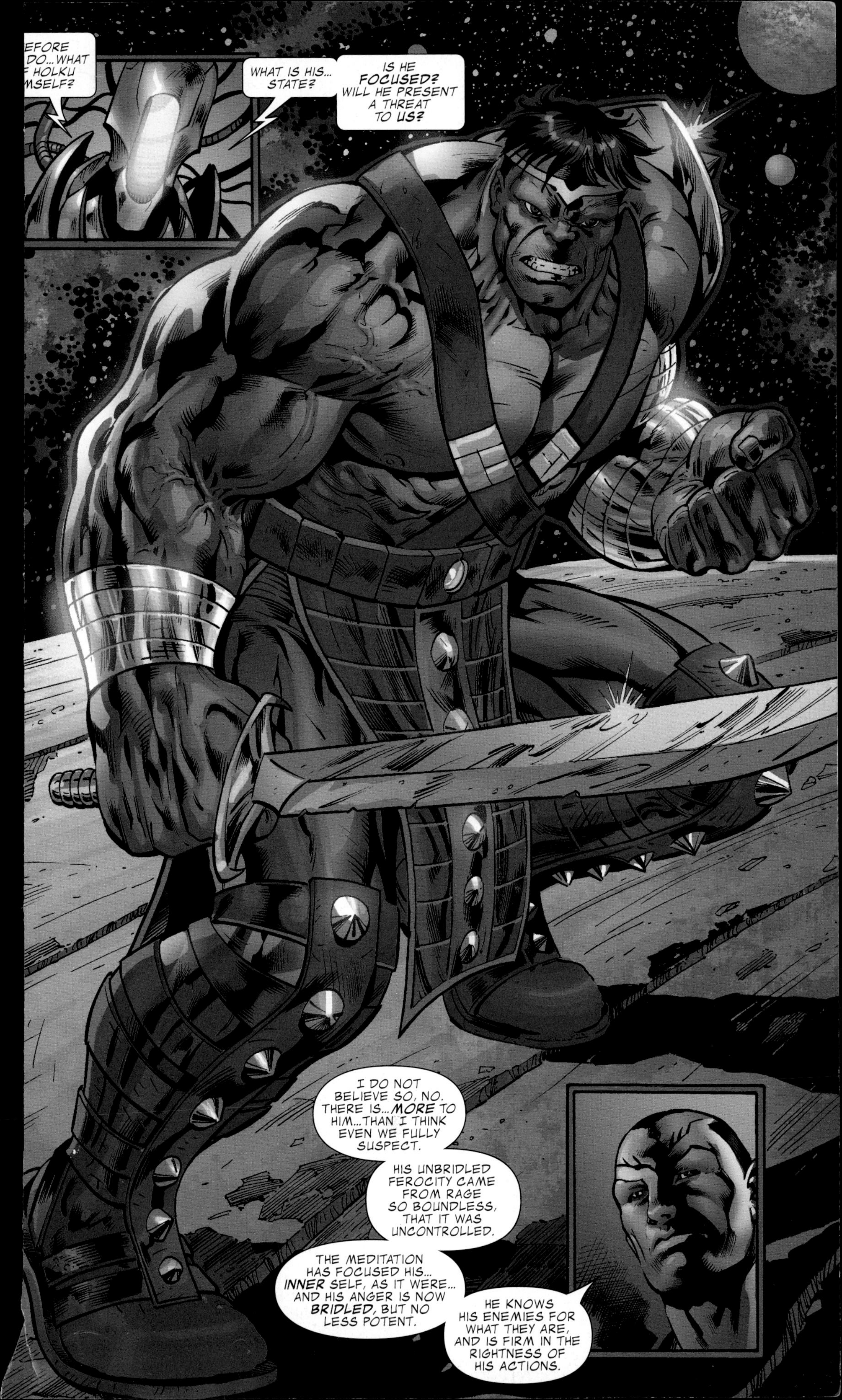

EFORE
DO...WHAT
F HOLKU
MSELF?
WHAT IS HIS... STATE?
IS HE FOCUSED? WILL HE PRESENT A THREAT TO US?
I DO NOT BELIEVE SO, NO. THERE IS...MORE TO HIM...THAN I THINK EVEN WE FULLY SUSPECT.
HIS UNBRIDLED FEROCITY CAME FROM RAGE SO BOUNDLESS, THAT IT WAS UNCONTROLLED.
THE MEDITATION HAS FOCUSED HIS... INNER SELF, AS IT WERE... AND HIS ANGER IS NOW BRIDLED, BUT NO LESS POTENT.
HE KNOWS HIS ENEMIES FOR WHAT THEY ARE, AND IS FIRM IN THE RIGHTNESS OF HIS ACTIONS.

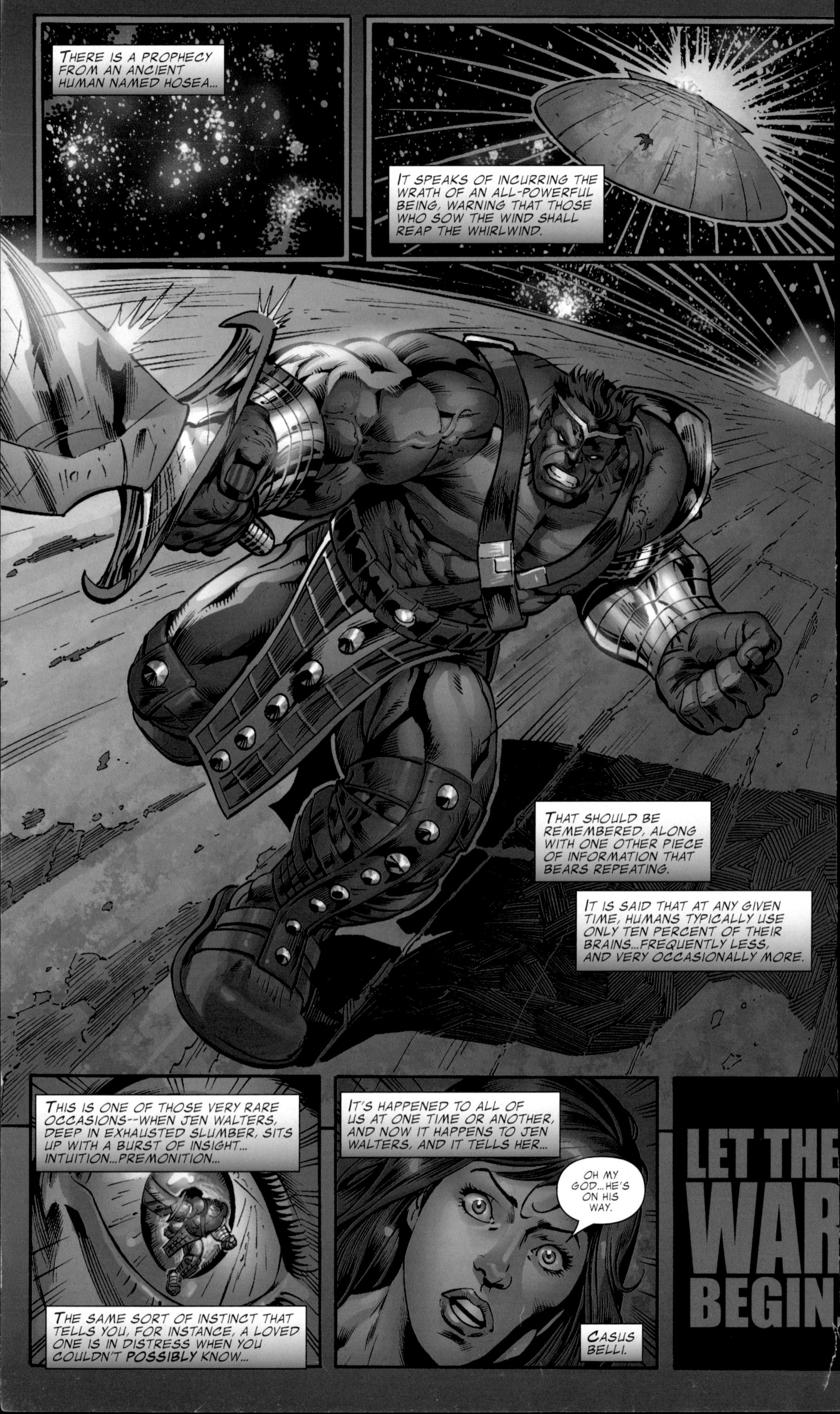
THERE IS A PROPHECY FROM AN ANCIENT HUMAN NAMED HOSEA...
IT SPEAKS OF INCURRING THE WRATH OF AN ALL-POWERFUL BEING, WARNING THAT THOSE WHO SOW THE WIND SHALL REAP THE WHIRLWIND.
THAT SHOULD BE REMEMBERED, ALONG WITH ONE OTHER PIECE OF INFORMATION THAT BEARS REPEATING.
IT IS SAID THAT AT ANY GIVEN TIME, HUMANS TYPICALLY USE ONLY TEN PERCENT OF THEIR BRAINS...FREQUENTLY LESS, AND VERY OCCASIONALLY MORE.
THIS IS ONE OF THOSE VERY RARE OCCASIONS--WHEN JEN WALTERS, DEEP IN EXHAUSTED SLUMBER, SITS UP WITH A BURST OF INSIGHT... INTUITION...PREMONITION...
THE SAME SORT OF INSTINCT THAT TELLS YOU, FOR INSTANCE, A LOVED ONE IS IN DISTRESS WHEN YOU COULDN'T POSSIBLY KNOW...
IT'S HAPPENED TO ALL OF US AT ONE TIME OR ANOTHER, AND NOW IT HAPPENS TO JEN WALTERS, AND IT TELLS HER...
OH MY GOD...HE'S ON HIS WAY.
CASUS BELLI.
LET THE WAR BEGIN

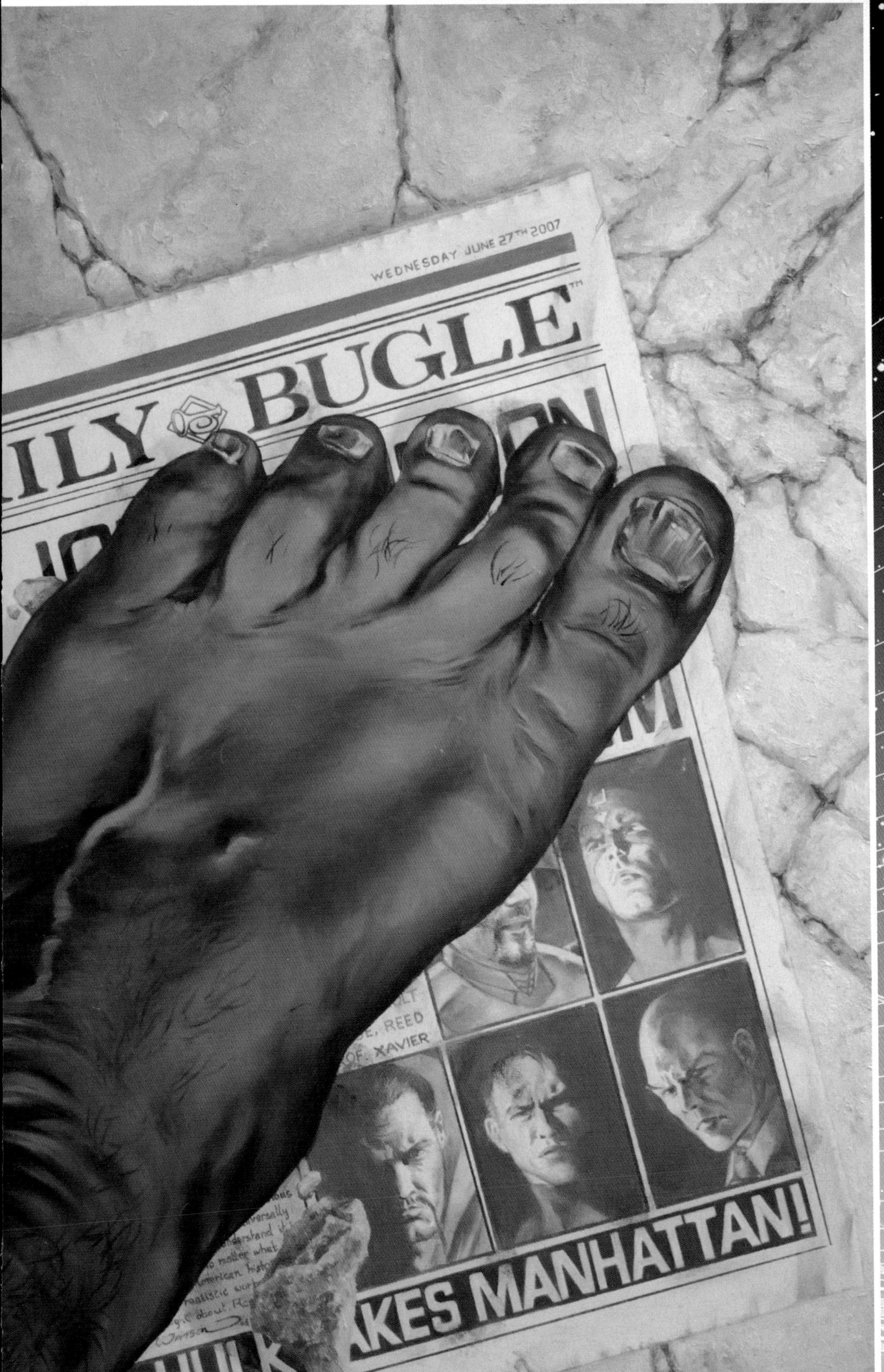
WEDNESDAY JUNE 27TH 2007
ILY BUGLE
HULK AKES MANHATTAN!

WORLD WAR HULK: FRONT LINE #1

WORLD WAR HULK
FRONT LINE

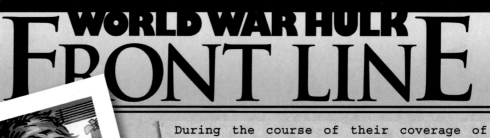

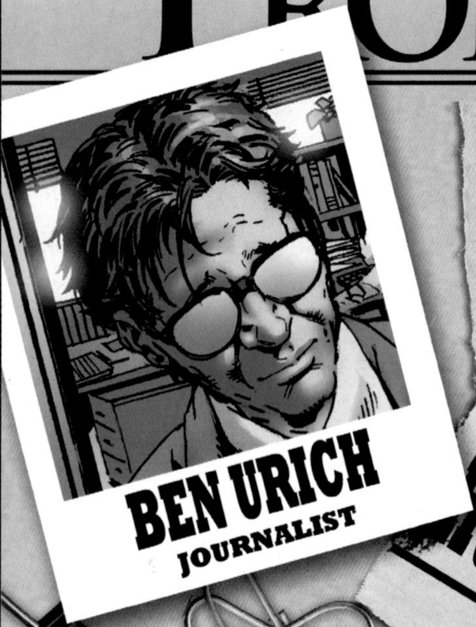
BEN URICH
JOURNALIST

During the course of their coverage of t recent superhuman Civil War, *Daily Bug* reporter **Ben Urich** and *Alternative* report **Sally Floyd** -- who is now dating Costu Division detective **Danny Granville** -- each qu their respective newspapers. Bonded by the shared experience, both journalists agreed form their own start-up newspaper, *Front Lin* through which they seek to expose the tru without corporate interferenc

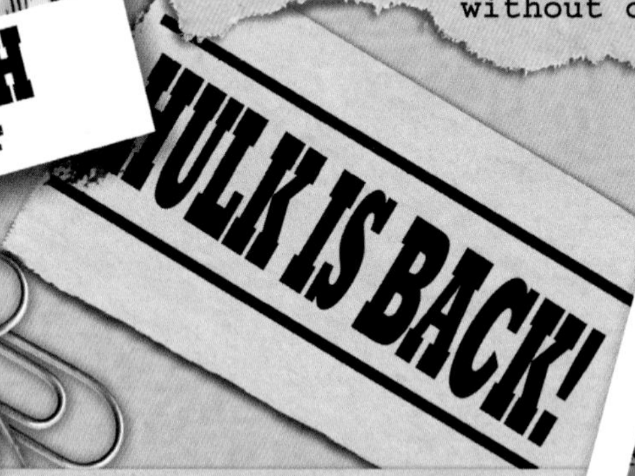
HULK IS BACK!

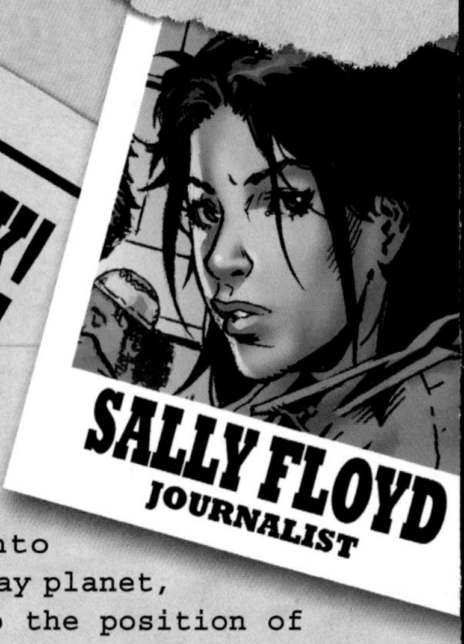
SALLY FLOYD
JOURNALIST

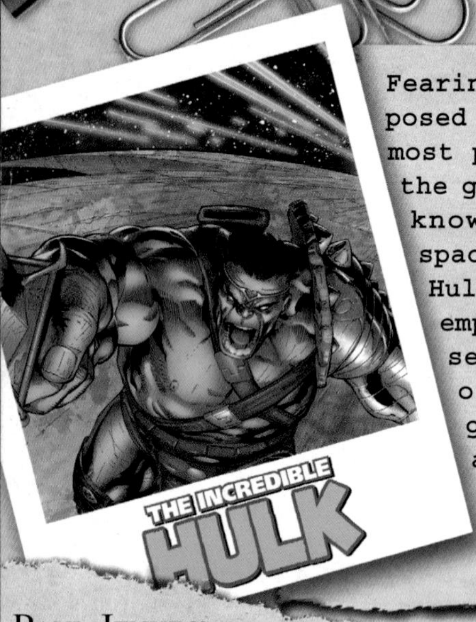
THE INCREDIBLE
HULK

Fearing the threat he posed to humanity, Earth's most powerful heroes shot the gamma-spawned monster known as the **Hulk** into space. Landing on a faraway planet, Hulk battled his way to the position of emperor and fell in love. But the shuttle that sent Hulk from Earth exploded, killing millions of people, including Hulk's queen and the baby growing inside her. Filled with rage, Hulk and his Warbound allies have set course for Earth, to bring revenge upon those he holds responsible for destroying his world.

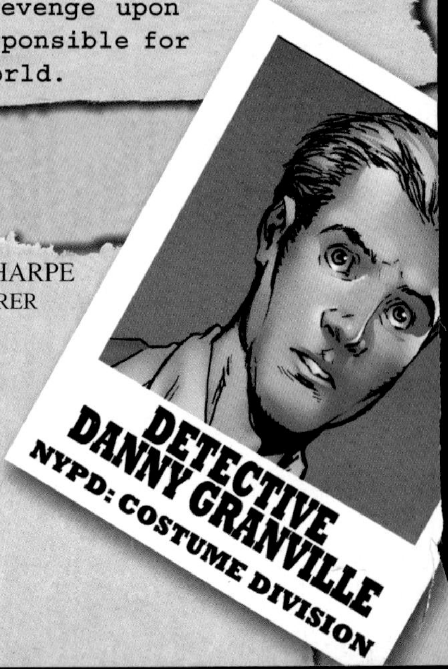
DETECTIVE
DANNY GRANVILLE
NYPD: COSTUME DIVISION

PAUL JENKINS
WRITER

RAMON BACHS
ARTIST

MATT MILLA
COLOR ARTIST

JOHN WATSON
COVER ARTIST

DAVE SHARPE
LETTERER

RICH GINTER
PRODUCTION

ALEJANDRO ARBONA
ASST. EDITOR

BILL ROSEMANN
EDITOR

JOE QUESADA
EDITOR-IN-CHIEF

DAN BUCKLEY
PUBLISHER

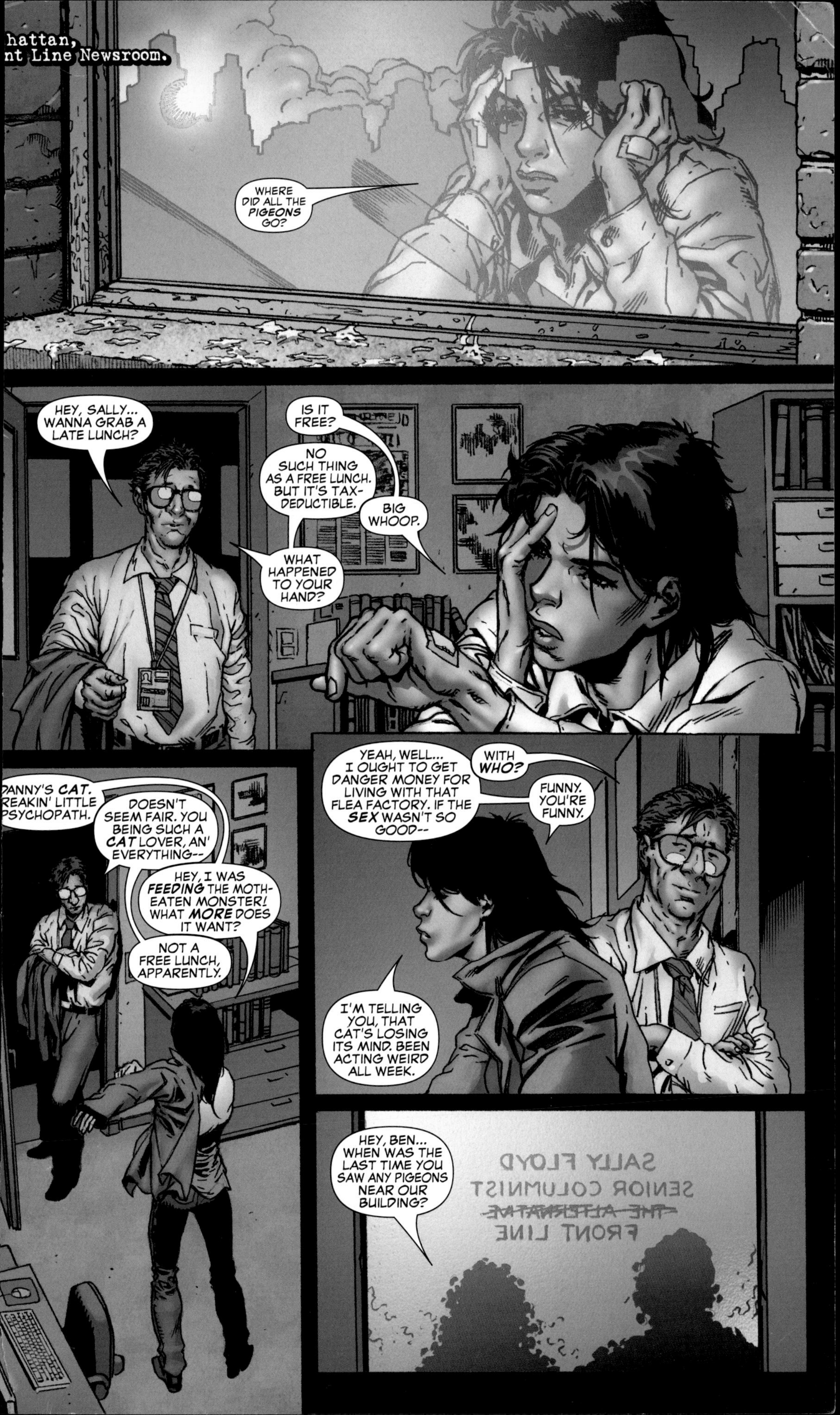
hattan,
nt Line Newsroom.
WHERE DID ALL THE *PIGEONS* GO?
HEY, SALLY... WANNA GRAB A LATE LUNCH?
IS IT FREE?
NO SUCH THING AS A FREE LUNCH. BUT IT'S TAX-DEDUCTIBLE.
BIG WHOOP.
WHAT HAPPENED TO YOUR HAND?
DANNY'S **CAT.** FREAKIN' LITTLE PSYCHOPATH.
DOESN'T SEEM FAIR. YOU BEING SUCH A **CAT** LOVER, AN' EVERYTHING--
HEY, I WAS ***FEEDING*** THE MOTH-EATEN MONSTER! WHAT ***MORE*** DOES IT WANT?
NOT A FREE LUNCH, APPARENTLY.
YEAH, WELL... I OUGHT TO GET DANGER MONEY FOR LIVING WITH THAT FLEA FACTORY. IF THE ***SEX*** WASN'T SO GOOD--
WITH ***WHO?***
FUNNY. YOU'RE FUNNY.
I'M TELLING YOU, THAT CAT'S LOSING ITS MIND. BEEN ACTING WEIRD ALL WEEK.
HEY, BEN... WHEN WAS THE LAST TIME YOU SAW ANY PIGEONS NEAR OUR BUILDING?
SALLY FLOYD
SENIOR COLUMNIST
~~THE ALTERNATIVE~~
FRONT LINE

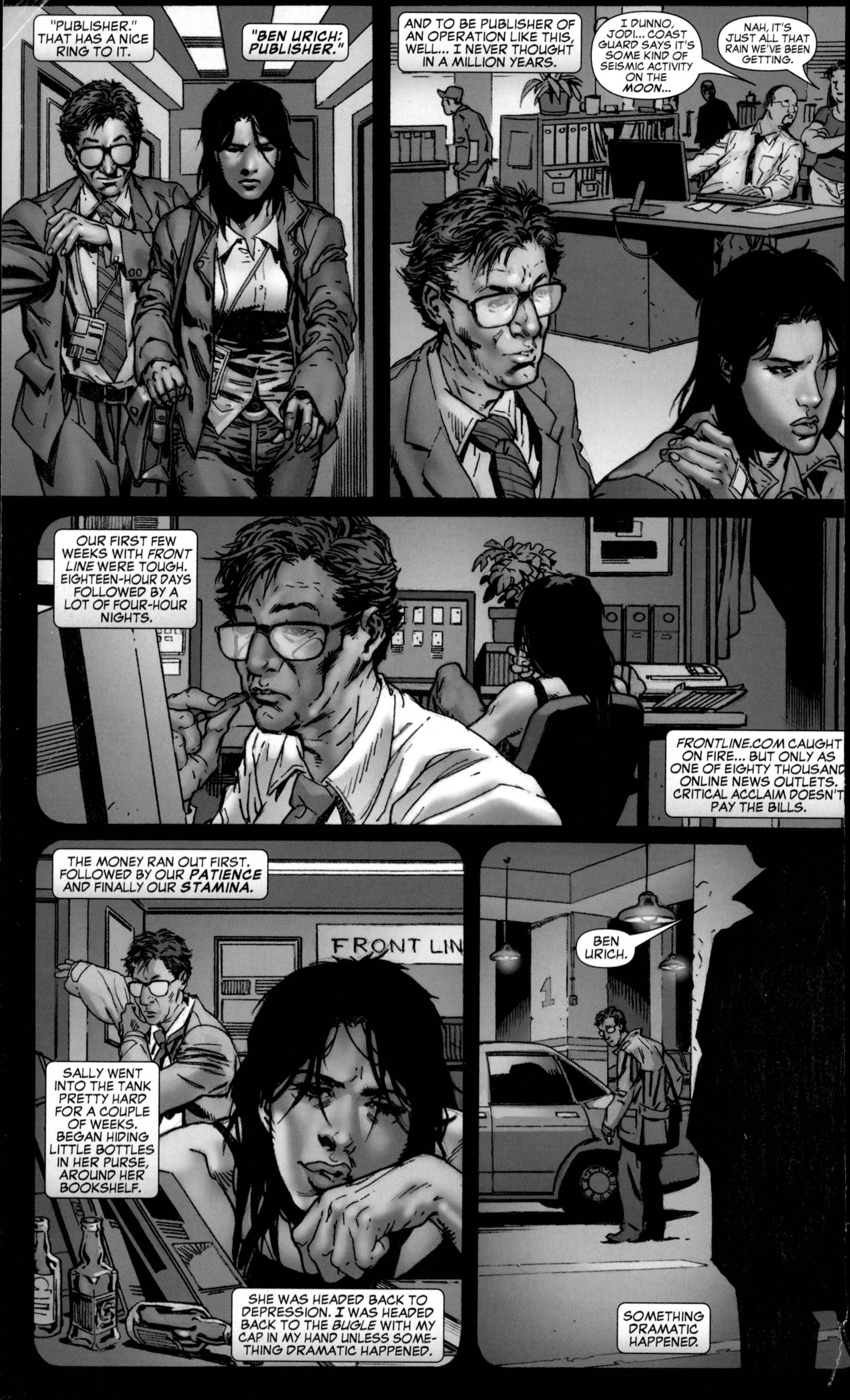
"PUBLISHER." THAT HAS A NICE RING TO IT.
"BEN URICH: PUBLISHER."
AND TO BE PUBLISHER OF AN OPERATION LIKE THIS, WELL... I NEVER THOUGHT IN A MILLION YEARS.
I DUNNO, JODI... COAST GUARD SAYS IT'S SOME KIND OF SEISMIC ACTIVITY ON THE MOON...
NAH, IT'S JUST ALL THAT RAIN WE'VE BEEN GETTING.
OUR FIRST FEW WEEKS WITH FRONT LINE WERE TOUGH. EIGHTEEN-HOUR DAYS FOLLOWED BY A LOT OF FOUR-HOUR NIGHTS.
FRONTLINE.COM CAUGHT ON FIRE... BUT ONLY AS ONE OF EIGHTY THOUSAND ONLINE NEWS OUTLETS. CRITICAL ACCLAIM DOESN'T PAY THE BILLS.
THE MONEY RAN OUT FIRST. FOLLOWED BY OUR PATIENCE AND FINALLY OUR STAMINA.
FRONT LIN
SALLY WENT INTO THE TANK PRETTY HARD FOR A COUPLE OF WEEKS. BEGAN HIDING LITTLE BOTTLES IN HER PURSE, AROUND HER BOOKSHELF.
SHE WAS HEADED BACK TO DEPRESSION. I WAS HEADED BACK TO THE BUGLE WITH MY CAP IN MY HAND UNLESS SOME-THING DRAMATIC HAPPENED.
BEN URICH.
SOMETHING DRAMATIC HAPPENED.

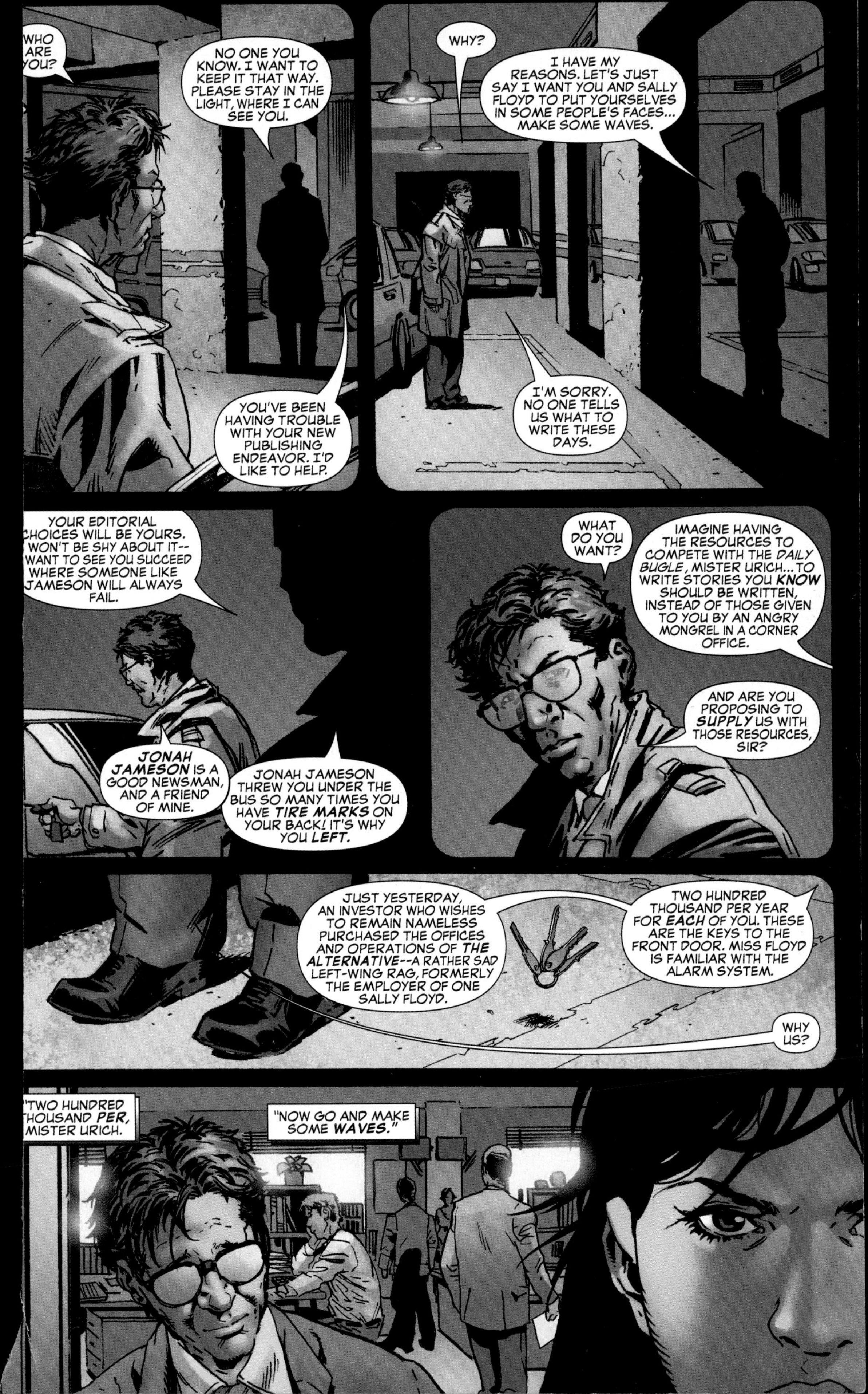
WHO ARE YOU?
NO ONE YOU KNOW. I WANT TO KEEP IT THAT WAY. PLEASE STAY IN THE LIGHT, WHERE I CAN SEE YOU.
YOU'VE BEEN HAVING TROUBLE WITH YOUR NEW PUBLISHING ENDEAVOR. I'D LIKE TO HELP.
WHY?
I HAVE MY REASONS. LET'S JUST SAY I WANT YOU AND SALLY FLOYD TO PUT YOURSELVES IN SOME PEOPLE'S FACES... MAKE SOME WAVES.
I'M SORRY. NO ONE TELLS US WHAT TO WRITE THESE DAYS.
YOUR EDITORIAL CHOICES WILL BE YOURS. WON'T BE SHY ABOUT IT-- WANT TO SEE YOU SUCCEED WHERE SOMEONE LIKE JAMESON WILL ALWAYS FAIL.
JONAH JAMESON IS A GOOD NEWSMAN, AND A FRIEND OF MINE.
JONAH JAMESON THREW YOU UNDER THE BUS SO MANY TIMES YOU HAVE TIRE MARKS ON YOUR BACK! IT'S WHY YOU LEFT.
WHAT DO YOU WANT?
IMAGINE HAVING THE RESOURCES TO COMPETE WITH THE DAILY BUGLE, MISTER URICH... TO WRITE STORIES YOU KNOW SHOULD BE WRITTEN, INSTEAD OF THOSE GIVEN TO YOU BY AN ANGRY MONGREL IN A CORNER OFFICE.
AND ARE YOU PROPOSING TO SUPPLY US WITH THOSE RESOURCES, SIR?
JUST YESTERDAY, AN INVESTOR WHO WISHES TO REMAIN NAMELESS PURCHASED THE OFFICES AND OPERATIONS OF THE ALTERNATIVE--A RATHER SAD LEFT-WING RAG, FORMERLY THE EMPLOYER OF ONE SALLY FLOYD.
TWO HUNDRED THOUSAND PER YEAR FOR EACH OF YOU. THESE ARE THE KEYS TO THE FRONT DOOR. MISS FLOYD IS FAMILIAR WITH THE ALARM SYSTEM.
WHY US?
"TWO HUNDRED THOUSAND PER, MISTER URICH.
"NOW GO AND MAKE SOME WAVES."

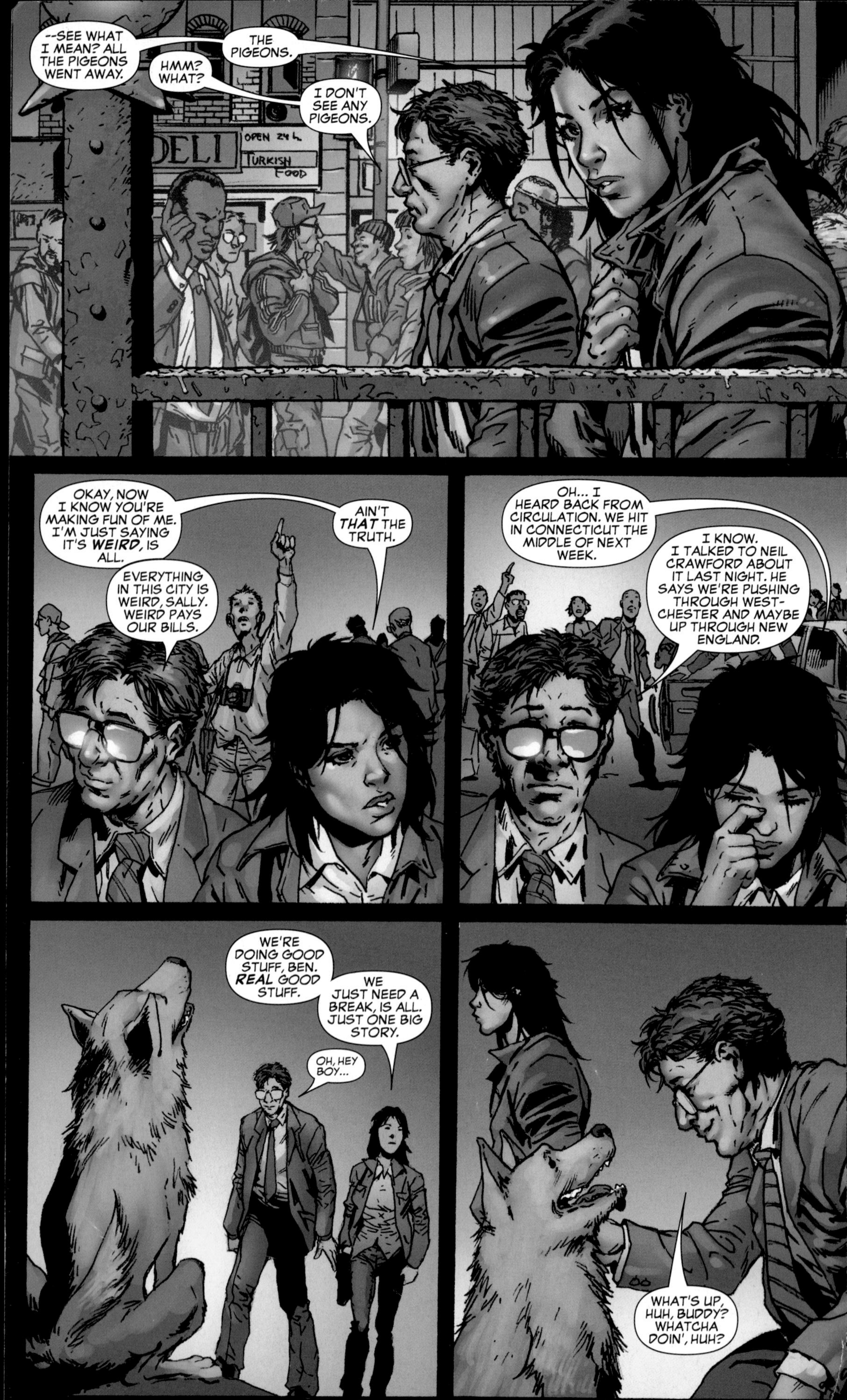
--SEE WHAT I MEAN? ALL THE PIGEONS WENT AWAY.
HMM? WHAT?
THE PIGEONS.
I DON'T SEE ANY PIGEONS.
DELI
OPEN 24 h.
TURKISH FOOD
OKAY, NOW I KNOW YOU'RE MAKING FUN OF ME. I'M JUST SAYING IT'S *WEIRD*, IS ALL.
EVERYTHING IN THIS CITY IS WEIRD, SALLY. WEIRD PAYS OUR BILLS.
AIN'T *THAT* THE TRUTH.
OH... I HEARD BACK FROM CIRCULATION. WE HIT IN CONNECTICUT THE MIDDLE OF NEXT WEEK.
I KNOW. I TALKED TO NEIL CRAWFORD ABOUT IT LAST NIGHT. HE SAYS WE'RE PUSHING THROUGH WEST-CHESTER AND MAYBE UP THROUGH NEW ENGLAND.
WE'RE DOING GOOD STUFF, BEN. *REAL* GOOD STUFF.
WE JUST NEED A BREAK, IS ALL. JUST ONE BIG STORY.
OH, HEY BOY...
WHAT'S UP, HUH, BUDDY? WHATCHA DOIN', HUH?

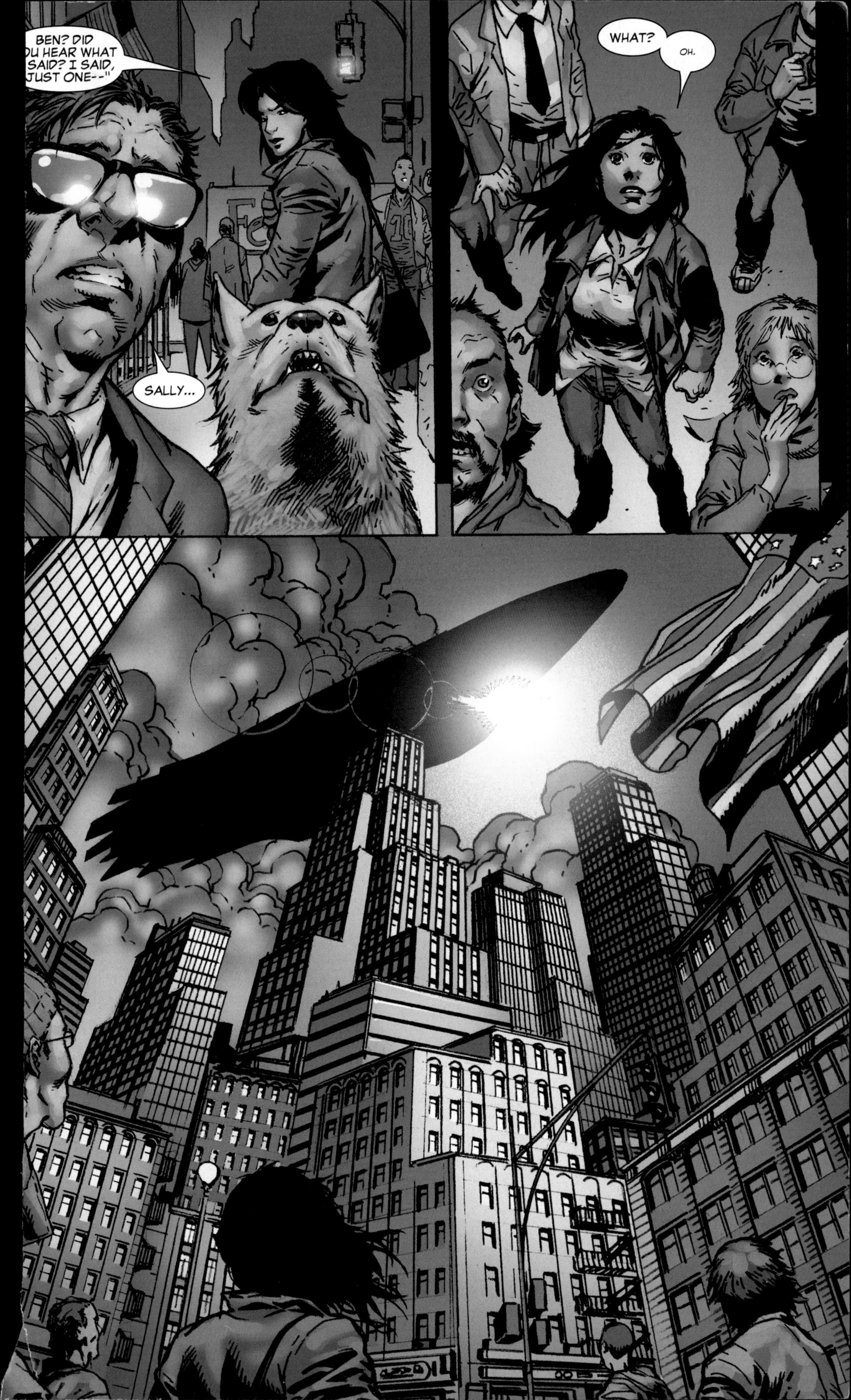
BEN? DID
U HEAR WHAT
SAID? I SAID,
JUST ONE--"
SALLY...
WHAT?
OH.

EVERYTHING MOVED REAL FAST AFTER THAT.

IT WAS *THE HULK* IN THAT SHIP, AND HE ISSUED AN *ULTIMATUM:* APPARENTLY, FOUR OF OUR BEST AND BRIGHTEST--MR. FANTASTIC, DR. STRANGE, BLACK BOLT AND IRON MAN--SHOT HIM INTO SPACE WITHOUT HIS PERMISSION AND THEN BLEW UP HIS LANDING SPOT.

WE HAD TWENTY-FO[UR] HOURS TO HAND TH[EM] OVER, OR WE HAD TWE[NTY-] FIVE HOURS TO LIV[E.]

FIVE HOURS AFTER THE SHIP FIRST APPEARED, MOST OF NEW YORK CITY'S INHABITANTS WERE GETTING OUT OF DODGE.

EVACUATION PROCEDURE IMPLEMENTE[D]

TAKE ONLY [ESSEN]TIAL [TH]INGS

THIS WAS A MASSIVE UNDER-TAKING. WE'D ALL SEEN THE REPORTS ON TV. PEOPLE KNEW BETTER THAN TO ARGUE WITH A FORCE OF NATURE.

SALLY AND GEOFF CRESWELL WENT TO MOTT HAVEN IN THE SOUTH BRONX TO CHECK ON EVACUATION PROCEEDINGS THERE.

IN SUCH A POOR AREA, THERE WAS NEITHER MONE[Y] NOR A SINGLE CITY OFFICIA[L] IN EVIDENCE TO HELP WITH THE EXODUS. THAT WAS TH[E] REALITY OF THIS SITUATION.

OKAY... GEORGE HUMMERT CAN TAKE THE BROOKLYN BRIDGE.

COPY, CHIEF.

AS FOR ME: I GOT READY TO *ENJOY* MYSELF.

WELL... AT LEAST NOW I KNOW WHERE ALL THE FREAKIN' *PIGEONS* WENT.

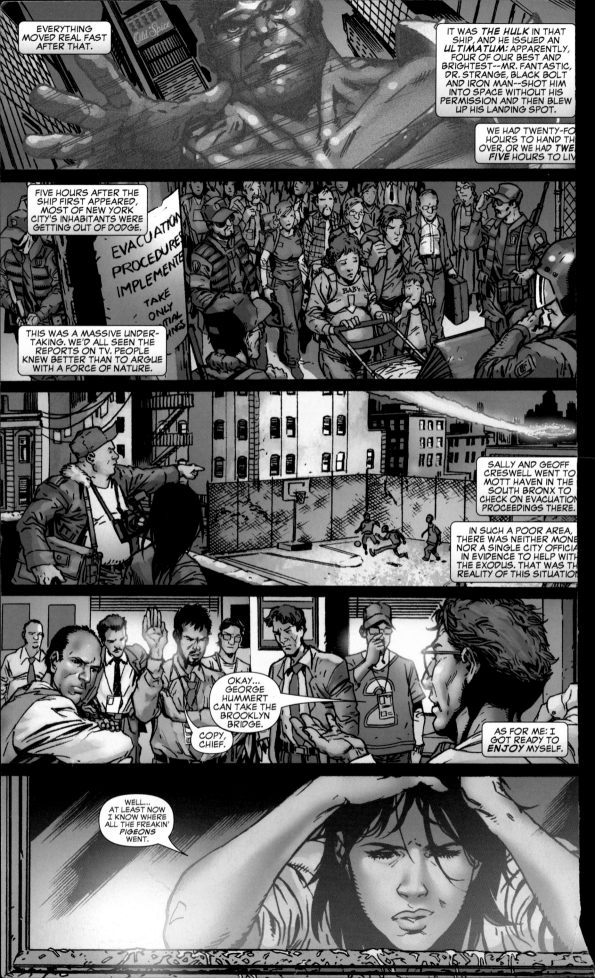

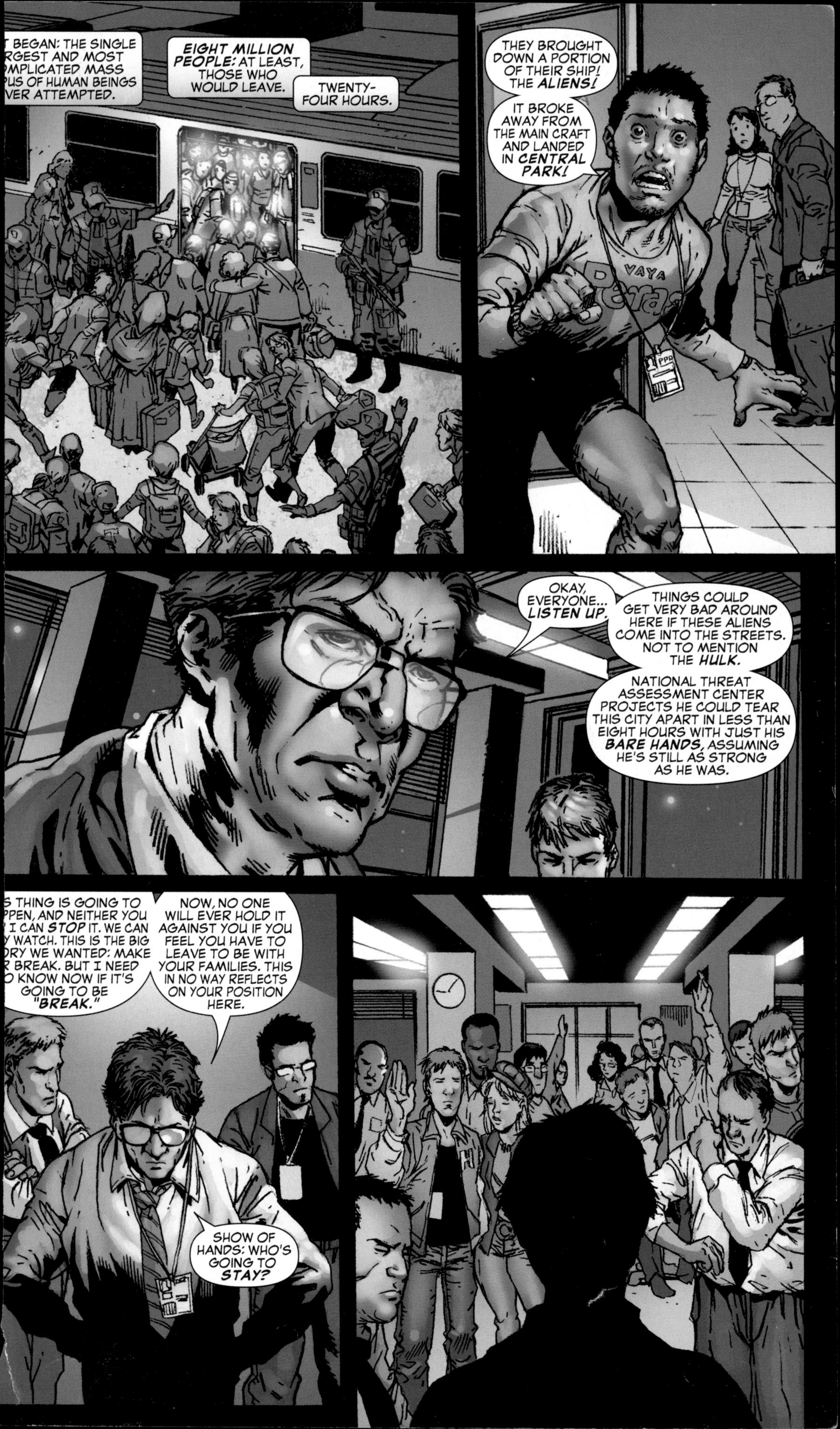
T BEGAN: THE SINGLE RGEST AND MOST OMPLICATED MASS PUS OF HUMAN BEINGS VER ATTEMPTED.
EIGHT MILLION PEOPLE: AT LEAST, THOSE WHO WOULD LEAVE.
TWENTY-FOUR HOURS.
THEY BROUGHT DOWN A PORTION OF THEIR SHIP! THE ALIENS!
IT BROKE AWAY FROM THE MAIN CRAFT AND LANDED IN CENTRAL PARK!
VAYA
OKAY, EVERYONE... LISTEN UP.
THINGS COULD GET VERY BAD AROUND HERE IF THESE ALIENS COME INTO THE STREETS. NOT TO MENTION THE HULK.
NATIONAL THREAT ASSESSMENT CENTER PROJECTS HE COULD TEAR THIS CITY APART IN LESS THAN EIGHT HOURS WITH JUST HIS BARE HANDS, ASSUMING HE'S STILL AS STRONG AS HE WAS.
S THING IS GOING TO PPEN, AND NEITHER YOU R I CAN STOP IT. WE CAN Y WATCH. THIS IS THE BIG ORY WE WANTED: MAKE R BREAK. BUT I NEED O KNOW NOW IF IT'S GOING TO BE "BREAK."
NOW, NO ONE WILL EVER HOLD IT AGAINST YOU IF YOU FEEL YOU HAVE TO LEAVE TO BE WITH YOUR FAMILIES. THIS IN NO WAY REFLECTS ON YOUR POSITION HERE.
SHOW OF HANDS: WHO'S GOING TO STAY?

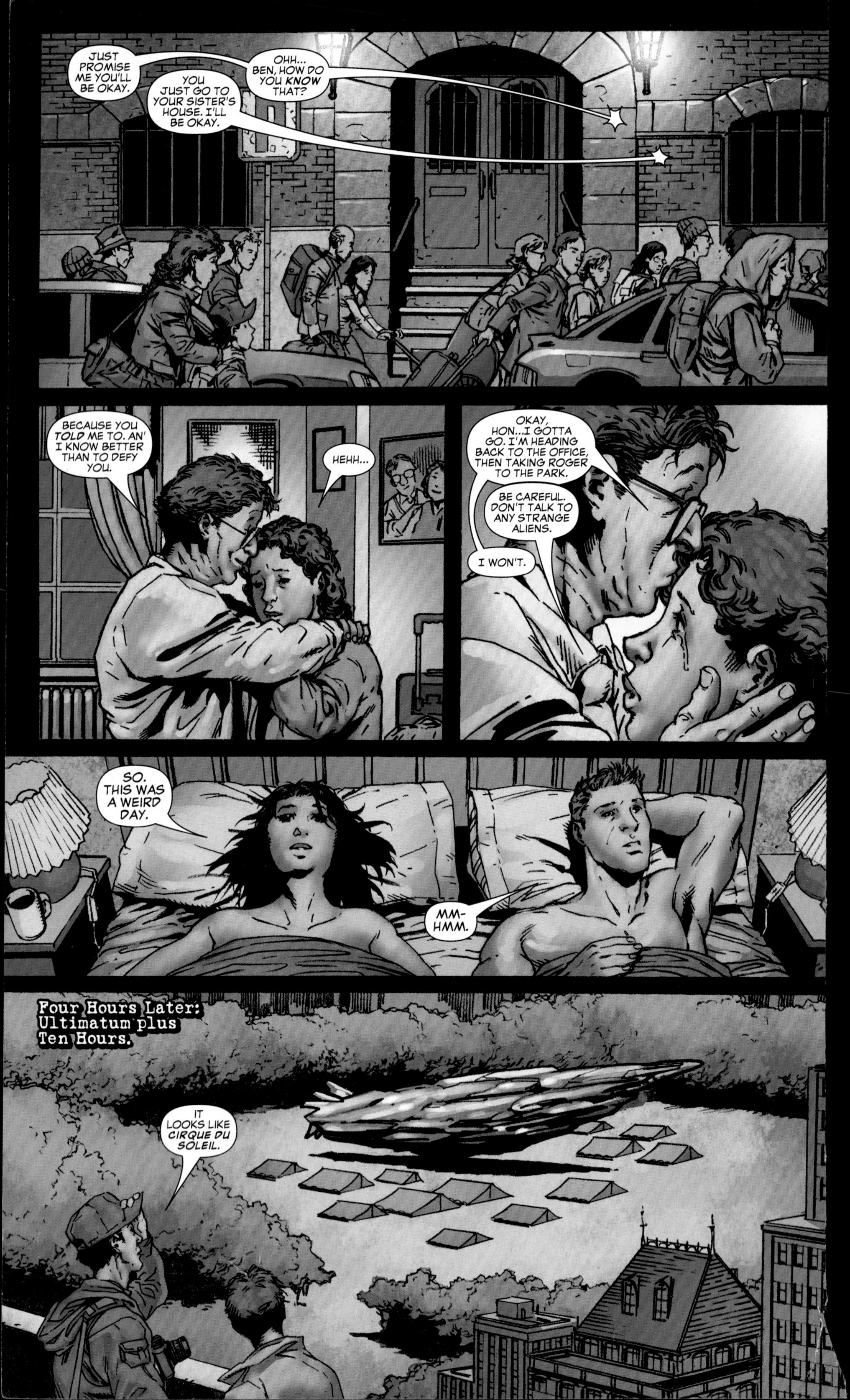

JUST PROMISE ME YOU'LL BE OKAY.
OHH... BEN, HOW DO YOU KNOW THAT?
YOU JUST GO TO YOUR SISTER'S HOUSE. I'LL BE OKAY.
BECAUSE YOU TOLD ME TO. AN' I KNOW BETTER THAN TO DEFY YOU.
HEHH...
OKAY, HON...I GOTTA GO. I'M HEADING BACK TO THE OFFICE, THEN TAKING ROGER TO THE PARK.
BE CAREFUL. DON'T TALK TO ANY STRANGE ALIENS.
I WON'T.
SO. THIS WAS A WEIRD DAY.
MM-HMM.
Four Hours Later: Ultimatum plus Ten Hours.
IT LOOKS LIKE CIRQUE DU SOLEIL.

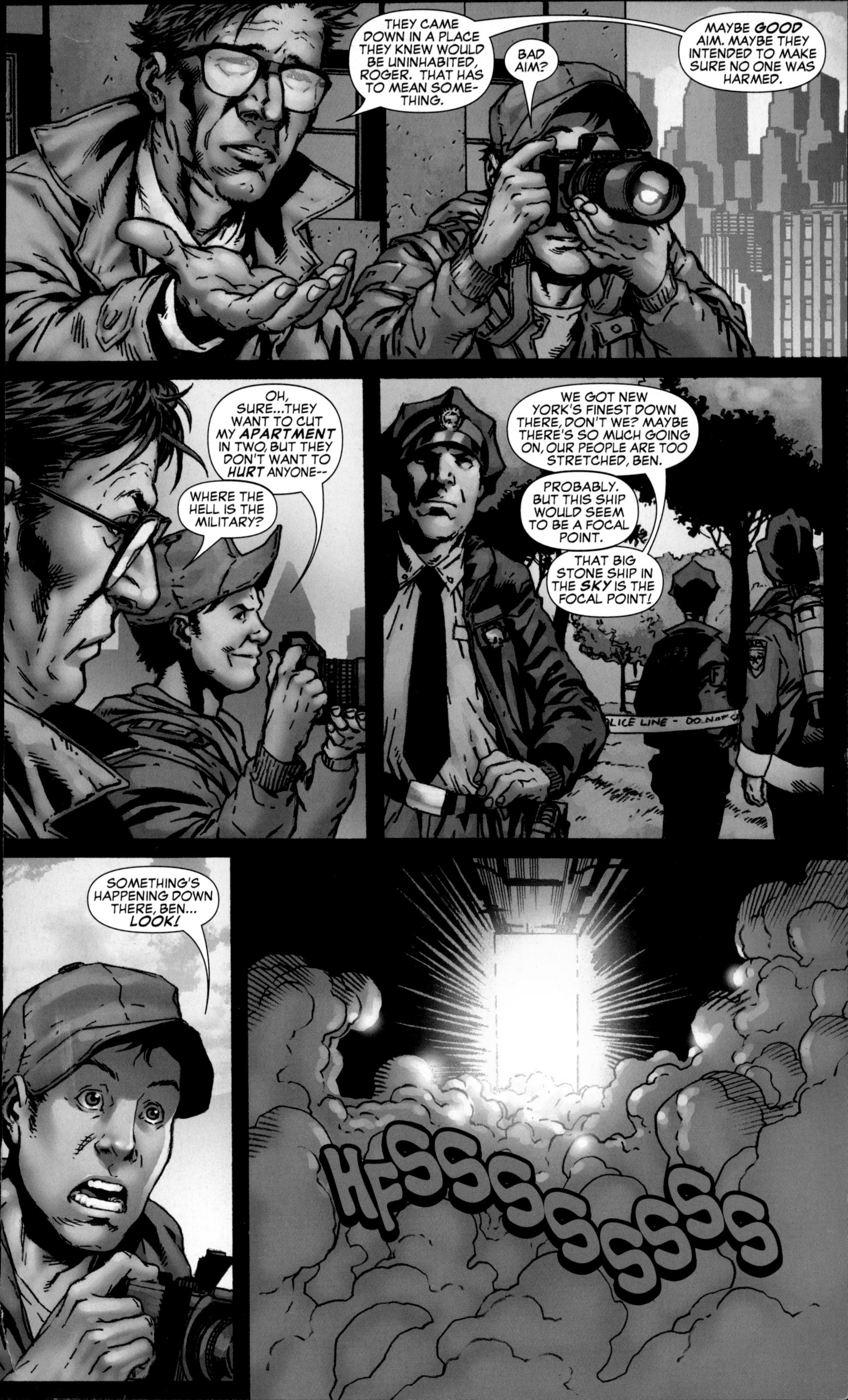
THEY CAME DOWN IN A PLACE THEY KNEW WOULD BE UNINHABITED, ROGER. THAT HAS TO MEAN SOMETHING.
BAD AIM?
MAYBE GOOD AIM. MAYBE THEY INTENDED TO MAKE SURE NO ONE WAS HARMED.
OH, SURE...THEY WANT TO CUT MY APARTMENT IN TWO, BUT THEY DON'T WANT TO HURT ANYONE--
WHERE THE HELL IS THE MILITARY?
WE GOT NEW YORK'S FINEST DOWN THERE, DON'T WE? MAYBE THERE'S SO MUCH GOING ON, OUR PEOPLE ARE TOO STRETCHED, BEN.
PROBABLY. BUT THIS SHIP WOULD SEEM TO BE A FOCAL POINT.
THAT BIG STONE SHIP IN THE SKY IS THE FOCAL POINT!
SOMETHING'S HAPPENING DOWN THERE, BEN... LOOK!
HFSSSSSSSSS

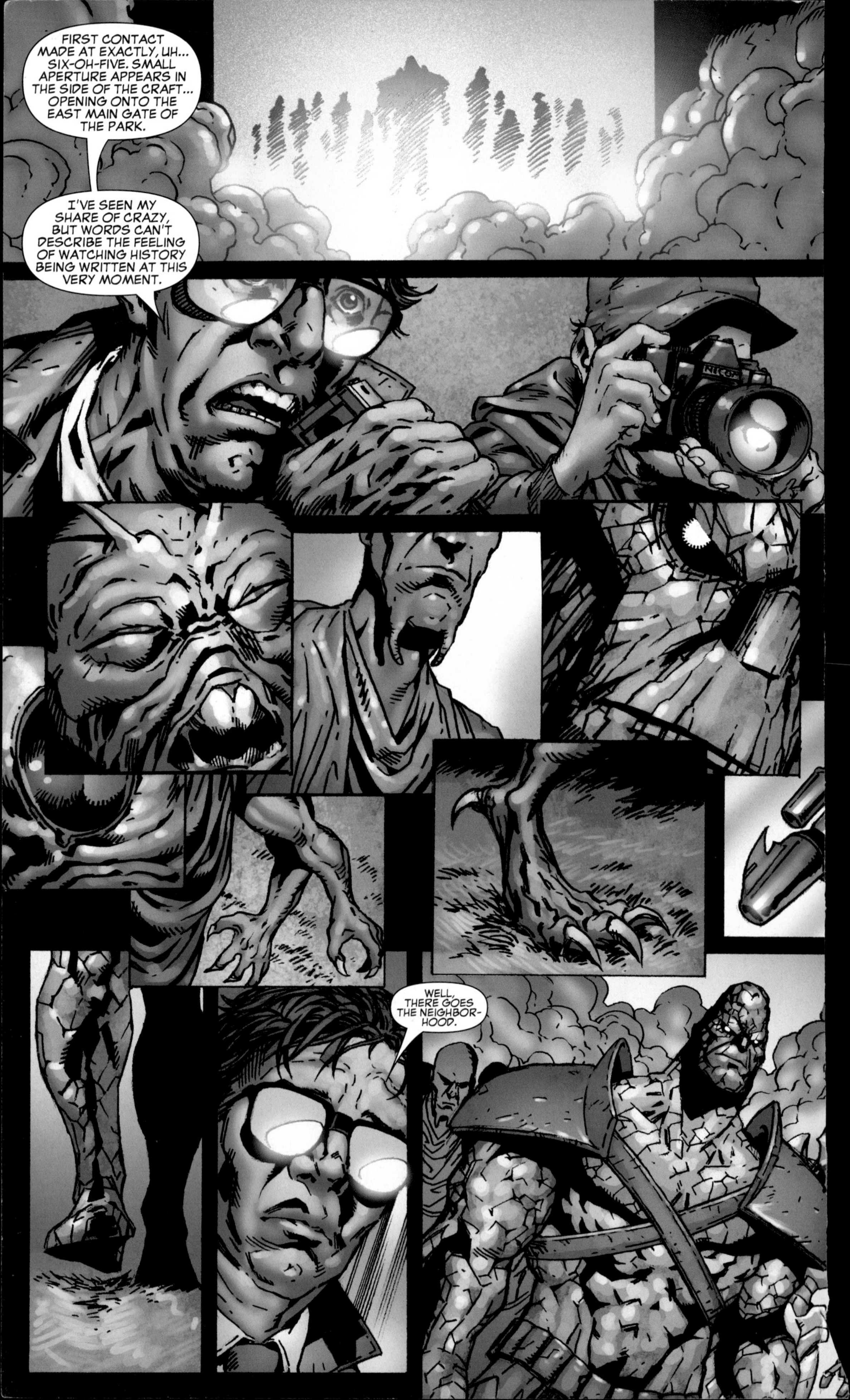
FIRST CONTACT MADE AT EXACTLY, UH... SIX-OH-FIVE. SMALL APERTURE APPEARS IN THE SIDE OF THE CRAFT... OPENING ONTO THE EAST MAIN GATE OF THE PARK.
I'VE SEEN MY SHARE OF CRAZY, BUT WORDS CAN'T DESCRIBE THE FEELING OF WATCHING HISTORY BEING WRITTEN AT THIS VERY MOMENT.
WELL, THERE GOES THE NEIGHBOR-HOOD.

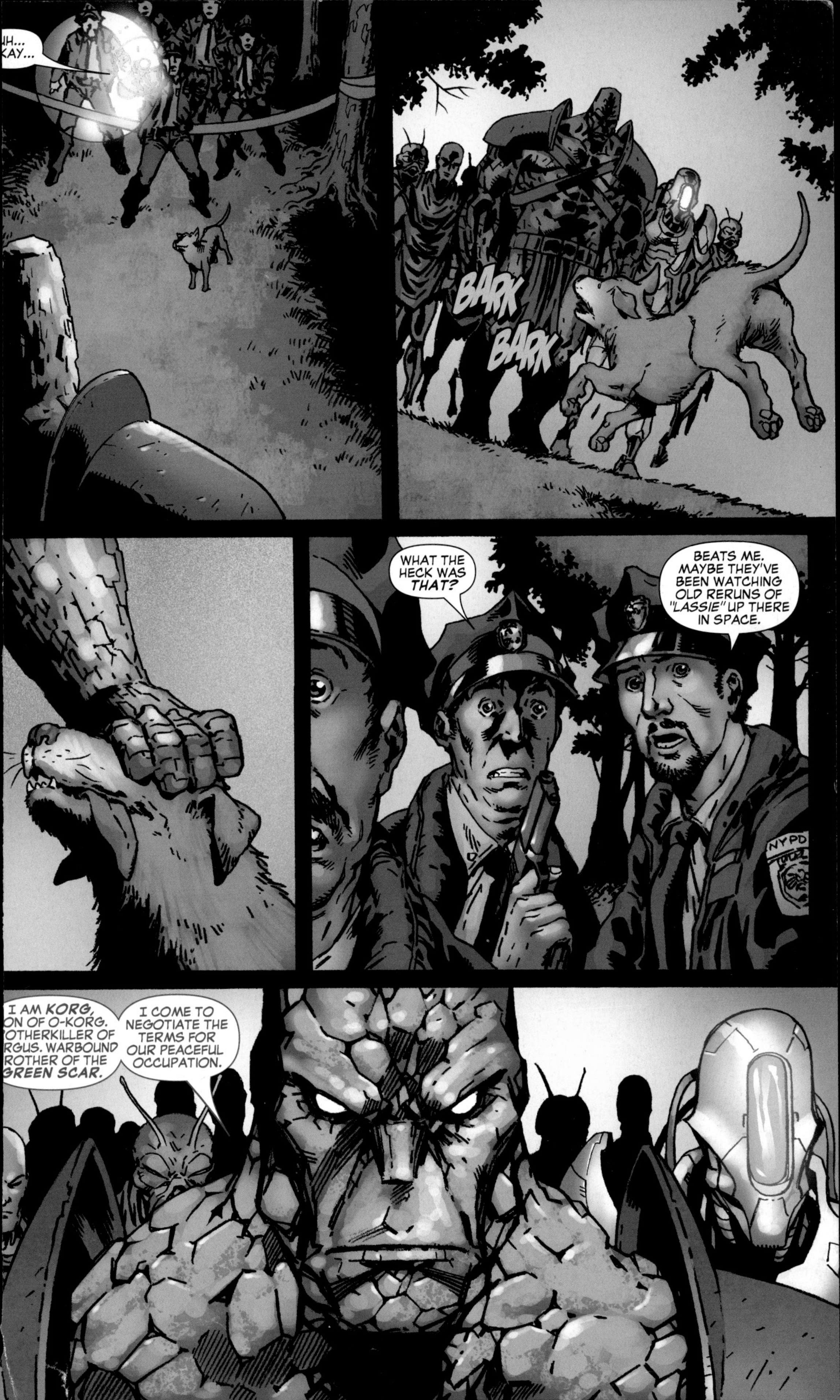
H... KAY...
BARK BARK
WHAT THE HECK WAS THAT?
BEATS ME. MAYBE THEY'VE BEEN WATCHING OLD RERUNS OF "LASSIE" UP THERE IN SPACE.
NYPD
I AM KORG, ON OF O-KORG. OTHERKILLER OF RGUS. WARBOUND ROTHER OF THE GREEN SCAR.
I COME TO NEGOTIATE THE TERMS FOR OUR PEACEFUL OCCUPATION.

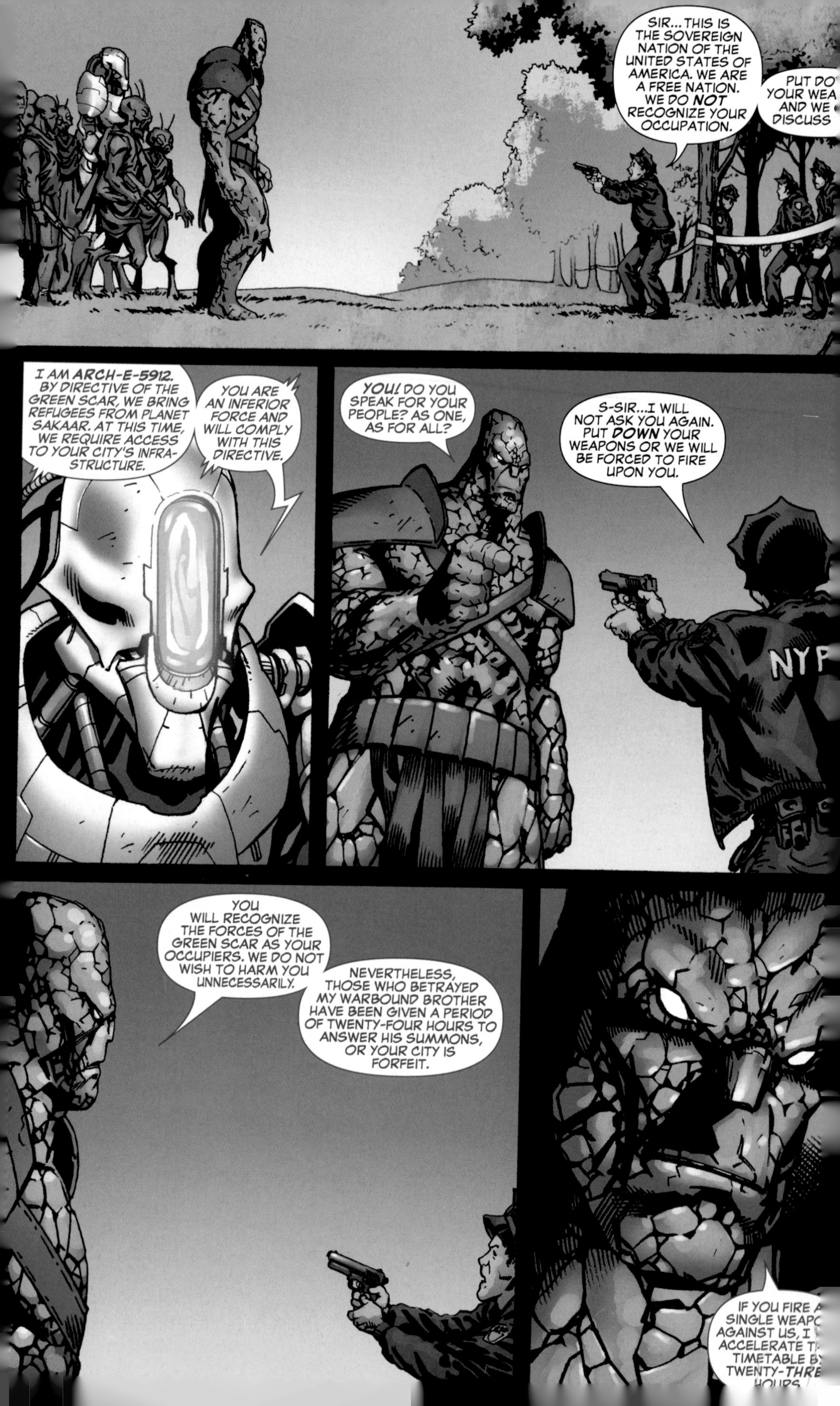
SIR... THIS IS THE SOVEREIGN NATION OF THE UNITED STATES OF AMERICA. WE ARE A FREE NATION. WE DO NOT RECOGNIZE YOUR OCCUPATION.
PUT DO YOUR WEA AND WE DISCUSS
I AM ARCH-E-5912. BY DIRECTIVE OF THE GREEN SCAR, WE BRING REFUGEES FROM PLANET SAKAAR. AT THIS TIME, WE REQUIRE ACCESS TO YOUR CITY'S INFRA-STRUCTURE.
YOU ARE AN INFERIOR FORCE AND WILL COMPLY WITH THIS DIRECTIVE.
YOU! DO YOU SPEAK FOR YOUR PEOPLE? AS ONE, AS FOR ALL?
S-SIR...I WILL NOT ASK YOU AGAIN. PUT DOWN YOUR WEAPONS OR WE WILL BE FORCED TO FIRE UPON YOU.
NYP
YOU WILL RECOGNIZE THE FORCES OF THE GREEN SCAR AS YOUR OCCUPIERS. WE DO NOT WISH TO HARM YOU UNNECESSARILY.
NEVERTHELESS, THOSE WHO BETRAYED MY WARBOUND BROTHER HAVE BEEN GIVEN A PERIOD OF TWENTY-FOUR HOURS TO ANSWER HIS SUMMONS, OR YOUR CITY IS FORFEIT.
IF YOU FIRE A SINGLE WEAPO AGAINST US, I ACCELERATE T TIMETABLE B TWENTY-THRE HOURS.

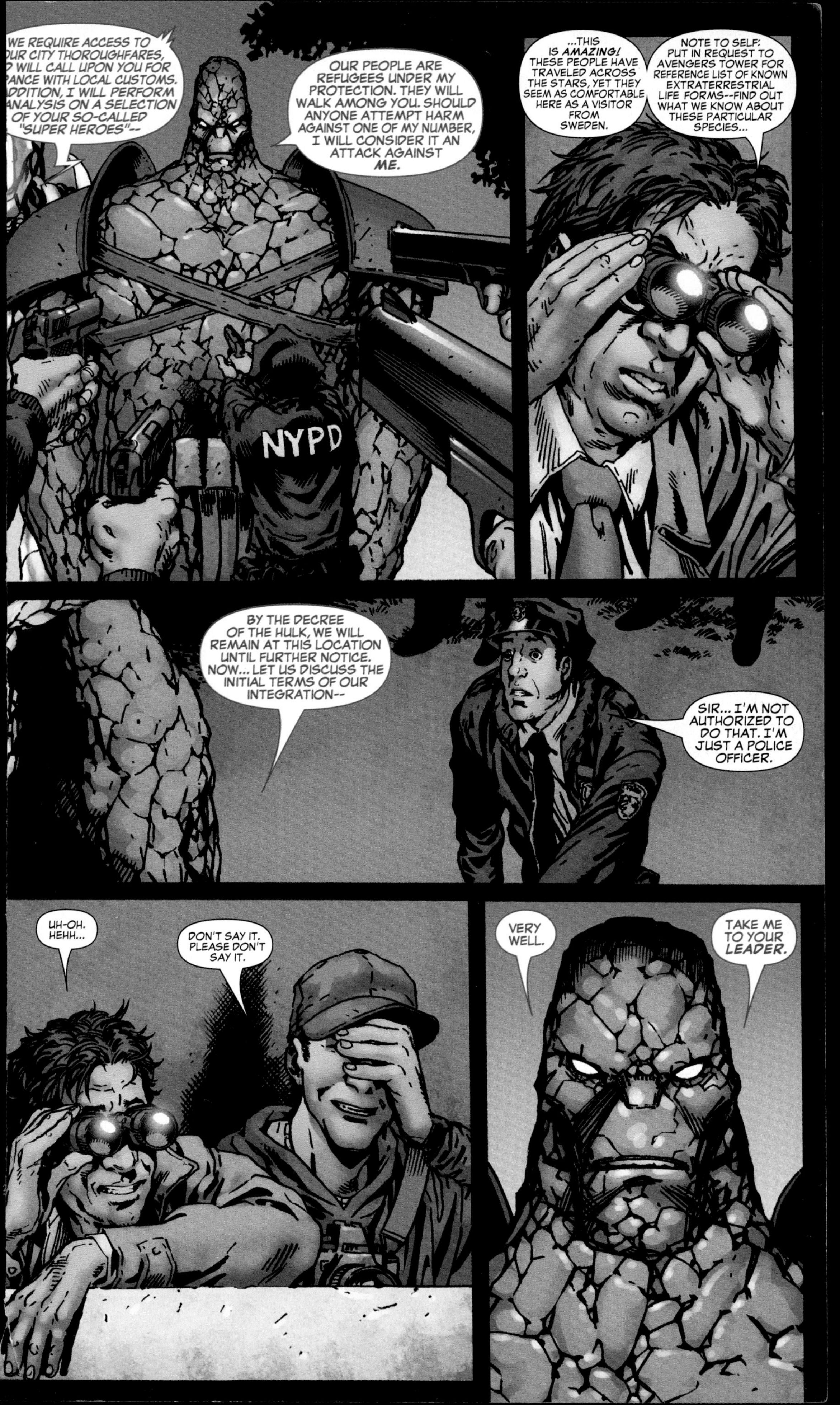

WE REQUIRE ACCESS TO OUR CITY THOROUGHFARES, D WILL CALL UPON YOU FOR ANCE WITH LOCAL CUSTOMS. DDITION, I WILL PERFORM ANALYSIS ON A SELECTION OF YOUR SO-CALLED "SUPER HEROES"--
OUR PEOPLE ARE REFUGEES UNDER MY PROTECTION. THEY WILL WALK AMONG YOU. SHOULD ANYONE ATTEMPT HARM AGAINST ONE OF MY NUMBER, I WILL CONSIDER IT AN ATTACK AGAINST ME.
NYPD
...THIS IS AMAZING! THESE PEOPLE HAVE TRAVELED ACROSS THE STARS, YET THEY SEEM AS COMFORTABLE HERE AS A VISITOR FROM SWEDEN.
NOTE TO SELF: PUT IN REQUEST TO AVENGERS TOWER FOR REFERENCE LIST OF KNOWN EXTRATERRESTRIAL LIFE FORMS--FIND OUT WHAT WE KNOW ABOUT THESE PARTICULAR SPECIES...
BY THE DECREE OF THE HULK, WE WILL REMAIN AT THIS LOCATION UNTIL FURTHER NOTICE. NOW... LET US DISCUSS THE INITIAL TERMS OF OUR INTEGRATION--
SIR... I'M NOT AUTHORIZED TO DO THAT. I'M JUST A POLICE OFFICER.
UH-OH. HEHH...
DON'T SAY IT. PLEASE DON'T SAY IT.
VERY WELL.
TAKE ME TO YOUR LEADER.

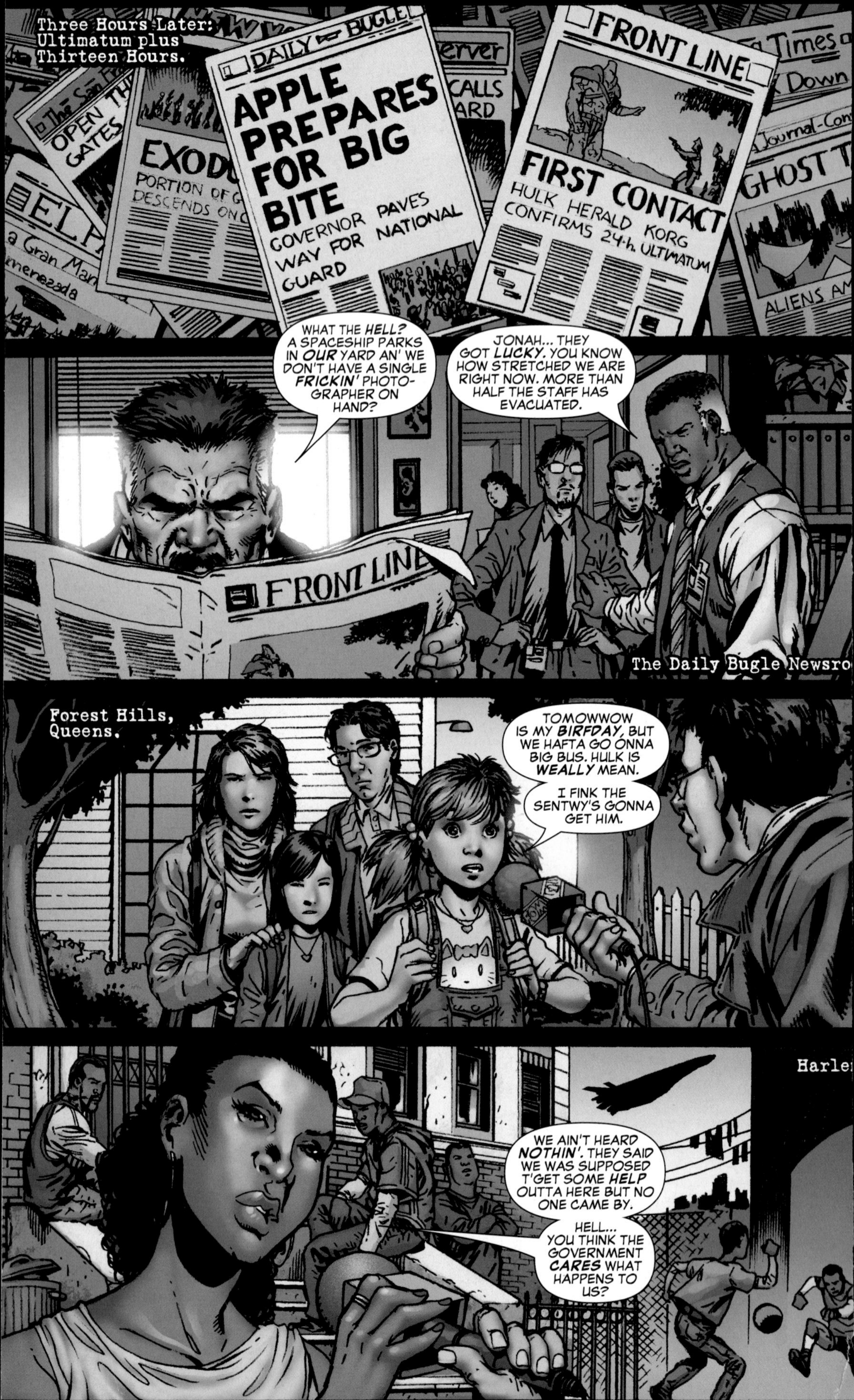
Three Hours Later: Ultimatum plus Thirteen Hours.
DAILY BUGLE
APPLE PREPARES FOR BIG BITE
GOVERNOR PAVES WAY FOR NATIONAL GUARD
FRONT LINE
FIRST CONTACT
HULK HERALD KORG CONFIRMS 24-h. ULTIMATUM
EXODU
PORTION OF G
DESCENDS ON C
OPEN TH GATES
CALLS
ARD
GHOST T
ALIENS AM
WHAT THE HELL? A SPACESHIP PARKS IN OUR YARD AN' WE DON'T HAVE A SINGLE FRICKIN' PHOTOGRAPHER ON HAND?
JONAH... THEY GOT LUCKY. YOU KNOW HOW STRETCHED WE ARE RIGHT NOW. MORE THAN HALF THE STAFF HAS EVACUATED.
FRONT LINE
The Daily Bugle Newsro
Forest Hills, Queens.
TOMOWWOW IS MY BIRFDAY, BUT WE HAFTA GO ONNA BIG BUS. HULK IS WEALLY MEAN.
I FINK THE SENTWY'S GONNA GET HIM.
Harle
WE AIN'T HEARD NOTHIN'. THEY SAID WE WAS SUPPOSED T'GET SOME HELP OUTTA HERE BUT NO ONE CAME BY.
HELL... YOU THINK THE GOVERNMENT CARES WHAT HAPPENS TO US?

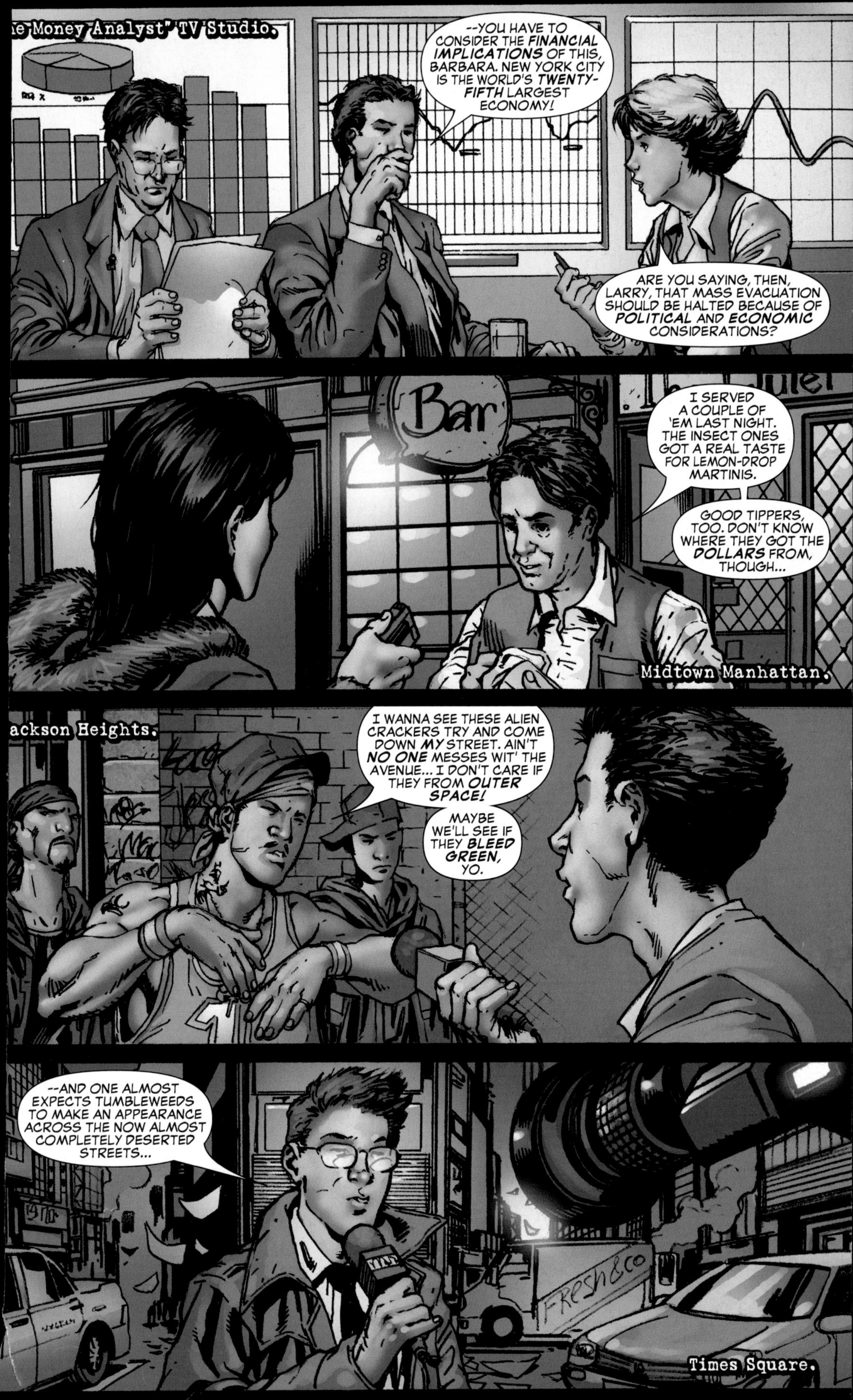
he Money Analyst" TV Studio.
--YOU HAVE TO CONSIDER THE FINANCIAL IMPLICATIONS OF THIS, BARBARA. NEW YORK CITY IS THE WORLD'S TWENTY-FIFTH LARGEST ECONOMY!
ARE YOU SAYING, THEN, LARRY, THAT MASS EVACUATION SHOULD BE HALTED BECAUSE OF POLITICAL AND ECONOMIC CONSIDERATIONS?
Bar
I SERVED A COUPLE OF 'EM LAST NIGHT. THE INSECT ONES GOT A REAL TASTE FOR LEMON-DROP MARTINIS.
GOOD TIPPERS, TOO. DON'T KNOW WHERE THEY GOT THE DOLLARS FROM, THOUGH...
Midtown Manhattan.
ackson Heights.
I WANNA SEE THESE ALIEN CRACKERS TRY AND COME DOWN MY STREET. AIN'T NO ONE MESSES WIT' THE AVENUE... I DON'T CARE IF THEY FROM OUTER SPACE!
MAYBE WE'LL SEE IF THEY BLEED GREEN, YO.
--AND ONE ALMOST EXPECTS TUMBLEWEEDS TO MAKE AN APPEARANCE ACROSS THE NOW ALMOST COMPLETELY DESERTED STREETS...
Times Square.

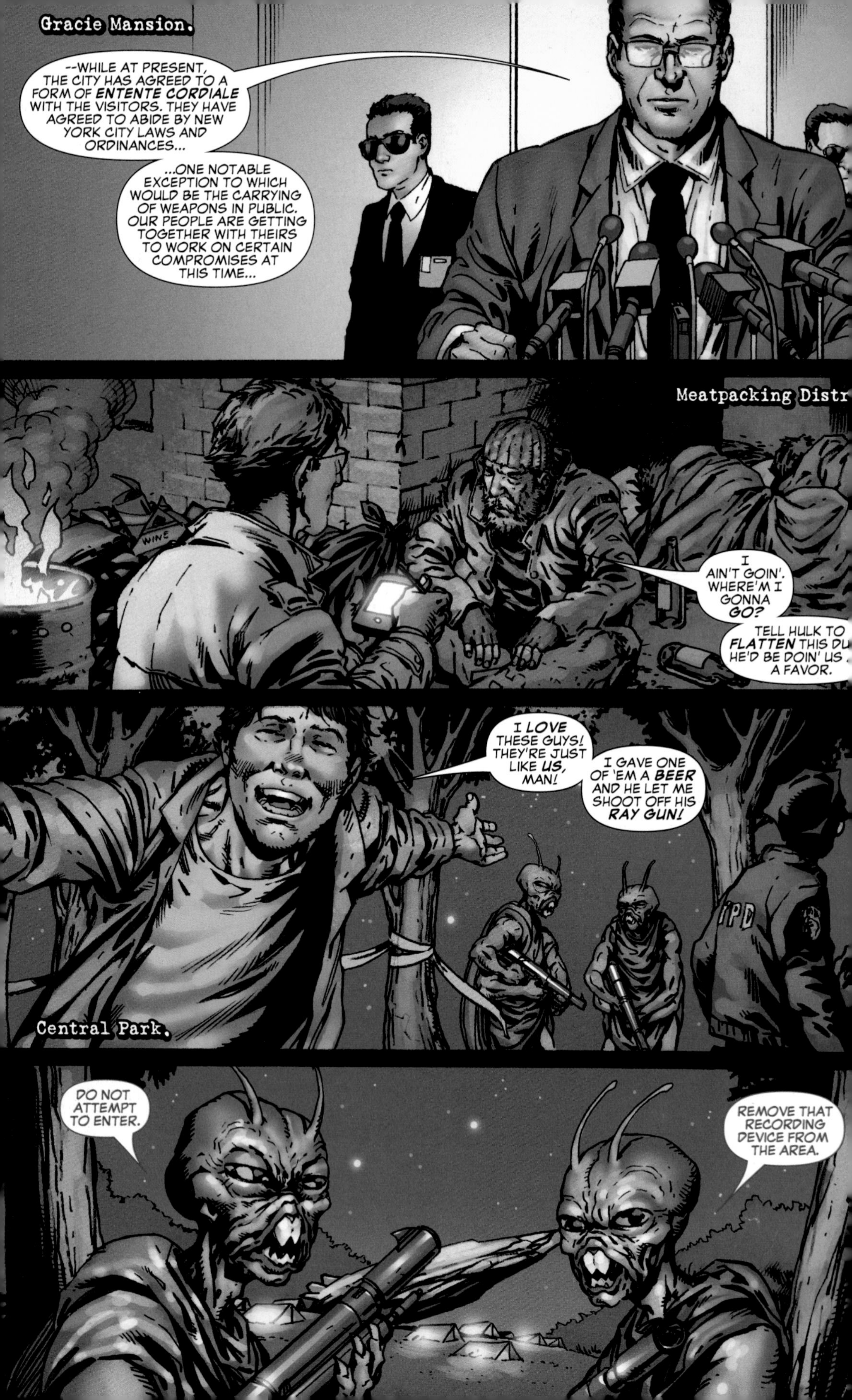
Gracie Mansion.
--WHILE AT PRESENT, THE CITY HAS AGREED TO A FORM OF ENTENTE CORDIALE WITH THE VISITORS. THEY HAVE AGREED TO ABIDE BY NEW YORK CITY LAWS AND ORDINANCES...
...ONE NOTABLE EXCEPTION TO WHICH WOULD BE THE CARRYING OF WEAPONS IN PUBLIC. OUR PEOPLE ARE GETTING TOGETHER WITH THEIRS TO WORK ON CERTAIN COMPROMISES AT THIS TIME...
Meatpacking Distr
WINE
I AIN'T GOIN'. WHERE'M I GONNA GO?
TELL HULK TO FLATTEN THIS DU HE'D BE DOIN' US A FAVOR.
I LOVE THESE GUYS! THEY'RE JUST LIKE US, MAN!
I GAVE ONE OF 'EM A BEER AND HE LET ME SHOOT OFF HIS RAY GUN!
Central Park.
DO NOT ATTEMPT TO ENTER.
REMOVE THAT RECORDING DEVICE FROM THE AREA.

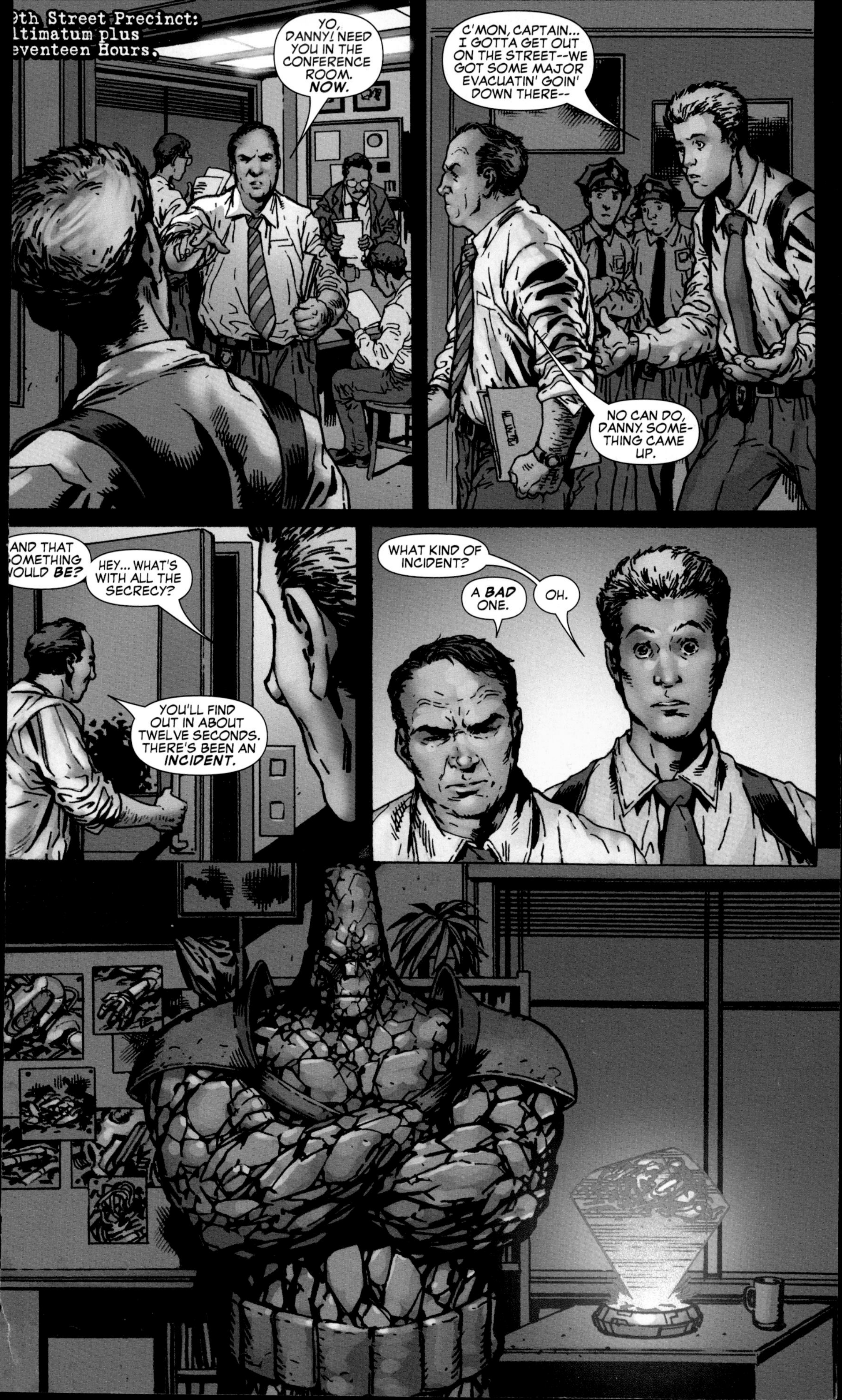
9th Street Precinct: Ultimatum plus Seventeen Hours.
YO, DANNY! NEED YOU IN THE CONFERENCE ROOM. NOW.
C'MON, CAPTAIN... I GOTTA GET OUT ON THE STREET--WE GOT SOME MAJOR EVACUATIN' GOIN' DOWN THERE--
NO CAN DO, DANNY. SOMETHING CAME UP.
AND THAT SOMETHING WOULD BE?
HEY... WHAT'S WITH ALL THE SECRECY?
YOU'LL FIND OUT IN ABOUT TWELVE SECONDS. THERE'S BEEN AN INCIDENT.
WHAT KIND OF INCIDENT?
A BAD ONE.
OH.

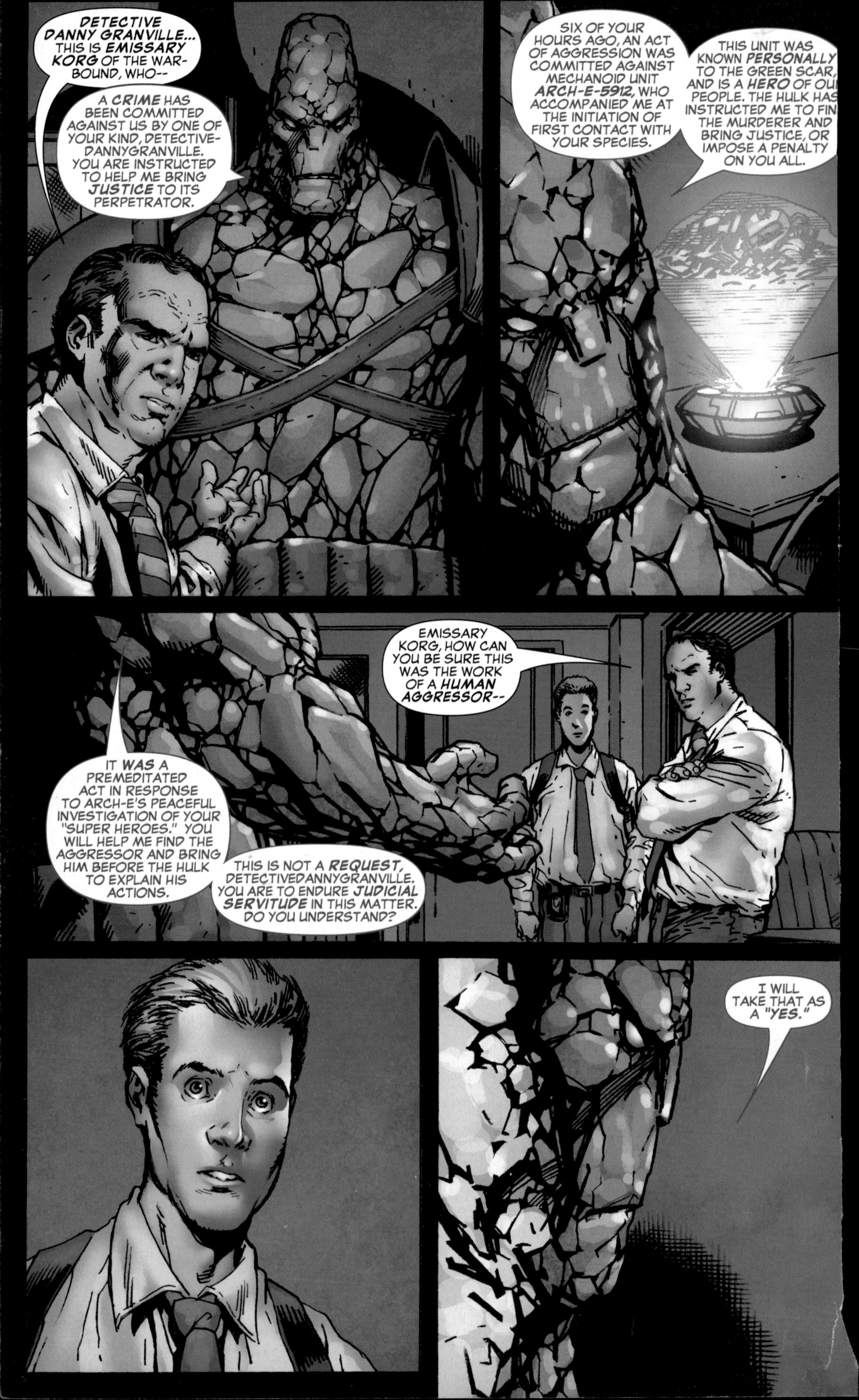
DETECTIVE DANNY GRANVILLE... THIS IS EMISSARY KORG OF THE WAR-BOUND, WHO--
A CRIME HAS BEEN COMMITTED AGAINST US BY ONE OF YOUR KIND, DETECTIVE-DANNYGRANVILLE. YOU ARE INSTRUCTED TO HELP ME BRING JUSTICE TO ITS PERPETRATOR.
SIX OF YOUR HOURS AGO, AN ACT OF AGGRESSION WAS COMMITTED AGAINST MECHANOID UNIT ARCH-E-5912, WHO ACCOMPANIED ME AT THE INITIATION OF FIRST CONTACT WITH YOUR SPECIES.
THIS UNIT WAS KNOWN PERSONALLY TO THE GREEN SCAR, AND IS A HERO OF OU PEOPLE. THE HULK HAS INSTRUCTED ME TO FIN THE MURDERER AND BRING JUSTICE, OR IMPOSE A PENALTY ON YOU ALL.
EMISSARY KORG, HOW CAN YOU BE SURE THIS WAS THE WORK OF A HUMAN AGGRESSOR--
IT WAS A PREMEDITATED ACT IN RESPONSE TO ARCH-E'S PEACEFUL INVESTIGATION OF YOUR "SUPER HEROES." YOU WILL HELP ME FIND THE AGGRESSOR AND BRING HIM BEFORE THE HULK TO EXPLAIN HIS ACTIONS.
THIS IS NOT A REQUEST, DETECTIVEDANNYGRANVILLE. YOU ARE TO ENDURE JUDICIAL SERVITUDE IN THIS MATTER. DO YOU UNDERSTAND?
I WILL TAKE THAT AS A "YES."

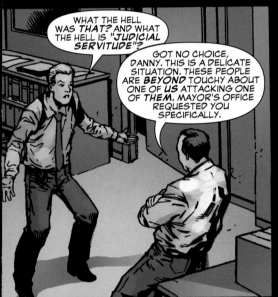

WHAT THE HELL WAS *THAT?* AND WHAT THE HELL IS *"JUDICIAL SERVITUDE"?*

GOT NO CHOICE, DANNY. THIS IS A DELICATE SITUATION. THESE PEOPLE ARE *BEYOND* TOUCHY ABOUT ONE OF *US* ATTACKING ONE OF *THEM.* MAYOR'S OFFICE REQUESTED YOU SPECIFICALLY.

AN' EXACTLY WHAT AM I SUPPOSED TO DO, CAP?

LOOK... THIS *KORG* GUY WANTS YOU TO HELP HIM PROCESS THE CRIME SCENE, GIVE HIM A LITTLE *LOCAL KNOWLEDGE.*

IT'S IMPORTANT RIGHT NOW THAT WE DON'T *START ANYTHING* WITH THESE PEOPLE. WE DON'T KNOW WHERE WE STAND UNTIL WE GET WORD FROM S.H.I.E.L.D.

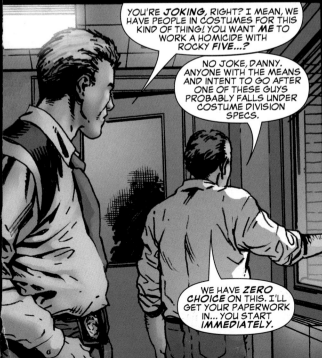

YOU'RE *JOKING,* RIGHT? I MEAN, WE HAVE PEOPLE IN COSTUMES FOR THIS KIND OF THING! YOU WANT *ME* TO WORK A HOMICIDE WITH ROCKY *FIVE...?*

NO JOKE, DANNY. ANYONE WITH THE MEANS AND INTENT TO GO AFTER ONE OF THESE GUYS PROBABLY FALLS UNDER COSTUME DIVISION SPECS.

WE HAVE *ZERO CHOICE* ON THIS. I'LL GET YOUR PAPERWORK IN... YOU START *IMMEDIATELY.*

GOD... WHERE IS IRON MAN WHEN YOU *NEED* HIM?

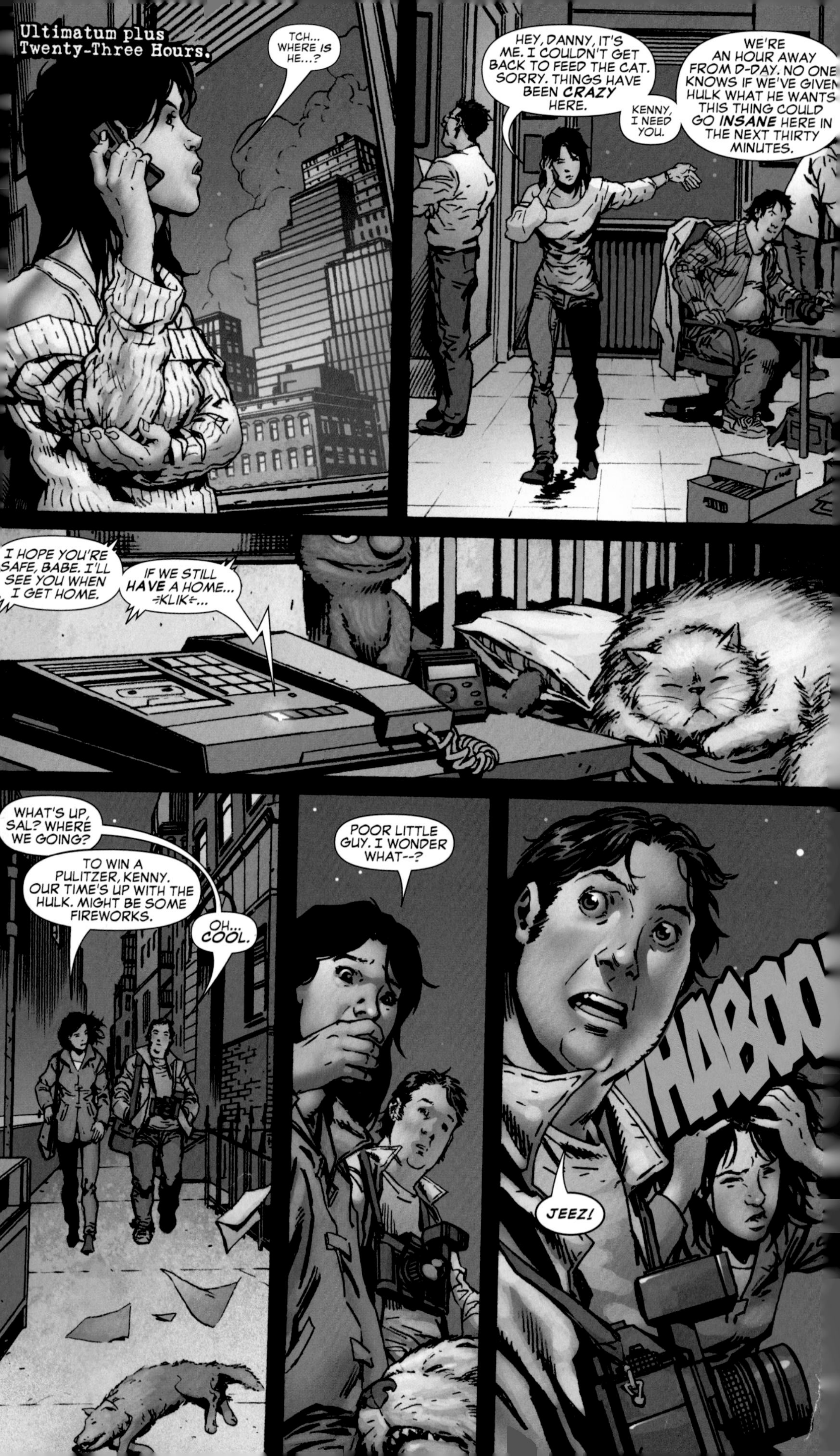
Ultimatum plus Twenty-Three Hours.
TCH... WHERE IS HE...?
HEY, DANNY, IT'S ME. I COULDN'T GET BACK TO FEED THE CAT. SORRY. THINGS HAVE BEEN CRAZY HERE.
KENNY, I NEED YOU.
WE'RE AN HOUR AWAY FROM D-DAY. NO ONE KNOWS IF WE'VE GIVEN HULK WHAT HE WANTS. THIS THING COULD GO INSANE HERE IN THE NEXT THIRTY MINUTES.
I HOPE YOU'RE SAFE, BABE. I'LL SEE YOU WHEN I GET HOME.
IF WE STILL HAVE A HOME... ⇗KLIK⇐...
WHAT'S UP, SAL? WHERE WE GOING?
TO WIN A PULITZER, KENNY. OUR TIME'S UP WITH THE HULK. MIGHT BE SOME FIREWORKS.
OH... COOL.
POOR LITTLE GUY. I WONDER WHAT--?
JEEZ!

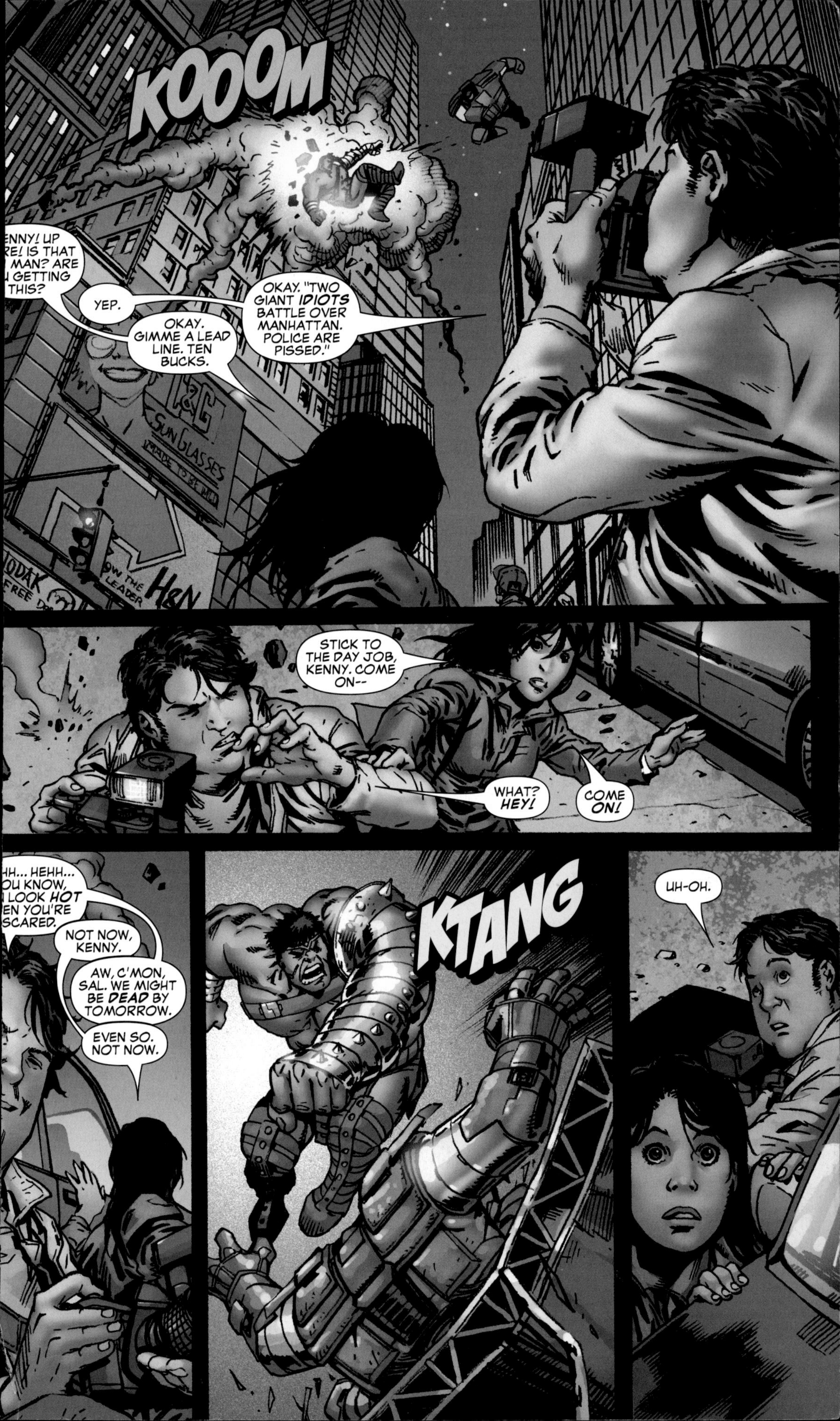
KOOOM
ENNY! UP
RE! IS THAT
MAN? ARE
U GETTING
THIS?
YEP.
OKAY. GIMME A LEAD LINE. TEN BUCKS.
OKAY. "TWO GIANT *IDIOTS* BATTLE OVER MANHATTAN. POLICE ARE PISSED."
SUN GLASSES
H&N
STICK TO THE DAY JOB, KENNY. COME ON--
WHAT? *HEY!*
COME *ON!*
HH... HEHH...
OU KNOW,
LOOK *HOT*
EN YOU'RE
SCARED.
NOT NOW, KENNY.
AW, C'MON, SAL. WE MIGHT BE *DEAD* BY TOMORROW.
EVEN SO. NOT NOW.
KTANG
UH-OH.

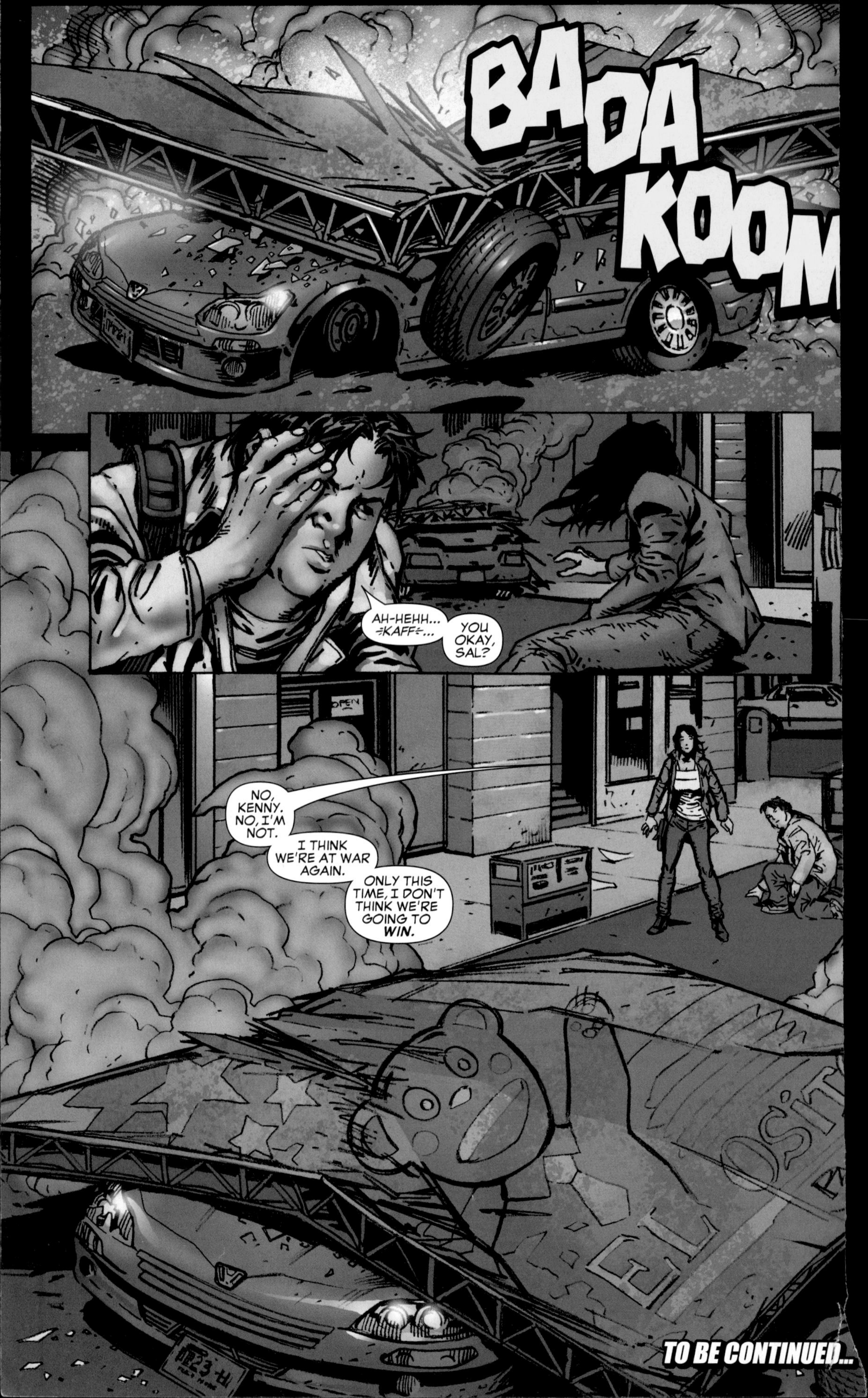
BADA KOOM
AH-HEHH... ≠KAFF≠...
YOU OKAY, SAL?
OPEN
NO, KENNY. NO, I'M NOT.
I THINK WE'RE AT WAR AGAIN.
ONLY THIS TIME, I DON'T THINK WE'RE GOING TO WIN.
TO BE CONTINUED...

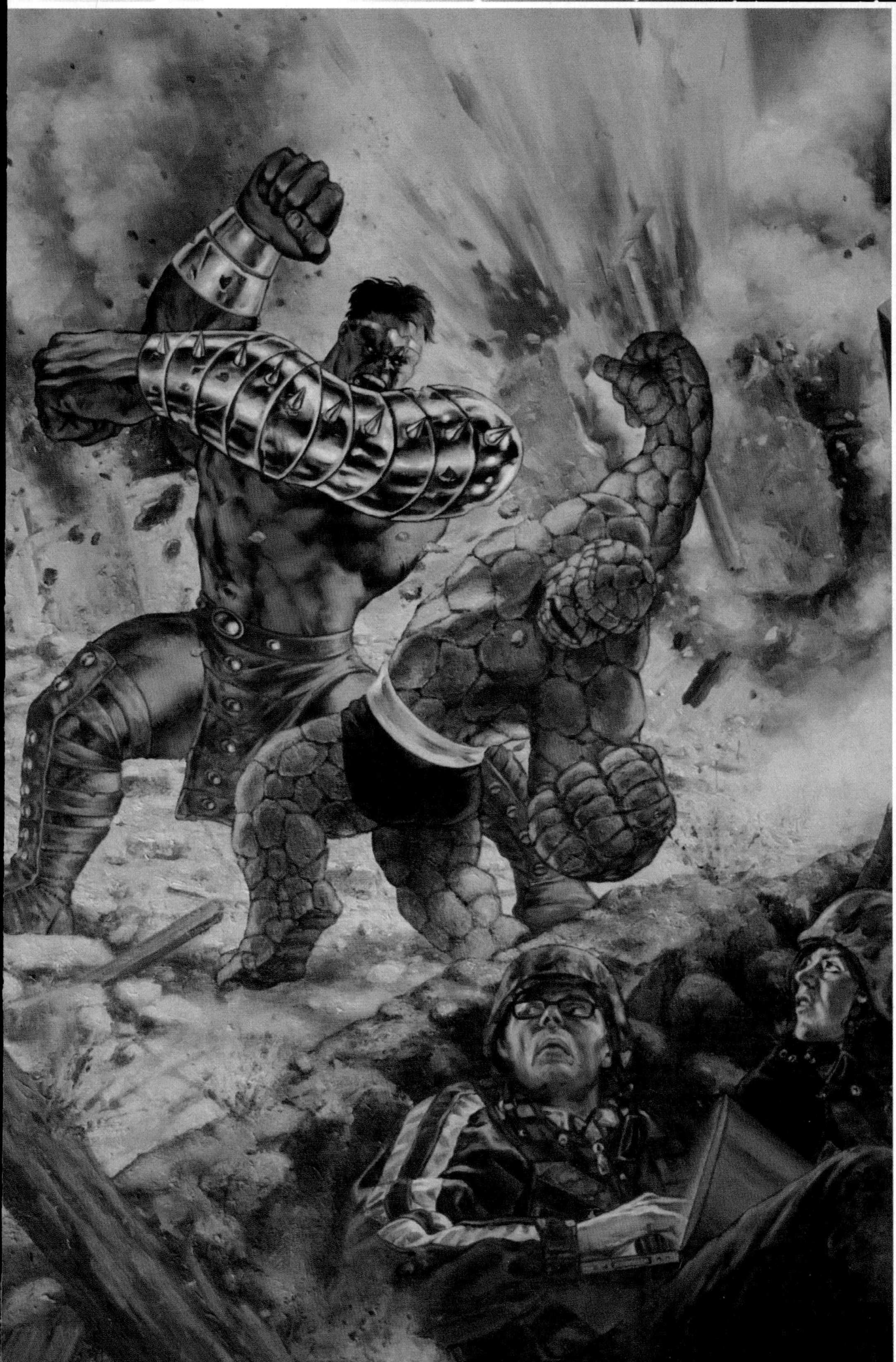

WORLD WAR HULK: FRONT LINE #2

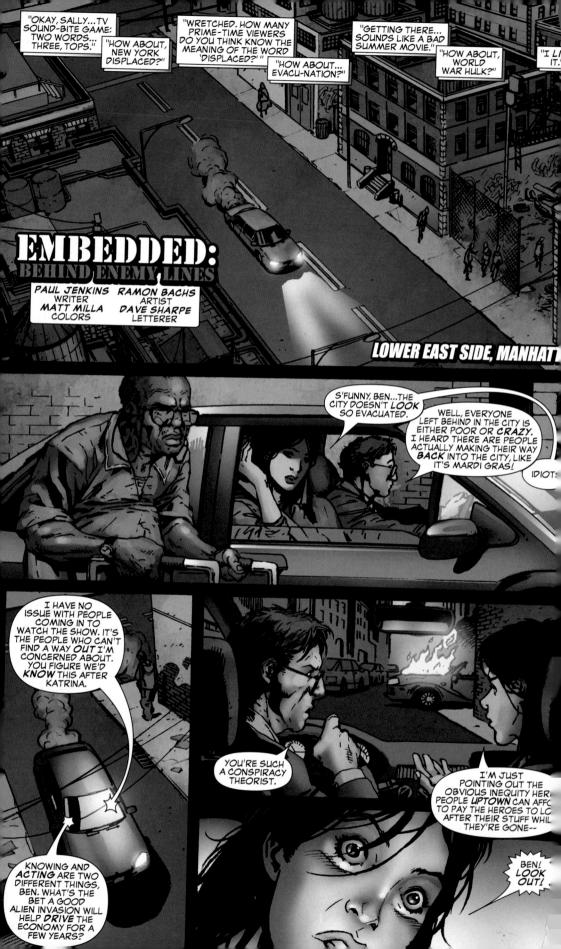

"OKAY, SALLY...TV SOUND-BITE GAME: TWO WORDS... THREE, TOPS."

"HOW ABOUT, NEW YORK DISPLACED?"

"WRETCHED. HOW MANY PRIME-TIME VIEWERS DO YOU THINK KNOW THE MEANING OF THE WORD 'DISPLACED?'"

"HOW ABOUT... EVACU-NATION?"

"GETTING THERE... SOUNDS LIKE A BAD SUMMER MOVIE."

"HOW ABOUT, WORLD WAR HULK?"

"I LI IT."

EMBEDDED:
BEHIND ENEMY LINES

PAUL JENKINS
WRITER

RAMON BACHS
ARTIST

MATT MILLA
COLORS

DAVE SHARPE
LETTERER

LOWER EAST SIDE, MANHATT

S'FUNNY, BEN...THE CITY DOESN'T *LOOK* SO EVACUATED.

WELL, EVERYONE LEFT BEHIND IN THE CITY IS EITHER POOR OR *CRAZY*. I HEARD THERE ARE PEOPLE ACTUALLY MAKING THEIR WAY *BACK* INTO THE CITY, LIKE IT'S MARDI GRAS!

IDIOTS

I HAVE NO ISSUE WITH PEOPLE COMING IN TO WATCH THE SHOW. IT'S THE PEOPLE WHO CAN'T FIND A WAY *OUT* I'M CONCERNED ABOUT. YOU FIGURE WE'D *KNOW* THIS AFTER KATRINA.

YOU'RE SUCH A CONSPIRACY THEORIST.

I'M JUST POINTING OUT THE OBVIOUS INEQUITY HER PEOPLE *UPTOWN* CAN AFFO TO PAY THE HEROES TO LO AFTER THEIR STUFF WHIL THEY'RE GONE--

KNOWING AND ACTING ARE TWO DIFFERENT THINGS, BEN. WHAT'S THE BET A GOOD ALIEN INVASION WILL HELP *DRIVE* THE ECONOMY FOR A FEW YEARS?

BEN! LOOK OUT!

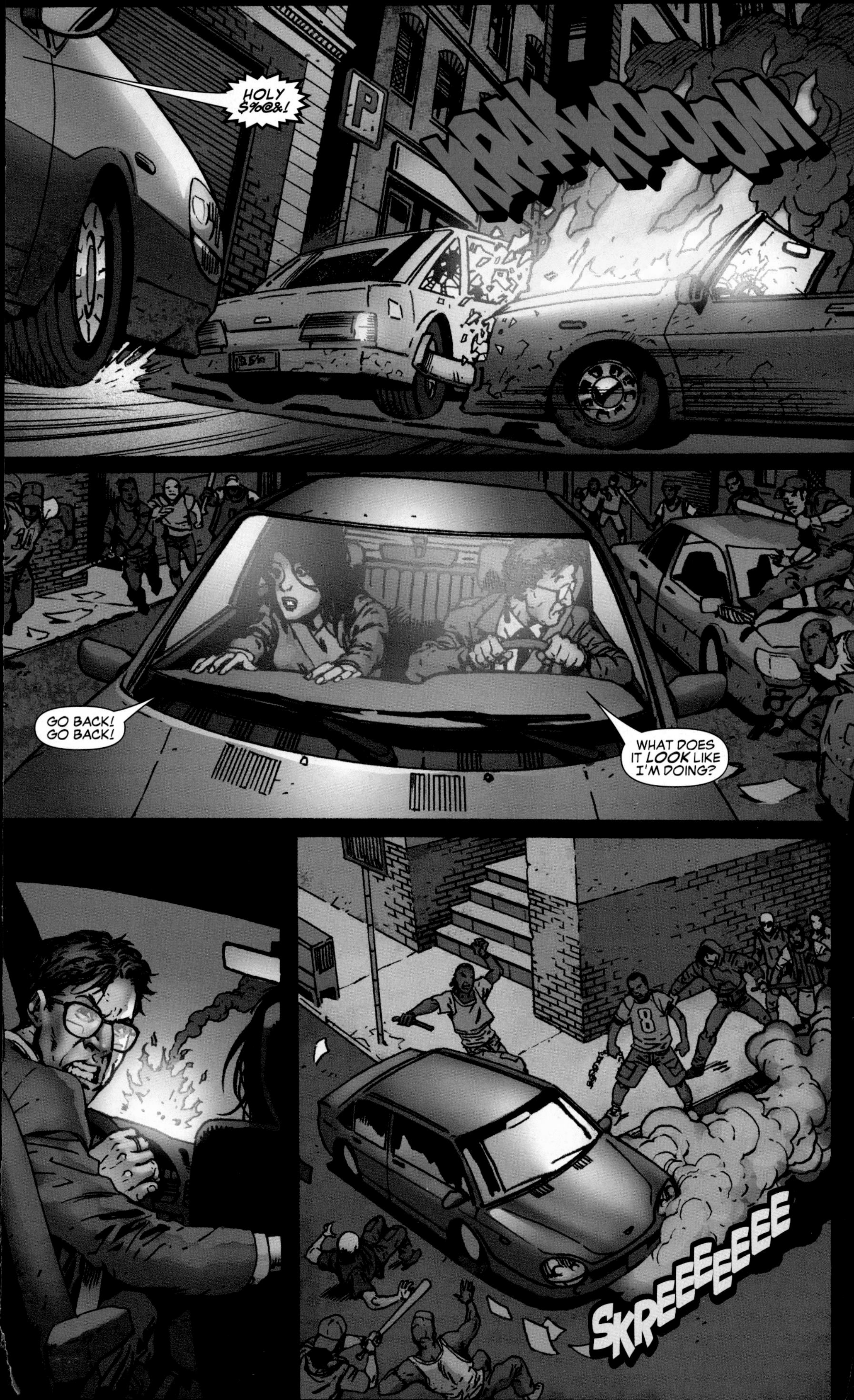
HOLY $%@&!
KRAKOOOM
GO BACK! GO BACK!
WHAT DOES IT LOOK LIKE I'M DOING?
SKREEEEEEEE

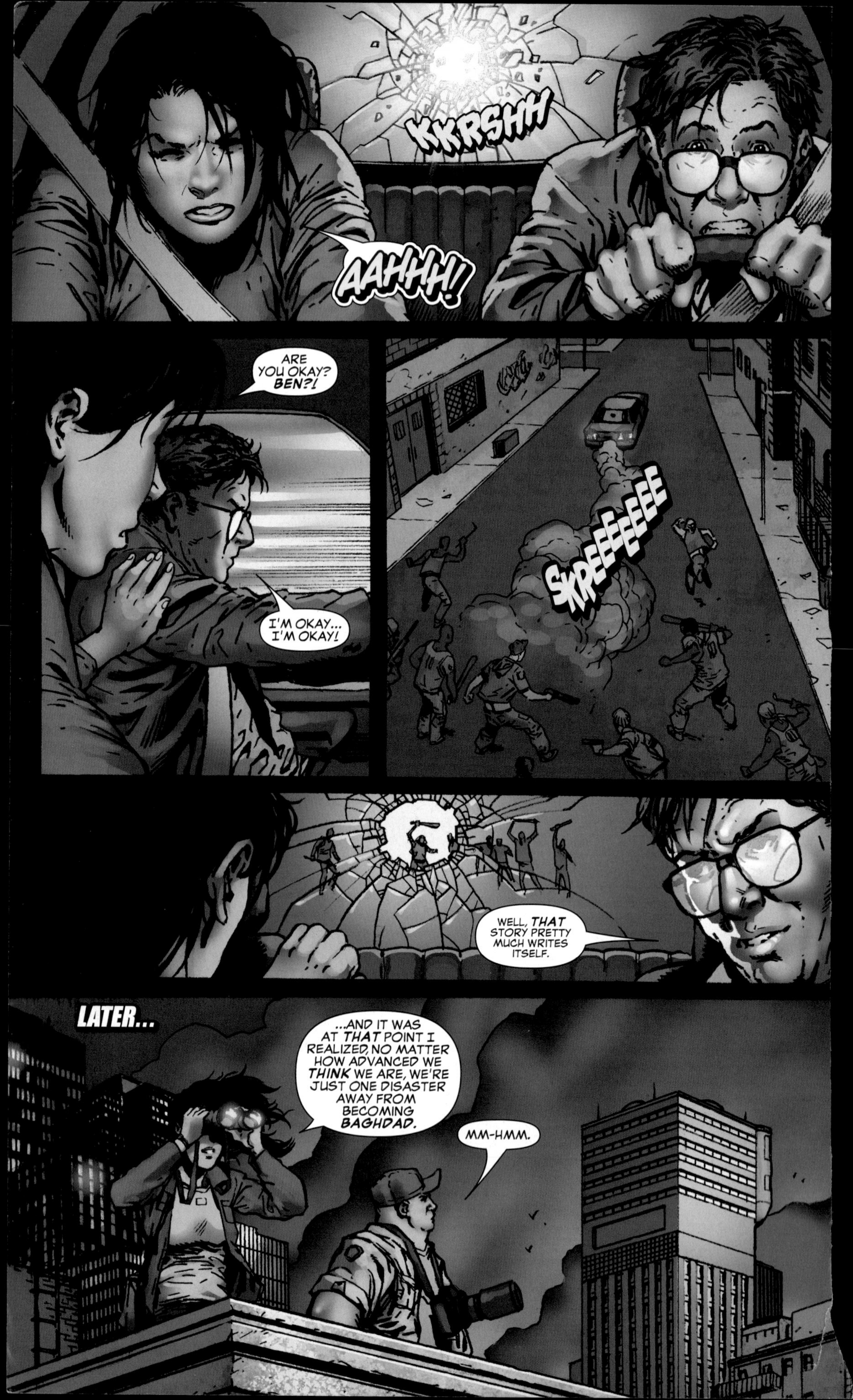
KKRSHH
AAHHH!
ARE YOU OKAY? BEN?!
I'M OKAY... I'M OKAY!
SKREEEEEEE
WELL, THAT STORY PRETTY MUCH WRITES ITSELF.
LATER...
...AND IT WAS AT THAT POINT I REALIZED, NO MATTER HOW ADVANCED WE THINK WE ARE, WE'RE JUST ONE DISASTER AWAY FROM BECOMING BAGHDAD.
MM-HMM.

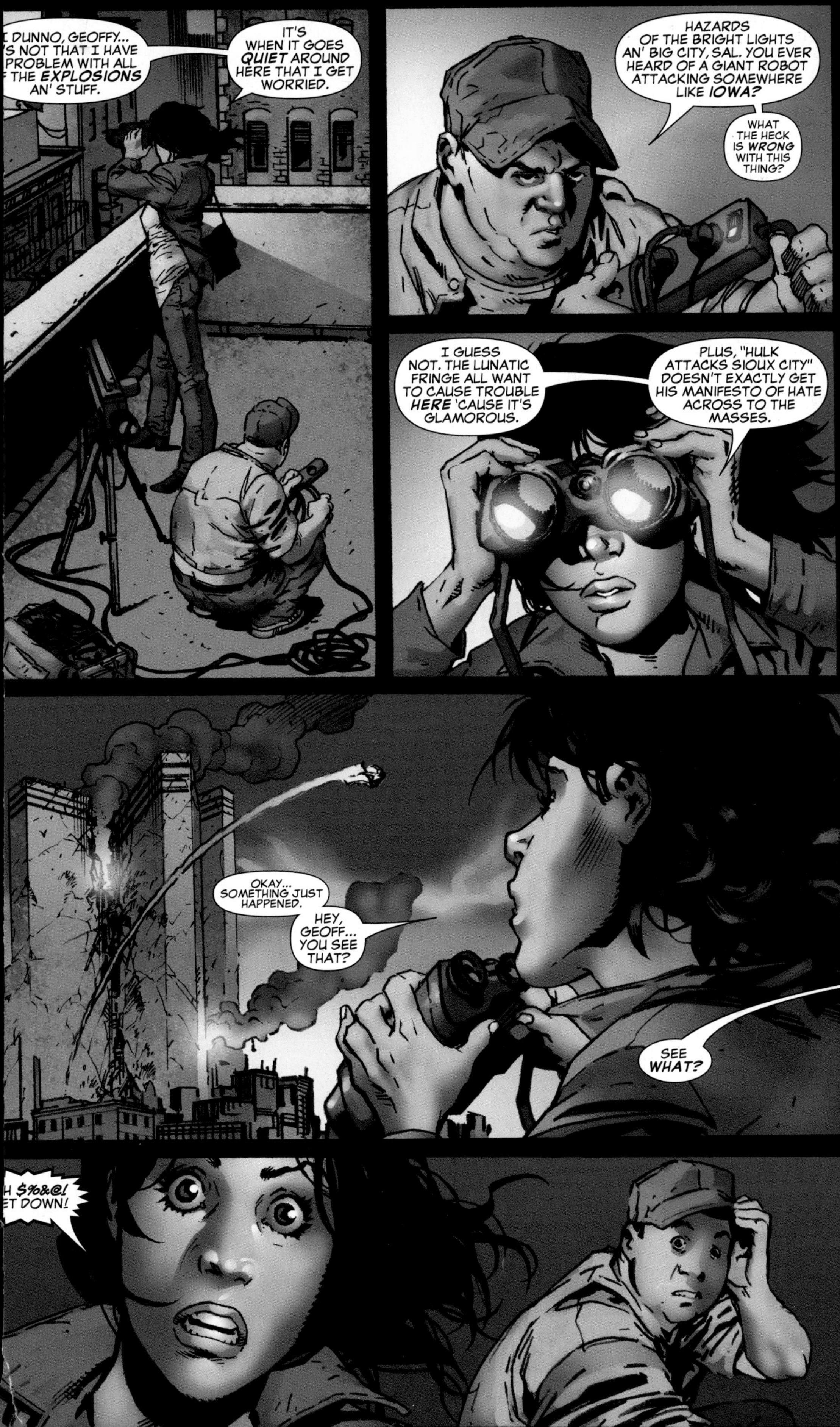
I DUNNO, GEOFFY... 'S NOT THAT I HAVE PROBLEM WITH ALL F THE EXPLOSIONS AN' STUFF.
IT'S WHEN IT GOES QUIET AROUND HERE THAT I GET WORRIED.
HAZARDS OF THE BRIGHT LIGHTS AN' BIG CITY, SAL. YOU EVER HEARD OF A GIANT ROBOT ATTACKING SOMEWHERE LIKE IOWA?
WHAT THE HECK IS WRONG WITH THIS THING?
I GUESS NOT. THE LUNATIC FRINGE ALL WANT TO CAUSE TROUBLE HERE 'CAUSE IT'S GLAMOROUS.
PLUS, "HULK ATTACKS SIOUX CITY" DOESN'T EXACTLY GET HIS MANIFESTO OF HATE ACROSS TO THE MASSES.
OKAY... SOMETHING JUST HAPPENED.
HEY, GEOFF... YOU SEE THAT?
SEE WHAT?
H $%&@! ET DOWN!

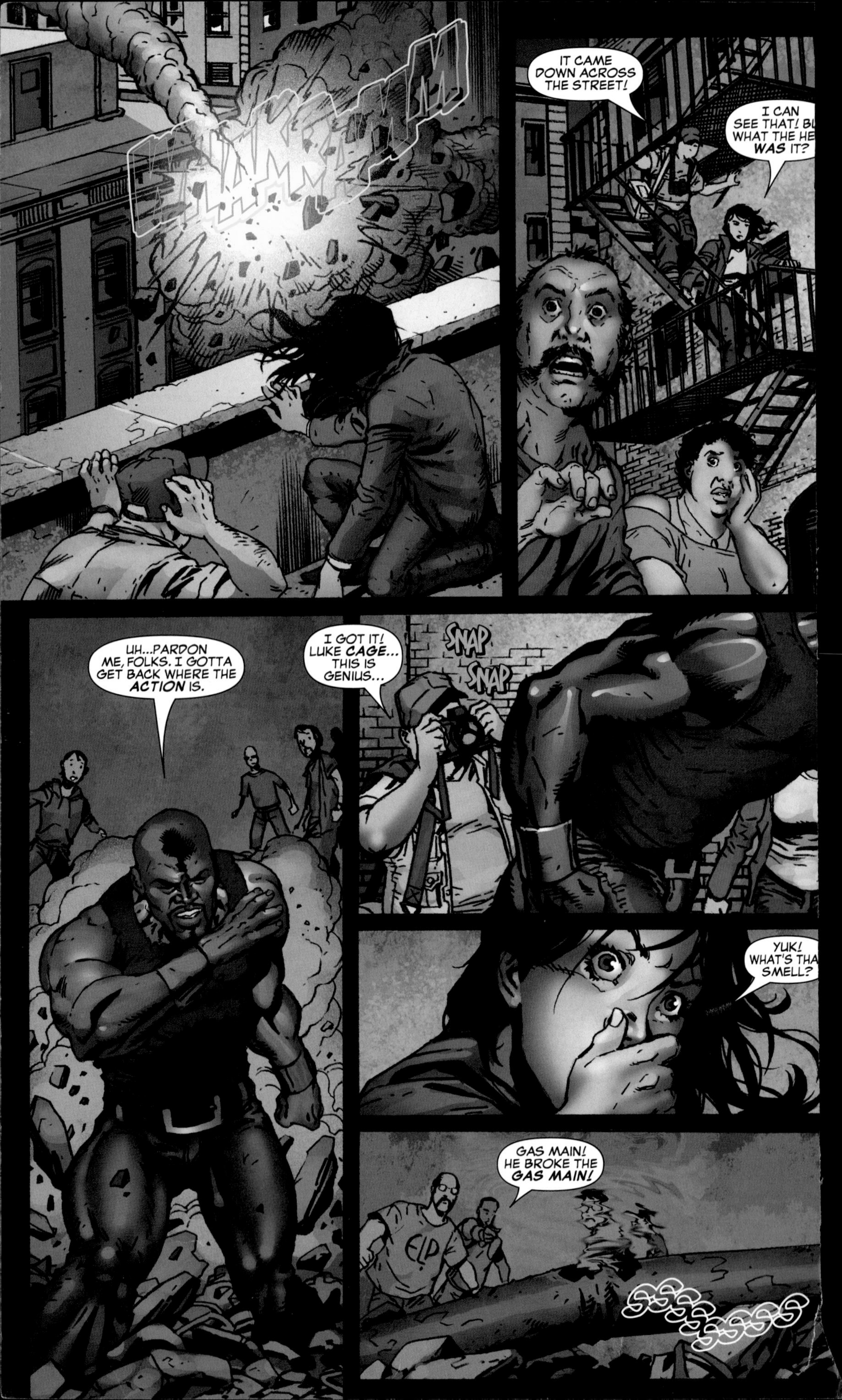
IT CAME DOWN ACROSS THE STREET!
I CAN SEE THAT! BU WHAT THE HE WAS IT?
UH...PARDON ME, FOLKS. I GOTTA GET BACK WHERE THE ACTION IS.
I GOT IT! LUKE CAGE... THIS IS GENIUS...
SNAP
SNAP
YUK! WHAT'S THA SMELL?
GAS MAIN! HE BROKE THE GAS MAIN!

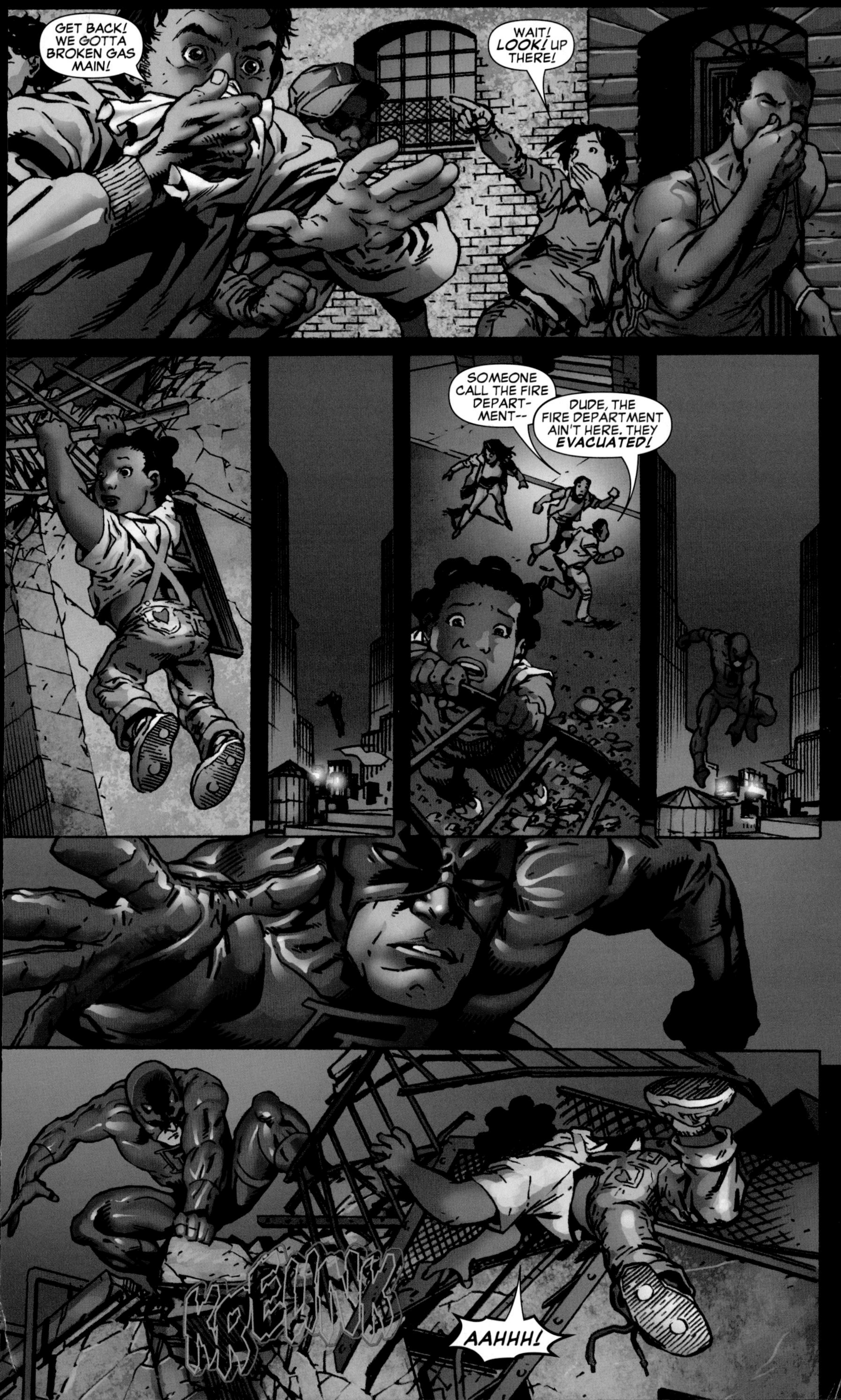
GET BACK! WE GOTTA BROKEN GAS MAIN!
WAIT! LOOK! UP THERE!
SOMEONE CALL THE FIRE DEPART-MENT--
DUDE, THE FIRE DEPARTMENT AIN'T HERE. THEY EVACUATED!
KRUNK
AAHHH!

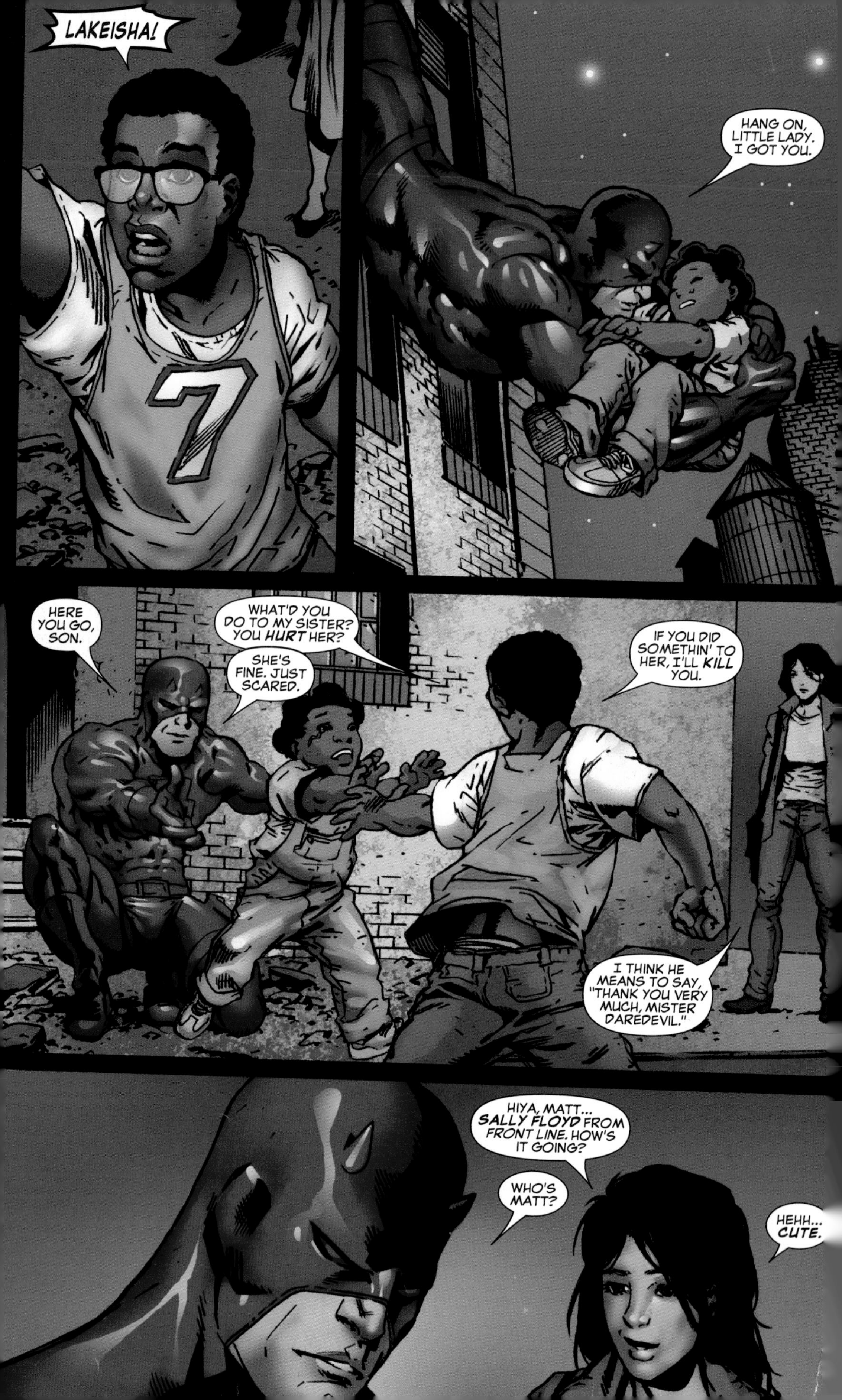
LAKEISHA!
HANG ON, LITTLE LADY. I GOT YOU.
HERE YOU GO, SON.
WHAT'D YOU DO TO MY SISTER? YOU HURT HER?
SHE'S FINE. JUST SCARED.
IF YOU DID SOMETHIN' TO HER, I'LL KILL YOU.
I THINK HE MEANS TO SAY, "THANK YOU VERY MUCH, MISTER DAREDEVIL."
HIYA, MATT... SALLY FLOYD FROM FRONT LINE. HOW'S IT GOING?
WHO'S MATT?
HEHH... CUTE.

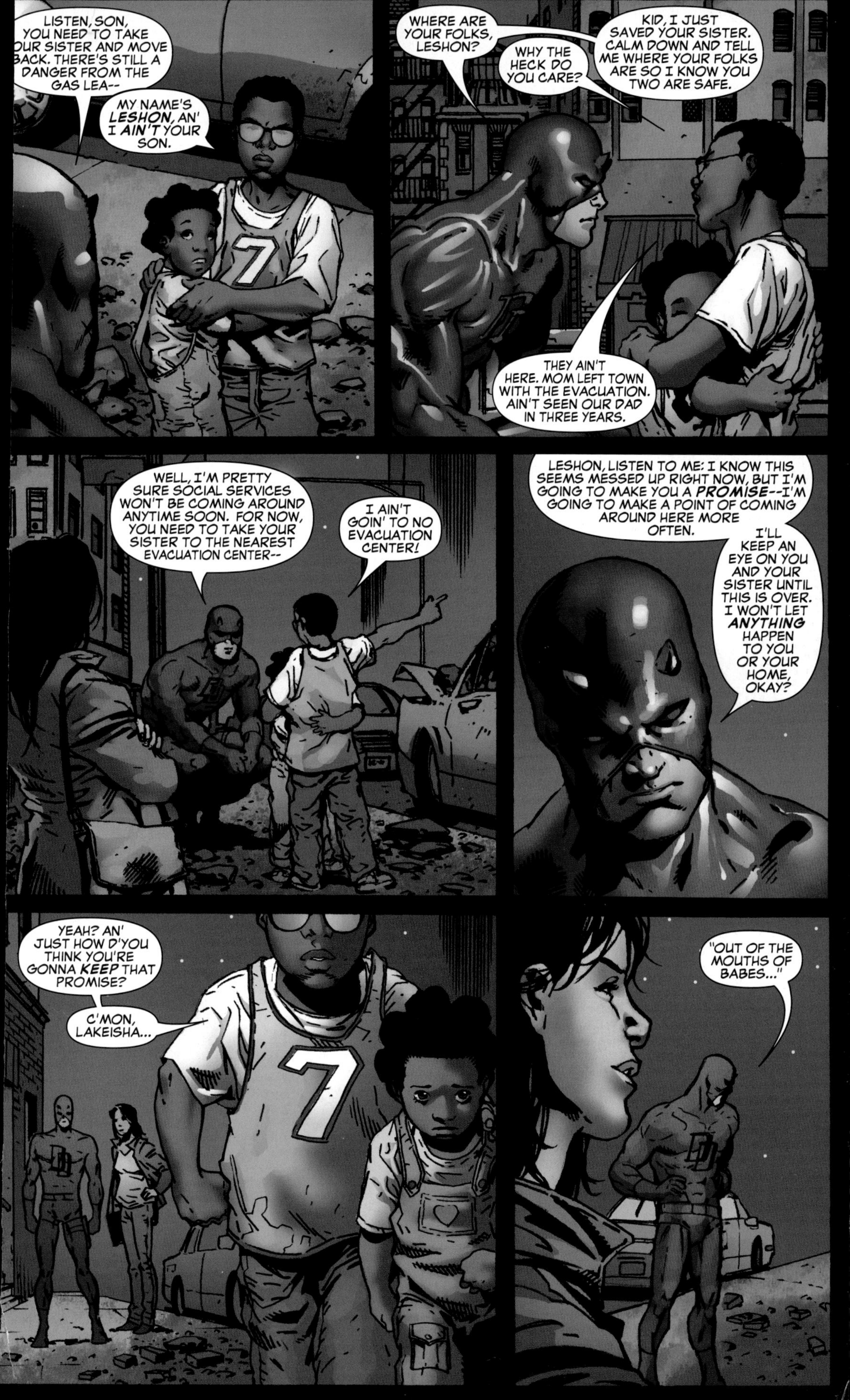
LISTEN, SON, YOU NEED TO TAKE YOUR SISTER AND MOVE BACK. THERE'S STILL A DANGER FROM THE GAS LEA--
MY NAME'S *LESHON*, AN' I *AIN'T* YOUR SON.
WHERE ARE YOUR FOLKS, LESHON?
WHY THE HECK DO YOU CARE?
KID, I JUST SAVED YOUR SISTER. CALM DOWN AND TELL ME WHERE YOUR FOLKS ARE SO I KNOW YOU TWO ARE SAFE.
THEY AIN'T HERE. MOM LEFT TOWN WITH THE EVACUATION. AIN'T SEEN OUR DAD IN THREE YEARS.
WELL, I'M PRETTY SURE SOCIAL SERVICES WON'T BE COMING AROUND ANYTIME SOON. FOR NOW, YOU NEED TO TAKE YOUR SISTER TO THE NEAREST EVACUATION CENTER--
I AIN'T GOIN' TO NO EVACUATION CENTER!
LESHON, LISTEN TO ME: I KNOW THIS SEEMS MESSED UP RIGHT NOW, BUT I'M GOING TO MAKE YOU A *PROMISE*--I'M GOING TO MAKE A POINT OF COMING AROUND HERE MORE OFTEN.
I'LL KEEP AN EYE ON YOU AND YOUR SISTER UNTIL THIS IS OVER. I WON'T LET *ANYTHING* HAPPEN TO YOU OR YOUR HOME, OKAY?
YEAH? AN' JUST HOW D'YOU THINK YOU'RE GONNA *KEEP* THAT PROMISE?
C'MON, LAKEISHA...
"OUT OF THE MOUTHS OF BABES..."

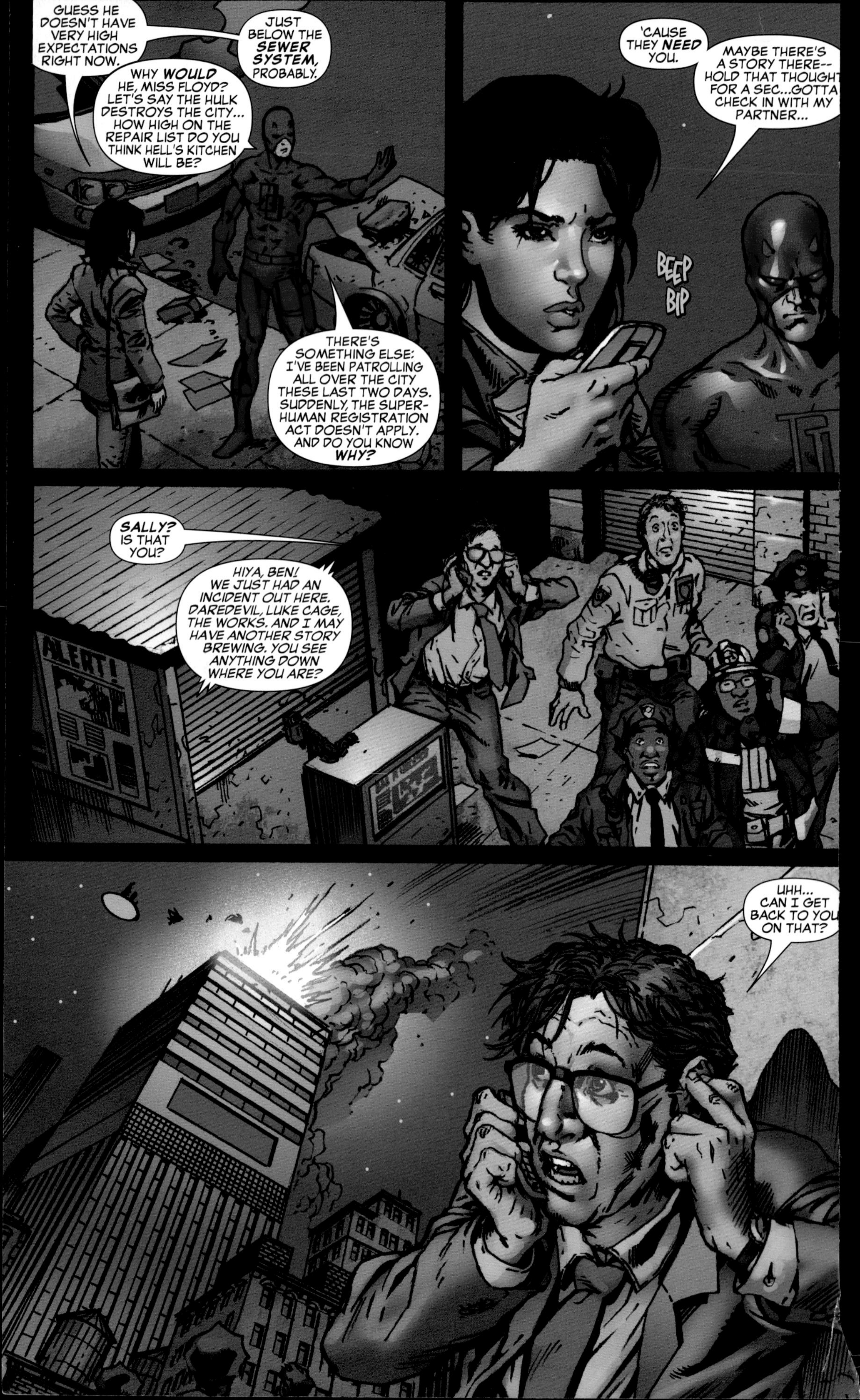
GUESS HE DOESN'T HAVE VERY HIGH EXPECTATIONS RIGHT NOW.
JUST BELOW THE SEWER SYSTEM, PROBABLY.
WHY WOULD HE, MISS FLOYD? LET'S SAY THE HULK DESTROYS THE CITY... HOW HIGH ON THE REPAIR LIST DO YOU THINK HELL'S KITCHEN WILL BE?
THERE'S SOMETHING ELSE: I'VE BEEN PATROLLING ALL OVER THE CITY THESE LAST TWO DAYS. SUDDENLY, THE SUPER-HUMAN REGISTRATION ACT DOESN'T APPLY. AND DO YOU KNOW WHY?
'CAUSE THEY NEED YOU.
MAYBE THERE'S A STORY THERE-- HOLD THAT THOUGHT FOR A SEC...GOTTA CHECK IN WITH MY PARTNER...
BEEP BIP
SALLY? IS THAT YOU?
HIYA, BEN! WE JUST HAD AN INCIDENT OUT HERE. DAREDEVIL, LUKE CAGE, THE WORKS. AND I MAY HAVE ANOTHER STORY BREWING. YOU SEE ANYTHING DOWN WHERE YOU ARE?
ALERT!
UHH... CAN I GET BACK TO YOU ON THAT?

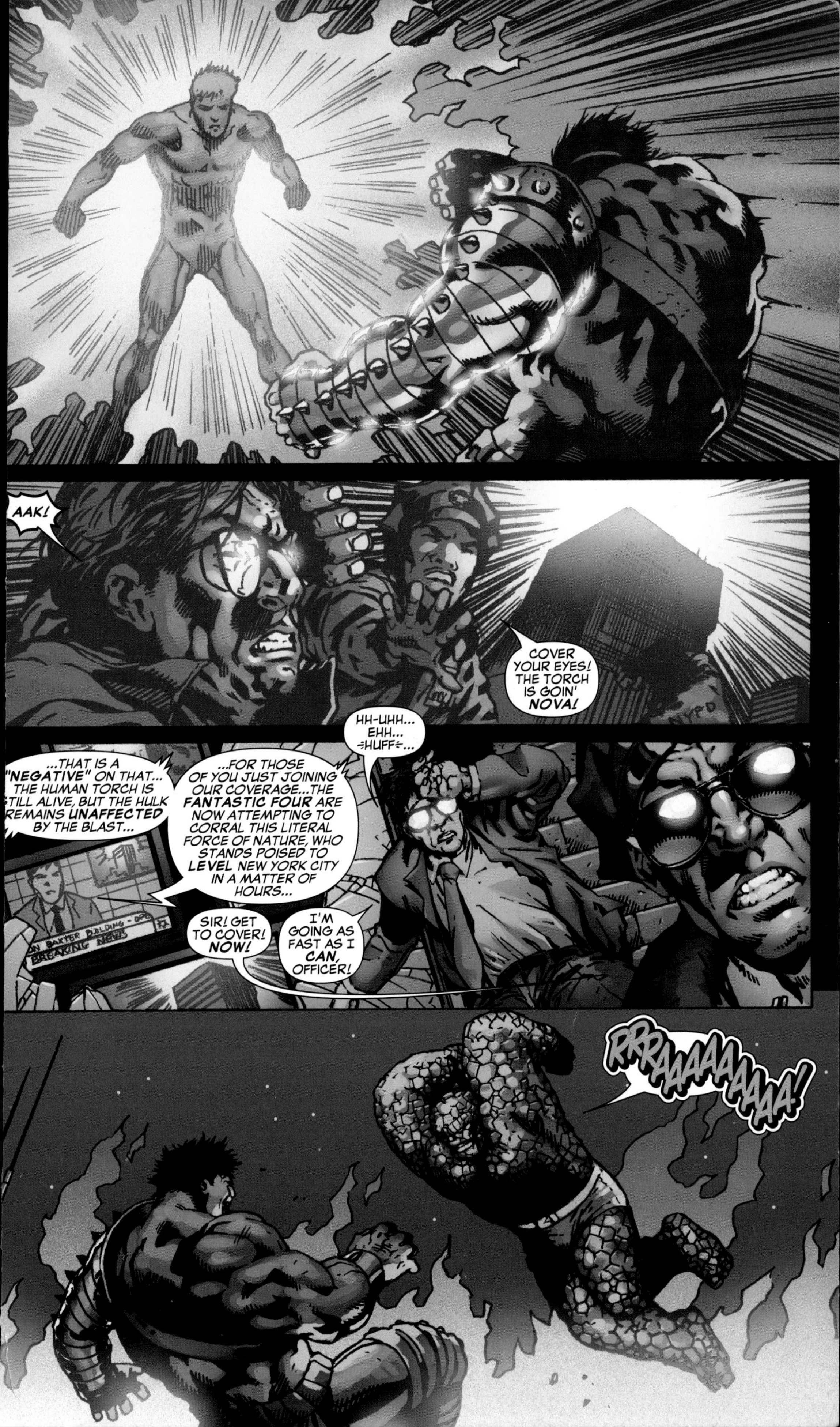
AAK!
COVER YOUR EYES! THE TORCH IS GOIN' NOVA!
NYPD
...THAT IS A "NEGATIVE" ON THAT... THE HUMAN TORCH IS STILL ALIVE, BUT THE HULK REMAINS UNAFFECTED BY THE BLAST...
...FOR THOSE OF YOU JUST JOINING OUR COVERAGE...THE FANTASTIC FOUR ARE NOW ATTEMPTING TO CORRAL THIS LITERAL FORCE OF NATURE, WHO STANDS POISED TO LEVEL NEW YORK CITY IN A MATTER OF HOURS...
BAXTER BUILDING
BREAKING NEWS
HH-UHH... EHH... HUFF...
SIR! GET TO COVER! NOW!
I'M GOING AS FAST AS I CAN, OFFICER!
RRRAAAAAAAAA!

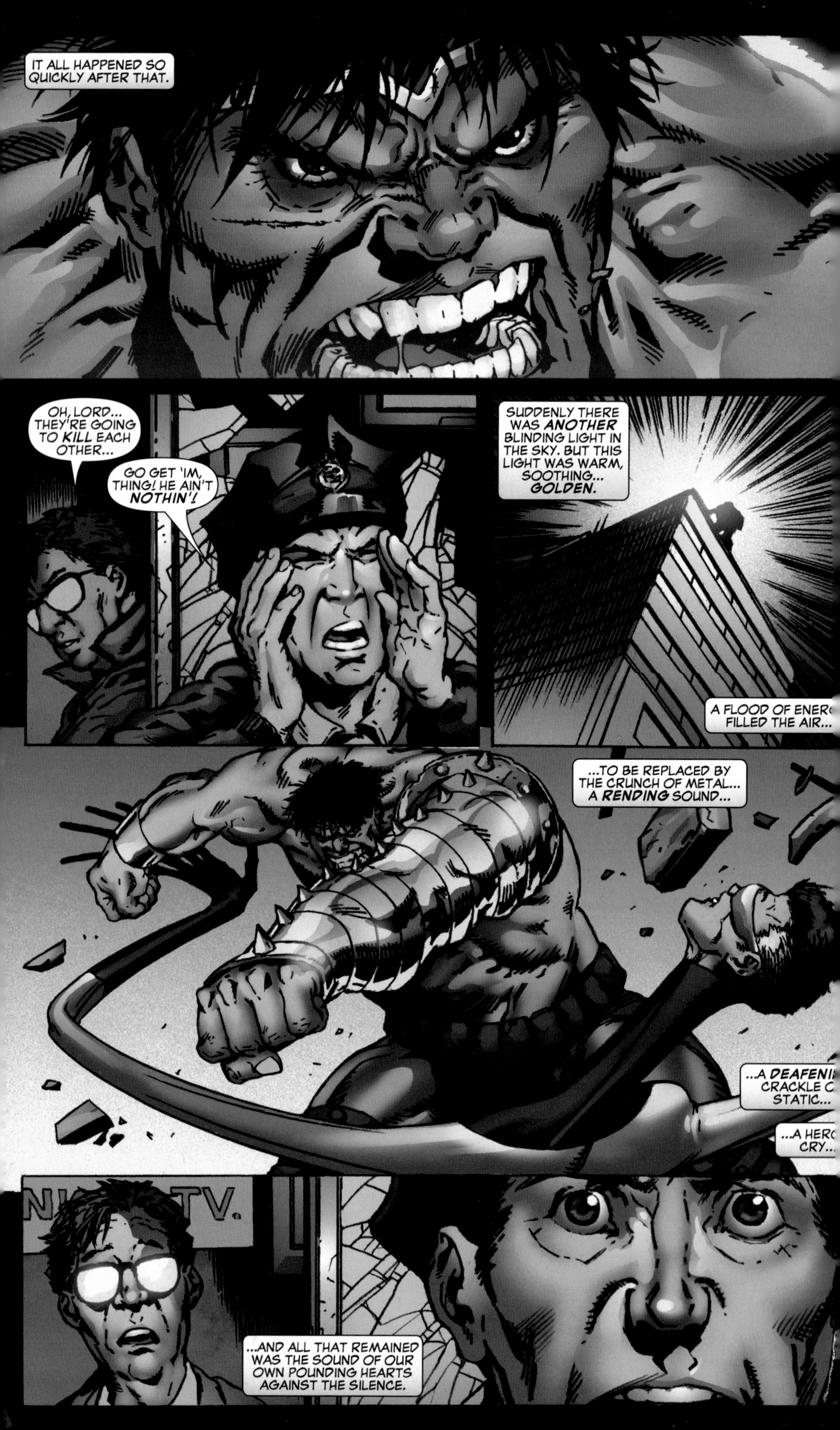
IT ALL HAPPENED SO QUICKLY AFTER THAT.
OH, LORD... THEY'RE GOING TO **KILL** EACH OTHER...
GO GET 'IM, THING! HE AIN'T **NOTHIN'!**
SUDDENLY THERE WAS **ANOTHER** BLINDING LIGHT IN THE SKY. BUT THIS LIGHT WAS WARM, SOOTHING... **GOLDEN.**
A FLOOD OF ENER
FILLED THE AIR...
...TO BE REPLACED BY THE CRUNCH OF METAL... A **RENDING** SOUND...
...A **DEAFENI**
CRACKLE C
STATIC...
...A HER
CRY...
TV.
...AND ALL THAT REMAINED WAS THE SOUND OF OUR OWN POUNDING HEARTS AGAINST THE SILENCE.

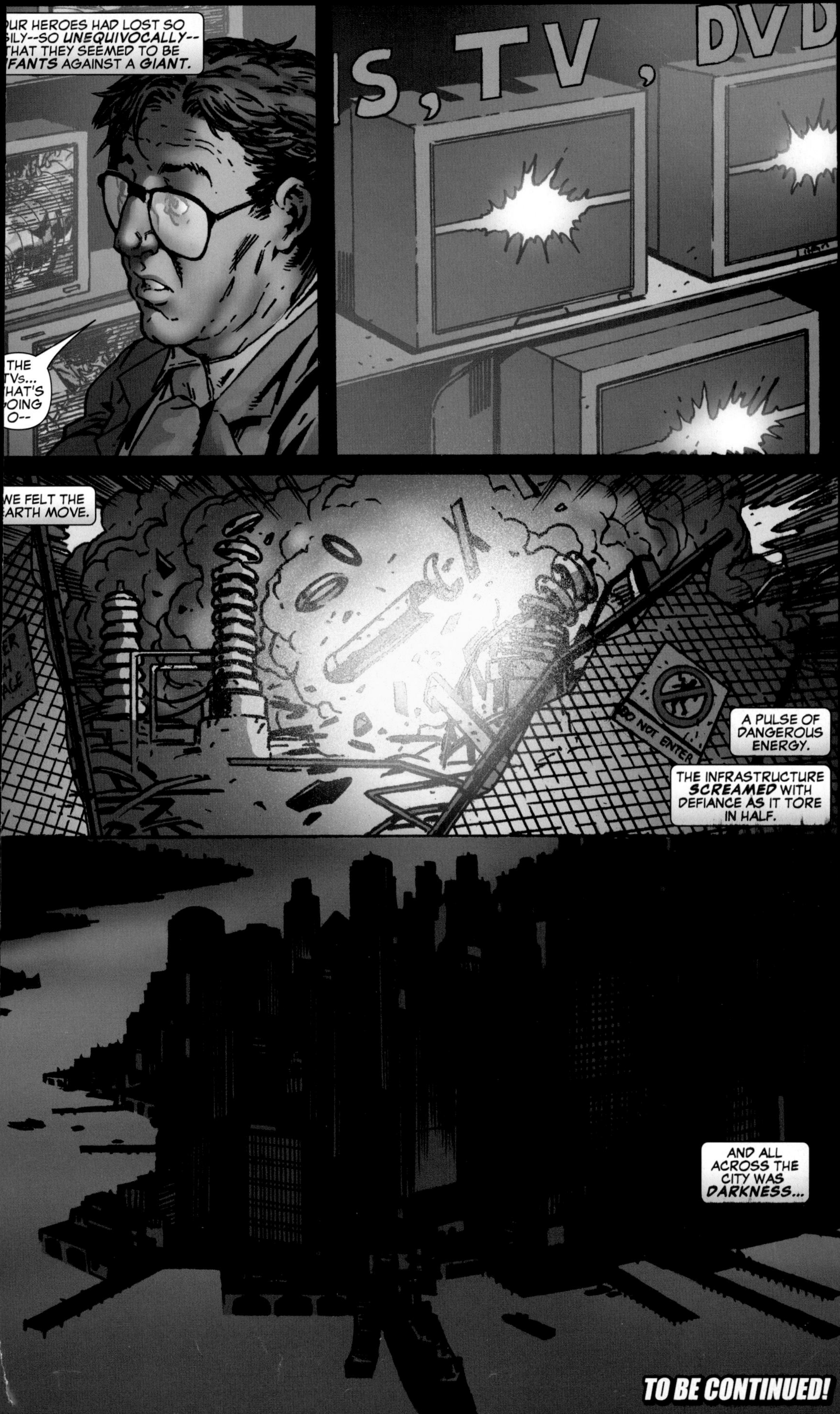
UR HEROES HAD LOST SO
SILY--SO UNEQUIVOCALLY--
THAT THEY SEEMED TO BE
FANTS AGAINST A GIANT.
THE
TVs...
HAT'S
OING
O--
S, TV , DVD
WE FELT THE
EARTH MOVE.
DO NOT ENTER
A PULSE OF
DANGEROUS
ENERGY.
THE INFRASTRUCTURE
SCREAMED WITH
DEFIANCE AS IT TORE
IN HALF.
AND ALL
ACROSS THE
CITY WAS
DARKNESS...
TO BE CONTINUED!

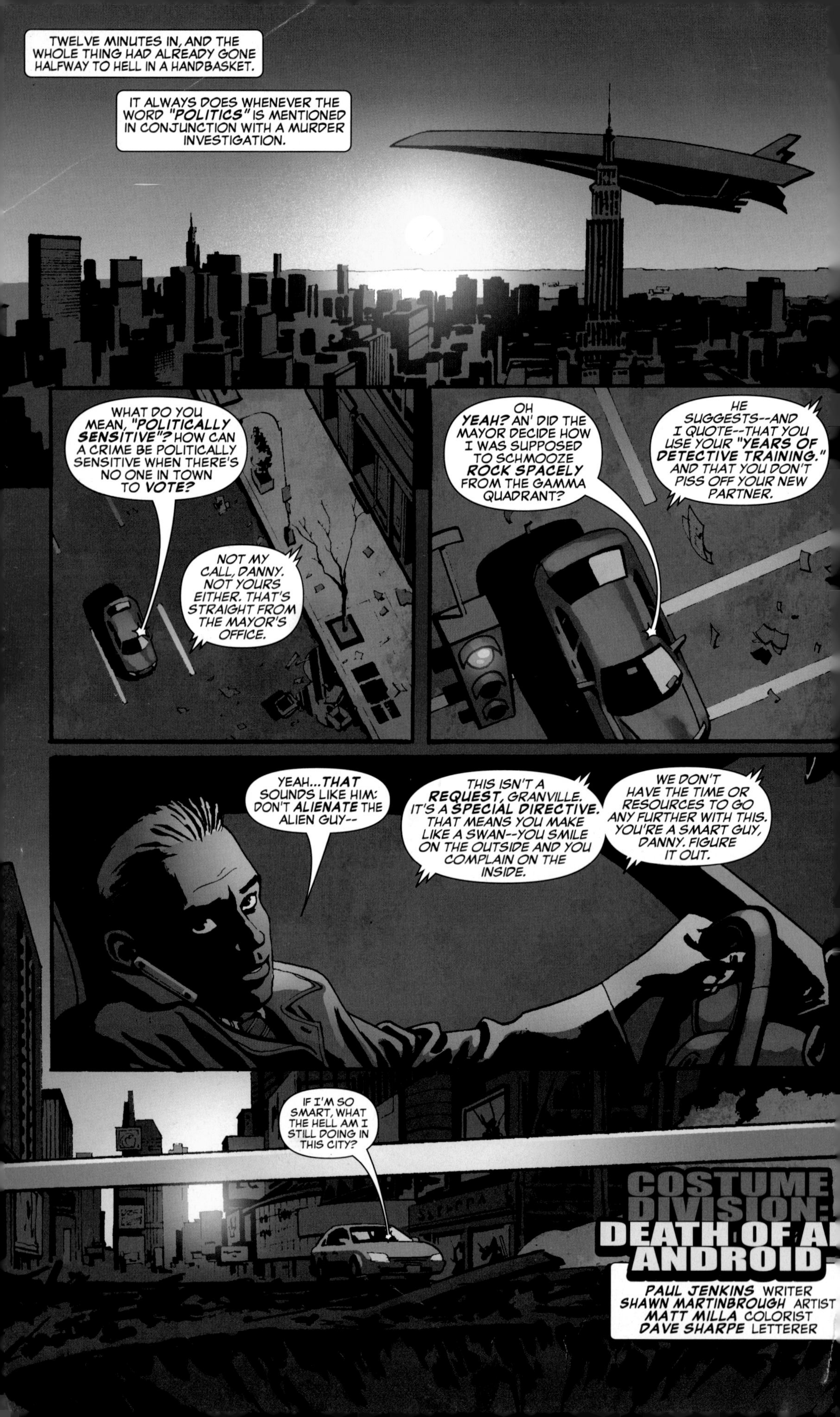

TWELVE MINUTES IN, AND THE WHOLE THING HAD ALREADY GONE HALFWAY TO HELL IN A HANDBASKET.
IT ALWAYS DOES WHENEVER THE WORD "POLITICS" IS MENTIONED IN CONJUNCTION WITH A MURDER INVESTIGATION.
WHAT DO YOU MEAN, "POLITICALLY SENSITIVE"? HOW CAN A CRIME BE POLITICALLY SENSITIVE WHEN THERE'S NO ONE IN TOWN TO VOTE?
NOT MY CALL, DANNY. NOT YOURS EITHER. THAT'S STRAIGHT FROM THE MAYOR'S OFFICE.
OH YEAH? AN' DID THE MAYOR DECIDE HOW I WAS SUPPOSED TO SCHMOOZE ROCK SPACELY FROM THE GAMMA QUADRANT?
HE SUGGESTS--AND I QUOTE--THAT YOU USE YOUR "YEARS OF DETECTIVE TRAINING." AND THAT YOU DON'T PISS OFF YOUR NEW PARTNER.
YEAH...THAT SOUNDS LIKE HIM: DON'T ALIENATE THE ALIEN GUY--
THIS ISN'T A REQUEST, GRANVILLE. IT'S A SPECIAL DIRECTIVE. THAT MEANS YOU MAKE LIKE A SWAN--YOU SMILE ON THE OUTSIDE AND YOU COMPLAIN ON THE INSIDE.
WE DON'T HAVE THE TIME OR RESOURCES TO GO ANY FURTHER WITH THIS. YOU'RE A SMART GUY, DANNY. FIGURE IT OUT.
IF I'M SO SMART, WHAT THE HELL AM I STILL DOING IN THIS CITY?
COSTUME DIVISION: DEATH OF AN ANDROID
PAUL JENKINS WRITER
SHAWN MARTINBROUGH ARTIST
MATT MILLA COLORIST
DAVE SHARPE LETTERER

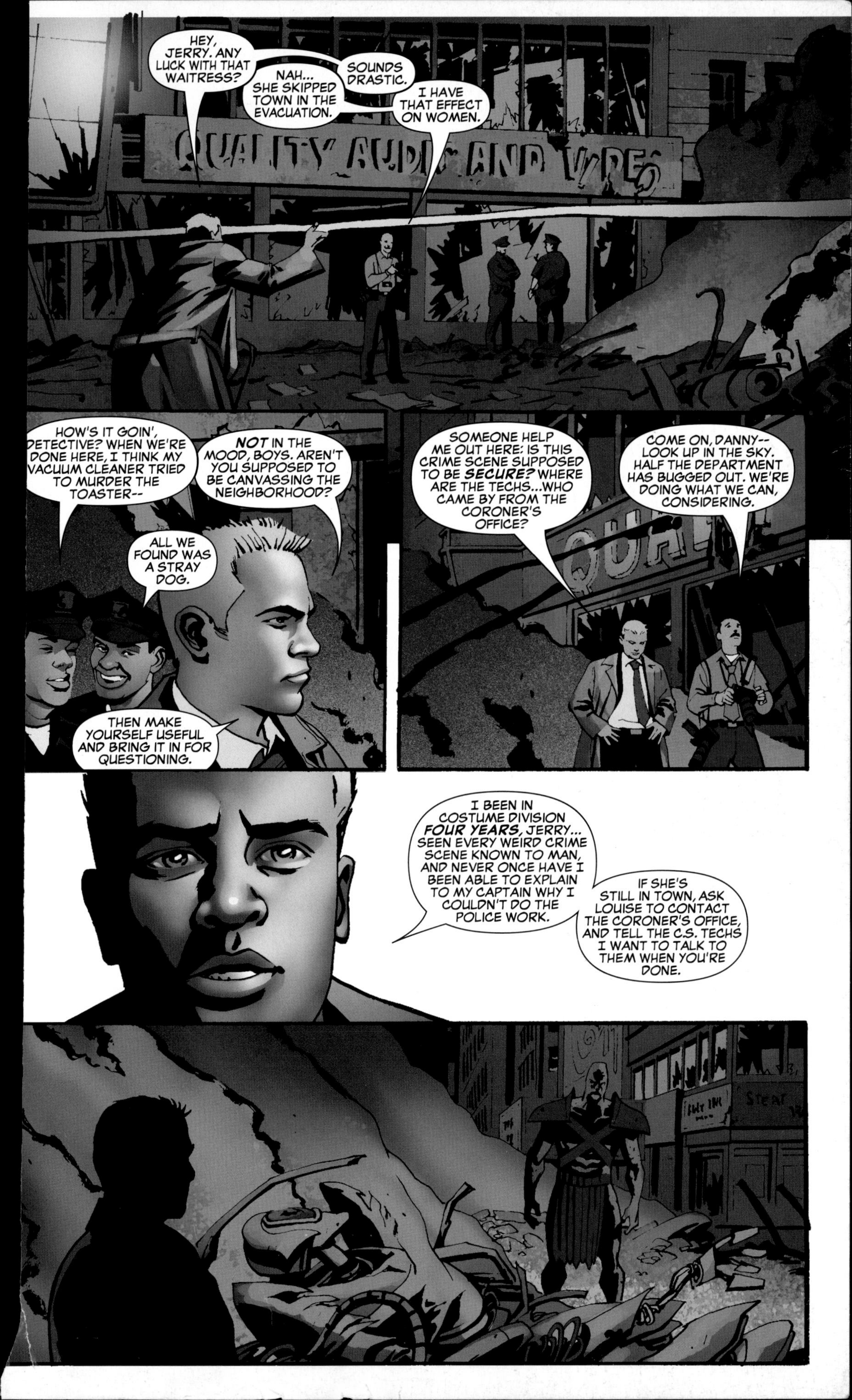

HEY, JERRY. ANY LUCK WITH THAT WAITRESS?
NAH... SHE SKIPPED TOWN IN THE EVACUATION.
SOUNDS DRASTIC.
I HAVE THAT EFFECT ON WOMEN.
HOW'S IT GOIN', DETECTIVE? WHEN WE'RE DONE HERE, I THINK MY VACUUM CLEANER TRIED TO MURDER THE TOASTER--
NOT IN THE MOOD, BOYS. AREN'T YOU SUPPOSED TO BE CANVASSING THE NEIGHBORHOOD?
ALL WE FOUND WAS A STRAY DOG.
THEN MAKE YOURSELF USEFUL AND BRING IT IN FOR QUESTIONING.
SOMEONE HELP ME OUT HERE: IS THIS CRIME SCENE SUPPOSED TO BE SECURE? WHERE ARE THE TECHS...WHO CAME BY FROM THE CORONER'S OFFICE?
COME ON, DANNY-- LOOK UP IN THE SKY. HALF THE DEPARTMENT HAS BUGGED OUT. WE'RE DOING WHAT WE CAN, CONSIDERING.
I BEEN IN COSTUME DIVISION FOUR YEARS, JERRY... SEEN EVERY WEIRD CRIME SCENE KNOWN TO MAN, AND NEVER ONCE HAVE I BEEN ABLE TO EXPLAIN TO MY CAPTAIN WHY I COULDN'T DO THE POLICE WORK.
IF SHE'S STILL IN TOWN, ASK LOUISE TO CONTACT THE CORONER'S OFFICE, AND TELL THE C.S. TECHS I WANT TO TALK TO THEM WHEN YOU'RE DONE.

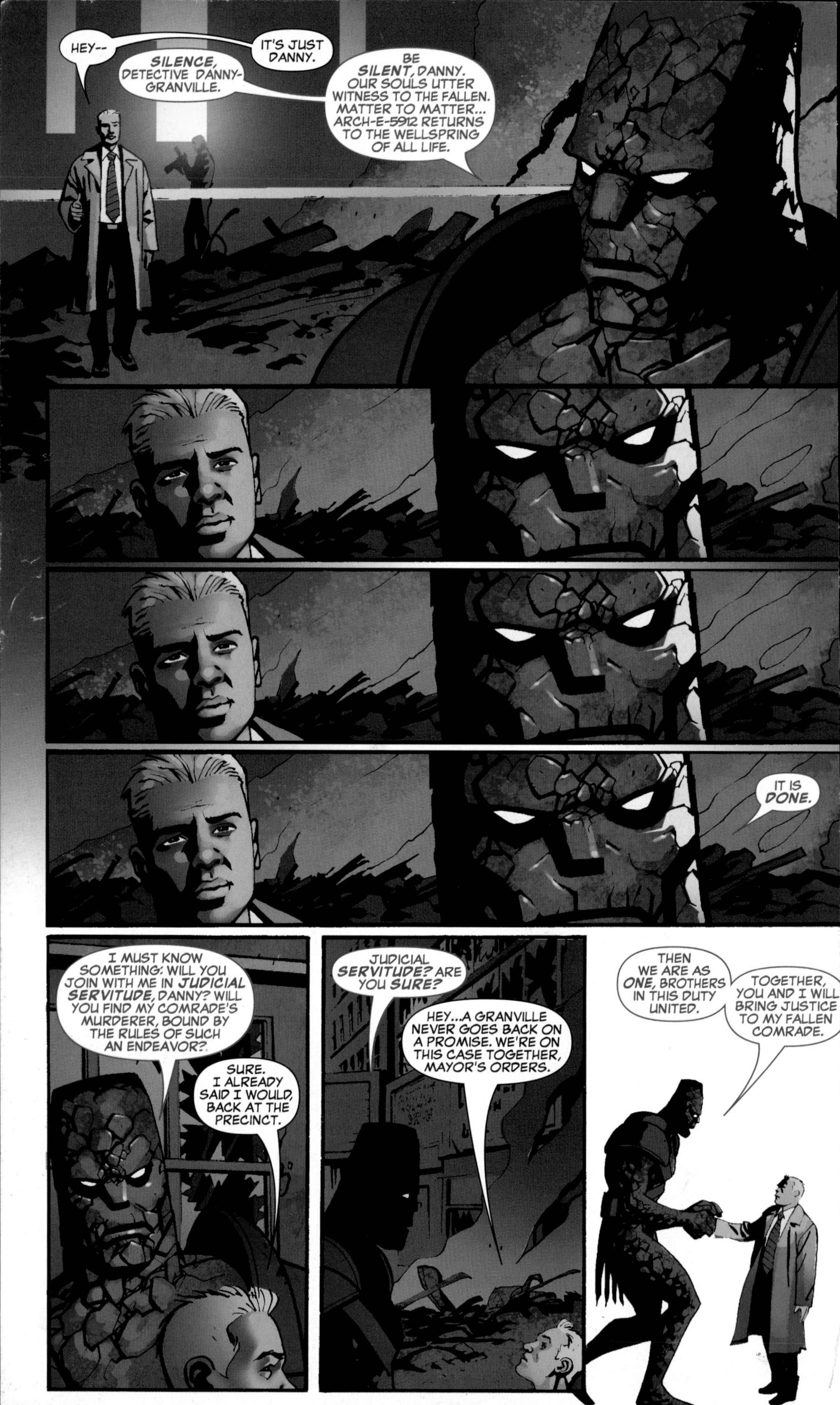
HEY--
IT'S JUST DANNY.
SILENCE, DETECTIVE DANNY-GRANVILLE.
BE SILENT, DANNY. OUR SOULS UTTER WITNESS TO THE FALLEN. MATTER TO MATTER... ARCH-E-5912 RETURNS TO THE WELLSPRING OF ALL LIFE.
IT IS DONE.
I MUST KNOW SOMETHING: WILL YOU JOIN WITH ME IN JUDICIAL SERVITUDE, DANNY? WILL YOU FIND MY COMRADE'S MURDERER, BOUND BY THE RULES OF SUCH AN ENDEAVOR?
SURE. I ALREADY SAID I WOULD, BACK AT THE PRECINCT.
JUDICIAL SERVITUDE? ARE YOU SURE?
HEY...A GRANVILLE NEVER GOES BACK ON A PROMISE. WE'RE ON THIS CASE TOGETHER, MAYOR'S ORDERS.
THEN WE ARE AS ONE, BROTHERS IN THIS DUTY UNITED.
TOGETHER, YOU AND I WILL BRING JUSTICE TO MY FALLEN COMRADE.

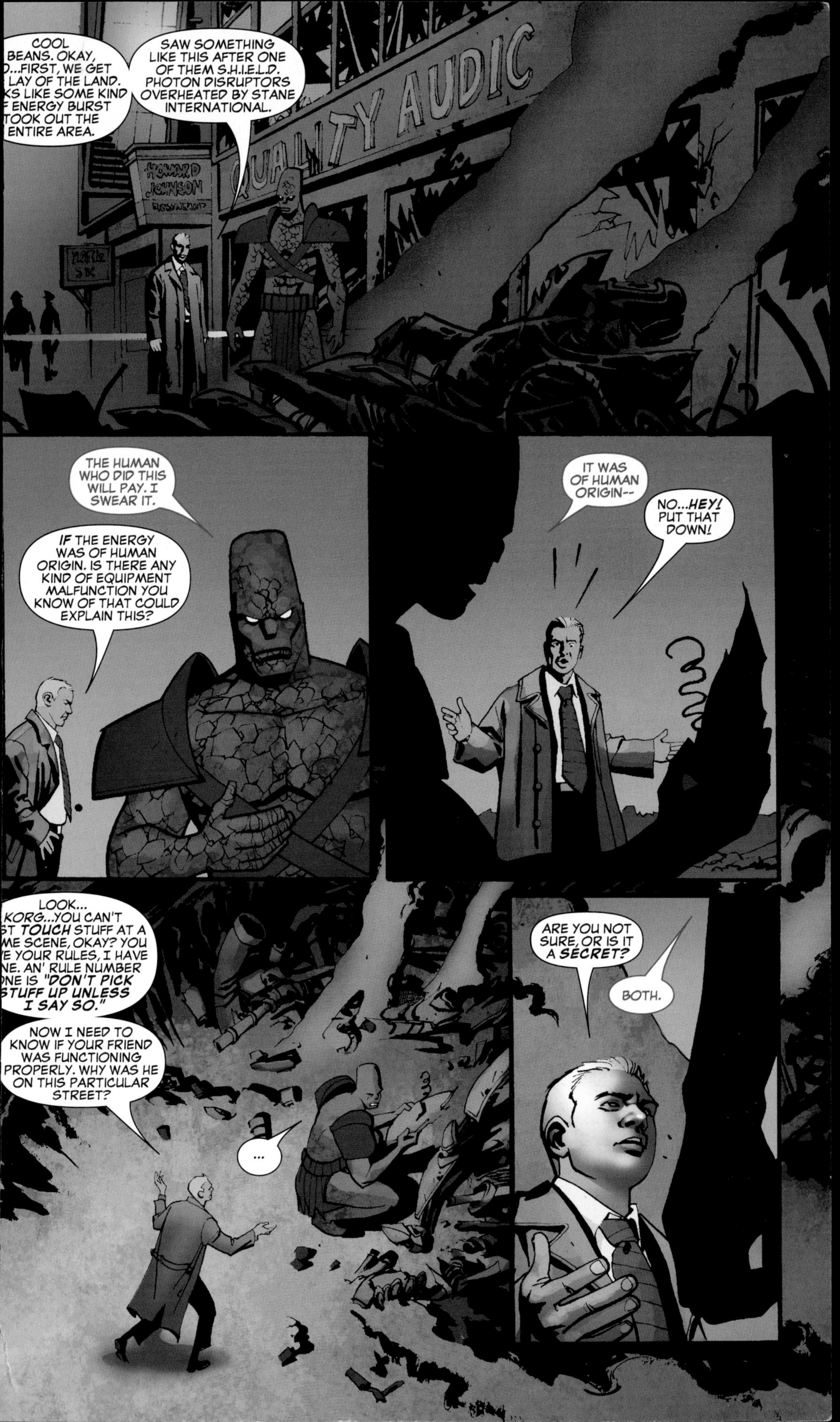
COOL BEANS. OKAY, D...FIRST, WE GET LAY OF THE LAND. KS LIKE SOME KIND F ENERGY BURST TOOK OUT THE ENTIRE AREA.
SAW SOMETHING LIKE THIS AFTER ONE OF THEM S.H.I.E.L.D. PHOTON DISRUPTORS OVERHEATED BY STANE INTERNATIONAL.
HOWARD JOHNSON
THE HUMAN WHO DID THIS WILL PAY. I SWEAR IT.
IF THE ENERGY WAS OF HUMAN ORIGIN. IS THERE ANY KIND OF EQUIPMENT MALFUNCTION YOU KNOW OF THAT COULD EXPLAIN THIS?
IT WAS OF HUMAN ORIGIN--
NO...*HEY!* PUT THAT DOWN!
LOOK... KORG...YOU CAN'T ST *TOUCH* STUFF AT A ME SCENE, OKAY? YOU E YOUR RULES, I HAVE NE. AN' RULE NUMBER ONE IS *"DON'T PICK STUFF UP UNLESS I SAY SO."*
NOW I NEED TO KNOW IF YOUR FRIEND WAS FUNCTIONING PROPERLY. WHY WAS HE ON THIS PARTICULAR STREET?
...
ARE YOU NOT SURE, OR IS IT A *SECRET?*
BOTH.

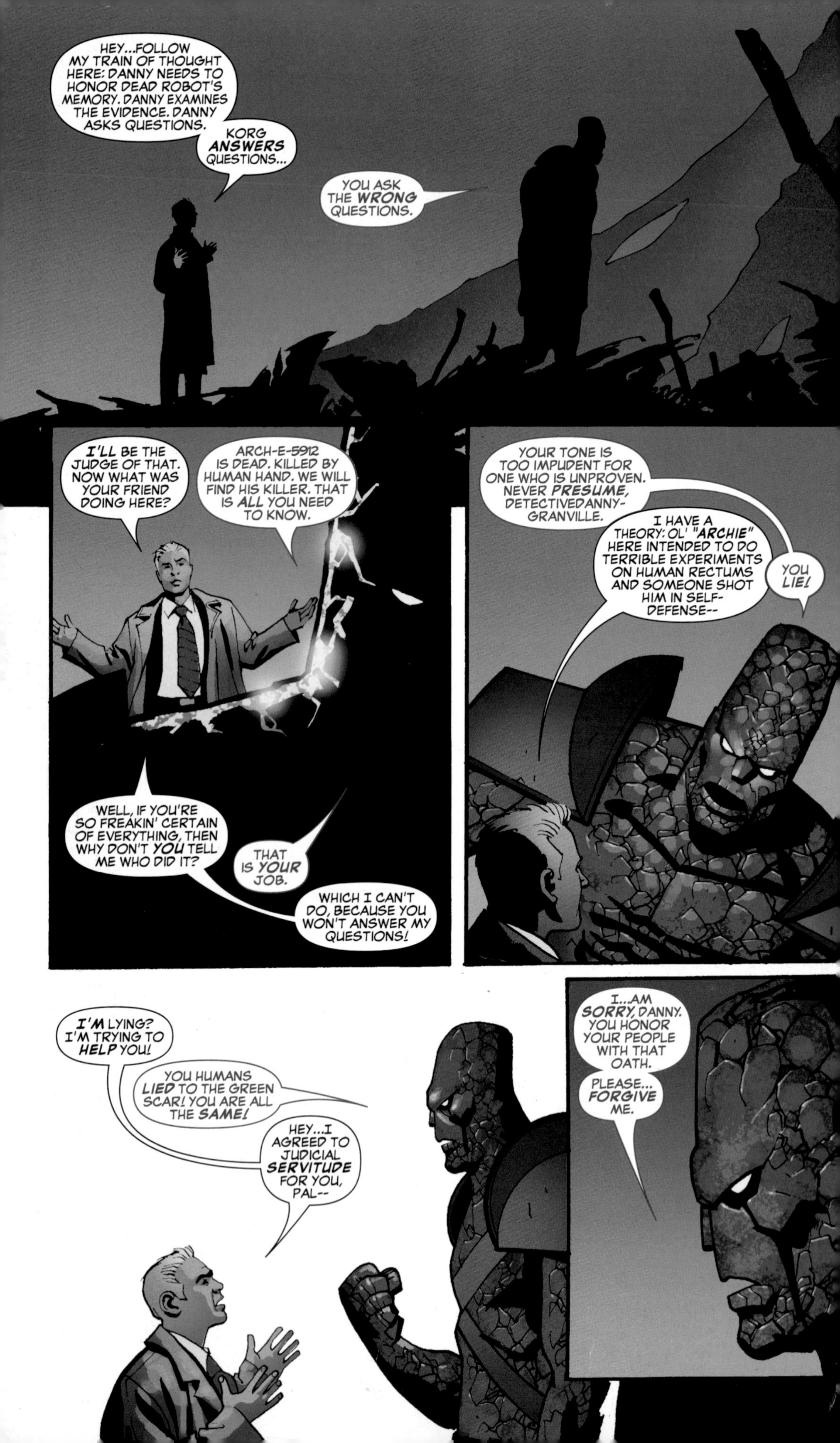

HEY...FOLLOW MY TRAIN OF THOUGHT HERE: DANNY NEEDS TO HONOR DEAD ROBOT'S MEMORY. DANNY EXAMINES THE EVIDENCE. DANNY ASKS QUESTIONS.
KORG ANSWERS QUESTIONS...
YOU ASK THE WRONG QUESTIONS.
I'LL BE THE JUDGE OF THAT. NOW WHAT WAS YOUR FRIEND DOING HERE?
ARCH-E-5912 IS DEAD. KILLED BY HUMAN HAND. WE WILL FIND HIS KILLER. THAT IS ALL YOU NEED TO KNOW.
WELL, IF YOU'RE SO FREAKIN' CERTAIN OF EVERYTHING, THEN WHY DON'T YOU TELL ME WHO DID IT?
THAT IS YOUR JOB.
WHICH I CAN'T DO, BECAUSE YOU WON'T ANSWER MY QUESTIONS!
YOUR TONE IS TOO IMPUDENT FOR ONE WHO IS UNPROVEN. NEVER PRESUME, DETECTIVEDANNY-GRANVILLE.
I HAVE A THEORY: OL' "ARCHIE" HERE INTENDED TO DO TERRIBLE EXPERIMENTS ON HUMAN RECTUMS AND SOMEONE SHOT HIM IN SELF-DEFENSE--
YOU LIE!
I'M LYING? I'M TRYING TO HELP YOU!
YOU HUMANS LIED TO THE GREEN SCAR! YOU ARE ALL THE SAME!
HEY...I AGREED TO JUDICIAL SERVITUDE FOR YOU, PAL--
I...AM SORRY, DANNY. YOU HONOR YOUR PEOPLE WITH THAT OATH.
PLEASE... FORGIVE ME.

ARCH-E-5912'S OBJECTIVES WERE CEABLE. HE INTENDED O EXAMINE HUMAN EACTIONS TO OUR PRESENCE HERE.

IF POSSIBLE, HE WAS TO OBSERVE THE MOVEMENTS AND ACTIVITIES OF YOUR SO-CALLED "SUPER HEROES."

--ALL HUMAN ACTIVITY HAS CEASED IN THIS SECTOR. NO EVIDENCE OF SENTIENT, BIO-ORGANIC LIFE FORMS WITHIN RANGE.

SENSORS INDICATE AN UNUSUAL DISTURBANCE IN THE ELECTROMAGNETIC FIELD NEARBY.

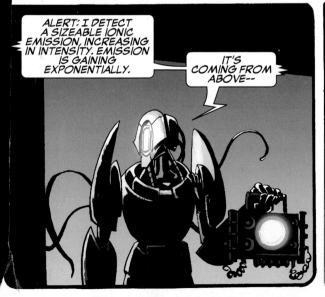

ALERT: I DETECT A SIZEABLE IONIC EMISSION, INCREASING IN INTENSITY. EMISSION IS GAINING EXPONENTIALLY.

IT'S COMING FROM ABOVE--

THAT WAS THE LAST TRANSMISSION WE RECEIVED.

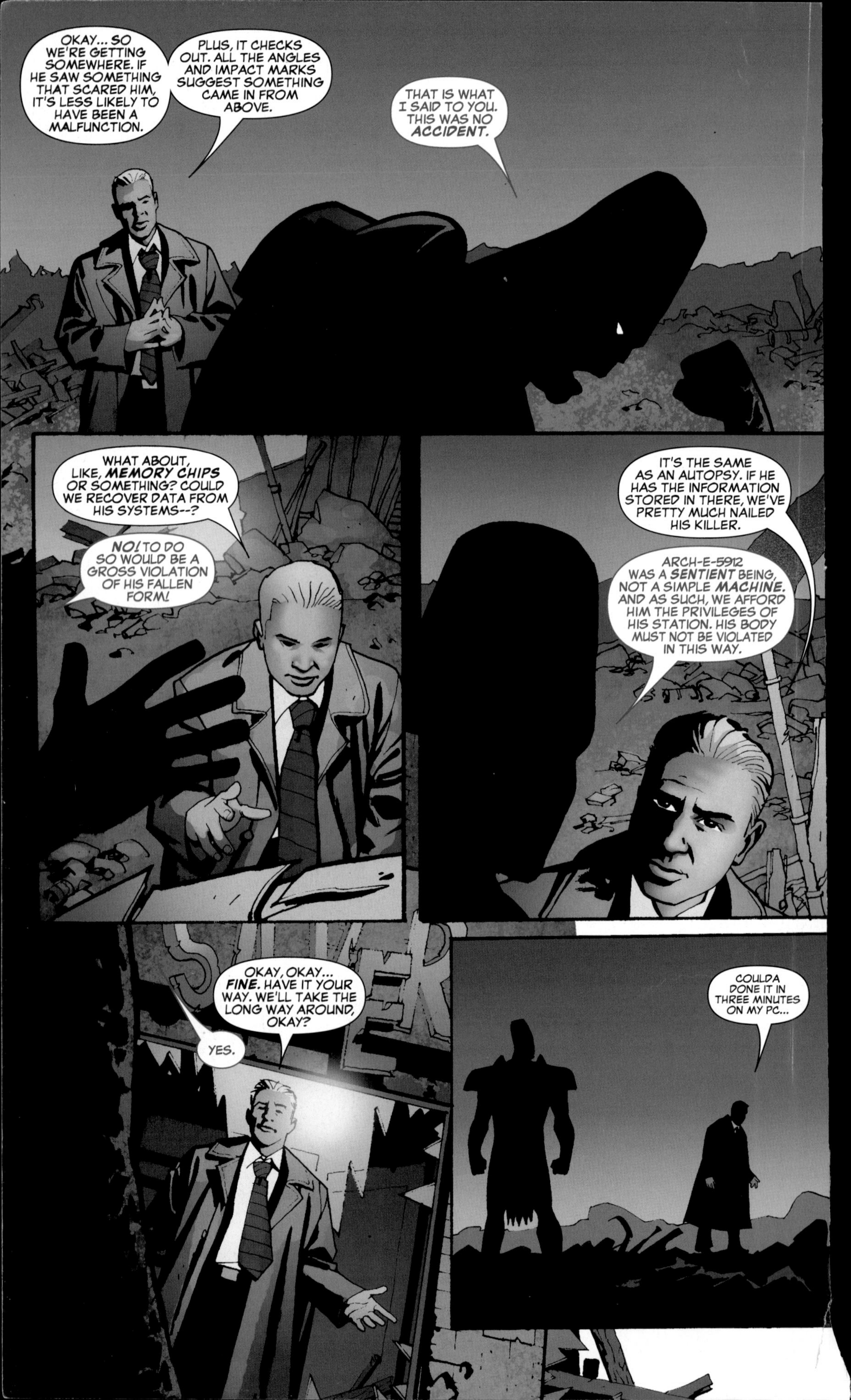
OKAY... SO WE'RE GETTING SOMEWHERE. IF HE SAW SOMETHING THAT SCARED HIM, IT'S LESS LIKELY TO HAVE BEEN A MALFUNCTION.
PLUS, IT CHECKS OUT. ALL THE ANGLES AND IMPACT MARKS SUGGEST SOMETHING CAME IN FROM ABOVE.
THAT IS WHAT I SAID TO YOU. THIS WAS NO ACCIDENT.
WHAT ABOUT, LIKE, MEMORY CHIPS OR SOMETHING? COULD WE RECOVER DATA FROM HIS SYSTEMS--?
NO! TO DO SO WOULD BE A GROSS VIOLATION OF HIS FALLEN FORM!
IT'S THE SAME AS AN AUTOPSY. IF HE HAS THE INFORMATION STORED IN THERE, WE'VE PRETTY MUCH NAILED HIS KILLER.
ARCH-E-5912 WAS A SENTIENT BEING, NOT A SIMPLE MACHINE. AND AS SUCH, WE AFFORD HIM THE PRIVILEGES OF HIS STATION. HIS BODY MUST NOT BE VIOLATED IN THIS WAY.
OKAY, OKAY... FINE. HAVE IT YOUR WAY. WE'LL TAKE THE LONG WAY AROUND, OKAY?
YES.
COULDA DONE IT IN THREE MINUTES ON MY PC...

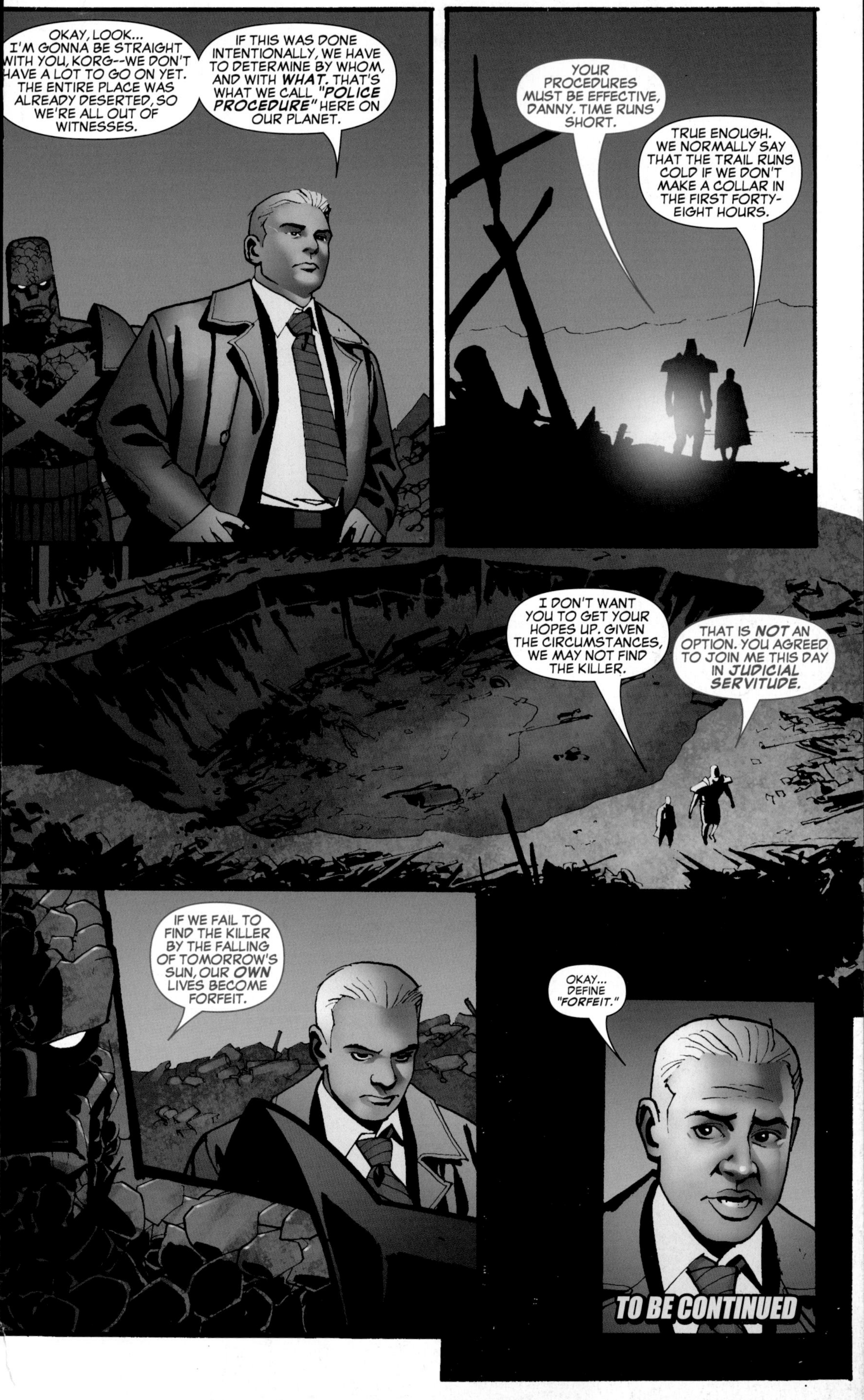
OKAY, LOOK... I'M GONNA BE STRAIGHT WITH YOU, KORG--WE DON'T HAVE A LOT TO GO ON YET. THE ENTIRE PLACE WAS ALREADY DESERTED, SO WE'RE ALL OUT OF WITNESSES.
IF THIS WAS DONE INTENTIONALLY, WE HAVE TO DETERMINE BY WHOM, AND WITH WHAT. THAT'S WHAT WE CALL "POLICE PROCEDURE" HERE ON OUR PLANET.
YOUR PROCEDURES MUST BE EFFECTIVE, DANNY. TIME RUNS SHORT.
TRUE ENOUGH. WE NORMALLY SAY THAT THE TRAIL RUNS COLD IF WE DON'T MAKE A COLLAR IN THE FIRST FORTY-EIGHT HOURS.
I DON'T WANT YOU TO GET YOUR HOPES UP. GIVEN THE CIRCUMSTANCES, WE MAY NOT FIND THE KILLER.
THAT IS NOT AN OPTION. YOU AGREED TO JOIN ME THIS DAY IN JUDICIAL SERVITUDE.
IF WE FAIL TO FIND THE KILLER BY THE FALLING OF TOMORROW'S SUN, OUR OWN LIVES BECOME FORFEIT.
OKAY... DEFINE "FORFEIT."
TO BE CONTINUED

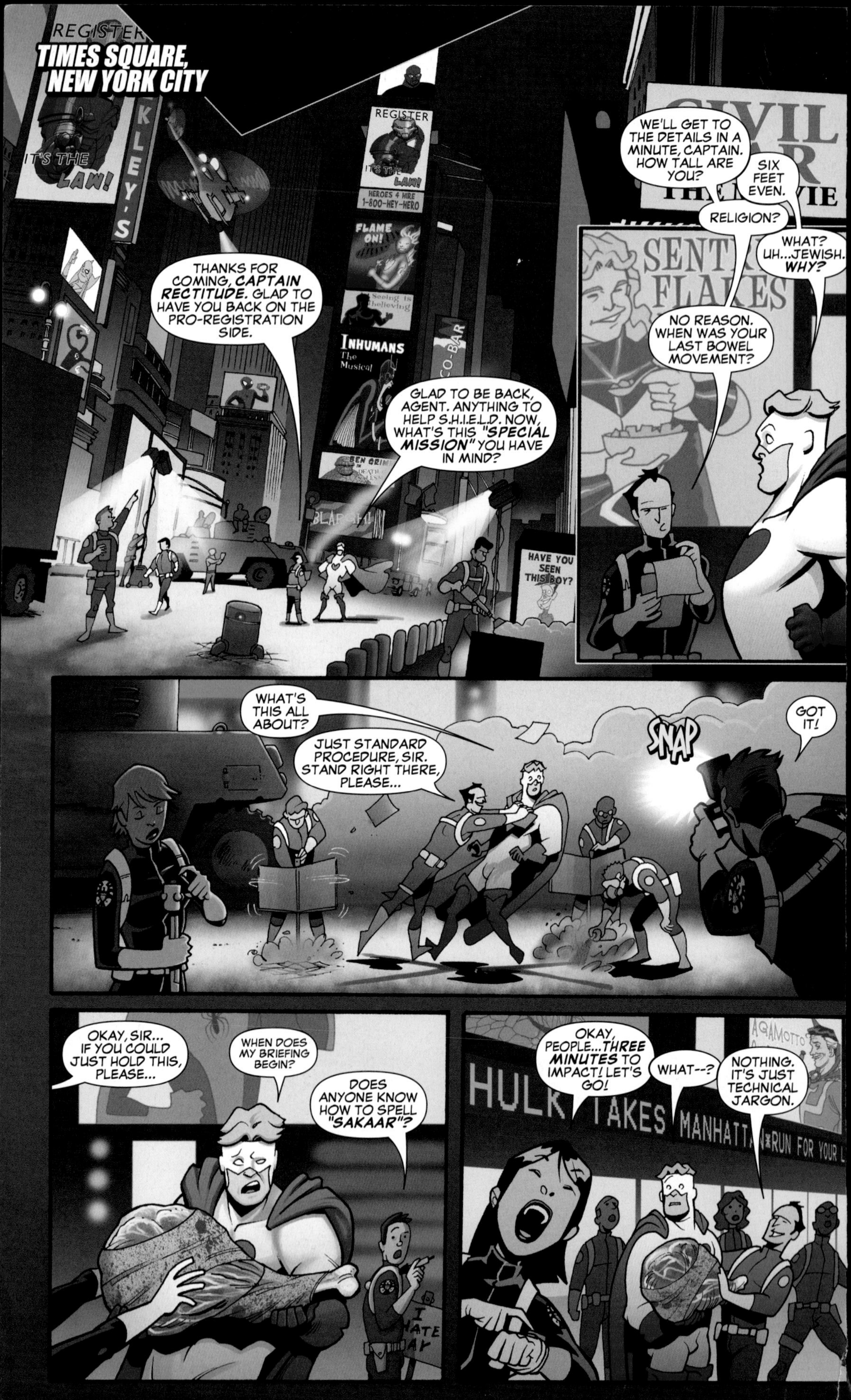
TIMES SQUARE, NEW YORK CITY
THANKS FOR COMING, CAPTAIN RECTITUDE. GLAD TO HAVE YOU BACK ON THE PRO-REGISTRATION SIDE.
GLAD TO BE BACK, AGENT. ANYTHING TO HELP S.H.I.E.L.D. NOW, WHAT'S THIS "SPECIAL MISSION" YOU HAVE IN MIND?
REGISTER IT'S THE LAW!
HEROES 4 HIRE 1-800-HEY-HERO
FLAME ON!
INHUMANS The Musical
HAVE YOU SEEN THIS BOY?
WE'LL GET TO THE DETAILS IN A MINUTE, CAPTAIN. HOW TALL ARE YOU?
SIX FEET EVEN.
RELIGION?
WHAT? UH...JEWISH. WHY?
NO REASON. WHEN WAS YOUR LAST BOWEL MOVEMENT?
WHAT'S THIS ALL ABOUT?
JUST STANDARD PROCEDURE, SIR. STAND RIGHT THERE, PLEASE...
SNAP
GOT IT!
OKAY, SIR... IF YOU COULD JUST HOLD THIS, PLEASE...
WHEN DOES MY BRIEFING BEGIN?
DOES ANYONE KNOW HOW TO SPELL "SAKAAR"?
OKAY, PEOPLE...THREE MINUTES TO IMPACT! LET'S GO!
WHAT--?
NOTHING. IT'S JUST TECHNICAL JARGON.
HULK TAKES MANHATTAN*RUN FOR YOUR L

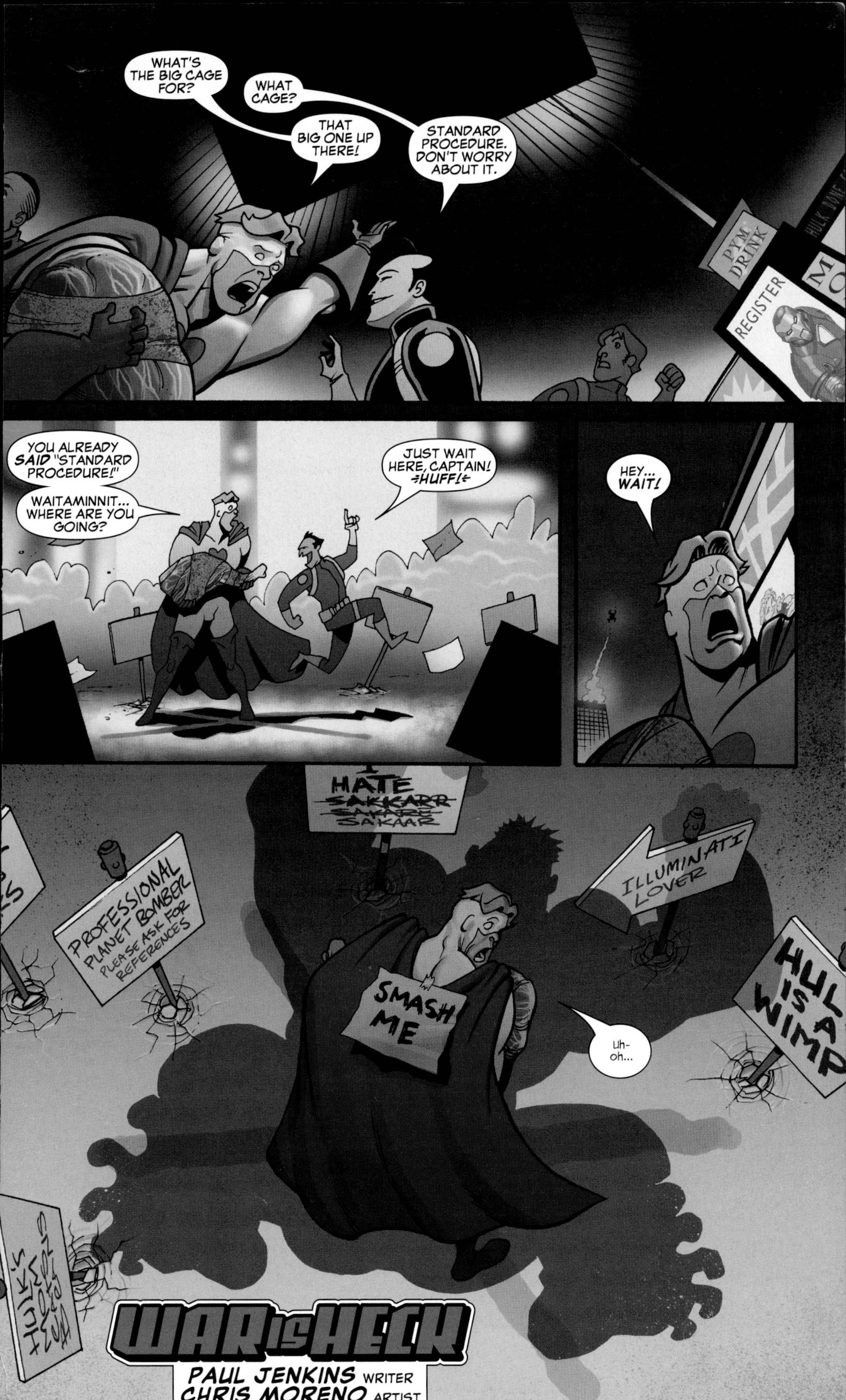
WHAT'S THE BIG CAGE FOR?
WHAT CAGE?
THAT BIG ONE UP THERE!
STANDARD PROCEDURE. DON'T WORRY ABOUT IT.
PYM DRINK
REGISTER
YOU ALREADY SAID "STANDARD PROCEDURE!"
WAITAMINNIT... WHERE ARE YOU GOING?
JUST WAIT HERE, CAPTAIN! HUFF!
HEY... WAIT!
HATE ~~SAKKARR~~ ~~SAKARE~~ SAKAAR
PROFESSIONAL PLANET BOMBER PLEASE ASK FOR REFERENCES
ILLUMINATI LOVER
SMASH ME
Uh-oh...
HULK IS A WIMP
WAR IS HECK
PAUL JENKINS WRITER
CHRIS MORENO ARTIST
DAVE SHARPE LETTERER

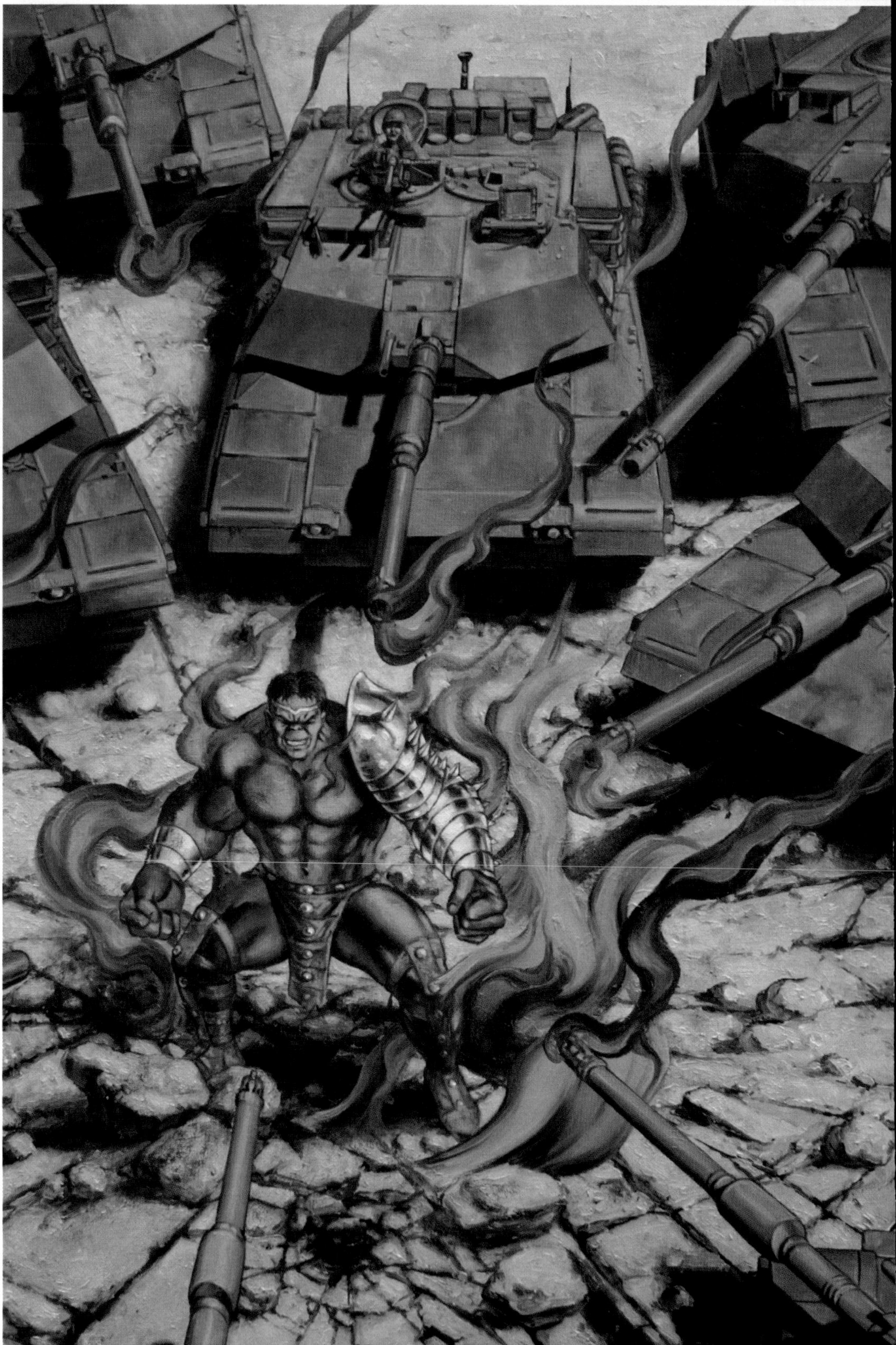

WORLD WAR HULK: FRONT LINE #3

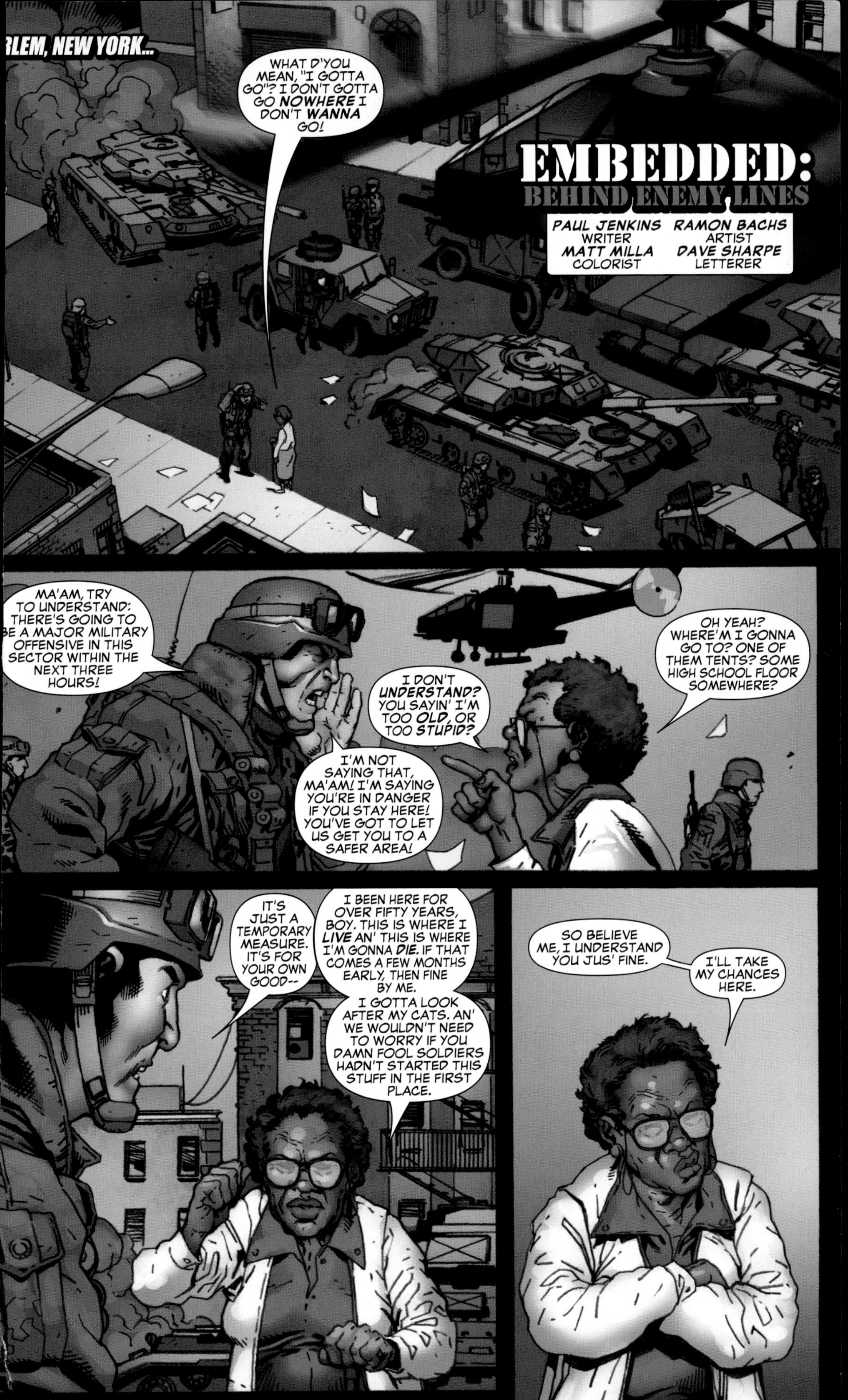

RLEM, NEW YORK...
WHAT D'YOU MEAN, "I GOTTA GO"? I DON'T GOTTA GO NOWHERE I DON'T WANNA GO!
EMBEDDED:
BEHIND ENEMY LINES
PAUL JENKINS WRITER
RAMON BACHS ARTIST
MATT MILLA COLORIST
DAVE SHARPE LETTERER
MA'AM, TRY TO UNDERSTAND: THERE'S GOING TO BE A MAJOR MILITARY OFFENSIVE IN THIS SECTOR WITHIN THE NEXT THREE HOURS!
I DON'T UNDERSTAND? YOU SAYIN' I'M TOO OLD, OR TOO STUPID?
I'M NOT SAYING THAT, MA'AM! I'M SAYING YOU'RE IN DANGER IF YOU STAY HERE! YOU'VE GOT TO LET US GET YOU TO A SAFER AREA!
OH YEAH? WHERE'M I GONNA GO TO? ONE OF THEM TENTS? SOME HIGH SCHOOL FLOOR SOMEWHERE?
IT'S JUST A TEMPORARY MEASURE. IT'S FOR YOUR OWN GOOD--
I BEEN HERE FOR OVER FIFTY YEARS, BOY. THIS IS WHERE I LIVE AN' THIS IS WHERE I'M GONNA DIE. IF THAT COMES A FEW MONTHS EARLY, THEN FINE BY ME.
I GOTTA LOOK AFTER MY CATS. AN' WE WOULDN'T NEED TO WORRY IF YOU DAMN FOOL SOLDIERS HADN'T STARTED THIS STUFF IN THE FIRST PLACE.
SO BELIEVE ME, I UNDERSTAND YOU JUS' FINE.
I'LL TAKE MY CHANCES HERE.

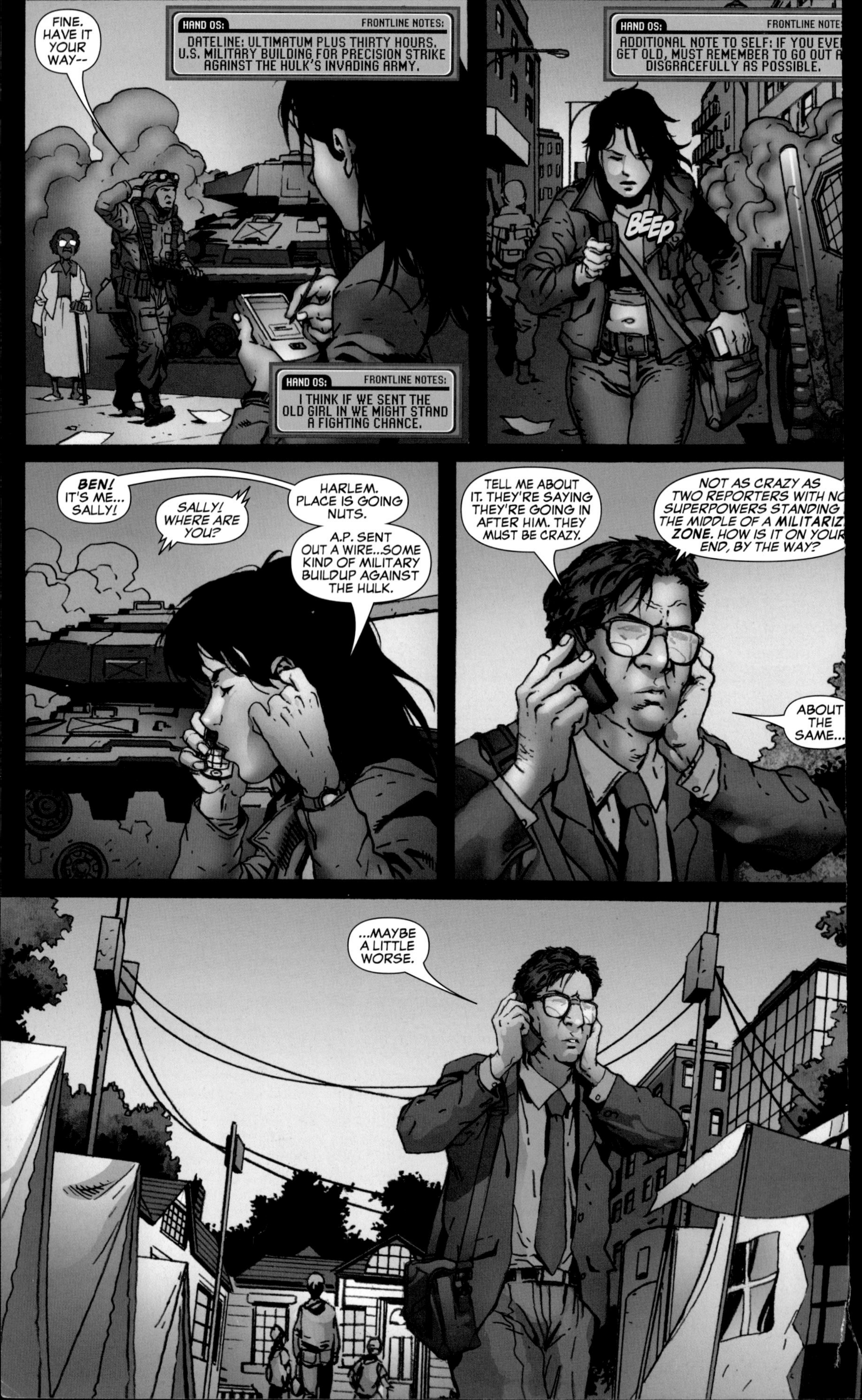
FINE. HAVE IT YOUR WAY--
HAND OS: FRONTLINE NOTES:
DATELINE: ULTIMATUM PLUS THIRTY HOURS. U.S. MILITARY BUILDING FOR PRECISION STRIKE AGAINST THE HULK'S INVADING ARMY.
HAND OS: FRONTLINE NOTES:
I THINK IF WE SENT THE OLD GIRL IN WE MIGHT STAND A FIGHTING CHANCE.
HAND OS: FRONTLINE NOTES:
ADDITIONAL NOTE TO SELF: IF YOU EVE GET OLD, MUST REMEMBER TO GO OUT A DISGRACEFULLY AS POSSIBLE.
BEEP
BEN! IT'S ME... SALLY!
SALLY! WHERE ARE YOU?
HARLEM. PLACE IS GOING NUTS.
A.P. SENT OUT A WIRE...SOME KIND OF MILITARY BUILDUP AGAINST THE HULK.
TELL ME ABOUT IT. THEY'RE SAYING THEY'RE GOING IN AFTER HIM. THEY MUST BE CRAZY.
NOT AS CRAZY AS TWO REPORTERS WITH NO SUPERPOWERS STANDING THE MIDDLE OF A MILITARIZ ZONE. HOW IS IT ON YOUR END, BY THE WAY?
ABOUT THE SAME...
...MAYBE A LITTLE WORSE.

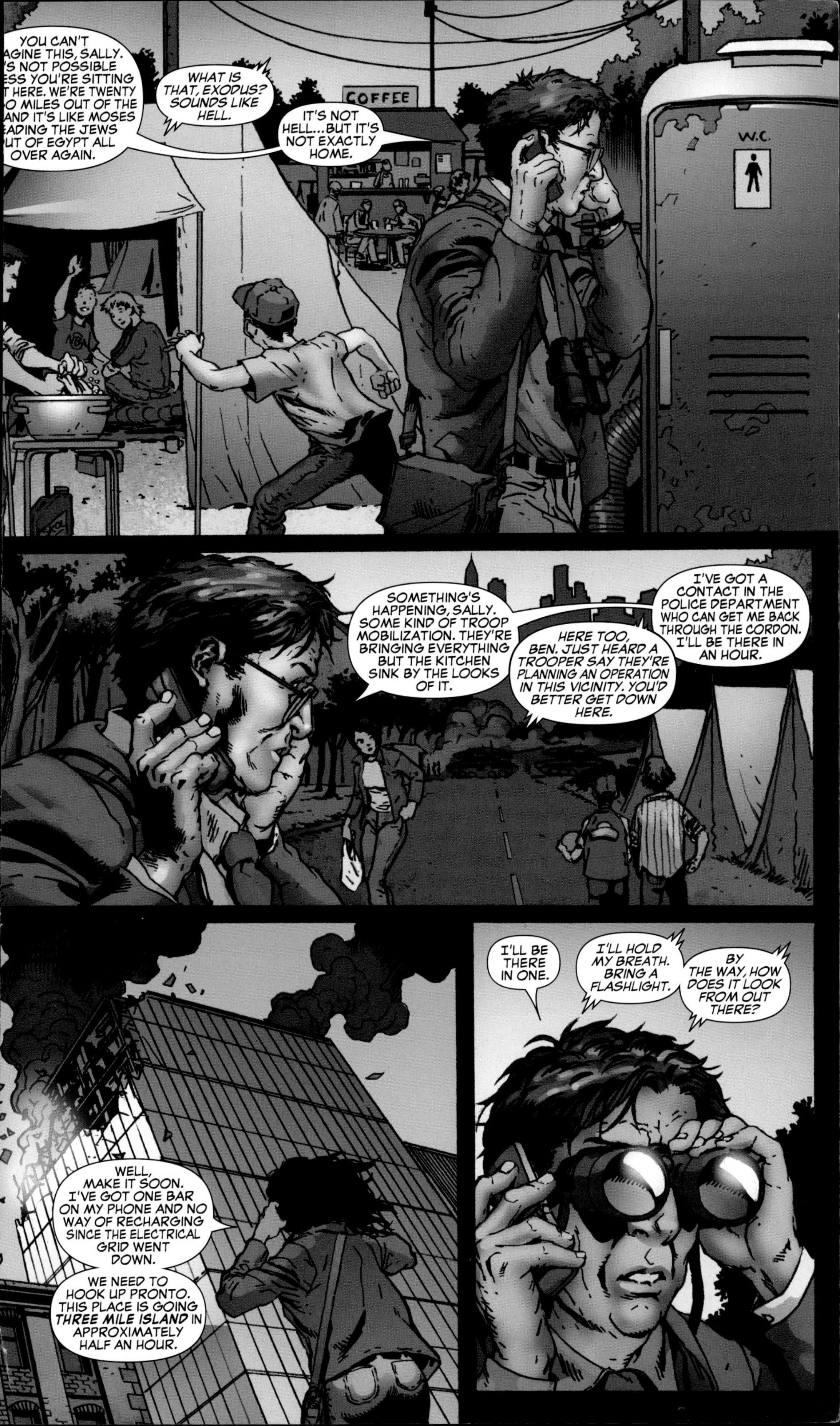
YOU CAN'T AGINE THIS, SALLY. 'S NOT POSSIBLE ESS YOU'RE SITTING T HERE. WE'RE TWENTY O MILES OUT OF THE AND IT'S LIKE MOSES EADING THE JEWS UT OF EGYPT ALL OVER AGAIN.
WHAT IS THAT, EXODUS? SOUNDS LIKE HELL.
COFFEE
IT'S NOT HELL...BUT IT'S NOT EXACTLY HOME.
W.C.
SOMETHING'S HAPPENING, SALLY. SOME KIND OF TROOP MOBILIZATION. THEY'RE BRINGING EVERYTHING BUT THE KITCHEN SINK BY THE LOOKS OF IT.
HERE TOO, BEN. JUST HEARD A TROOPER SAY THEY'RE PLANNING AN OPERATION IN THIS VICINITY. YOU'D BETTER GET DOWN HERE.
I'VE GOT A CONTACT IN THE POLICE DEPARTMENT WHO CAN GET ME BACK THROUGH THE CORDON. I'LL BE THERE IN AN HOUR.
WELL, MAKE IT SOON. I'VE GOT ONE BAR ON MY PHONE AND NO WAY OF RECHARGING SINCE THE ELECTRICAL GRID WENT DOWN.
WE NEED TO HOOK UP PRONTO. THIS PLACE IS GOING THREE MILE ISLAND IN APPROXIMATELY HALF AN HOUR.
I'LL BE THERE IN ONE.
I'LL HOLD MY BREATH. BRING A FLASHLIGHT.
BY THE WAY, HOW DOES IT LOOK FROM OUT THERE?

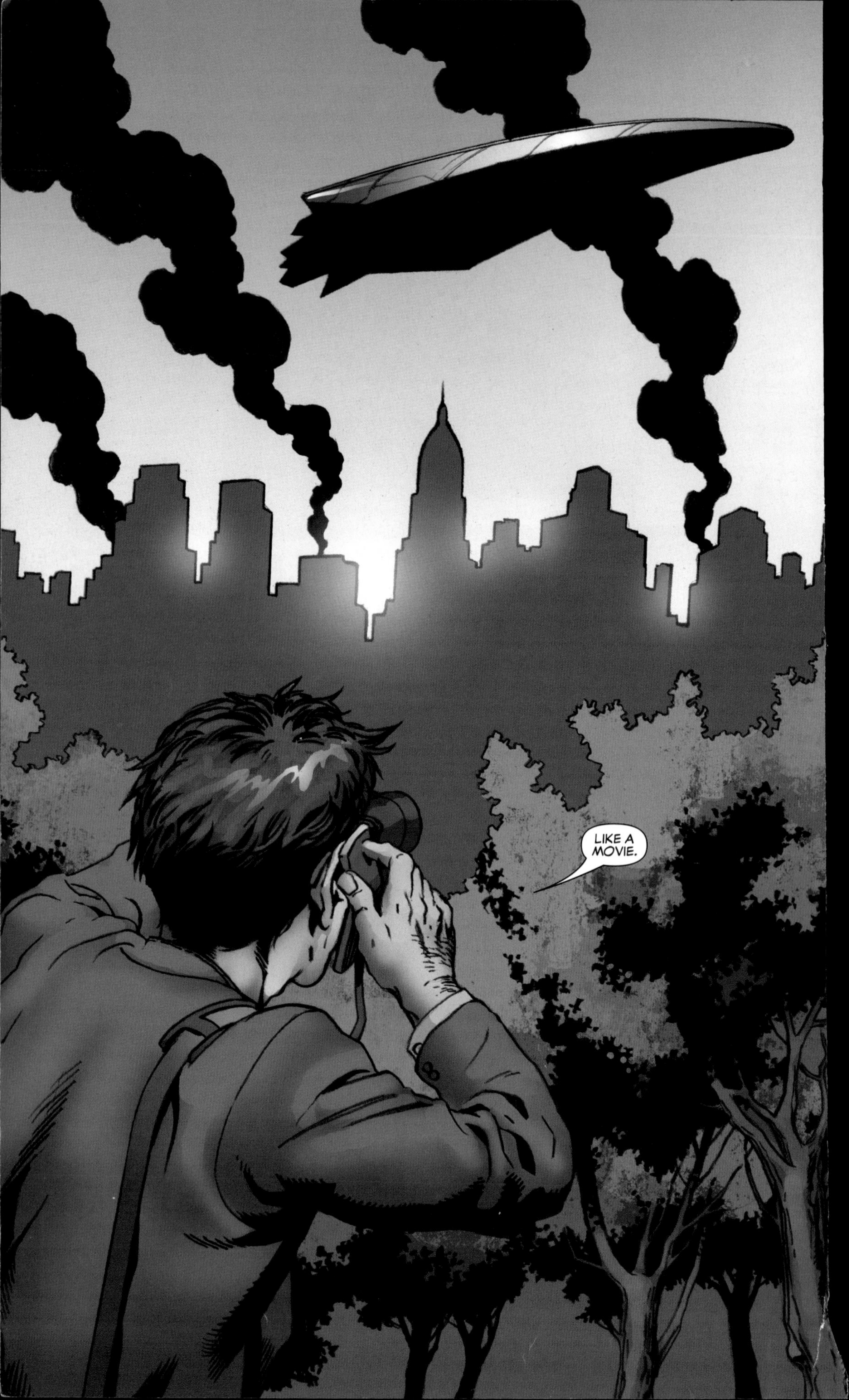
LIKE A MOVIE.

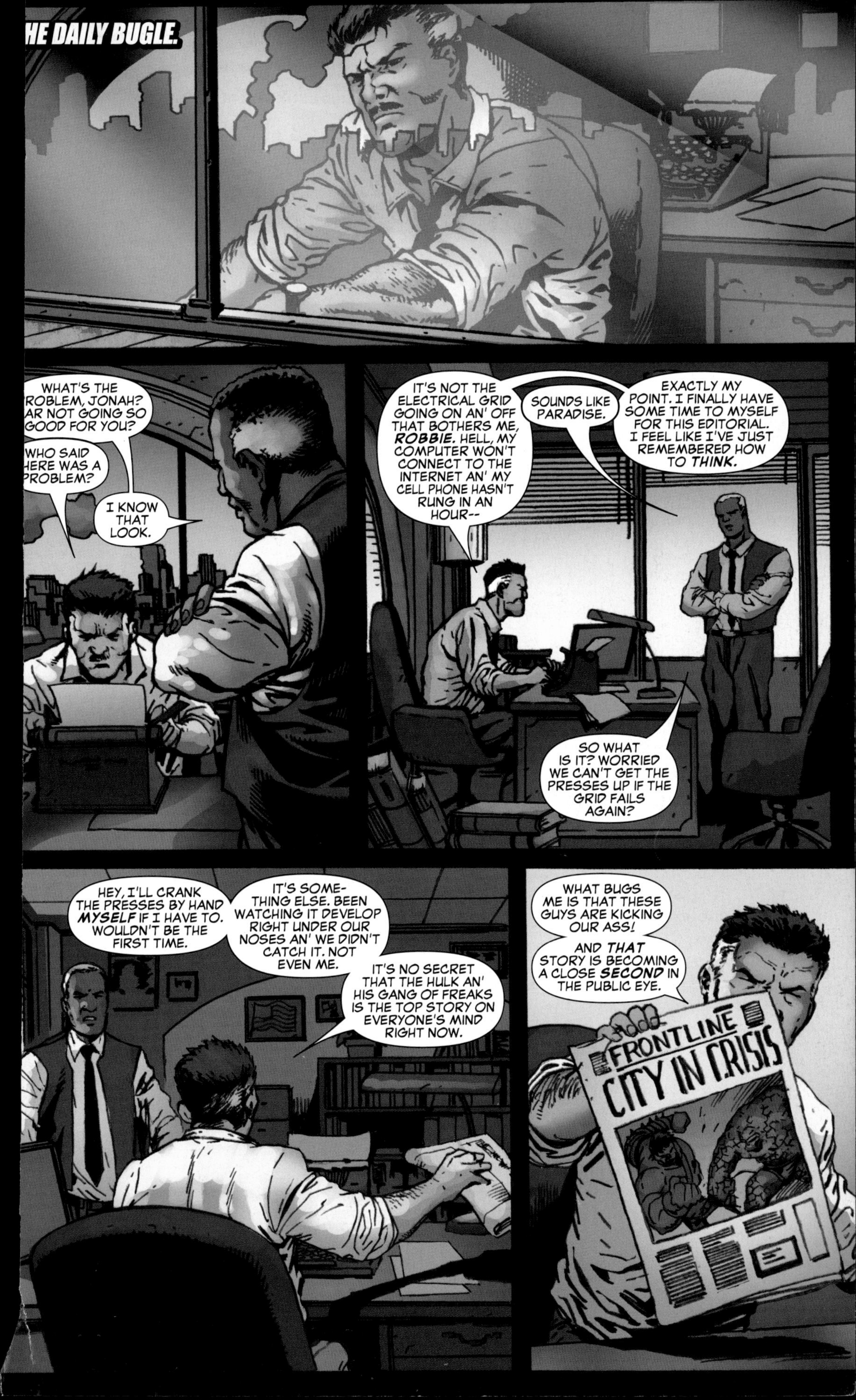
HE DAILY BUGLE.
WHAT'S THE ROBLEM, JONAH? AR NOT GOING SO GOOD FOR YOU?
WHO SAID HERE WAS A PROBLEM?
I KNOW THAT LOOK.
IT'S NOT THE ELECTRICAL GRID GOING ON AN' OFF THAT BOTHERS ME, ROBBIE. HELL, MY COMPUTER WON'T CONNECT TO THE INTERNET AN' MY CELL PHONE HASN'T RUNG IN AN HOUR--
SOUNDS LIKE PARADISE.
EXACTLY MY POINT. I FINALLY HAVE SOME TIME TO MYSELF FOR THIS EDITORIAL. I FEEL LIKE I'VE JUST REMEMBERED HOW TO THINK.
SO WHAT IS IT? WORRIED WE CAN'T GET THE PRESSES UP IF THE GRID FAILS AGAIN?
HEY, I'LL CRANK THE PRESSES BY HAND MYSELF IF I HAVE TO. WOULDN'T BE THE FIRST TIME.
IT'S SOME-THING ELSE. BEEN WATCHING IT DEVELOP RIGHT UNDER OUR NOSES AN' WE DIDN'T CATCH IT. NOT EVEN ME.
IT'S NO SECRET THAT THE HULK AN' HIS GANG OF FREAKS IS THE TOP STORY ON EVERYONE'S MIND RIGHT NOW.
WHAT BUGS ME IS THAT THESE GUYS ARE KICKING OUR ASS!
AND THAT STORY IS BECOMING A CLOSE SECOND IN THE PUBLIC EYE.
FRONTLINE
CITY IN CRISIS

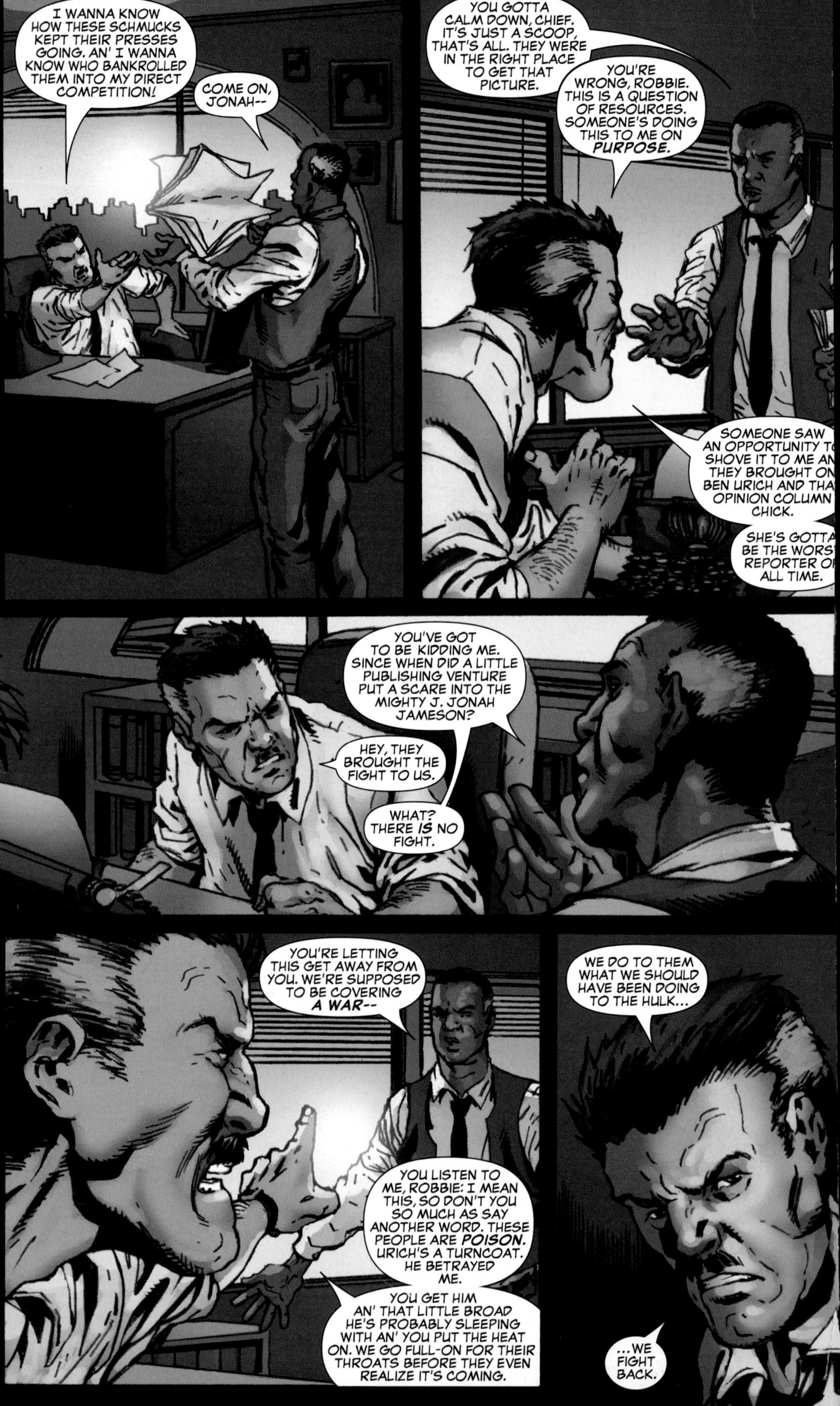
I WANNA KNOW HOW THESE SCHMUCKS KEPT THEIR PRESSES GOING. AN' I WANNA KNOW WHO BANKROLLED THEM INTO MY DIRECT COMPETITION!
COME ON, JONAH--
YOU GOTTA CALM DOWN, CHIEF. IT'S JUST A SCOOP, THAT'S ALL. THEY WERE IN THE RIGHT PLACE TO GET THAT PICTURE.
YOU'RE WRONG, ROBBIE. THIS IS A QUESTION OF RESOURCES. SOMEONE'S DOING THIS TO ME ON PURPOSE.
SOMEONE SAW AN OPPORTUNITY T SHOVE IT TO ME AN THEY BROUGHT ON BEN URICH AND THA OPINION COLUMN CHICK.
SHE'S GOTTA BE THE WORS REPORTER O ALL TIME.
YOU'VE GOT TO BE KIDDING ME. SINCE WHEN DID A LITTLE PUBLISHING VENTURE PUT A SCARE INTO THE MIGHTY J. JONAH JAMESON?
HEY, THEY BROUGHT THE FIGHT TO US.
WHAT? THERE IS NO FIGHT.
YOU'RE LETTING THIS GET AWAY FROM YOU. WE'RE SUPPOSED TO BE COVERING A WAR--
YOU LISTEN TO ME, ROBBIE: I MEAN THIS, SO DON'T YOU SO MUCH AS SAY ANOTHER WORD. THESE PEOPLE ARE POISON. URICH'S A TURNCOAT. HE BETRAYED ME.
YOU GET HIM AN' THAT LITTLE BROAD HE'S PROBABLY SLEEPING WITH AN' YOU PUT THE HEAT ON. WE GO FULL-ON FOR THEIR THROATS BEFORE THEY EVEN REALIZE IT'S COMING.
WE DO TO THEM WHAT WE SHOULD HAVE BEEN DOING TO THE HULK...
...WE FIGHT BACK.

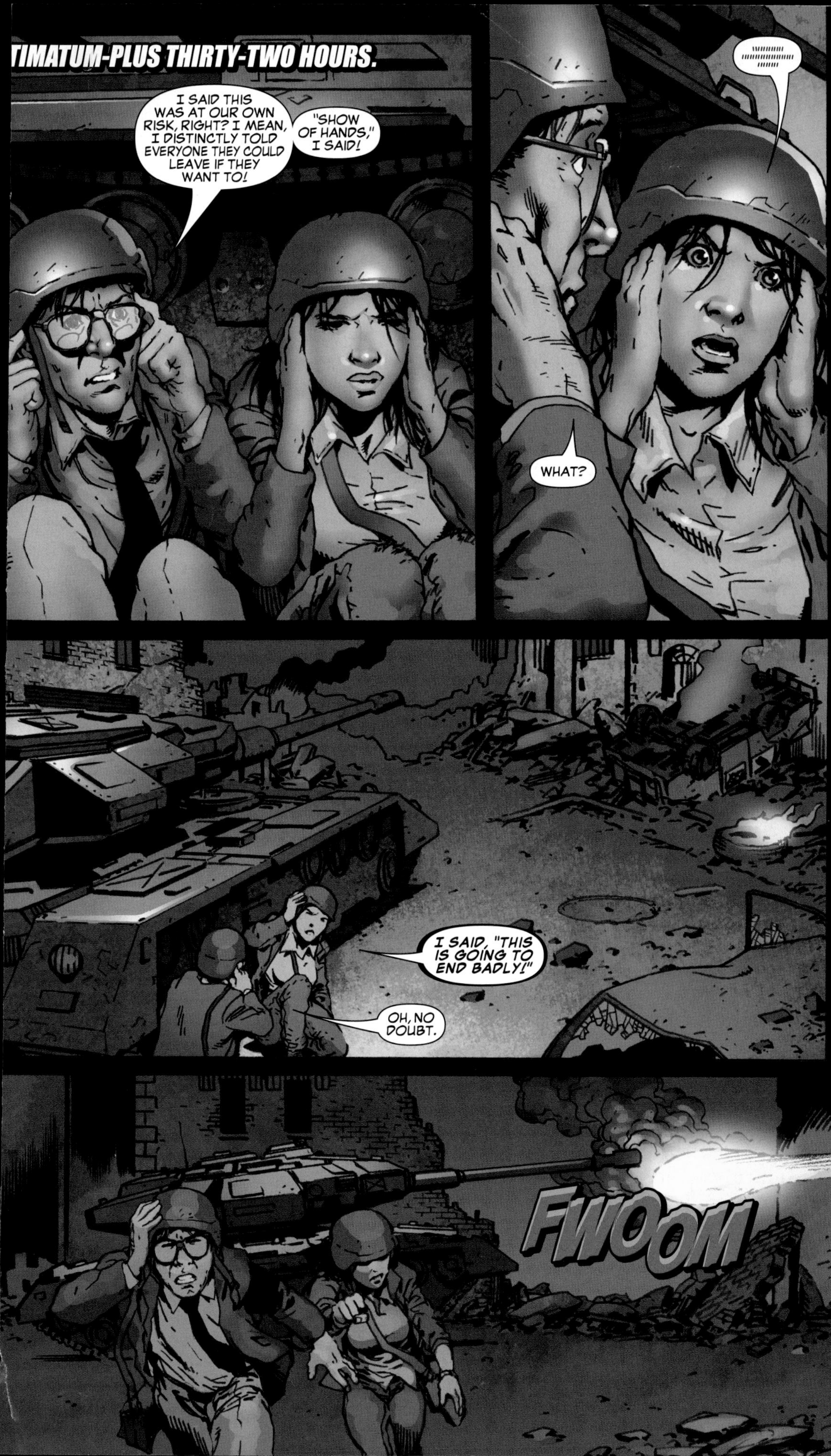
TIMATUM-PLUS THIRTY-TWO HOURS.
I SAID THIS WAS AT OUR OWN RISK, RIGHT? I MEAN, I DISTINCTLY TOLD EVERYONE THEY COULD LEAVE IF THEY WANT TO!
"SHOW OF HANDS," I SAID!
WHAT?
I SAID, "THIS IS GOING TO END BADLY!"
OH, NO DOUBT.
FWOOM

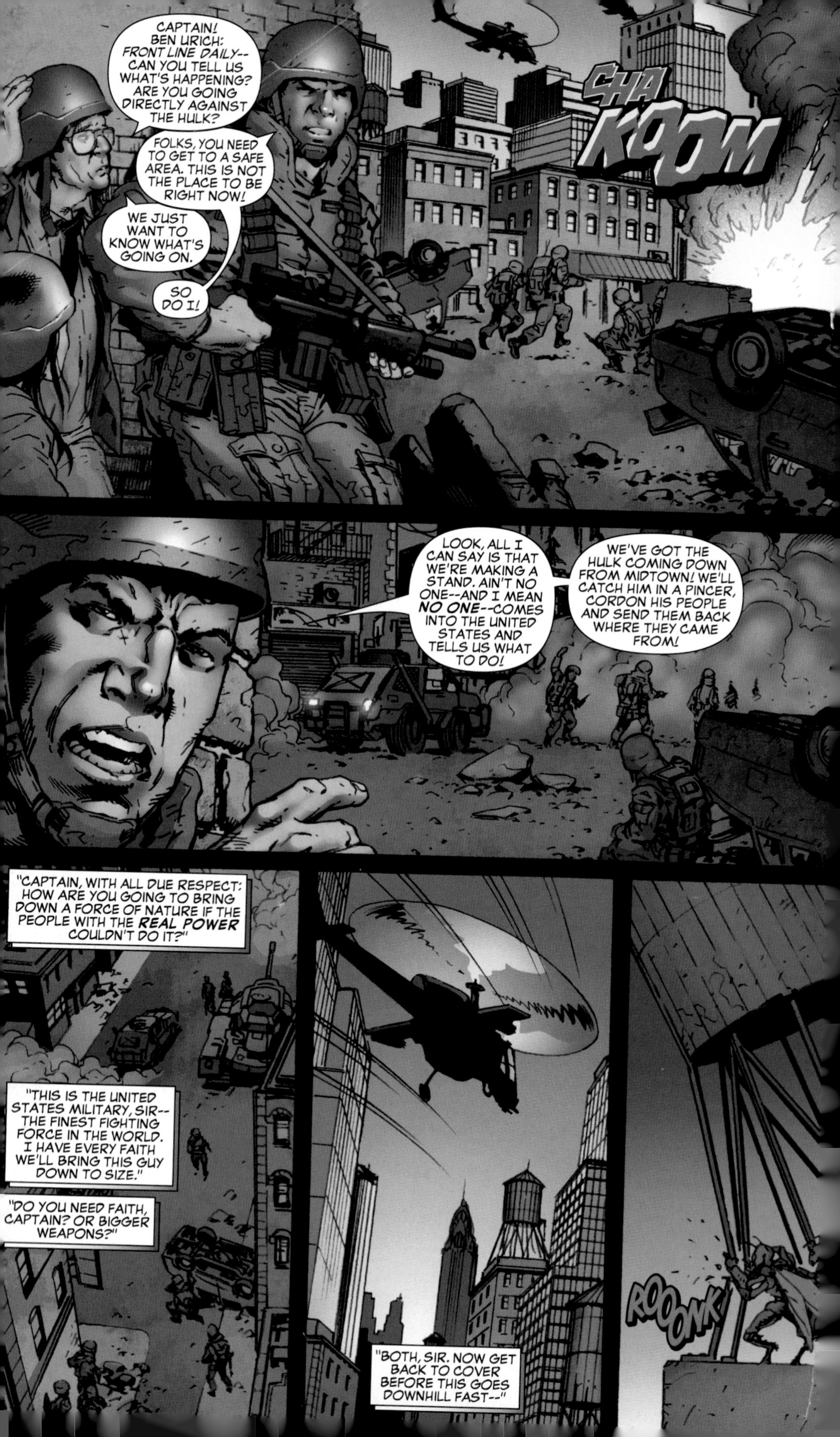
CAPTAIN! BEN URICH: FRONT LINE DAILY-- CAN YOU TELL US WHAT'S HAPPENING? ARE YOU GOING DIRECTLY AGAINST THE HULK?
FOLKS, YOU NEED TO GET TO A SAFE AREA. THIS IS NOT THE PLACE TO BE RIGHT NOW!
WE JUST WANT TO KNOW WHAT'S GOING ON.
SO DO I!
CHA KOOM
LOOK, ALL I CAN SAY IS THAT WE'RE MAKING A STAND. AIN'T NO ONE--AND I MEAN NO ONE--COMES INTO THE UNITED STATES AND TELLS US WHAT TO DO!
WE'VE GOT THE HULK COMING DOWN FROM MIDTOWN! WE'LL CATCH HIM IN A PINCER, CORDON HIS PEOPLE AND SEND THEM BACK WHERE THEY CAME FROM!
"CAPTAIN, WITH ALL DUE RESPECT: HOW ARE YOU GOING TO BRING DOWN A FORCE OF NATURE IF THE PEOPLE WITH THE REAL POWER COULDN'T DO IT?"
"THIS IS THE UNITED STATES MILITARY, SIR-- THE FINEST FIGHTING FORCE IN THE WORLD. I HAVE EVERY FAITH WE'LL BRING THIS GUY DOWN TO SIZE."
"DO YOU NEED FAITH, CAPTAIN? OR BIGGER WEAPONS?"
"BOTH, SIR. NOW GET BACK TO COVER BEFORE THIS GOES DOWNHILL FAST--"
ROOONK

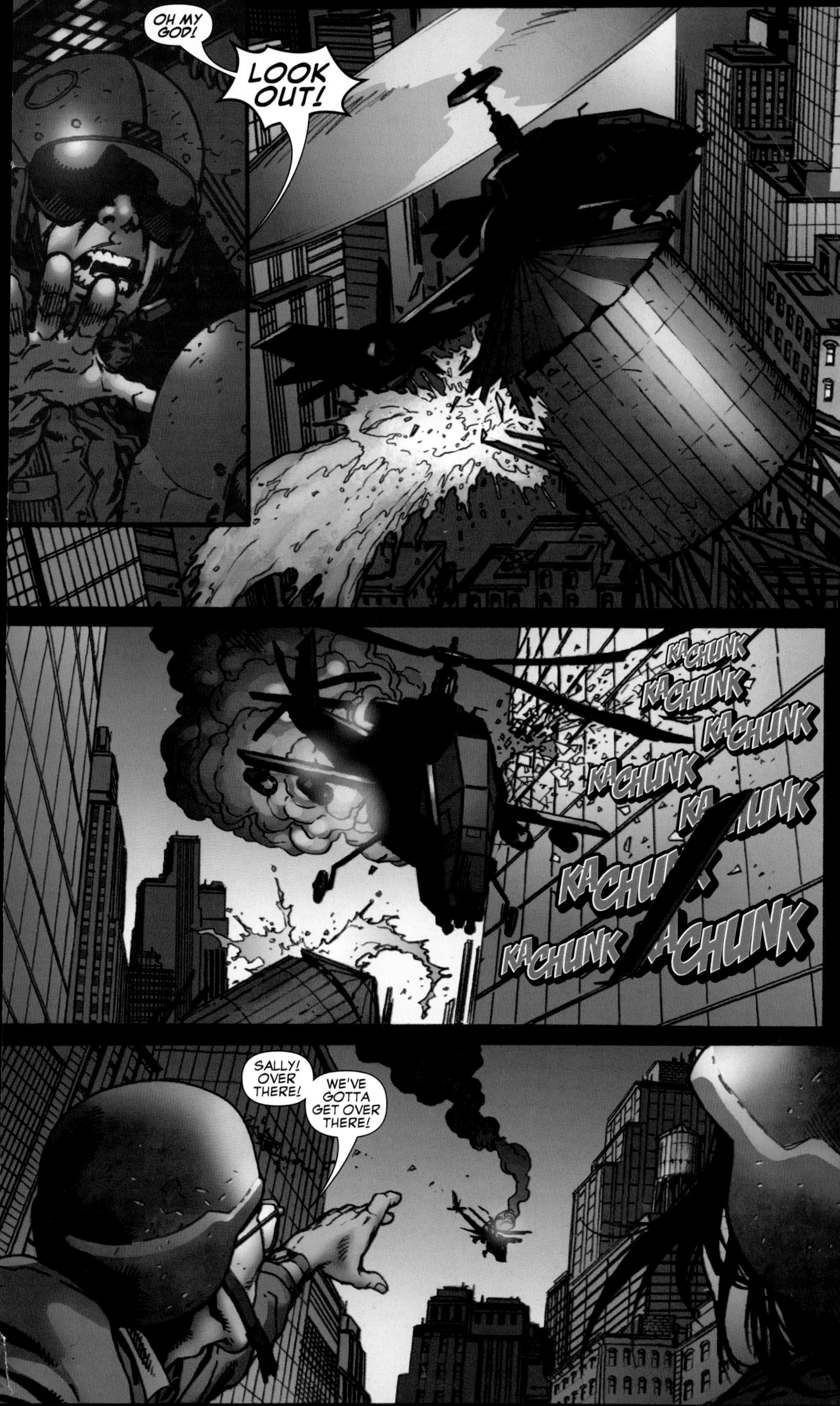
OH MY GOD!
LOOK OUT!
KA CHUNK
KA CHUNK
KA CHUNK
KA CHUNK
KA CHUNK
KA CHUNK
KA CHUNK
KA CHUNK
SALLY! OVER THERE!
WE'VE GOTTA GET OVER THERE!

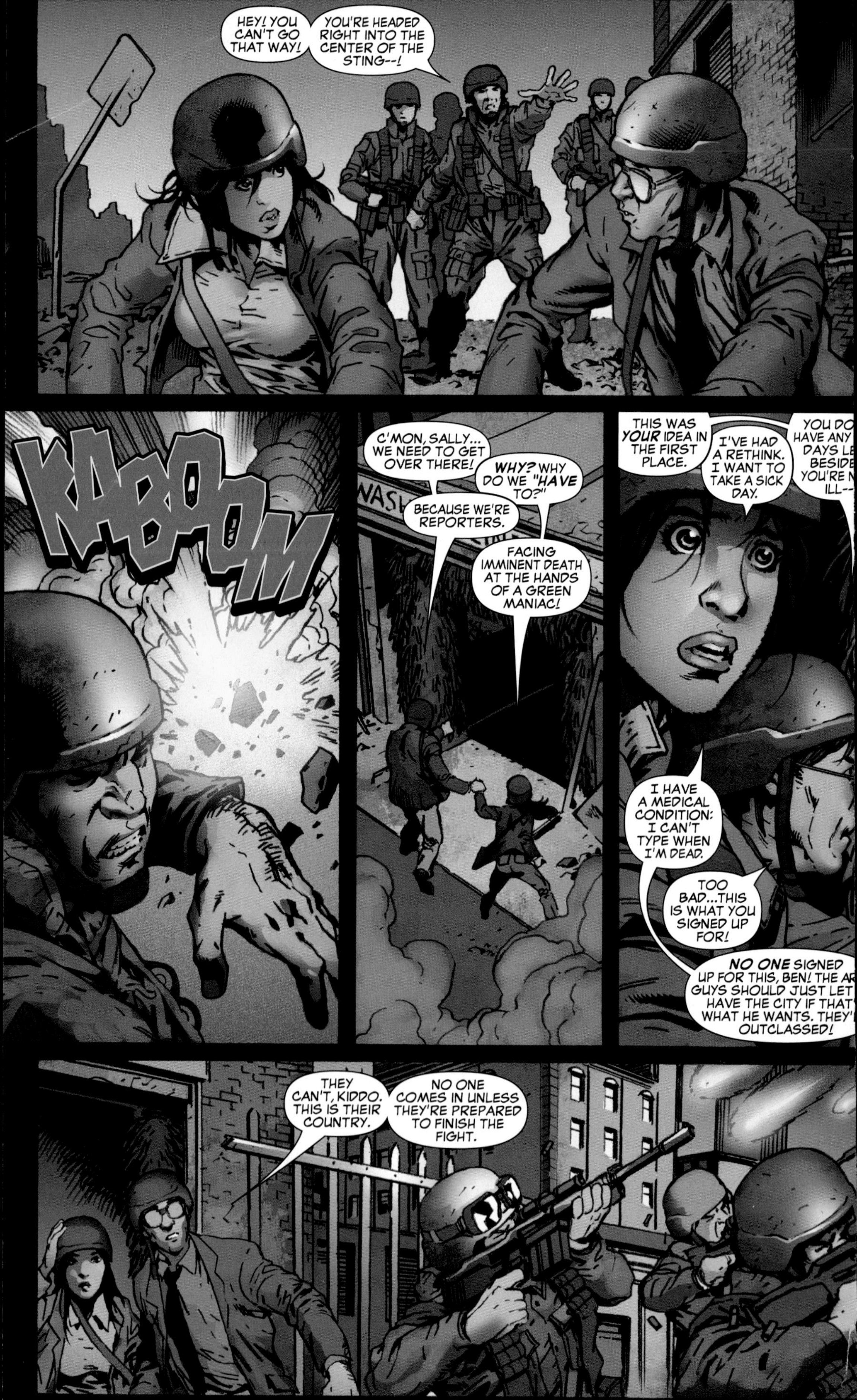
HEY! YOU CAN'T GO THAT WAY!
YOU'RE HEADED RIGHT INTO THE CENTER OF THE STING--!
KABOOM
C'MON, SALLY... WE NEED TO GET OVER THERE!
WHY? WHY DO WE "HAVE TO?"
BECAUSE WE'RE REPORTERS.
FACING IMMINENT DEATH AT THE HANDS OF A GREEN MANIAC!
WASH
THIS WAS YOUR IDEA IN THE FIRST PLACE.
I'VE HAD A RETHINK. I WANT TO TAKE A SICK DAY.
YOU DO HAVE ANY DAYS LE BESIDE YOU'RE N ILL--
I HAVE A MEDICAL CONDITION: I CAN'T TYPE WHEN I'M DEAD.
TOO BAD...THIS IS WHAT YOU SIGNED UP FOR!
NO ONE SIGNED UP FOR THIS, BEN! THE AR GUYS SHOULD JUST LET HAVE THE CITY IF THAT WHAT HE WANTS. THEY' OUTCLASSED!
THEY CAN'T, KIDDO. THIS IS THEIR COUNTRY.
NO ONE COMES IN UNLESS THEY'RE PREPARED TO FINISH THE FIGHT.

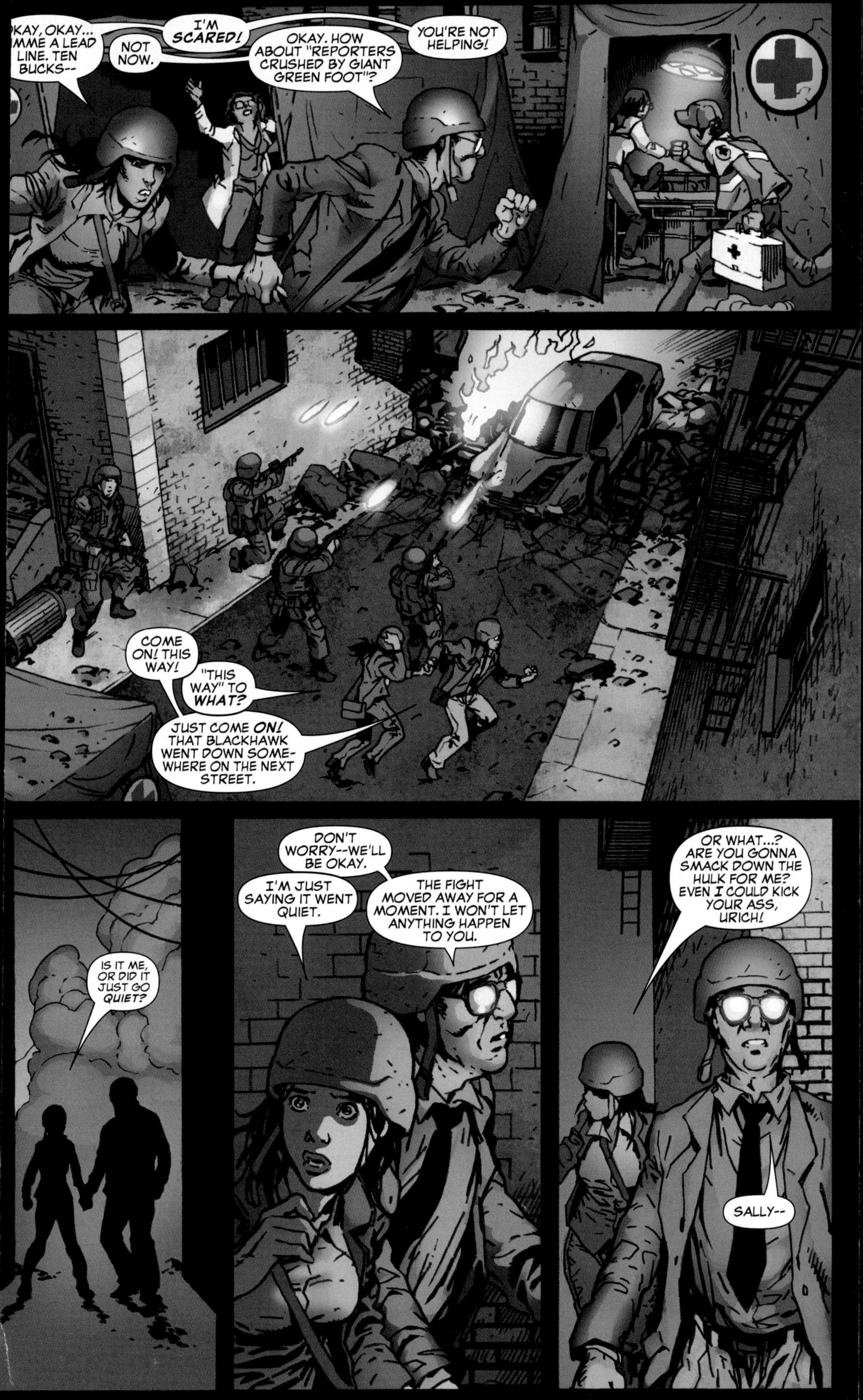
OKAY, OKAY... GIMME A LEAD LINE. TEN BUCKS--
I'M SCARED!
NOT NOW.
OKAY. HOW ABOUT "REPORTERS CRUSHED BY GIANT GREEN FOOT"?
YOU'RE NOT HELPING!
COME ON! THIS WAY!
"THIS WAY" TO WHAT?
JUST COME ON! THAT BLACKHAWK WENT DOWN SOMEWHERE ON THE NEXT STREET.
IS IT ME, OR DID IT JUST GO QUIET?
DON'T WORRY--WE'LL BE OKAY.
I'M JUST SAYING IT WENT QUIET.
THE FIGHT MOVED AWAY FOR A MOMENT. I WON'T LET ANYTHING HAPPEN TO YOU.
OR WHAT...? ARE YOU GONNA SMACK DOWN THE HULK FOR ME? EVEN I COULD KICK YOUR ASS, URICH!
SALLY--

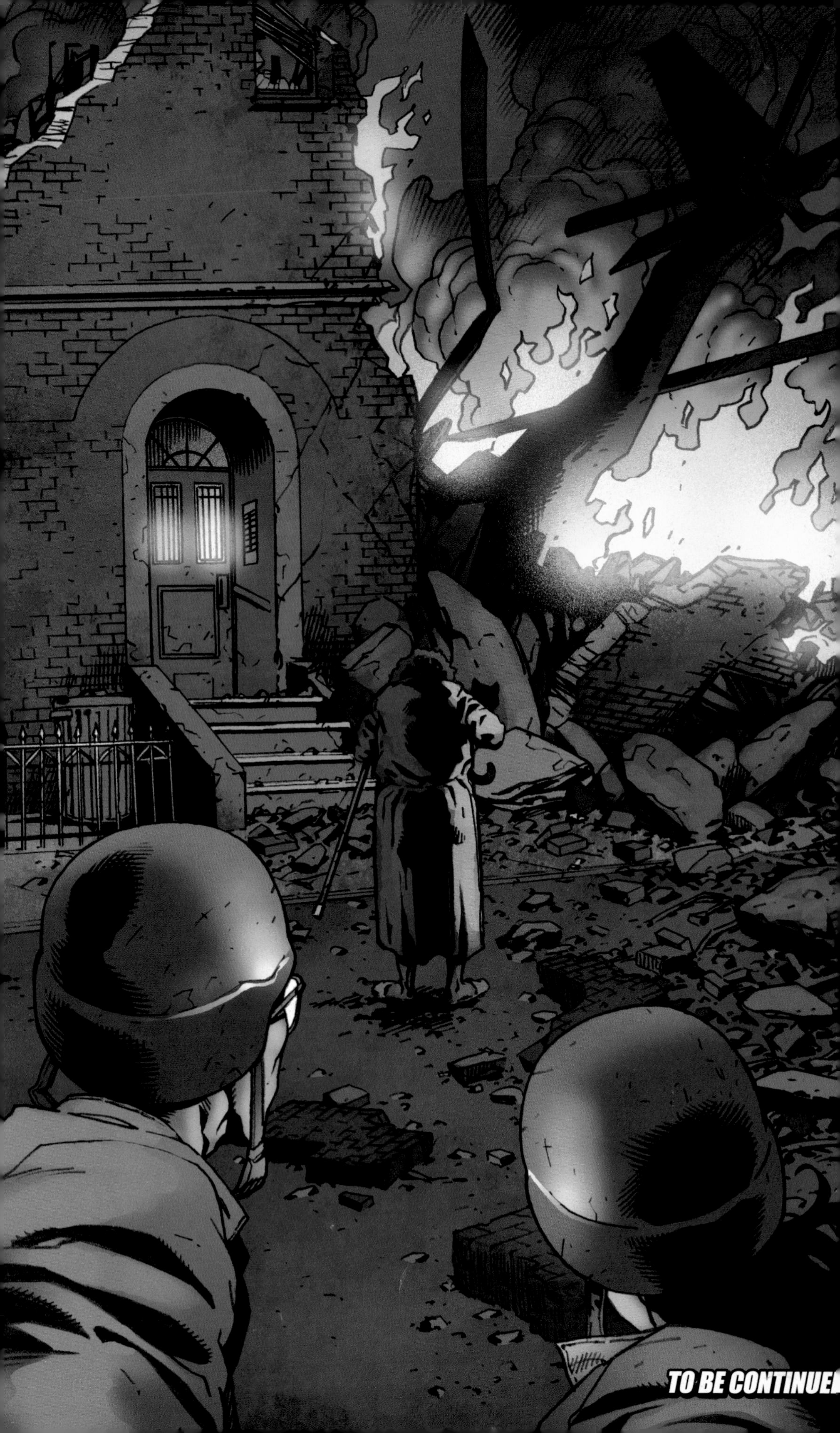
TO BE CONTINUED

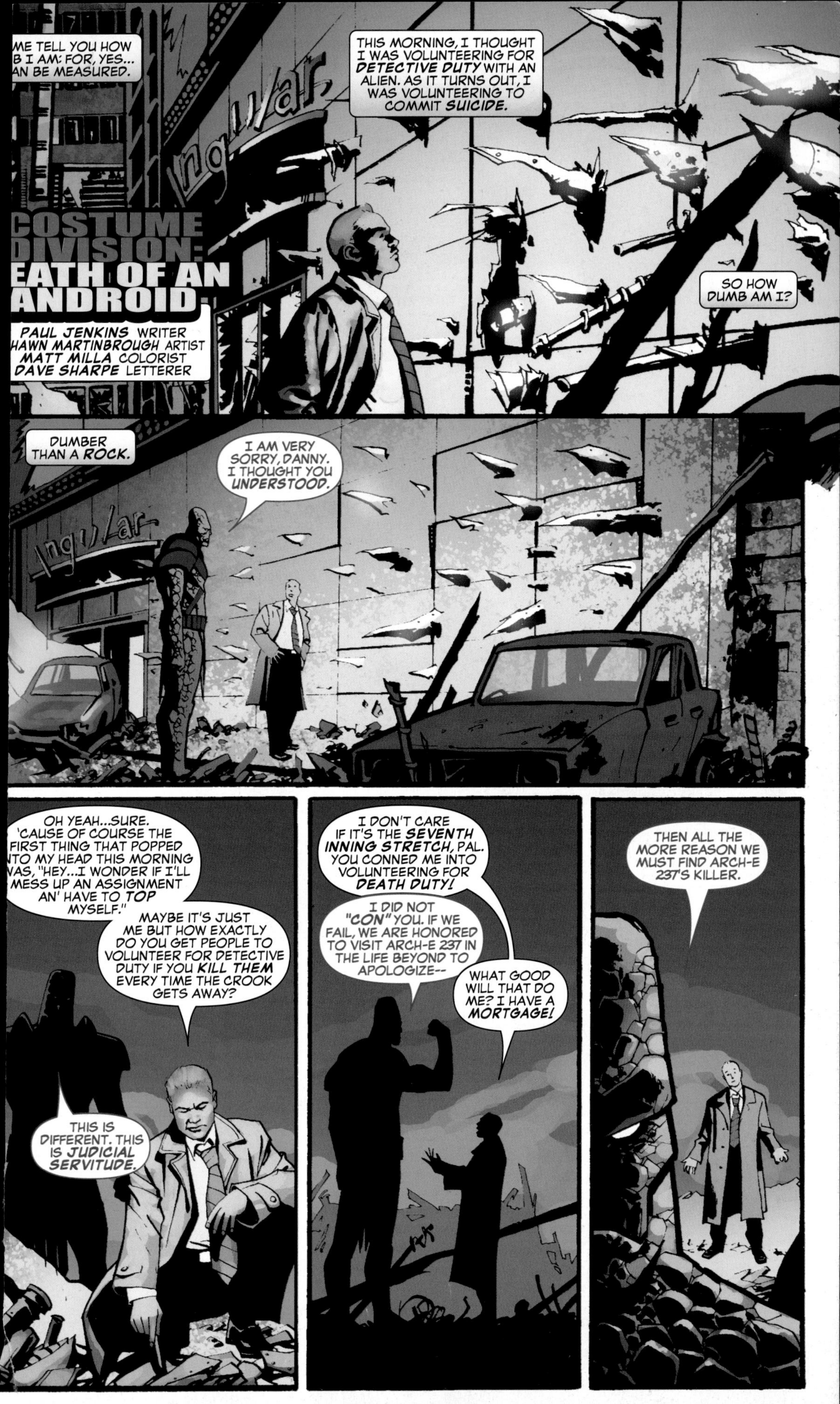
ME TELL YOU HOW
B I AM: FOR, YES...
AN BE MEASURED.
THIS MORNING, I THOUGHT I WAS VOLUNTEERING FOR DETECTIVE DUTY WITH AN ALIEN. AS IT TURNS OUT, I WAS VOLUNTEERING TO COMMIT SUICIDE.
COSTUME DIVISION: EATH OF AN ANDROID
PAUL JENKINS WRITER
HAWN MARTINBROUGH ARTIST
MATT MILLA COLORIST
DAVE SHARPE LETTERER
SO HOW DUMB AM I?
DUMBER THAN A ROCK.
I AM VERY SORRY, DANNY. I THOUGHT YOU UNDERSTOOD.
OH YEAH...SURE. 'CAUSE OF COURSE THE FIRST THING THAT POPPED NTO MY HEAD THIS MORNING VAS, "HEY...I WONDER IF I'LL MESS UP AN ASSIGNMENT AN' HAVE TO TOP MYSELF."
MAYBE IT'S JUST ME BUT HOW EXACTLY DO YOU GET PEOPLE TO VOLUNTEER FOR DETECTIVE DUTY IF YOU KILL THEM EVERY TIME THE CROOK GETS AWAY?
THIS IS DIFFERENT. THIS IS JUDICIAL SERVITUDE.
I DON'T CARE IF IT'S THE SEVENTH INNING STRETCH, PAL. YOU CONNED ME INTO VOLUNTEERING FOR DEATH DUTY!
I DID NOT "CON" YOU. IF WE FAIL, WE ARE HONORED TO VISIT ARCH-E 237 IN THE LIFE BEYOND TO APOLOGIZE--
WHAT GOOD WILL THAT DO ME? I HAVE A MORTGAGE!
THEN ALL THE MORE REASON WE MUST FIND ARCH-E 237'S KILLER.

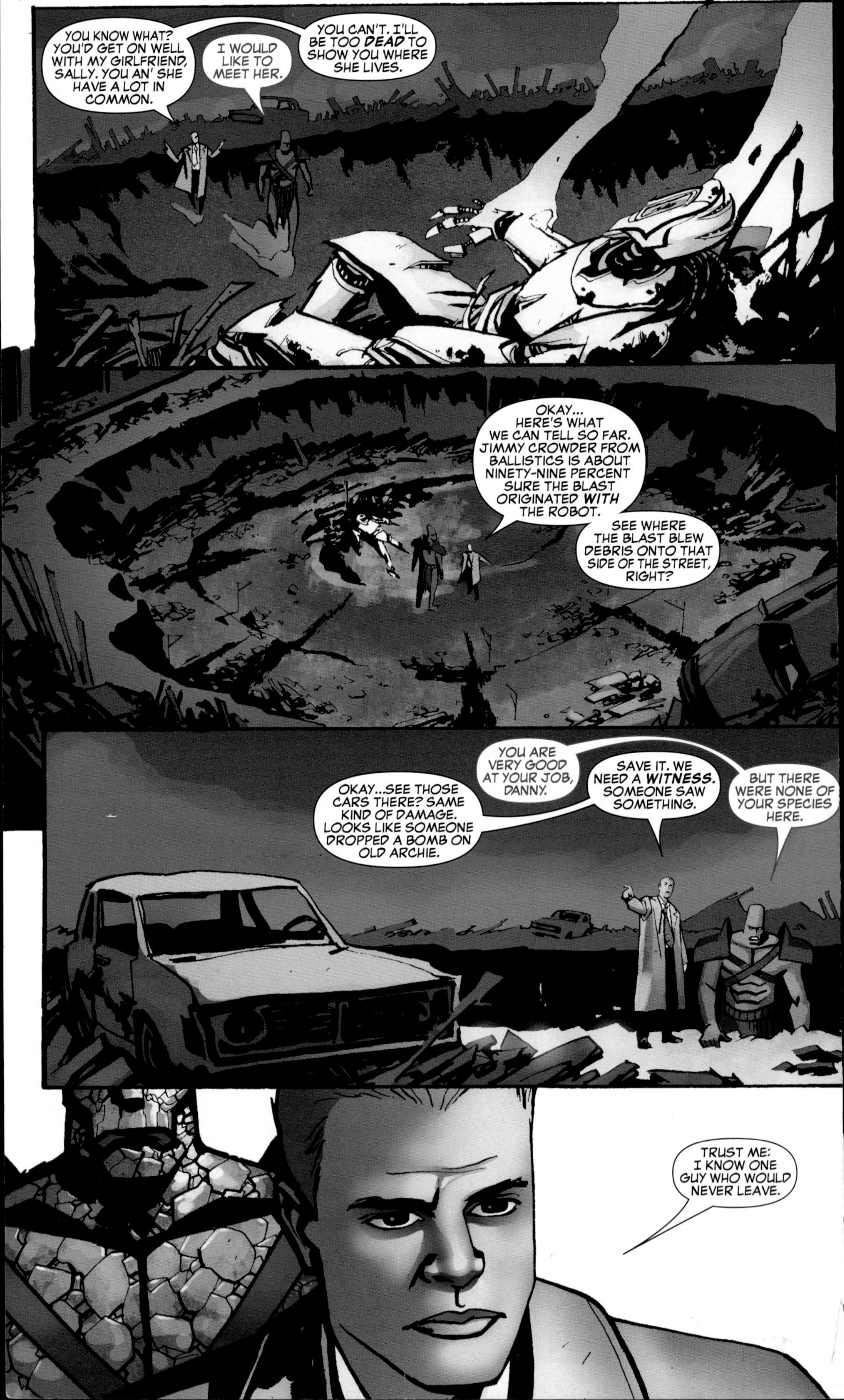
YOU KNOW WHAT? YOU'D GET ON WELL WITH MY GIRLFRIEND, SALLY. YOU AN' SHE HAVE A LOT IN COMMON.
I WOULD LIKE TO MEET HER.
YOU CAN'T. I'LL BE TOO **DEAD** TO SHOW YOU WHERE SHE LIVES.
OKAY... HERE'S WHAT WE CAN TELL SO FAR. JIMMY CROWDER FROM BALLISTICS IS ABOUT NINETY-NINE PERCENT SURE THE BLAST ORIGINATED **WITH** THE ROBOT.
SEE WHERE THE BLAST BLEW DEBRIS ONTO THAT SIDE OF THE STREET, RIGHT?
OKAY...SEE THOSE CARS THERE? SAME KIND OF DAMAGE. LOOKS LIKE SOMEONE DROPPED A BOMB ON OLD ARCHIE.
YOU ARE VERY GOOD AT YOUR JOB, DANNY.
SAVE IT. WE NEED A **WITNESS.** SOMEONE SAW SOMETHING.
BUT THERE WERE NONE OF YOUR SPECIES HERE.
TRUST ME: I KNOW ONE GUY WHO WOULD NEVER LEAVE.

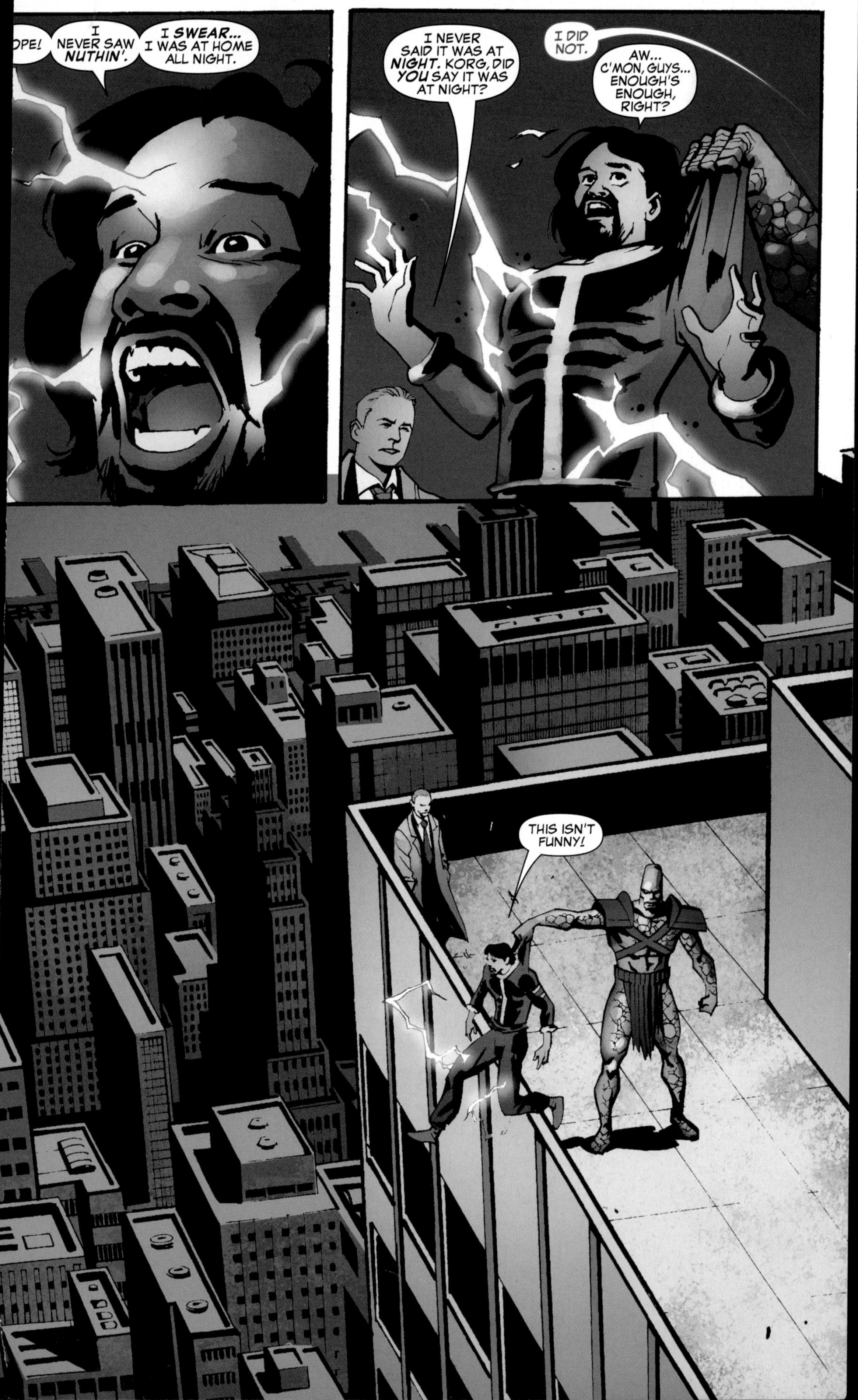
OPE!
I NEVER SAW NUTHIN'.
I SWEAR... I WAS AT HOME ALL NIGHT.
I NEVER SAID IT WAS AT NIGHT. KORG, DID YOU SAY IT WAS AT NIGHT?
I DID NOT.
AW... C'MON, GUYS... ENOUGH'S ENOUGH, RIGHT?
THIS ISN'T FUNNY!

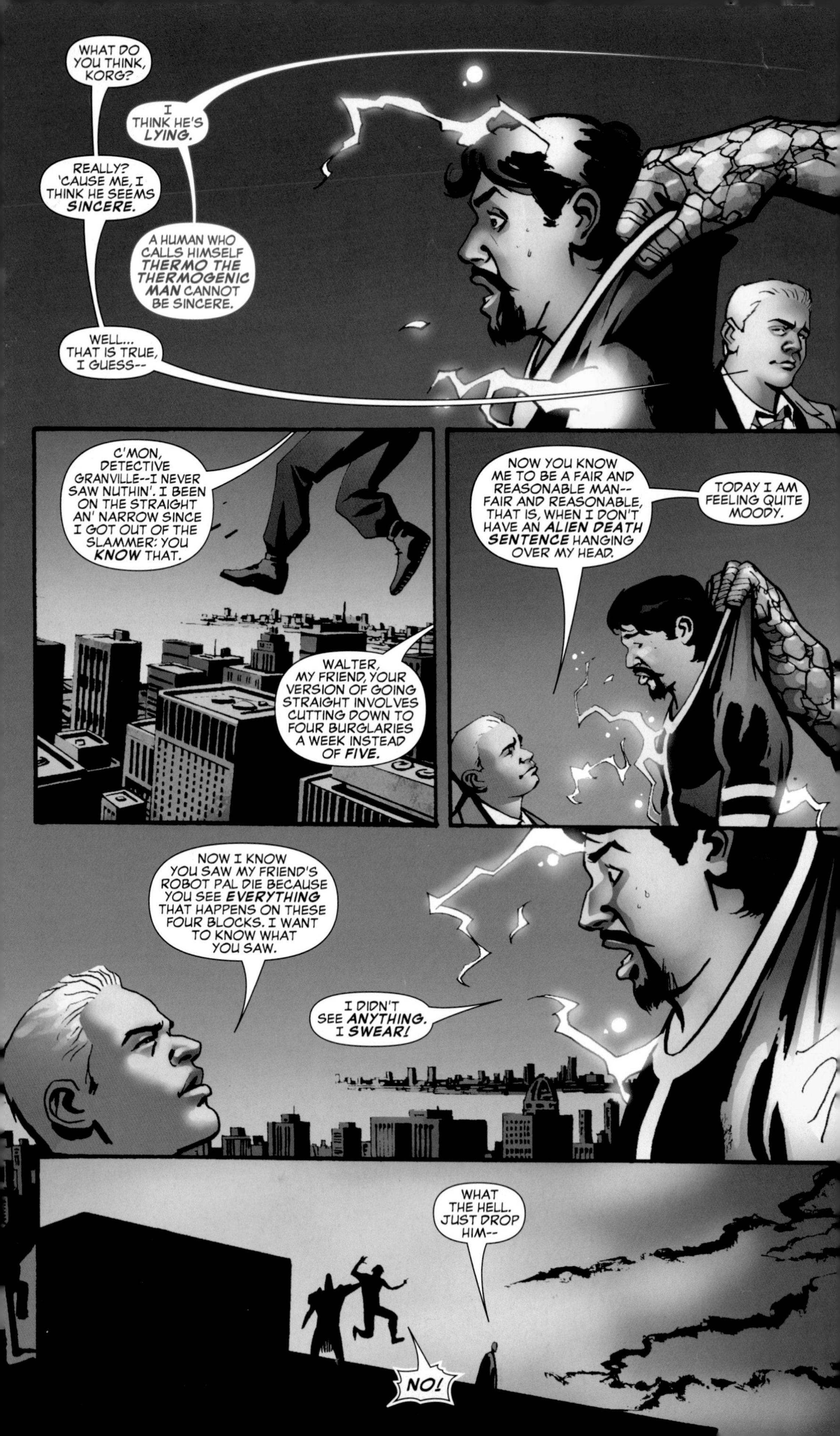
WHAT DO YOU THINK, KORG?
I THINK HE'S LYING.
REALLY? 'CAUSE ME, I THINK HE SEEMS SINCERE.
A HUMAN WHO CALLS HIMSELF THERMO THE THERMOGENIC MAN CANNOT BE SINCERE.
WELL... THAT IS TRUE, I GUESS--
C'MON, DETECTIVE GRANVILLE--I NEVER SAW NUTHIN'. I BEEN ON THE STRAIGHT AN' NARROW SINCE I GOT OUT OF THE SLAMMER: YOU KNOW THAT.
WALTER, MY FRIEND, YOUR VERSION OF GOING STRAIGHT INVOLVES CUTTING DOWN TO FOUR BURGLARIES A WEEK INSTEAD OF FIVE.
NOW YOU KNOW ME TO BE A FAIR AND REASONABLE MAN--FAIR AND REASONABLE, THAT IS, WHEN I DON'T HAVE AN ALIEN DEATH SENTENCE HANGING OVER MY HEAD.
TODAY I AM FEELING QUITE MOODY.
NOW I KNOW YOU SAW MY FRIEND'S ROBOT PAL DIE BECAUSE YOU SEE EVERYTHING THAT HAPPENS ON THESE FOUR BLOCKS. I WANT TO KNOW WHAT YOU SAW.
I DIDN'T SEE ANYTHING. I SWEAR!
WHAT THE HELL. JUST DROP HIM--
NO!

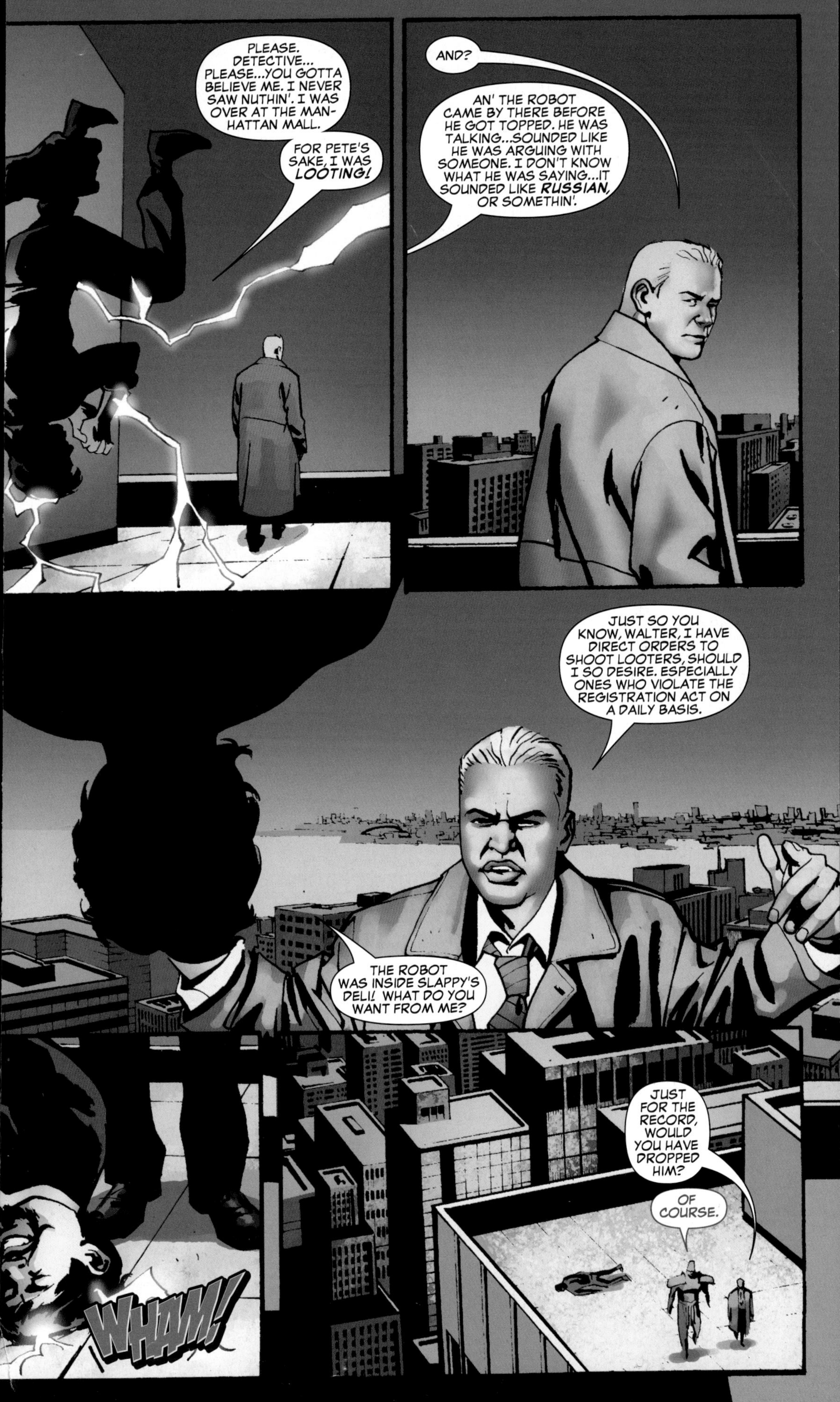
PLEASE. DETECTIVE... PLEASE...YOU GOTTA BELIEVE ME. I NEVER SAW NUTHIN'. I WAS OVER AT THE MAN-HATTAN MALL.
FOR PETE'S SAKE, I WAS *LOOTING!*
AND?
AN' THE ROBOT CAME BY THERE BEFORE HE GOT TOPPED. HE WAS TALKING...SOUNDED LIKE HE WAS ARGUING WITH SOMEONE. I DON'T KNOW WHAT HE WAS SAYING...IT SOUNDED LIKE *RUSSIAN,* OR SOMETHIN'.
JUST SO YOU KNOW, WALTER, I HAVE DIRECT ORDERS TO SHOOT LOOTERS, SHOULD I SO DESIRE. ESPECIALLY ONES WHO VIOLATE THE REGISTRATION ACT ON A DAILY BASIS.
THE ROBOT WAS INSIDE SLAPPY'S DELI! WHAT DO YOU WANT FROM ME?
WHAM!
JUST FOR THE RECORD, WOULD YOU HAVE DROPPED HIM?
OF COURSE.

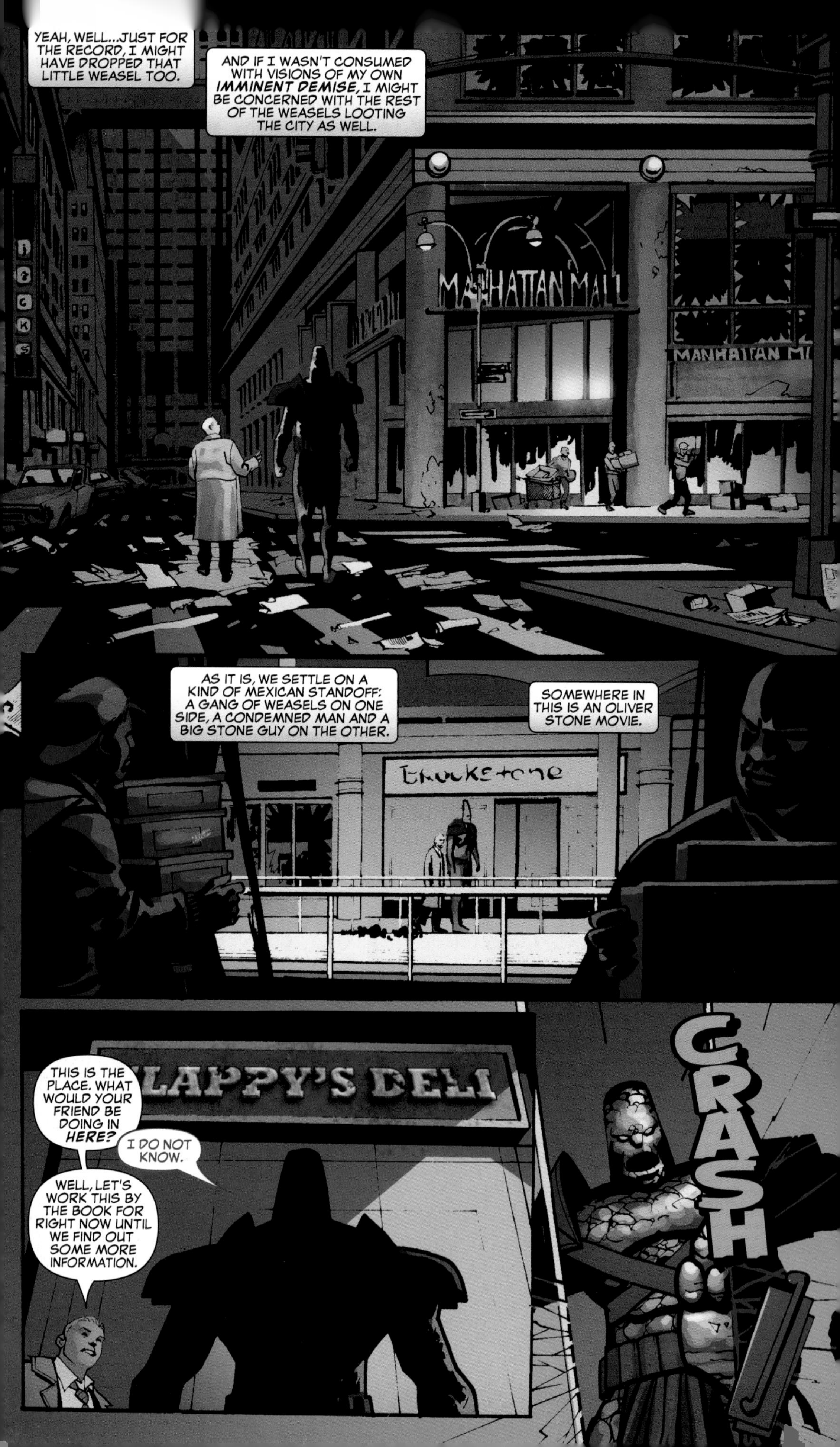
YEAH, WELL...JUST FOR THE RECORD, I MIGHT HAVE DROPPED THAT LITTLE WEASEL TOO.
AND IF I WASN'T CONSUMED WITH VISIONS OF MY OWN IMMINENT DEMISE, I MIGHT BE CONCERNED WITH THE REST OF THE WEASELS LOOTING THE CITY AS WELL.
MANHATTAN MALL
MANHATTAN M
AS IT IS, WE SETTLE ON A KIND OF MEXICAN STANDOFF: A GANG OF WEASELS ON ONE SIDE, A CONDEMNED MAN AND A BIG STONE GUY ON THE OTHER.
SOMEWHERE IN THIS IS AN OLIVER STONE MOVIE.
LAPPY'S DELI
THIS IS THE PLACE. WHAT WOULD YOUR FRIEND BE DOING IN HERE?
I DO NOT KNOW.
WELL, LET'S WORK THIS BY THE BOOK FOR RIGHT NOW UNTIL WE FIND OUT SOME MORE INFORMATION.
CRASH

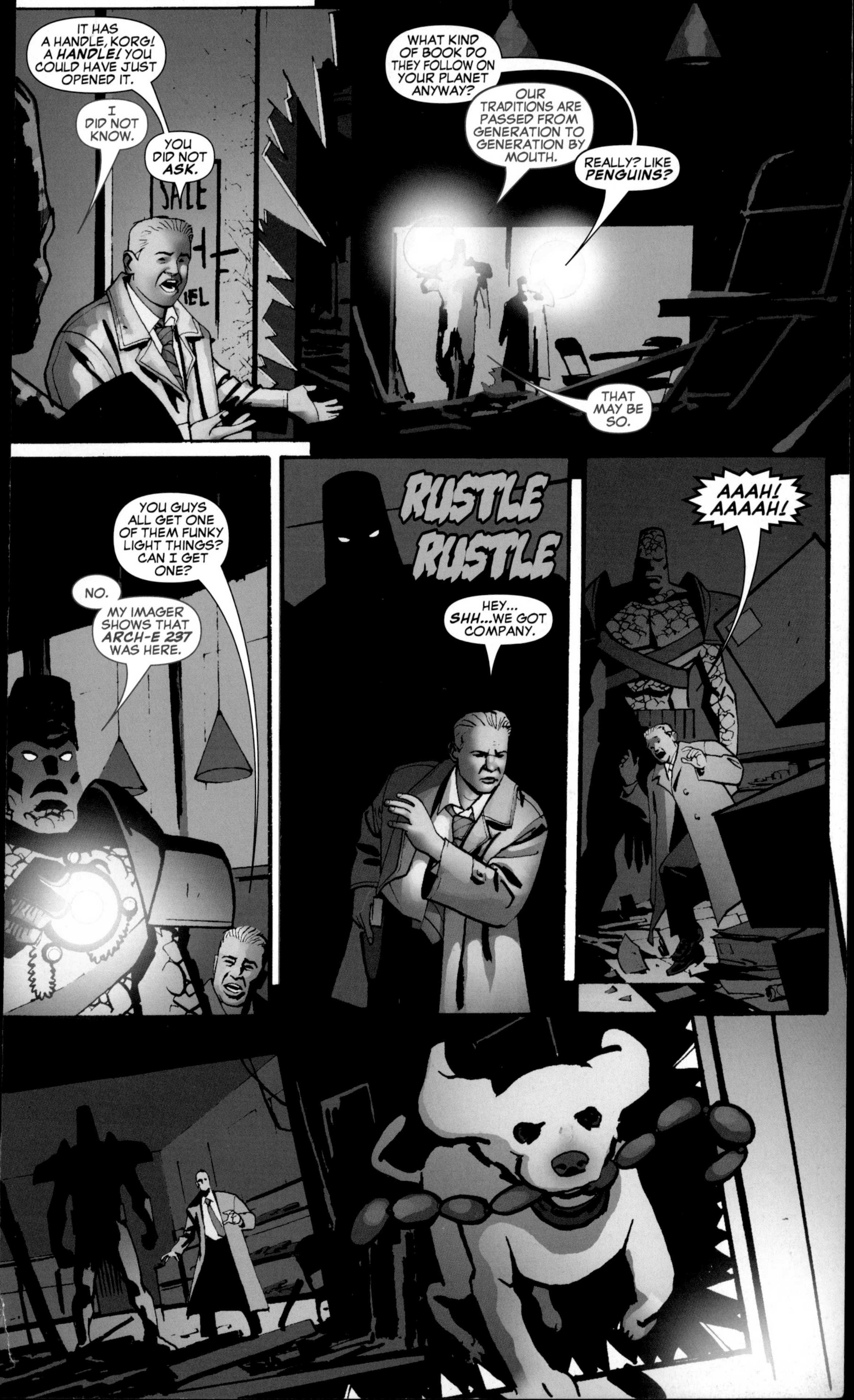

IT HAS A HANDLE, KORG! A *HANDLE!* YOU COULD HAVE JUST OPENED IT.
I DID NOT KNOW.
YOU DID NOT *ASK.*
SALE
WHAT KIND OF BOOK DO THEY FOLLOW ON YOUR PLANET ANYWAY?
OUR TRADITIONS ARE PASSED FROM GENERATION TO GENERATION BY MOUTH.
REALLY? LIKE *PENGUINS?*
THAT MAY BE SO.
YOU GUYS ALL GET ONE OF THEM FUNKY LIGHT THINGS? CAN I GET ONE?
NO.
MY IMAGER SHOWS THAT *ARCH-E 237* WAS HERE.
RUSTLE RUSTLE
HEY... *SHH*...WE GOT COMPANY.
AAAH! AAAAH!

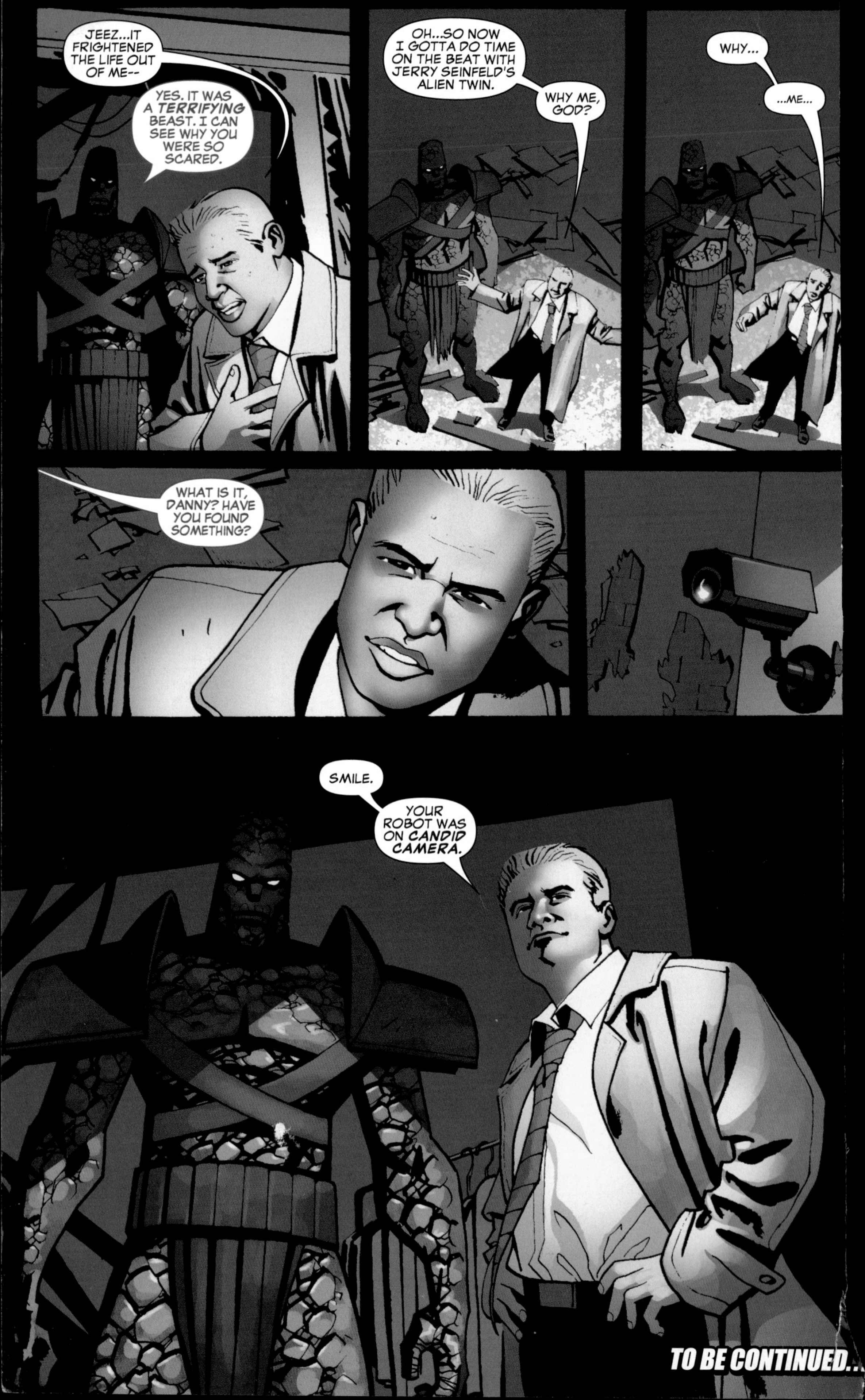
JEEZ...IT FRIGHTENED THE LIFE OUT OF ME--
YES. IT WAS A TERRIFYING BEAST. I CAN SEE WHY YOU WERE SO SCARED.
OH...SO NOW I GOTTA DO TIME ON THE BEAT WITH JERRY SEINFELD'S ALIEN TWIN.
WHY ME, GOD?
WHY...
...ME...
WHAT IS IT, DANNY? HAVE YOU FOUND SOMETHING?
SMILE.
YOUR ROBOT WAS ON CANDID CAMERA.
TO BE CONTINUED...

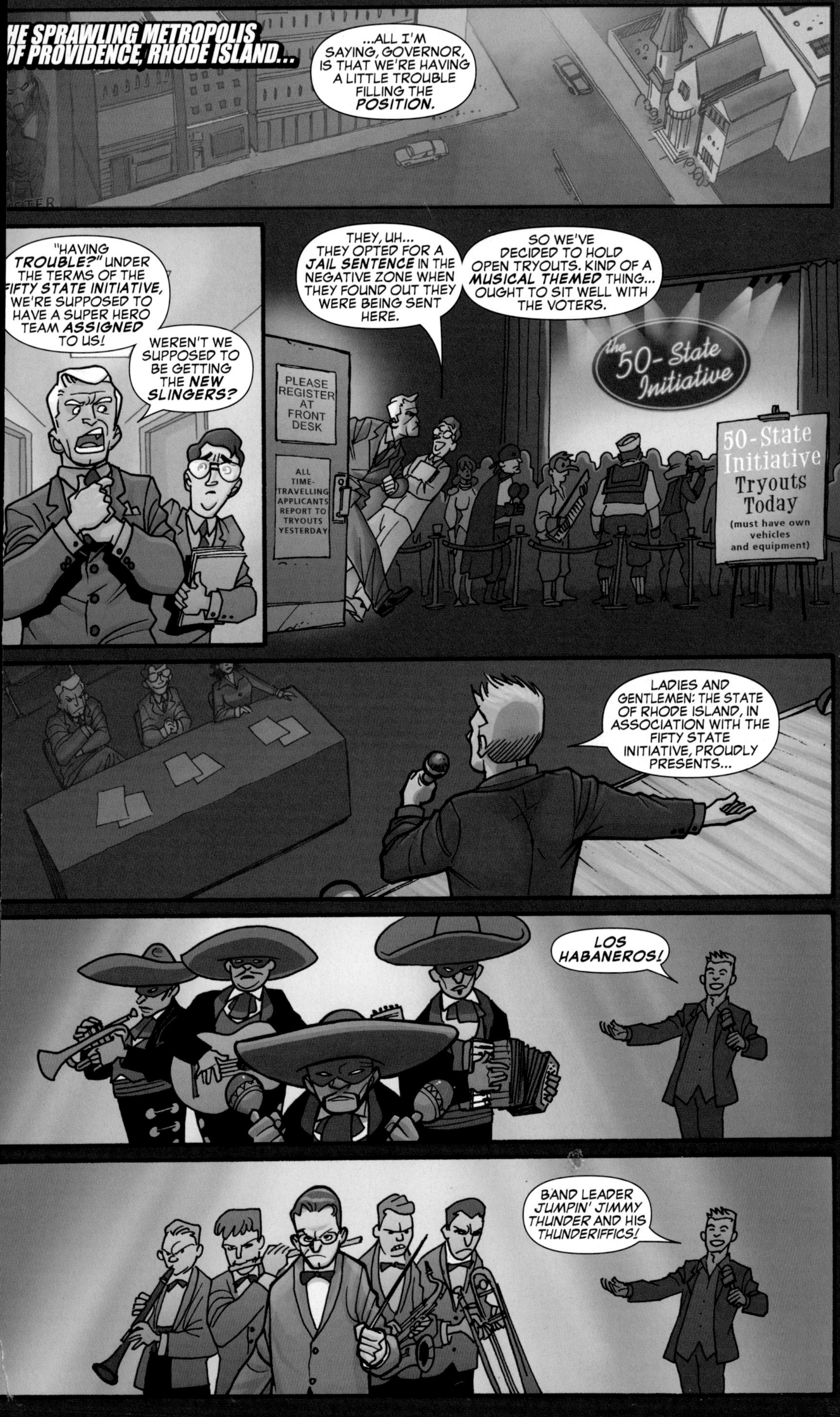
HE SPRAWLING METROPOLIS
OF PROVIDENCE, RHODE ISLAND...
...ALL I'M SAYING, GOVERNOR, IS THAT WE'RE HAVING A LITTLE TROUBLE FILLING THE POSITION.
"HAVING TROUBLE?" UNDER THE TERMS OF THE FIFTY STATE INITIATIVE, WE'RE SUPPOSED TO HAVE A SUPER HERO TEAM ASSIGNED TO US!
WEREN'T WE SUPPOSED TO BE GETTING THE NEW SLINGERS?
THEY, UH... THEY OPTED FOR A JAIL SENTENCE IN THE NEGATIVE ZONE WHEN THEY FOUND OUT THEY WERE BEING SENT HERE.
SO WE'VE DECIDED TO HOLD OPEN TRYOUTS. KIND OF A MUSICAL THEMED THING... OUGHT TO SIT WELL WITH THE VOTERS.
PLEASE REGISTER AT FRONT DESK
ALL TIME-TRAVELLING APPLICANTS REPORT TO TRYOUTS YESTERDAY
the 50-State Initiative
50-State Initiative Tryouts Today
(must have own vehicles and equipment)
LADIES AND GENTLEMEN: THE STATE OF RHODE ISLAND, IN ASSOCIATION WITH THE FIFTY STATE INITIATIVE, PROUDLY PRESENTS...
LOS HABANEROS!
BAND LEADER JUMPIN' JIMMY THUNDER AND HIS THUNDERIFFICS!

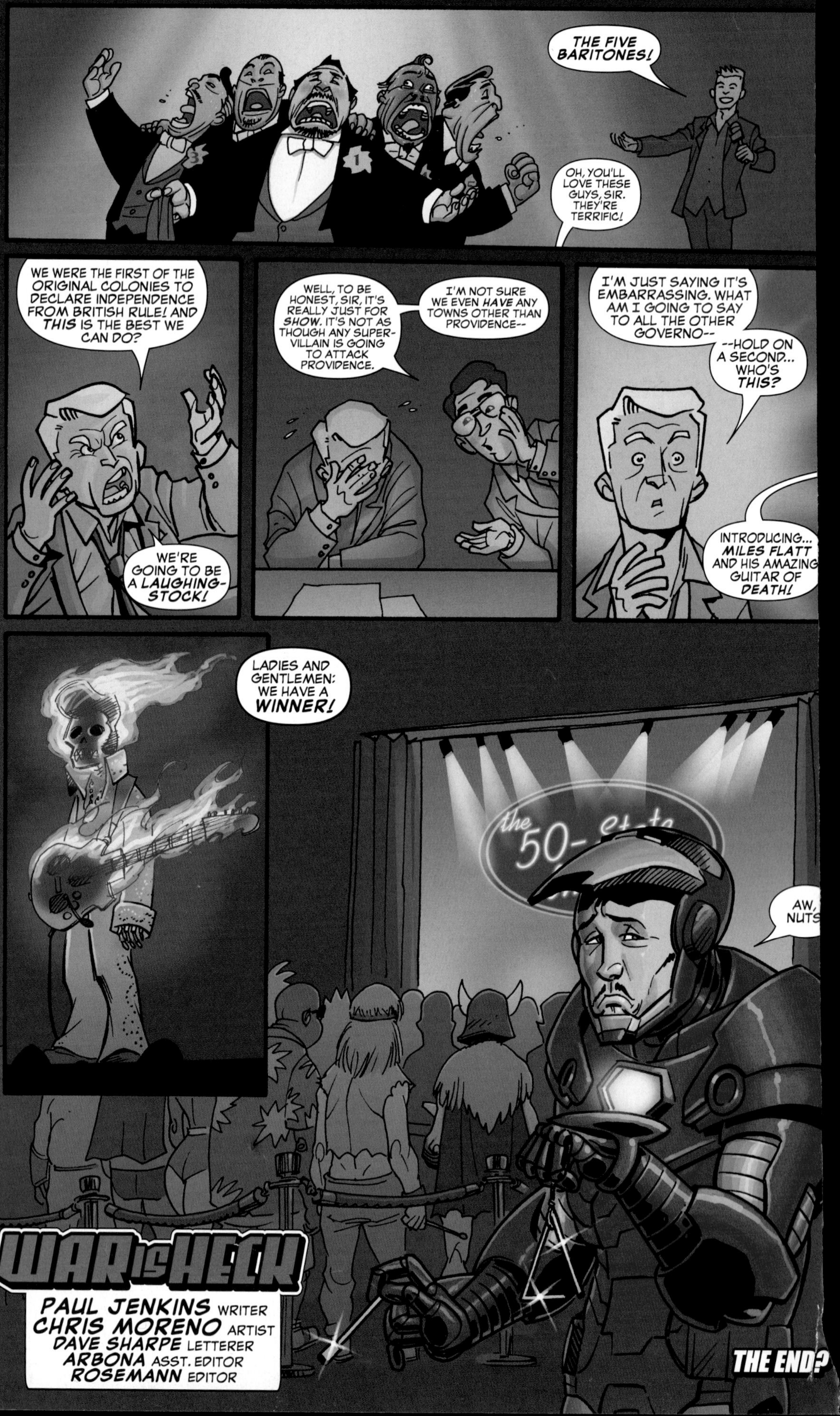
THE FIVE BARITONES!
OH, YOU'LL LOVE THESE GUYS, SIR. THEY'RE TERRIFIC!
WE WERE THE FIRST OF THE ORIGINAL COLONIES TO DECLARE INDEPENDENCE FROM BRITISH RULE! AND THIS IS THE BEST WE CAN DO?
WE'RE GOING TO BE A LAUGHING-STOCK!
WELL, TO BE HONEST, SIR, IT'S REALLY JUST FOR SHOW. IT'S NOT AS THOUGH ANY SUPER-VILLAIN IS GOING TO ATTACK PROVIDENCE.
I'M NOT SURE WE EVEN HAVE ANY TOWNS OTHER THAN PROVIDENCE--
I'M JUST SAYING IT'S EMBARRASSING. WHAT AM I GOING TO SAY TO ALL THE OTHER GOVERNO--
--HOLD ON A SECOND... WHO'S THIS?
INTRODUCING... MILES FLATT AND HIS AMAZING GUITAR OF DEATH!
LADIES AND GENTLEMEN: WE HAVE A WINNER!
the 50-
AW, NUTS
WAR IS HECK
PAUL JENKINS WRITER
CHRIS MORENO ARTIST
DAVE SHARPE LETTERER
ARBONA ASST. EDITOR
ROSEMANN EDITOR
THE END?

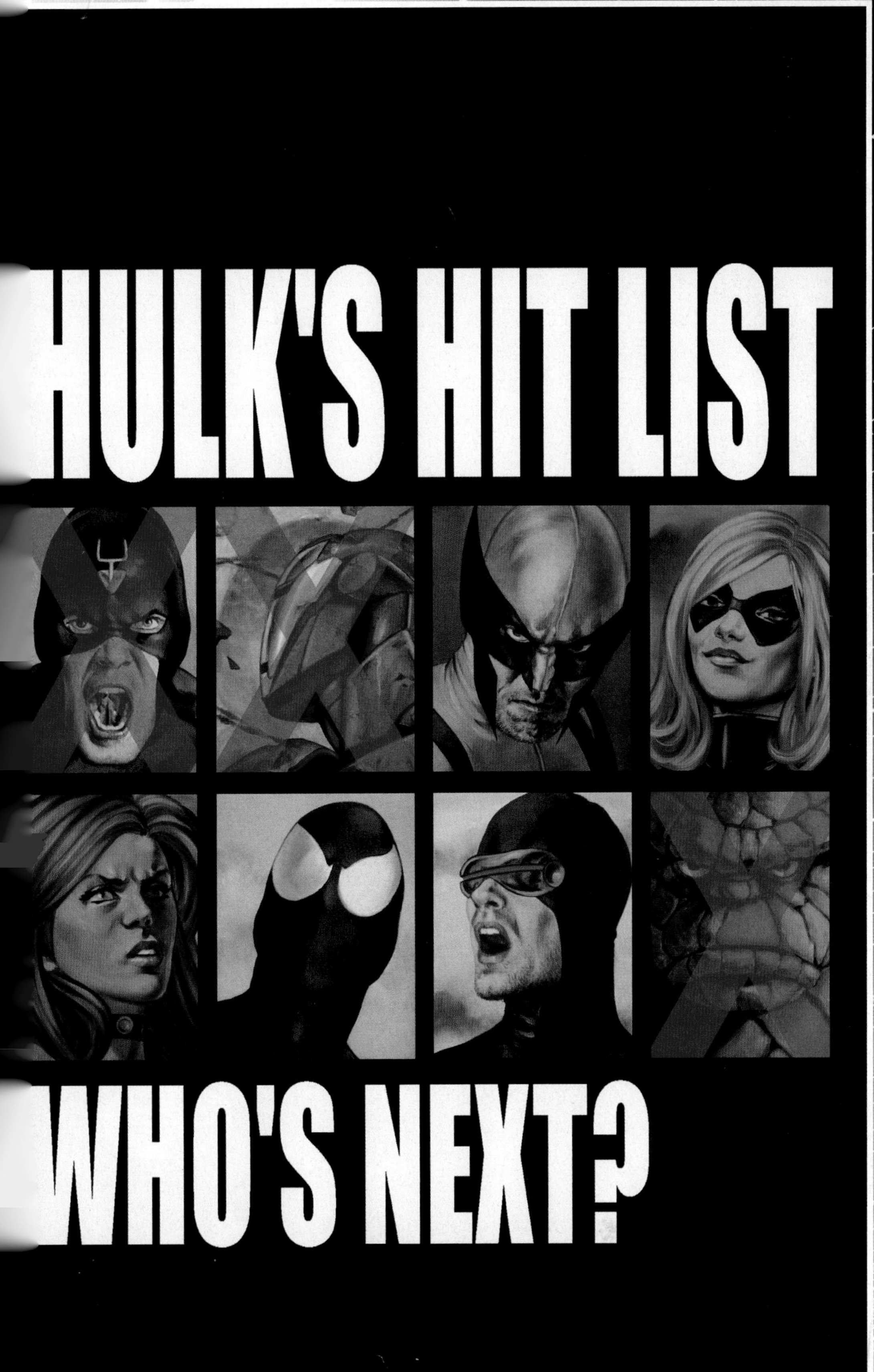
HULK'S HIT LIST
WHO'S NEXT?

WORLD WAR HULK: FRONT LINE #4

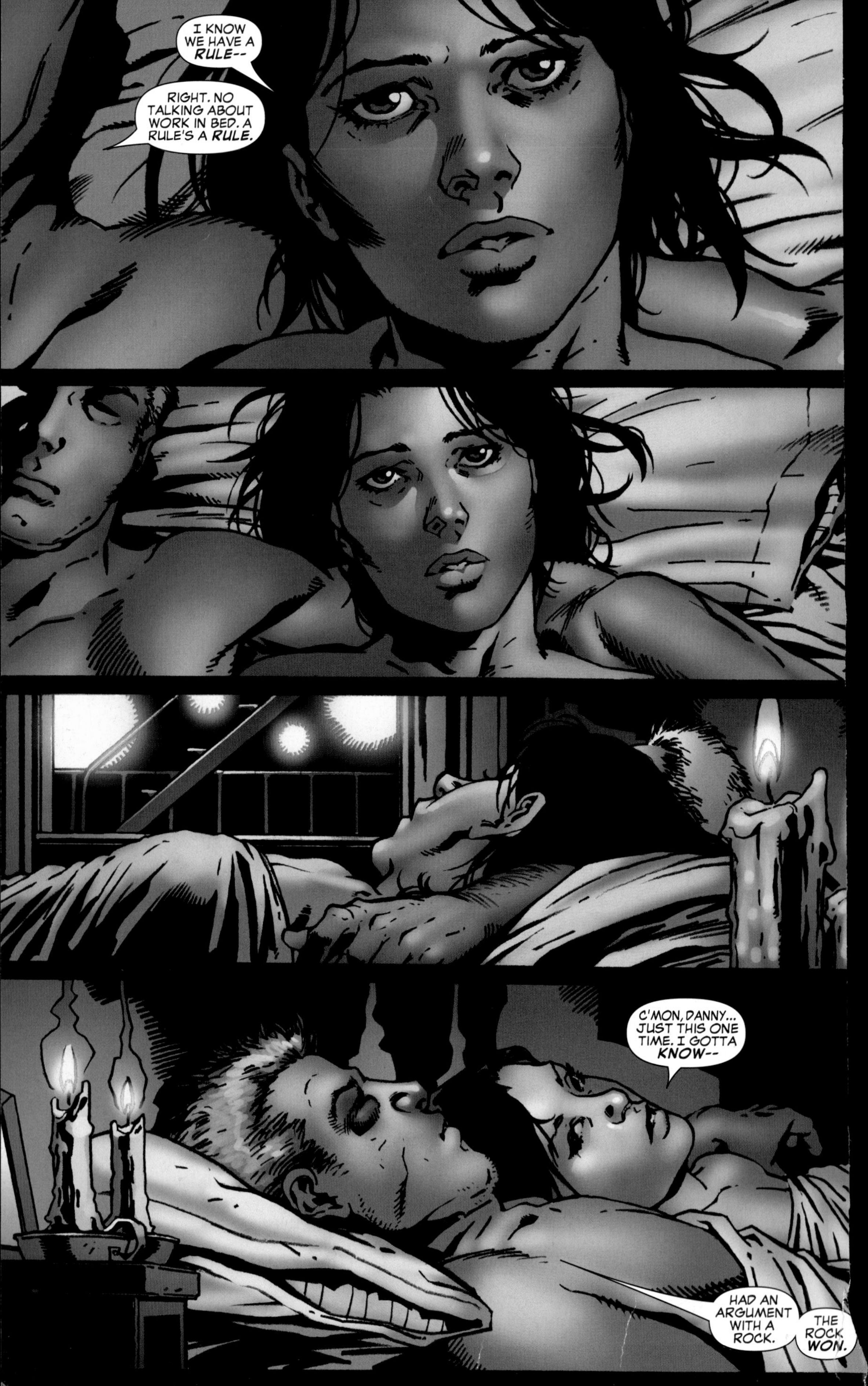
I KNOW WE HAVE A RULE--
RIGHT. NO TALKING ABOUT WORK IN BED. A RULE'S A RULE.
C'MON, DANNY... JUST THIS ONE TIME. I GOTTA KNOW--
HAD AN ARGUMENT WITH A ROCK.
THE ROCK WON.

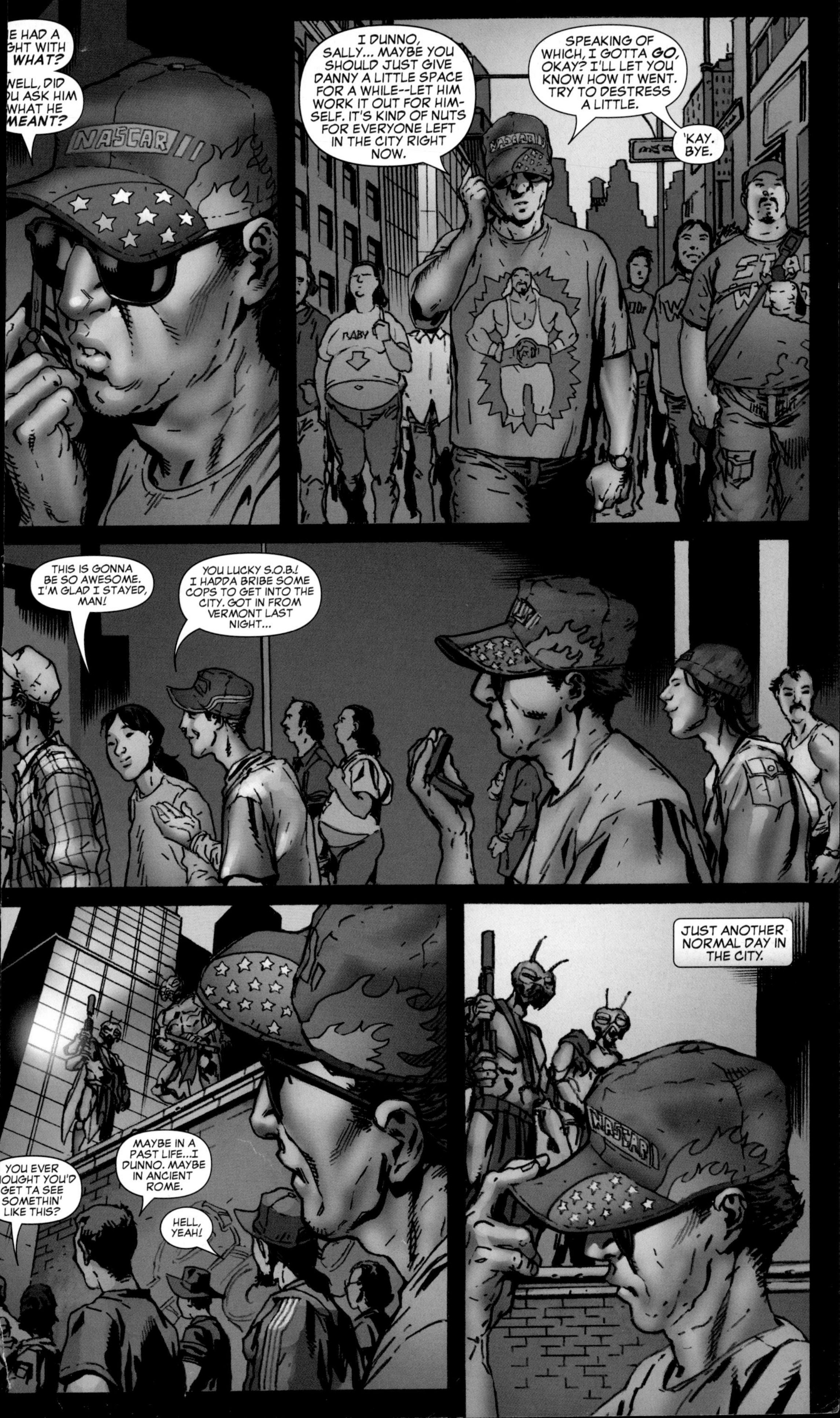

E HAD A
GHT WITH
WHAT?
WELL, DID
OU ASK HIM
WHAT HE
MEANT?
NASCAR
I DUNNO, SALLY... MAYBE YOU SHOULD JUST GIVE DANNY A LITTLE SPACE FOR A WHILE--LET HIM WORK IT OUT FOR HIMSELF. IT'S KIND OF NUTS FOR EVERYONE LEFT IN THE CITY RIGHT NOW.
SPEAKING OF WHICH, I GOTTA GO, OKAY? I'LL LET YOU KNOW HOW IT WENT. TRY TO DESTRESS A LITTLE.
'KAY. BYE.
THIS IS GONNA BE SO AWESOME. I'M GLAD I STAYED, MAN!
YOU LUCKY S.O.B.! I HADDA BRIBE SOME COPS TO GET INTO THE CITY. GOT IN FROM VERMONT LAST NIGHT...
YOU EVER
HOUGHT YOU'D
GET TA SEE
SOMETHIN'
LIKE THIS?
MAYBE IN A PAST LIFE...I DUNNO. MAYBE IN ANCIENT ROME.
HELL, YEAH!
JUST ANOTHER NORMAL DAY IN THE CITY.

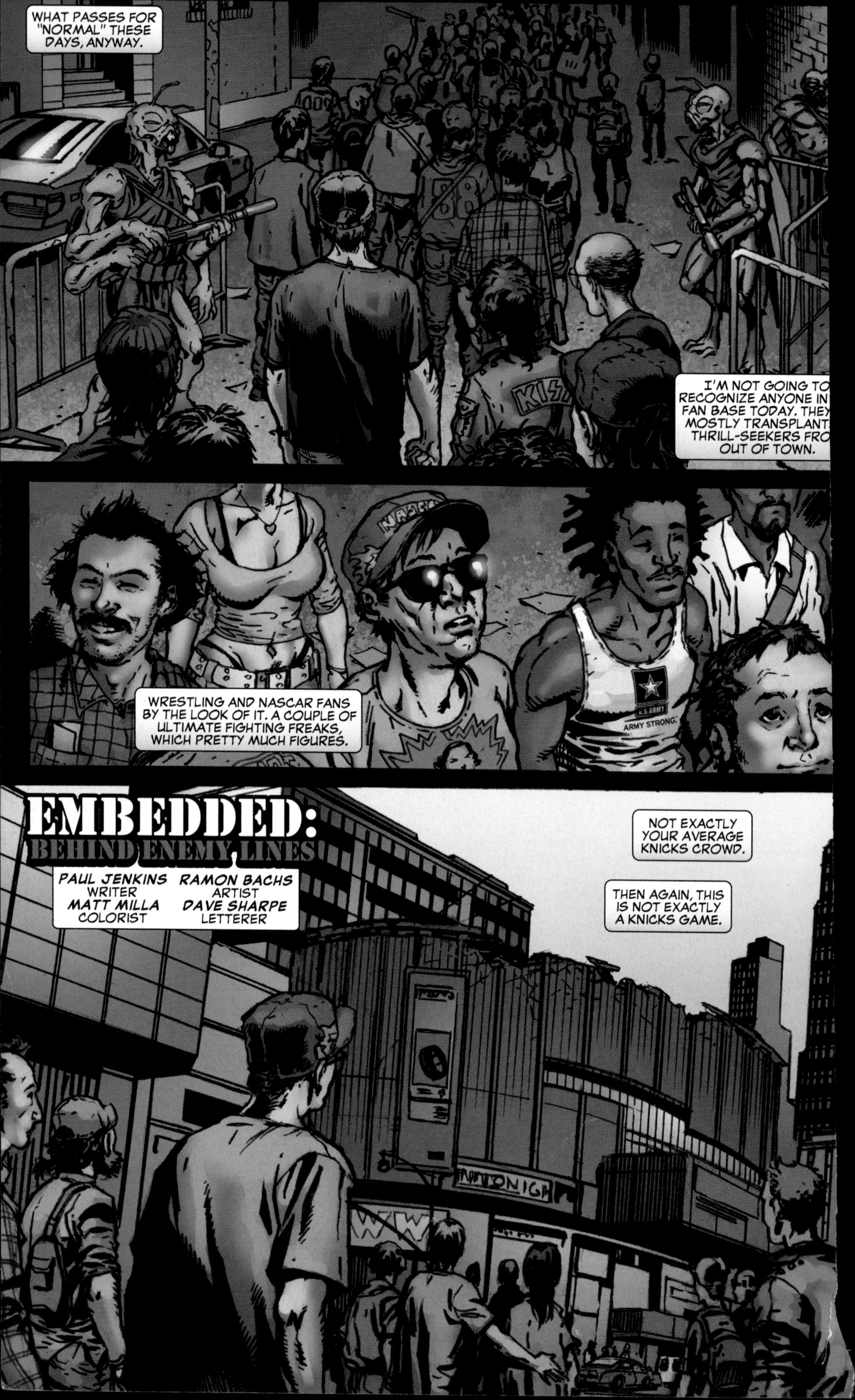
WHAT PASSES FOR "NORMAL" THESE DAYS, ANYWAY.
I'M NOT GOING TO RECOGNIZE ANYONE IN FAN BASE TODAY. THEY MOSTLY TRANSPLANT THRILL-SEEKERS FRO OUT OF TOWN.
WRESTLING AND NASCAR FANS BY THE LOOK OF IT. A COUPLE OF ULTIMATE FIGHTING FREAKS, WHICH PRETTY MUCH FIGURES.
ARMY STRONG.
EMBEDDED:
BEHIND ENEMY LINES
PAUL JENKINS WRITER
RAMON BACHS ARTIST
MATT MILLA COLORIST
DAVE SHARPE LETTERER
NOT EXACTLY YOUR AVERAGE KNICKS CROWD.
THEN AGAIN, THIS IS NOT EXACTLY A KNICKS GAME.

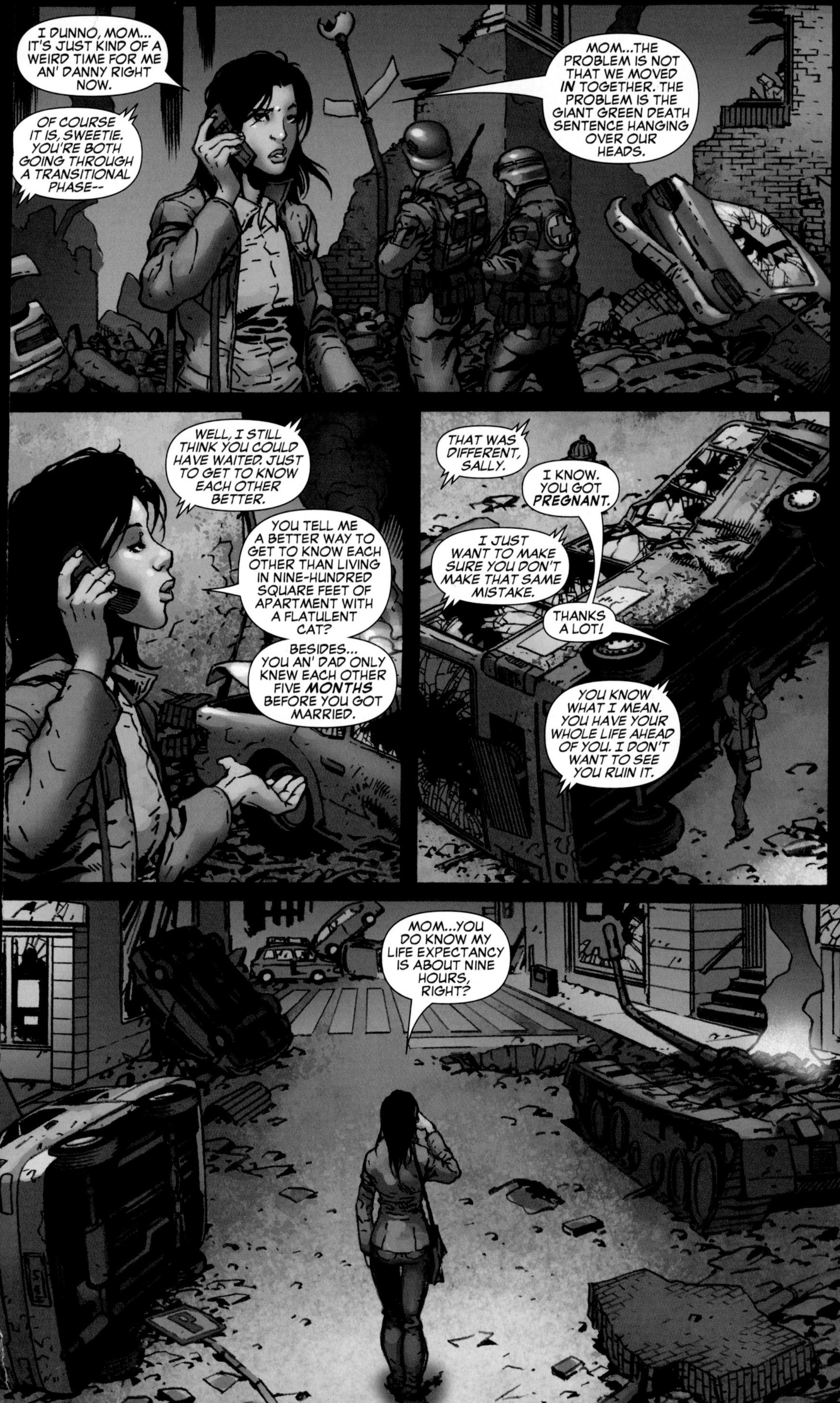
I DUNNO, MOM... IT'S JUST KIND OF A WEIRD TIME FOR ME AN' DANNY RIGHT NOW.
OF COURSE IT IS, SWEETIE. YOU'RE BOTH GOING THROUGH A TRANSITIONAL PHASE--
MOM...THE PROBLEM IS NOT THAT WE MOVED IN TOGETHER. THE PROBLEM IS THE GIANT GREEN DEATH SENTENCE HANGING OVER OUR HEADS.
WELL, I STILL THINK YOU COULD HAVE WAITED. JUST TO GET TO KNOW EACH OTHER BETTER.
YOU TELL ME A BETTER WAY TO GET TO KNOW EACH OTHER THAN LIVING IN NINE-HUNDRED SQUARE FEET OF APARTMENT WITH A FLATULENT CAT?
BESIDES... YOU AN' DAD ONLY KNEW EACH OTHER FIVE MONTHS BEFORE YOU GOT MARRIED.
THAT WAS DIFFERENT, SALLY.
I KNOW. YOU GOT PREGNANT.
I JUST WANT TO MAKE SURE YOU DON'T MAKE THAT SAME MISTAKE.
THANKS A LOT!
YOU KNOW WHAT I MEAN. YOU HAVE YOUR WHOLE LIFE AHEAD OF YOU. I DON'T WANT TO SEE YOU RUIN IT.
MOM...YOU DO KNOW MY LIFE EXPECTANCY IS ABOUT NINE HOURS, RIGHT?

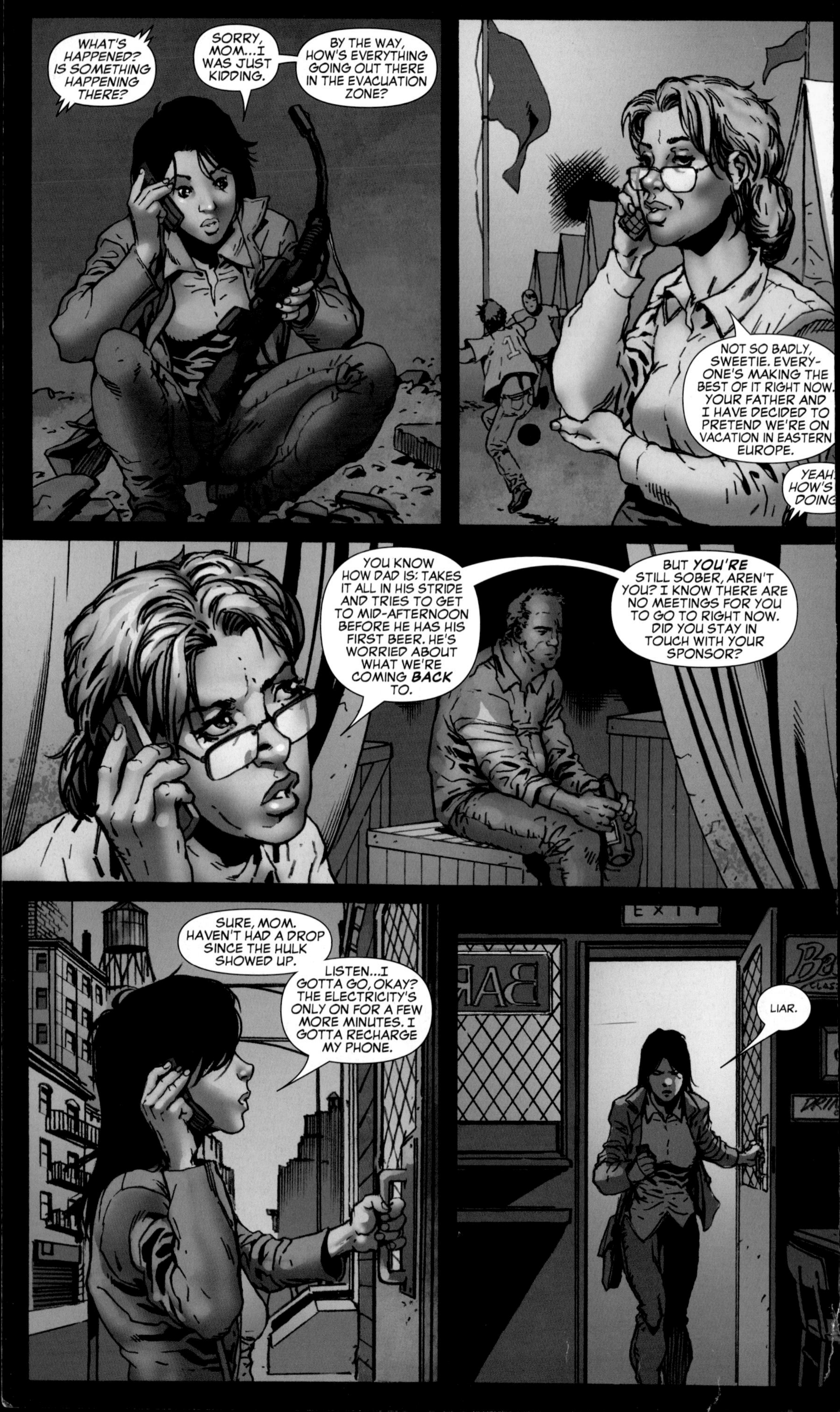
WHAT'S HAPPENED? IS SOMETHING HAPPENING THERE?
SORRY, MOM...I WAS JUST KIDDING.
BY THE WAY, HOW'S EVERYTHING GOING OUT THERE IN THE EVACUATION ZONE?
NOT SO BADLY, SWEETIE. EVERYONE'S MAKING THE BEST OF IT RIGHT NOW. YOUR FATHER AND I HAVE DECIDED TO PRETEND WE'RE ON VACATION IN EASTERN EUROPE.
YEAH HOW'S DOING
YOU KNOW HOW DAD IS: TAKES IT ALL IN HIS STRIDE AND TRIES TO GET TO MID-AFTERNOON BEFORE HE HAS HIS FIRST BEER. HE'S WORRIED ABOUT WHAT WE'RE COMING **BACK** TO.
BUT ***YOU'RE*** STILL SOBER, AREN'T YOU? I KNOW THERE ARE NO MEETINGS FOR YOU TO GO TO RIGHT NOW. DID YOU STAY IN TOUCH WITH YOUR SPONSOR?
SURE, MOM. HAVEN'T HAD A DROP SINCE THE HULK SHOWED UP.
LISTEN...I GOTTA GO, OKAY? THE ELECTRICITY'S ONLY ON FOR A FEW MORE MINUTES. I GOTTA RECHARGE MY PHONE.
EXIT
LIAR.

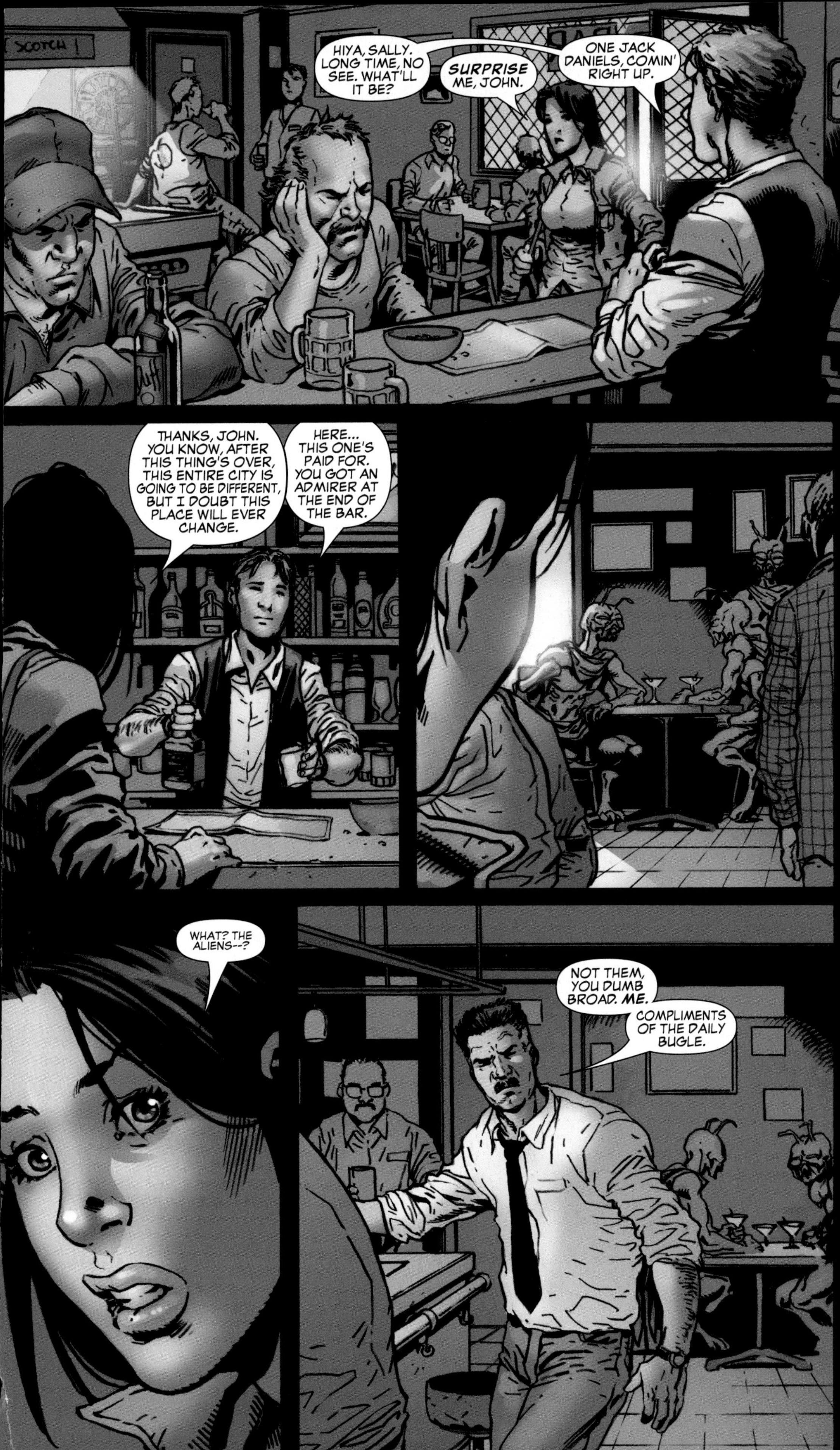
HIYA, SALLY. LONG TIME, NO SEE. WHAT'LL IT BE?
SURPRISE ME, JOHN.
ONE JACK DANIELS, COMIN' RIGHT UP.
THANKS, JOHN. YOU KNOW, AFTER THIS THING'S OVER, THIS ENTIRE CITY IS GOING TO BE DIFFERENT, BUT I DOUBT THIS PLACE WILL EVER CHANGE.
HERE... THIS ONE'S PAID FOR. YOU GOT AN ADMIRER AT THE END OF THE BAR.
WHAT? THE ALIENS--?
NOT THEM, YOU DUMB BROAD. ***ME.***
COMPLIMENTS OF THE DAILY BUGLE.

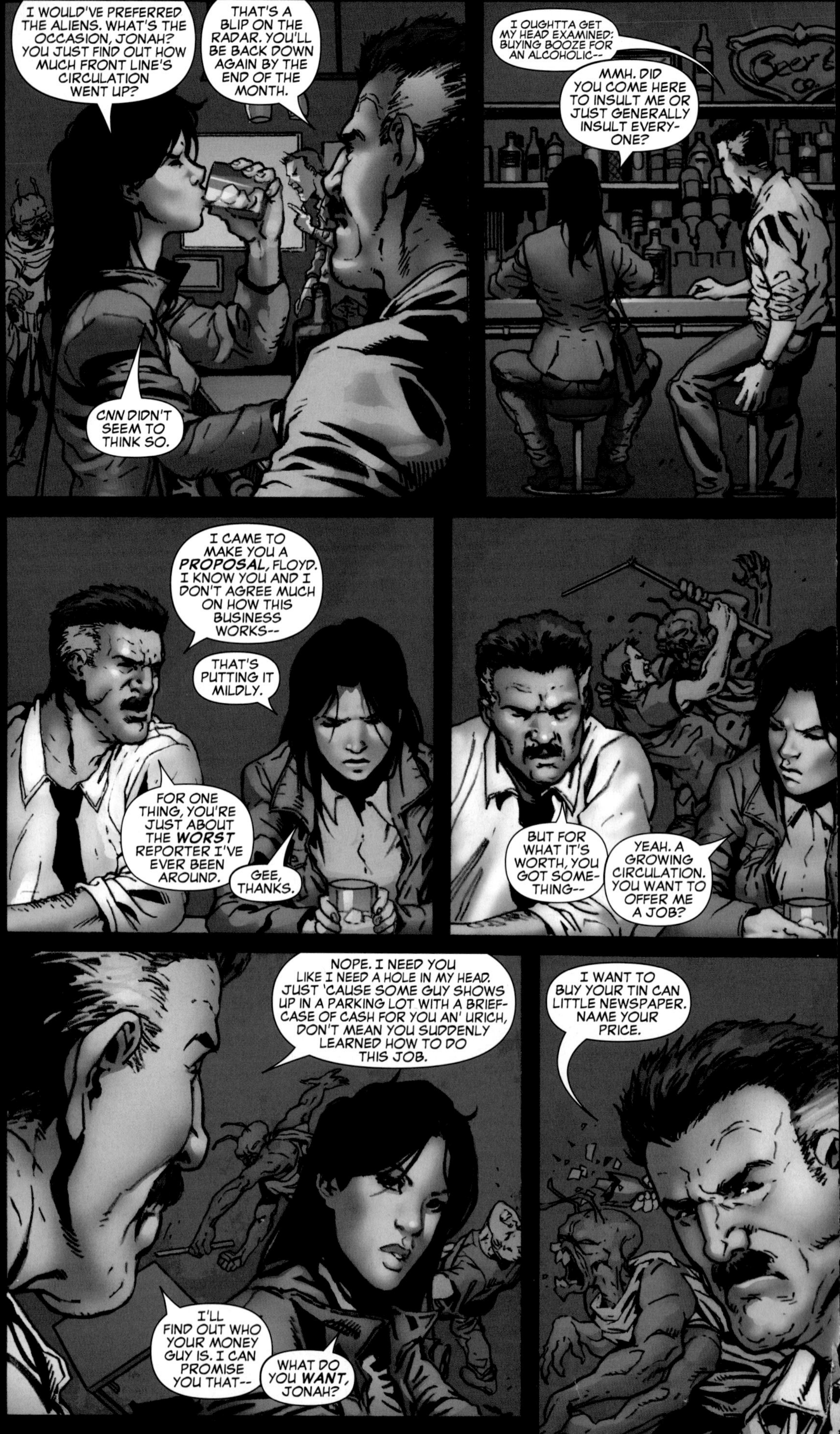
I WOULD'VE PREFERRED THE ALIENS. WHAT'S THE OCCASION, JONAH? YOU JUST FIND OUT HOW MUCH FRONT LINE'S CIRCULATION WENT UP?
THAT'S A BLIP ON THE RADAR. YOU'LL BE BACK DOWN AGAIN BY THE END OF THE MONTH.
CNN DIDN'T SEEM TO THINK SO.
I OUGHTTA GET MY HEAD EXAMINED: BUYING BOOZE FOR AN ALCOHOLIC--
MMH. DID YOU COME HERE TO INSULT ME OR JUST GENERALLY INSULT EVERY-ONE?
I CAME TO MAKE YOU A PROPOSAL, FLOYD. I KNOW YOU AND I DON'T AGREE MUCH ON HOW THIS BUSINESS WORKS--
THAT'S PUTTING IT MILDLY.
FOR ONE THING, YOU'RE JUST ABOUT THE WORST REPORTER I'VE EVER BEEN AROUND.
GEE, THANKS.
BUT FOR WHAT IT'S WORTH, YOU GOT SOME-THING--
YEAH. A GROWING CIRCULATION. YOU WANT TO OFFER ME A JOB?
NOPE. I NEED YOU LIKE I NEED A HOLE IN MY HEAD. JUST 'CAUSE SOME GUY SHOWS UP IN A PARKING LOT WITH A BRIEF-CASE OF CASH FOR YOU AN' URICH, DON'T MEAN YOU SUDDENLY LEARNED HOW TO DO THIS JOB.
I'LL FIND OUT WHO YOUR MONEY GUY IS. I CAN PROMISE YOU THAT--
WHAT DO YOU WANT, JONAH?
I WANT TO BUY YOUR TIN CAN LITTLE NEWSPAPER. NAME YOUR PRICE.

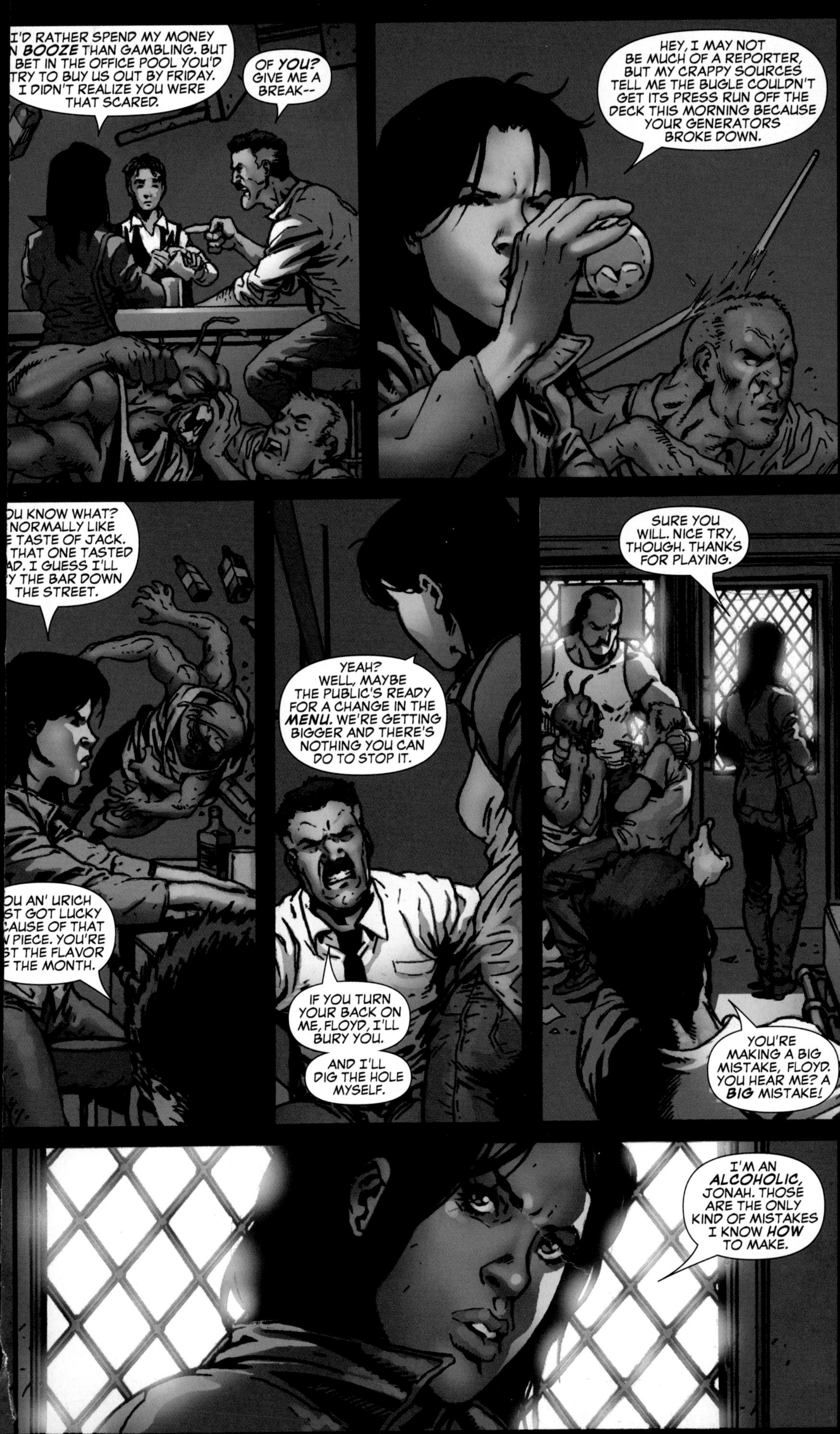

I'D RATHER SPEND MY MONEY N **BOOZE** THAN GAMBLING. BUT BET IN THE OFFICE POOL YOU'D TRY TO BUY US OUT BY FRIDAY. I DIDN'T REALIZE YOU WERE THAT SCARED.
OF ***YOU?*** GIVE ME A BREAK--
HEY, I MAY NOT BE MUCH OF A REPORTER, BUT MY CRAPPY SOURCES TELL ME THE BUGLE COULDN'T GET ITS PRESS RUN OFF THE DECK THIS MORNING BECAUSE YOUR GENERATORS BROKE DOWN.
OU KNOW WHAT? NORMALLY LIKE E TASTE OF JACK. THAT ONE TASTED AD. I GUESS I'LL Y THE BAR DOWN THE STREET.
OU AN' URICH ST GOT LUCKY CAUSE OF THAT W PIECE. YOU'RE ST THE FLAVOR F THE MONTH.
YEAH? WELL, MAYBE THE PUBLIC'S READY FOR A CHANGE IN THE ***MENU.*** WE'RE GETTING BIGGER AND THERE'S NOTHING YOU CAN DO TO STOP IT.
IF YOU TURN YOUR BACK ON ME, FLOYD, I'LL BURY YOU.
AND I'LL DIG THE HOLE MYSELF.
SURE YOU WILL. NICE TRY, THOUGH. THANKS FOR PLAYING.
YOU'RE MAKING A BIG MISTAKE, FLOYD. YOU HEAR ME? A ***BIG*** MISTAKE!
I'M AN ***ALCOHOLIC,*** JONAH. THOSE ARE THE ONLY KIND OF MISTAKES I KNOW ***HOW*** TO MAKE.

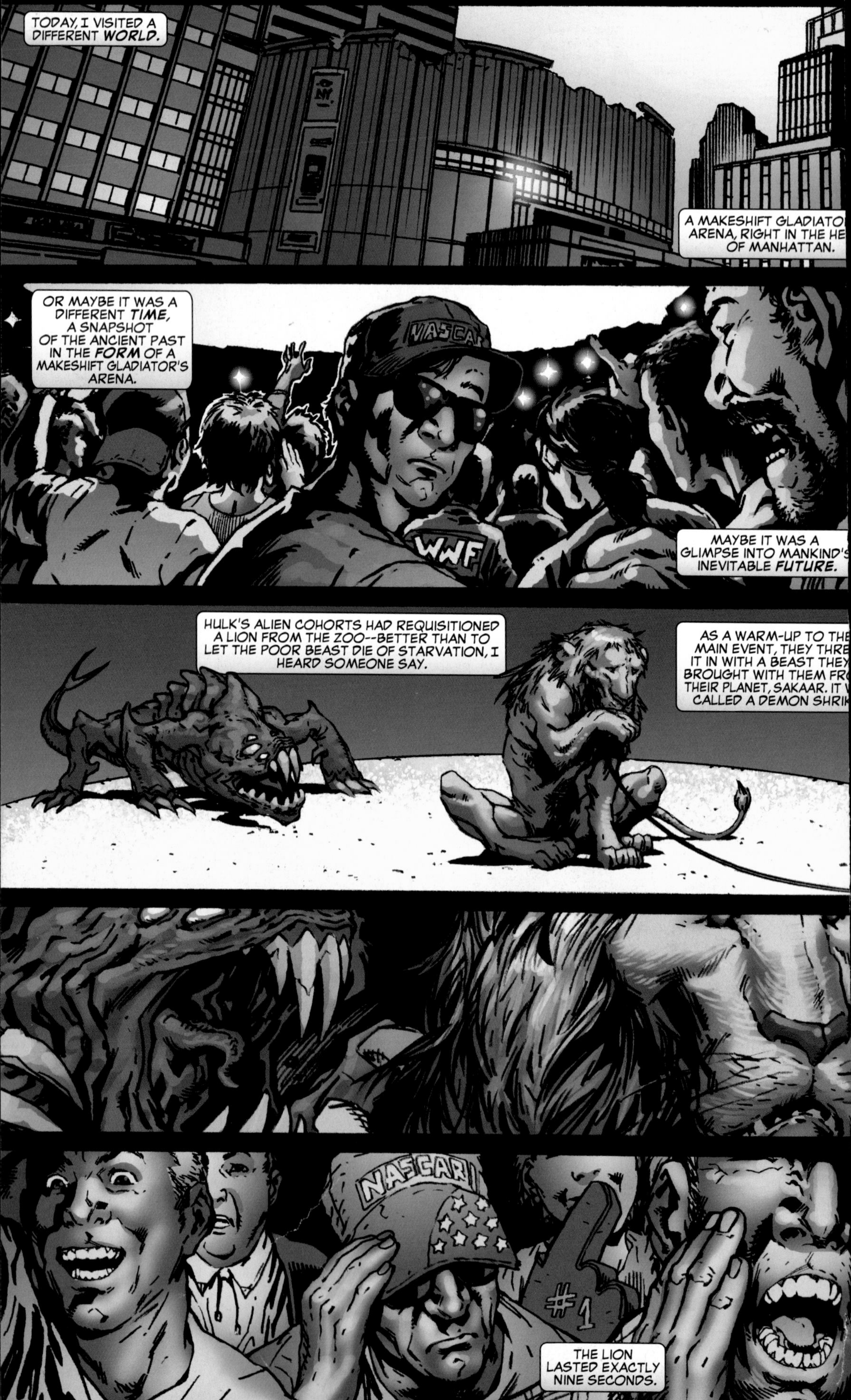
TODAY, I VISITED A DIFFERENT *WORLD*.
A MAKESHIFT GLADIATO ARENA, RIGHT IN THE HE OF MANHATTAN.
OR MAYBE IT WAS A DIFFERENT *TIME*, A SNAPSHOT OF THE ANCIENT PAST IN THE *FORM* OF A MAKESHIFT GLADIATOR'S ARENA.
NASCAR
WWF
MAYBE IT WAS A GLIMPSE INTO MANKIND'S INEVITABLE *FUTURE*.
HULK'S ALIEN COHORTS HAD REQUISITIONED A LION FROM THE ZOO--BETTER THAN TO LET THE POOR BEAST DIE OF STARVATION, I HEARD SOMEONE SAY.
AS A WARM-UP TO THE MAIN EVENT, THEY THRE IT IN WITH A BEAST THEY BROUGHT WITH THEM FR THEIR PLANET, SAKAAR. IT W CALLED A DEMON SHRIK
NASCAR
#1
THE LION LASTED EXACTLY NINE SECONDS.

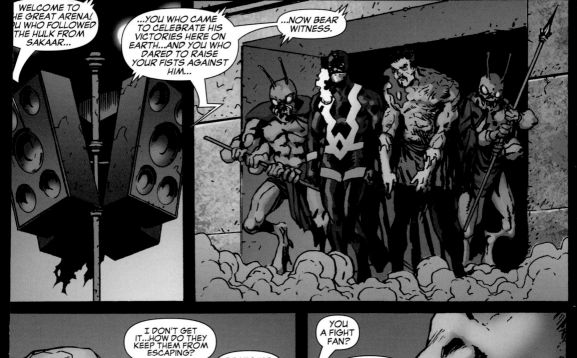

WELCOME TO THE GREAT ARENA! YOU WHO FOLLOWED THE HULK FROM SAKAAR...
...YOU WHO CAME TO CELEBRATE HIS VICTORIES HERE ON EARTH...AND YOU WHO DARED TO RAISE YOUR FISTS AGAINST HIM...
...NOW BEAR WITNESS.
I DON'T GET IT...HOW DO THEY KEEP THEM FROM ESCAPING?
BEATS ME. PRETTY COOL, THOUGH, HUH?
NASCAR
YOU A FIGHT FAN?
DAMN RIGHT! I SEEN JOHNNY PETERS TAKE ON IVAN THE HIDEOUS IN THAT SUPERIOR FIGHTING LEAGUE ONE TIME.
NASCAR
MAN...HE JUST ABOUT GOT ALL OF HIS RIBS BROKE BEFORE THEY DRAGGED HIM OUT ONTO THE RESPIRATOR!
AIN'T NEVER SEEN NOTHING LIKE *THIS*, THOUGH! THEY OUGHTTA DO THIS ON PAY-PER-VIEW!
HOT DANG! YOU SEE THAT LION GET FRIED? DAMN THING'S SPLIT IN TWO LIKE A PEACH IN A MICROWAVE--!
NASCAR
JUST OUT OF CURIOSITY, YOU HAVE ANY PETS AT HOME?
SURE I DO. COUPLA DOGS. WHY?
NASCAR
NO REASON.

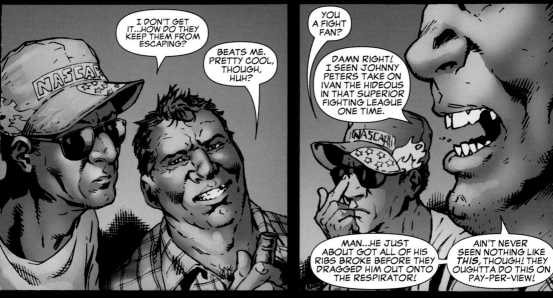

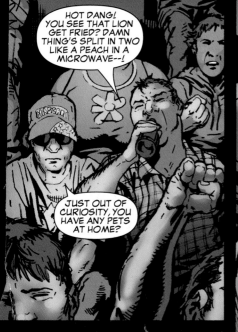

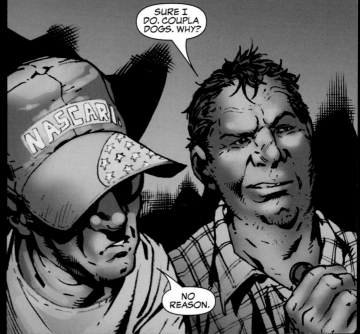

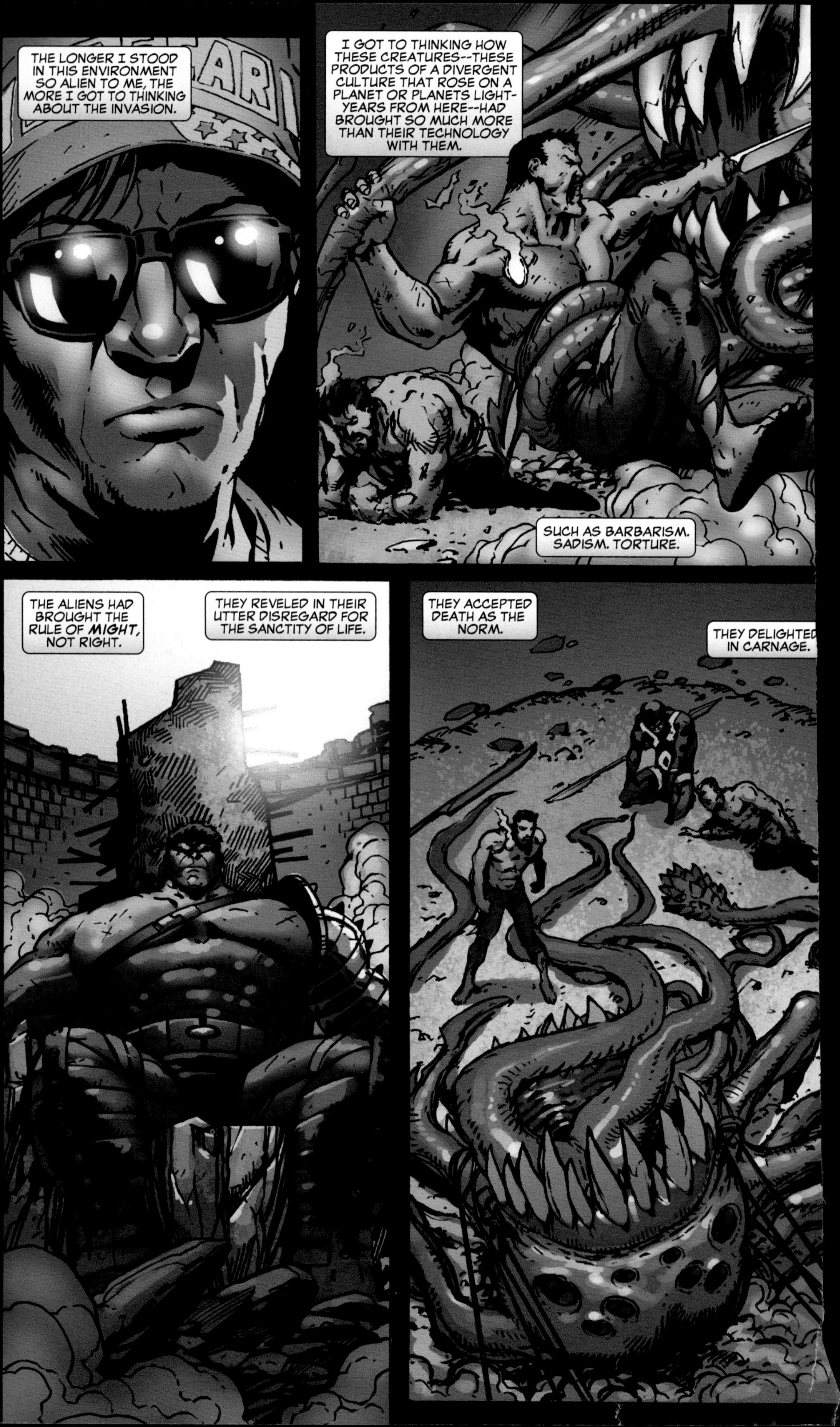
THE LONGER I STOOD IN THIS ENVIRONMENT SO ALIEN TO ME, THE MORE I GOT TO THINKING ABOUT THE INVASION.
I GOT TO THINKING HOW THESE CREATURES--THESE PRODUCTS OF A DIVERGENT CULTURE THAT ROSE ON A PLANET OR PLANETS LIGHT-YEARS FROM HERE--HAD BROUGHT SO MUCH MORE THAN THEIR TECHNOLOGY WITH THEM.
SUCH AS BARBARISM. SADISM. TORTURE.
THE ALIENS HAD BROUGHT THE RULE OF *MIGHT*, NOT RIGHT.
THEY REVELED IN THEIR UTTER DISREGARD FOR THE SANCTITY OF LIFE.
THEY ACCEPTED DEATH AS THE NORM.
THEY DELIGHTED IN CARNAGE.

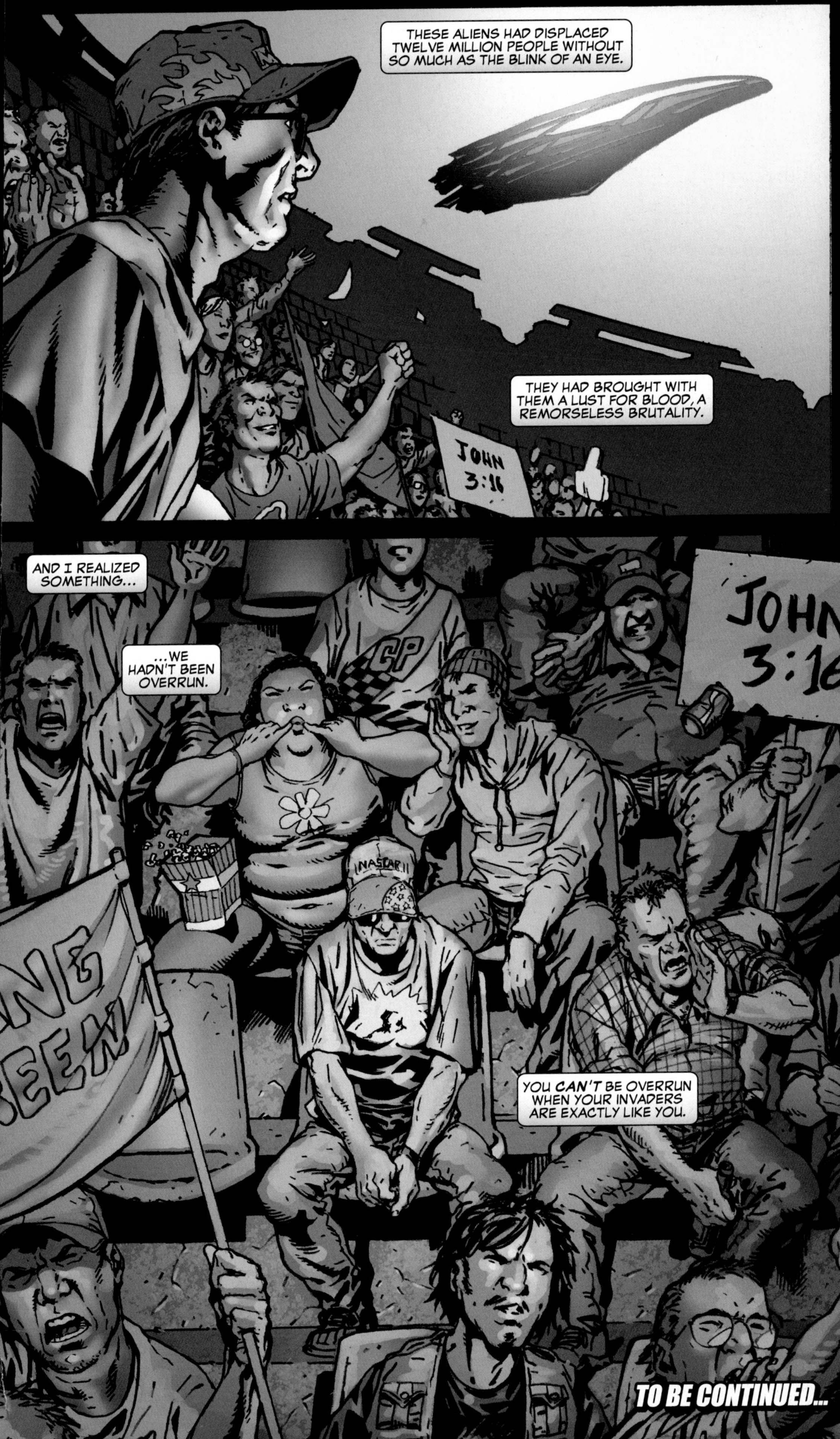
THESE ALIENS HAD DISPLACED TWELVE MILLION PEOPLE WITHOUT SO MUCH AS THE BLINK OF AN EYE.
THEY HAD BROUGHT WITH THEM A LUST FOR BLOOD, A REMORSELESS BRUTALITY.
JOHN 3:16
AND I REALIZED SOMETHING...
...WE HADN'T BEEN OVERRUN.
JOHN 3:16
NASCAR
YOU **CAN'T** BE OVERRUN WHEN YOUR INVADERS ARE EXACTLY LIKE YOU.
TO BE CONTINUED...

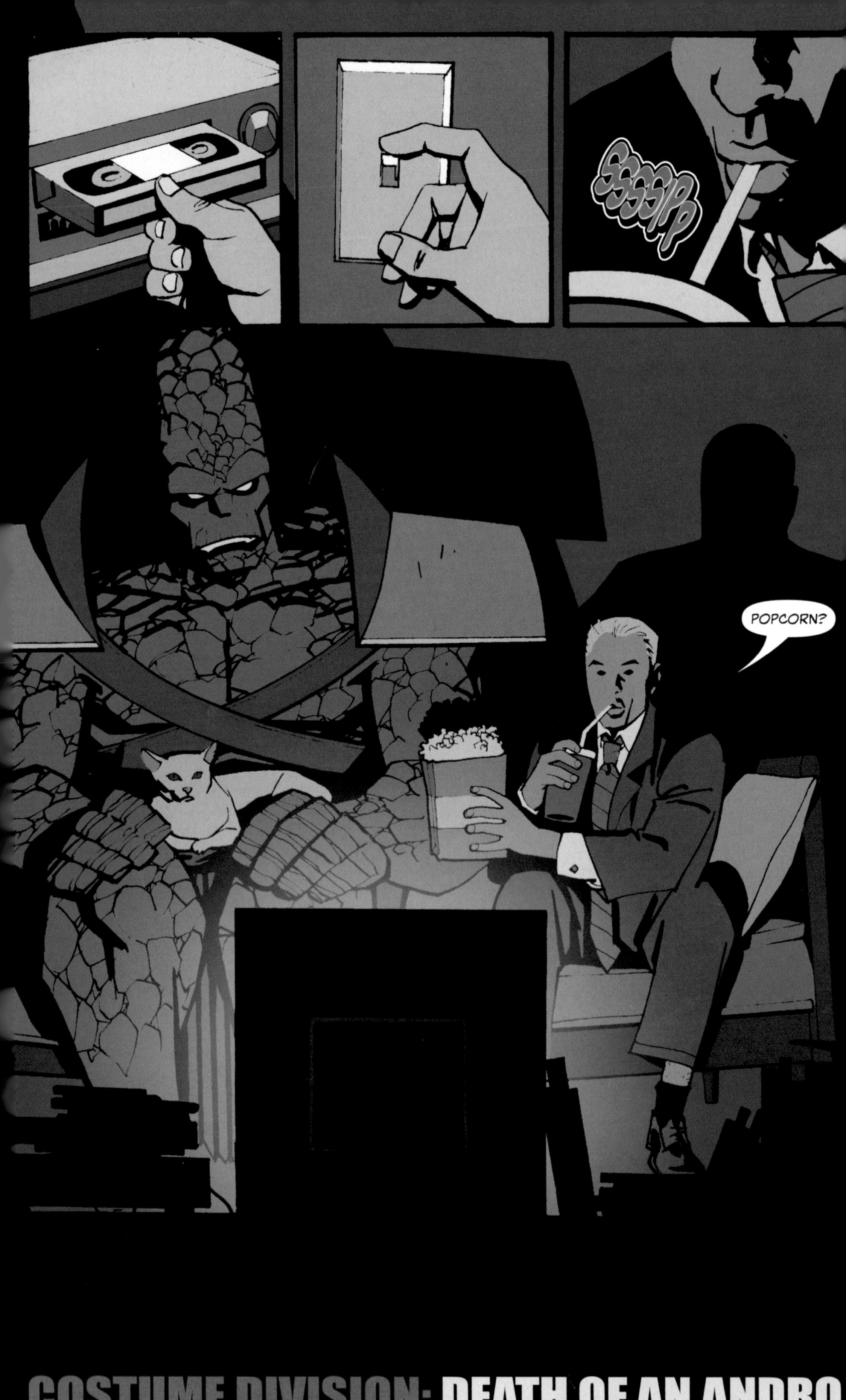
SSSSIPP
POPCORN?

COSTUME DIVISION: DEATH OF AN ANDRO

PAUL JENKINS WRITER ***SHAWN MARTINBROUGH*** ARTIST ***MATT MILLA*** COLORIST ***DAVE SHARPE*** LETT

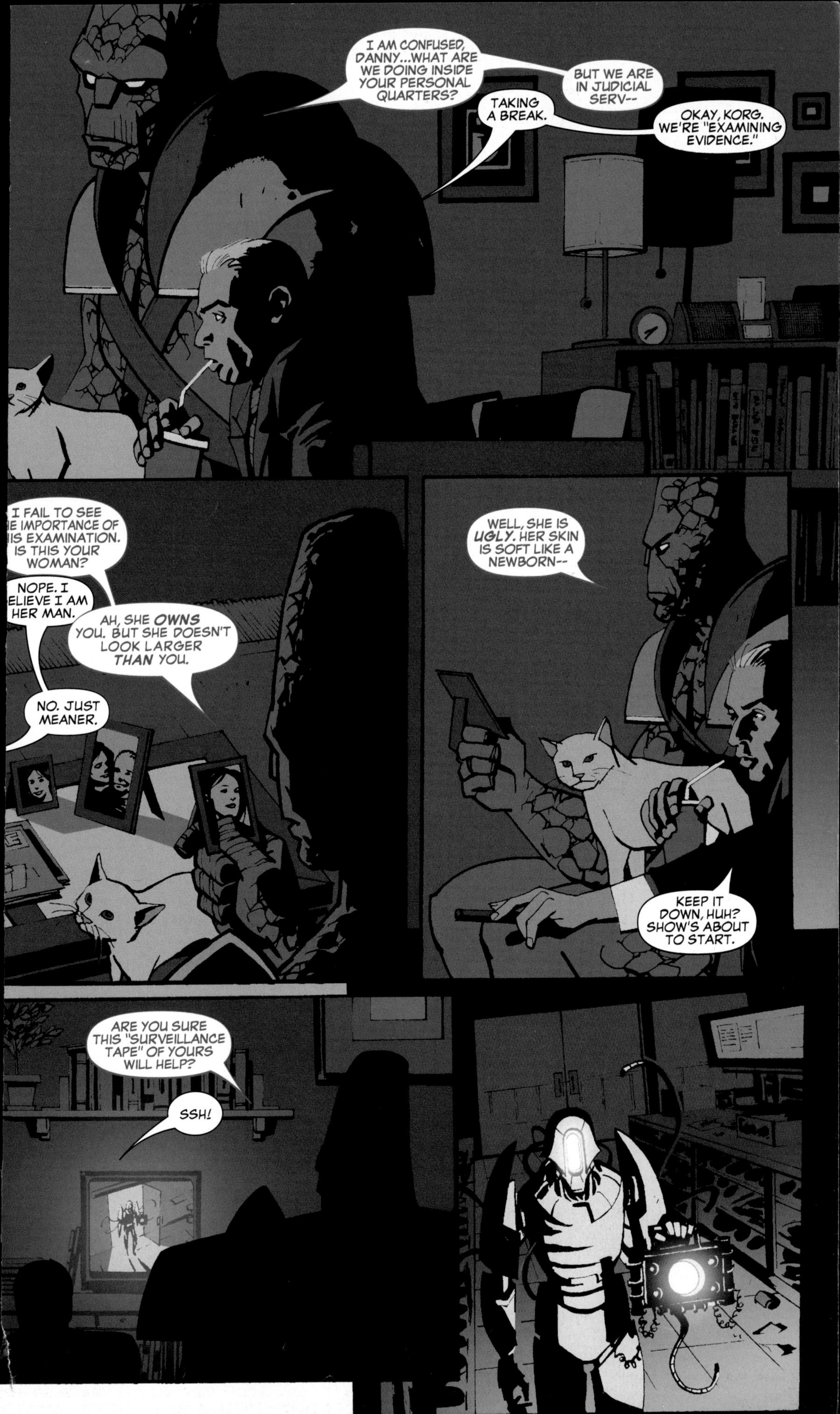
I AM CONFUSED, DANNY...WHAT ARE WE DOING INSIDE YOUR PERSONAL QUARTERS?
TAKING A BREAK.
BUT WE ARE IN JUDICIAL SERV--
OKAY, KORG. WE'RE "EXAMINING EVIDENCE."
I FAIL TO SEE THE IMPORTANCE OF THIS EXAMINATION. IS THIS YOUR WOMAN?
NOPE. I BELIEVE I AM HER MAN.
AH, SHE OWNS YOU. BUT SHE DOESN'T LOOK LARGER THAN YOU.
NO. JUST MEANER.
WELL, SHE IS UGLY. HER SKIN IS SOFT LIKE A NEWBORN--
KEEP IT DOWN, HUH? SHOW'S ABOUT TO START.
ARE YOU SURE THIS "SURVEILLANCE TAPE" OF YOURS WILL HELP?
SSH!

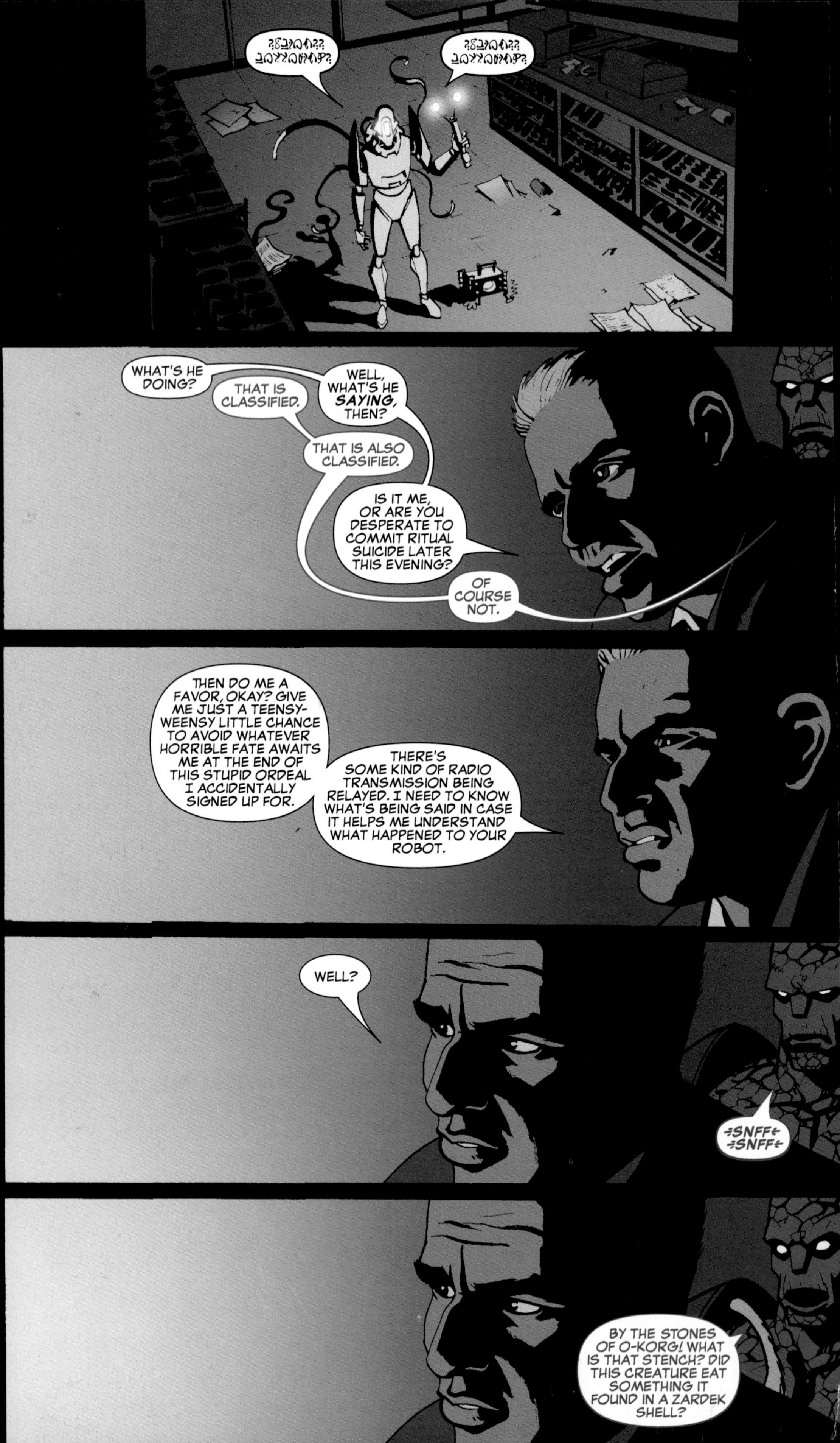
WHAT'S HE DOING?
THAT IS CLASSIFIED.
WELL, WHAT'S HE *SAYING,* THEN?
THAT IS ALSO CLASSIFIED.
IS IT ME, OR ARE YOU DESPERATE TO COMMIT RITUAL SUICIDE LATER THIS EVENING?
OF COURSE NOT.
THEN DO ME A FAVOR, OKAY? GIVE ME JUST A TEENSY-WEENSY LITTLE CHANCE TO AVOID WHATEVER HORRIBLE FATE AWAITS ME AT THE END OF THIS STUPID ORDEAL I ACCIDENTALLY SIGNED UP FOR.
THERE'S SOME KIND OF RADIO TRANSMISSION BEING RELAYED. I NEED TO KNOW WHAT'S BEING SAID IN CASE IT HELPS ME UNDERSTAND WHAT HAPPENED TO YOUR ROBOT.
WELL?
SNFF SNFF
BY THE STONES OF O-KORG! WHAT IS THAT STENCH? DID THIS CREATURE EAT SOMETHING IT FOUND IN A ZARDEK SHELL?

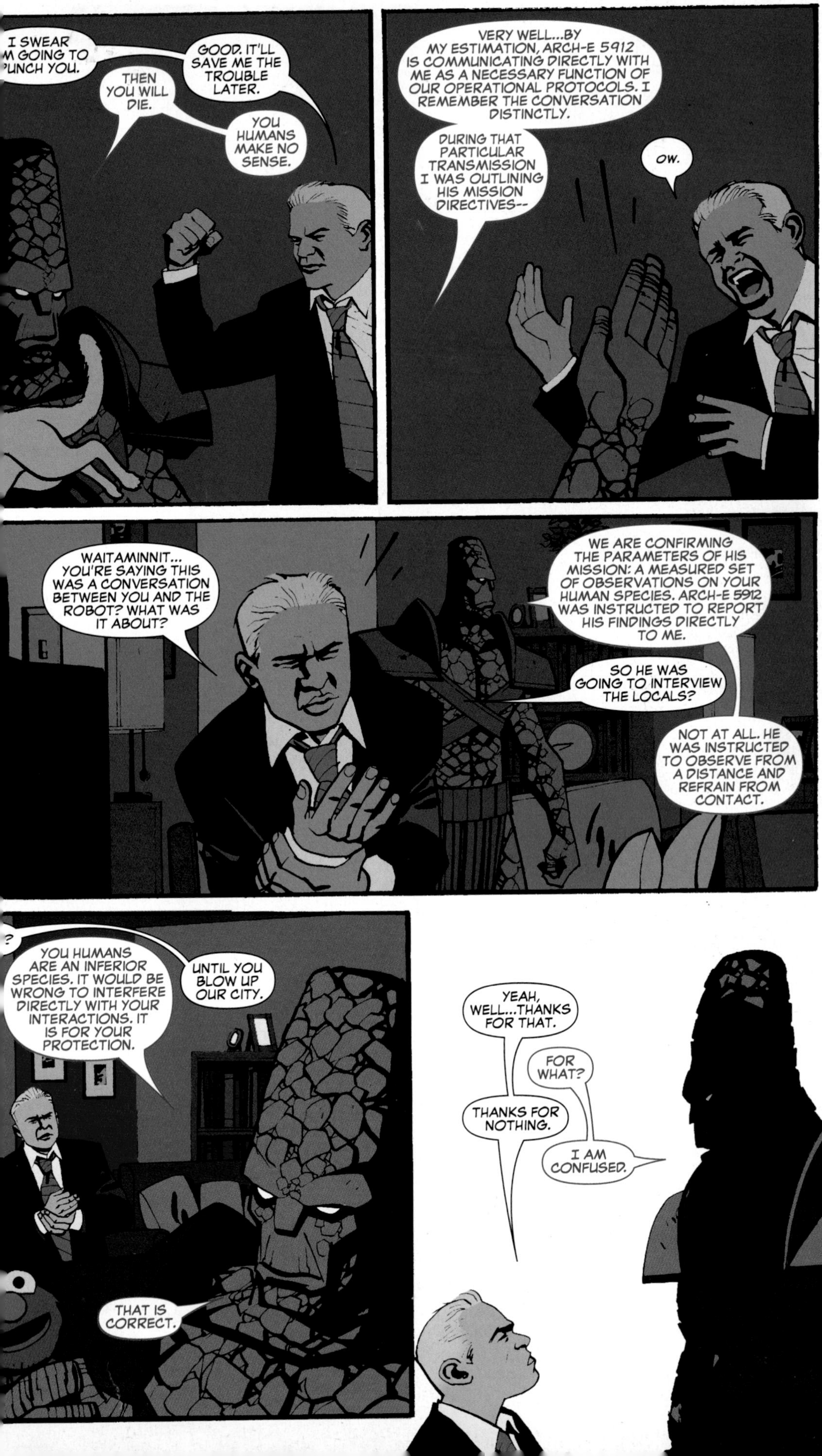

I SWEAR
M GOING TO
PUNCH YOU.
GOOD. IT'LL SAVE ME THE TROUBLE LATER.
THEN YOU WILL DIE.
YOU HUMANS MAKE NO SENSE.
VERY WELL...BY MY ESTIMATION, ARCH-E 5912 IS COMMUNICATING DIRECTLY WITH ME AS A NECESSARY FUNCTION OF OUR OPERATIONAL PROTOCOLS. I REMEMBER THE CONVERSATION DISTINCTLY.
DURING THAT PARTICULAR TRANSMISSION I WAS OUTLINING HIS MISSION DIRECTIVES--
OW.
WAITAMINNIT... YOU'RE SAYING THIS WAS A CONVERSATION BETWEEN YOU AND THE ROBOT? WHAT WAS IT ABOUT?
WE ARE CONFIRMING THE PARAMETERS OF HIS MISSION: A MEASURED SET OF OBSERVATIONS ON YOUR HUMAN SPECIES. ARCH-E 5912 WAS INSTRUCTED TO REPORT HIS FINDINGS DIRECTLY TO ME.
SO HE WAS GOING TO INTERVIEW THE LOCALS?
NOT AT ALL. HE WAS INSTRUCTED TO OBSERVE FROM A DISTANCE AND REFRAIN FROM CONTACT.
?
YOU HUMANS ARE AN INFERIOR SPECIES. IT WOULD BE WRONG TO INTERFERE DIRECTLY WITH YOUR INTERACTIONS. IT IS FOR YOUR PROTECTION.
UNTIL YOU BLOW UP OUR CITY.
THAT IS CORRECT.
YEAH, WELL...THANKS FOR THAT.
FOR WHAT?
THANKS FOR NOTHING.
I AM CONFUSED.

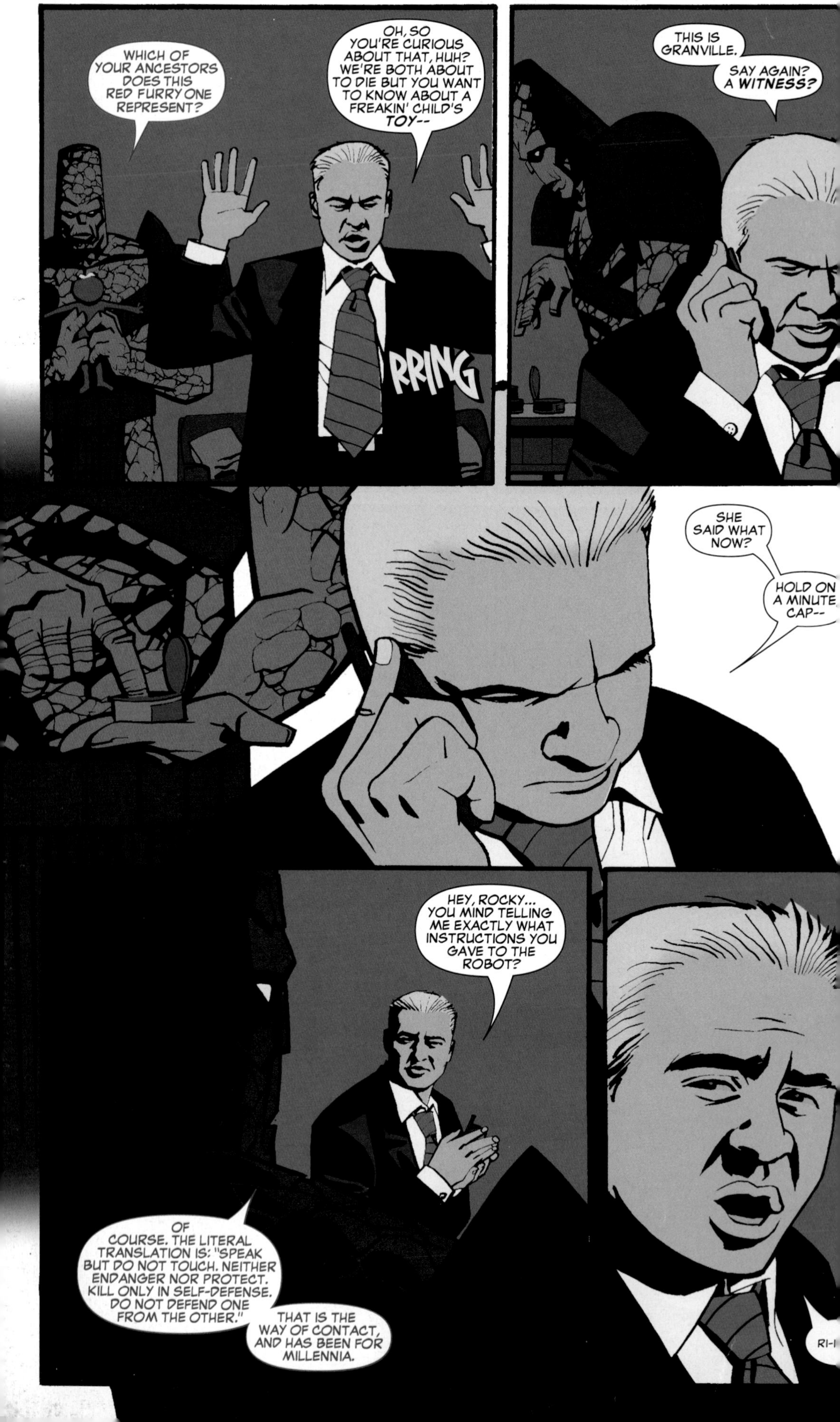
WHICH OF YOUR ANCESTORS DOES THIS RED FURRY ONE REPRESENT?
OH, SO YOU'RE CURIOUS ABOUT THAT, HUH? WE'RE BOTH ABOUT TO DIE BUT YOU WANT TO KNOW ABOUT A FREAKIN' CHILD'S *TOY*--
RRING
THIS IS GRANVILLE.
SAY AGAIN? A ***WITNESS?***
SHE SAID WHAT NOW?
HOLD ON A MINUTE CAP--
HEY, ROCKY... YOU MIND TELLING ME EXACTLY WHAT INSTRUCTIONS YOU GAVE TO THE ROBOT?
OF COURSE. THE LITERAL TRANSLATION IS: "SPEAK BUT DO NOT TOUCH. NEITHER ENDANGER NOR PROTECT. KILL ONLY IN SELF-DEFENSE. DO NOT DEFEND ONE FROM THE OTHER."
THAT IS THE WAY OF CONTACT, AND HAS BEEN FOR MILLENNIA.

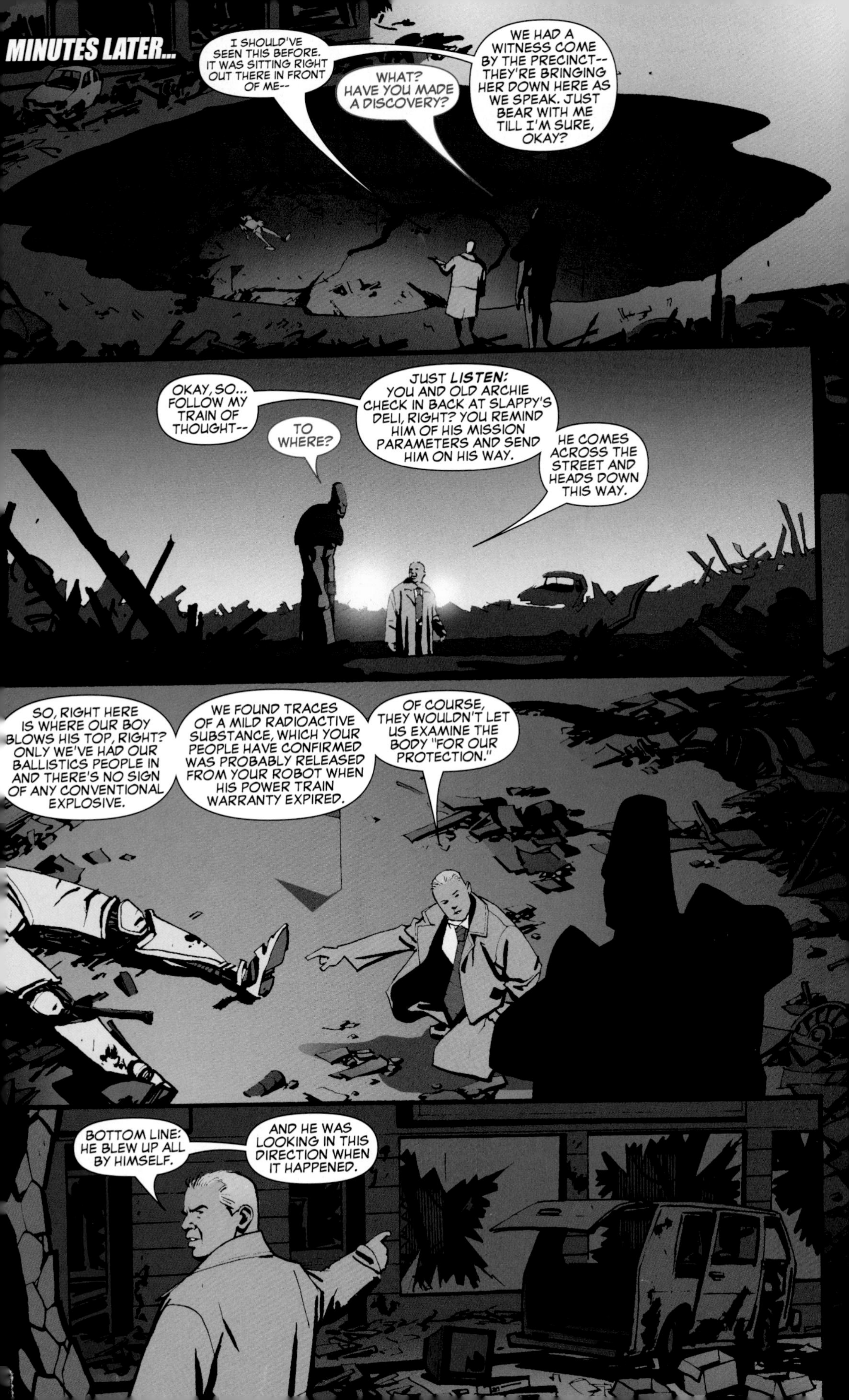
MINUTES LATER...
I SHOULD'VE SEEN THIS BEFORE. IT WAS SITTING RIGHT OUT THERE IN FRONT OF ME--
WHAT? HAVE YOU MADE A DISCOVERY?
WE HAD A WITNESS COME BY THE PRECINCT-- THEY'RE BRINGING HER DOWN HERE AS WE SPEAK. JUST BEAR WITH ME TILL I'M SURE, OKAY?
OKAY, SO... FOLLOW MY TRAIN OF THOUGHT--
TO WHERE?
JUST LISTEN: YOU AND OLD ARCHIE CHECK IN BACK AT SLAPPY'S DELI, RIGHT? YOU REMIND HIM OF HIS MISSION PARAMETERS AND SEND HIM ON HIS WAY.
HE COMES ACROSS THE STREET AND HEADS DOWN THIS WAY.
SO, RIGHT HERE IS WHERE OUR BOY BLOWS HIS TOP, RIGHT? ONLY WE'VE HAD OUR BALLISTICS PEOPLE IN AND THERE'S NO SIGN OF ANY CONVENTIONAL EXPLOSIVE.
WE FOUND TRACES OF A MILD RADIOACTIVE SUBSTANCE, WHICH YOUR PEOPLE HAVE CONFIRMED WAS PROBABLY RELEASED FROM YOUR ROBOT WHEN HIS POWER TRAIN WARRANTY EXPIRED.
OF COURSE, THEY WOULDN'T LET US EXAMINE THE BODY "FOR OUR PROTECTION."
BOTTOM LINE: HE BLEW UP ALL BY HIMSELF.
AND HE WAS LOOKING IN THIS DIRECTION WHEN IT HAPPENED.

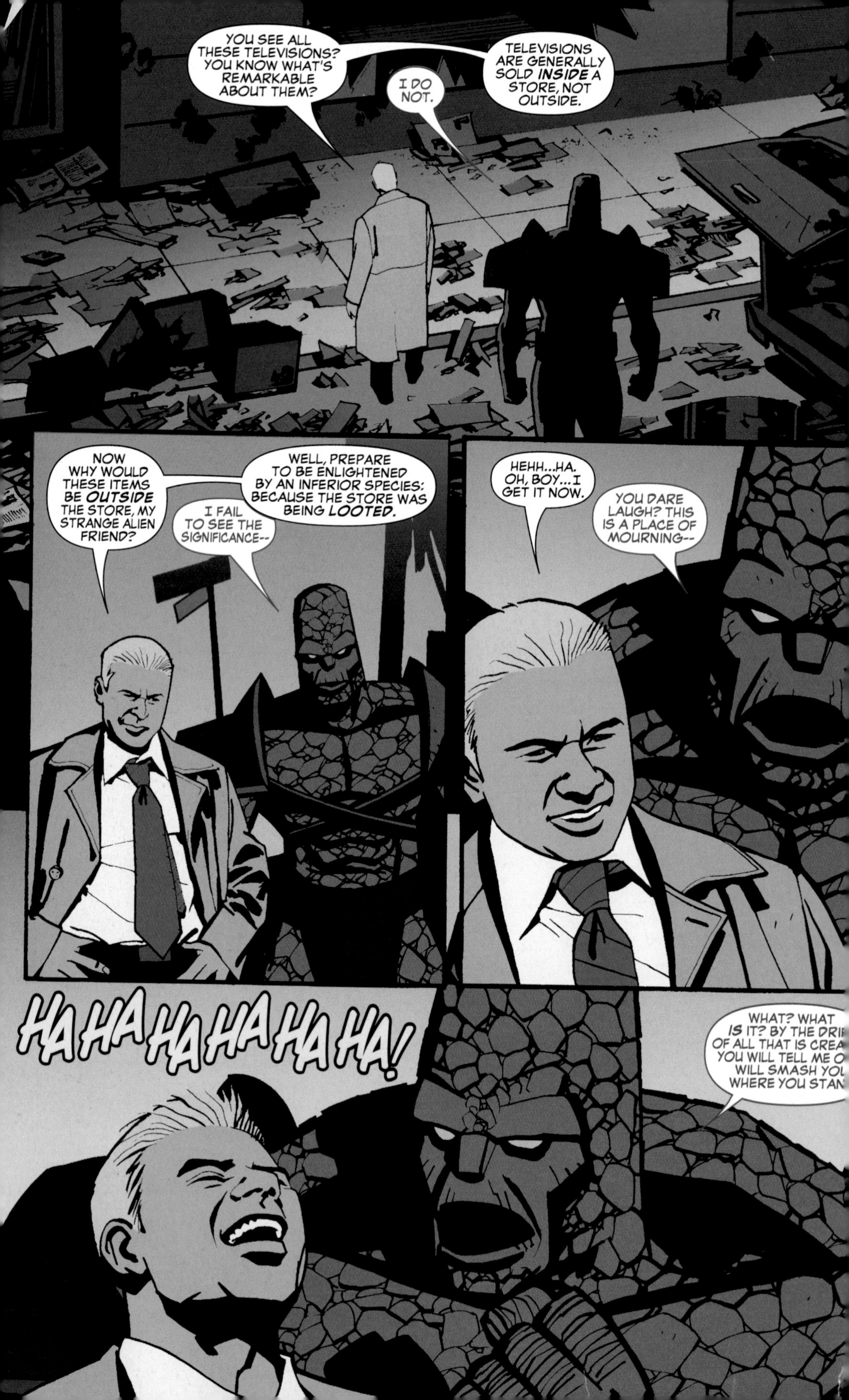

YOU SEE ALL THESE TELEVISIONS? YOU KNOW WHAT'S REMARKABLE ABOUT THEM?
I DO NOT.
TELEVISIONS ARE GENERALLY SOLD **INSIDE** A STORE, NOT OUTSIDE.
NOW WHY WOULD THESE ITEMS BE **OUTSIDE** THE STORE, MY STRANGE ALIEN FRIEND?
I FAIL TO SEE THE SIGNIFICANCE--
WELL, PREPARE TO BE ENLIGHTENED BY AN INFERIOR SPECIES: BECAUSE THE STORE WAS BEING **LOOTED**.
HEHH...HA. OH, BOY...I GET IT NOW.
YOU DARE LAUGH? THIS IS A PLACE OF MOURNING--
HA HA HA HA HA HA HA!
WHAT? WHAT **IS** IT? BY THE DRI OF ALL THAT IS CREA YOU WILL TELL ME O WILL SMASH YO WHERE YOU STAN

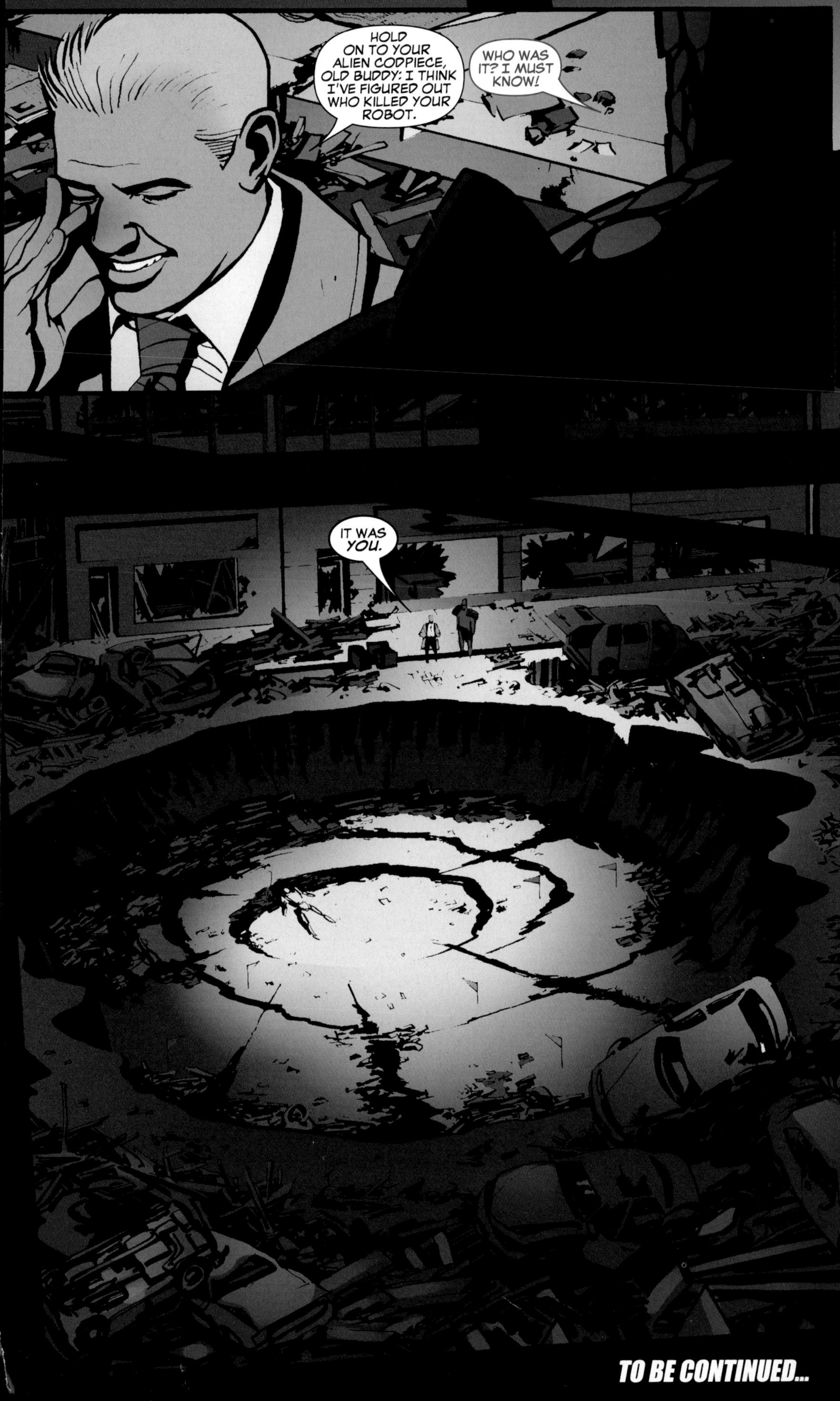
HOLD ON TO YOUR ALIEN CODPIECE, OLD BUDDY: I THINK I'VE FIGURED OUT WHO KILLED YOUR ROBOT.
WHO WAS IT? I MUST KNOW!
IT WAS YOU.
TO BE CONTINUED...

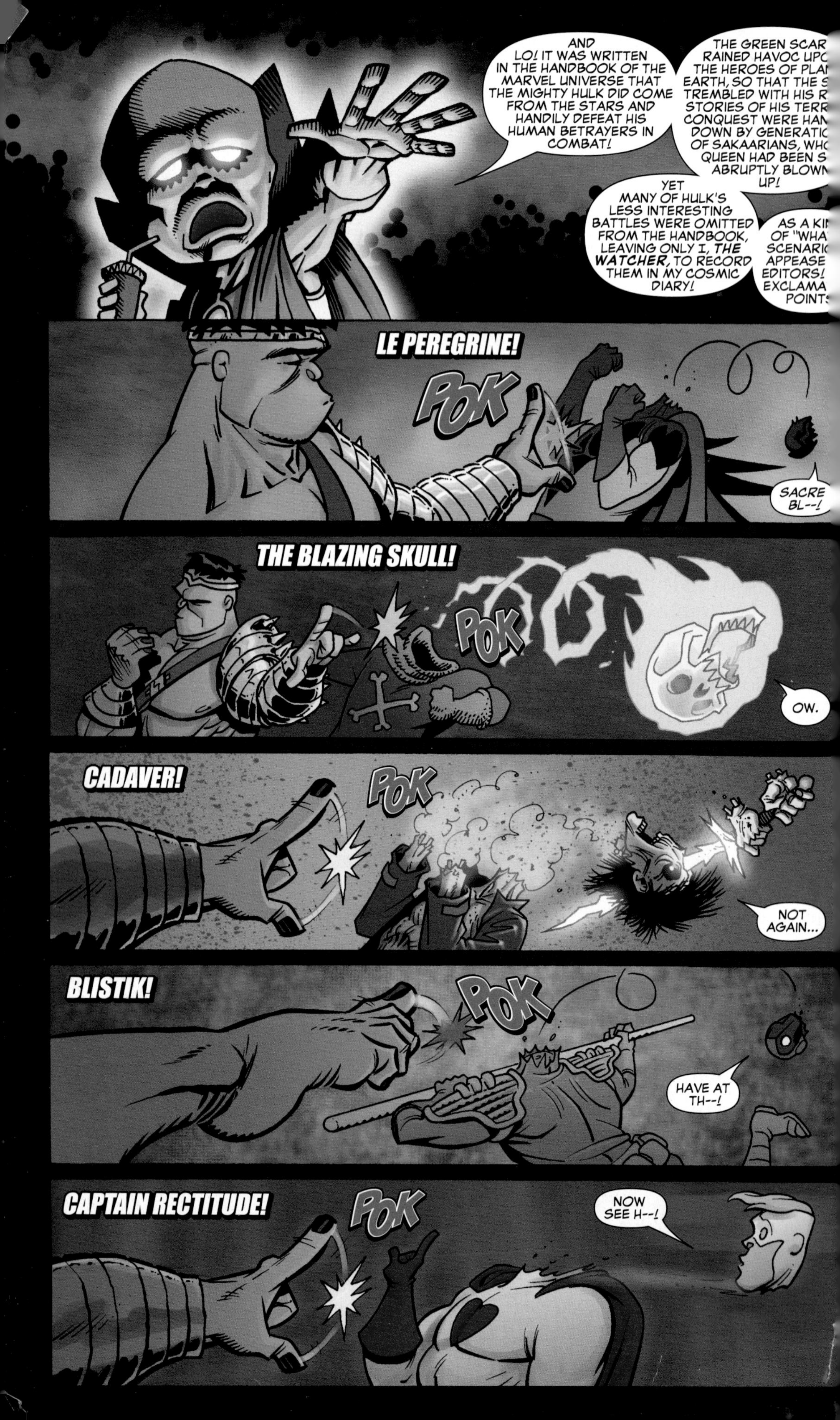
AND LO! IT WAS WRITTEN IN THE HANDBOOK OF THE MARVEL UNIVERSE THAT THE MIGHTY HULK DID COME FROM THE STARS AND HANDILY DEFEAT HIS HUMAN BETRAYERS IN COMBAT!
YET MANY OF HULK'S LESS INTERESTING BATTLES WERE OMITTED FROM THE HANDBOOK, LEAVING ONLY I, THE WATCHER, TO RECORD THEM IN MY COSMIC DIARY!
LE PEREGRINE!
POK
SACRE BL--!
THE BLAZING SKULL!
POK
OW.
CADAVER!
POK
NOT AGAIN...
BLISTIK!
POK
HAVE AT TH--!
CAPTAIN RECTITUDE!
POK
NOW SEE H--!

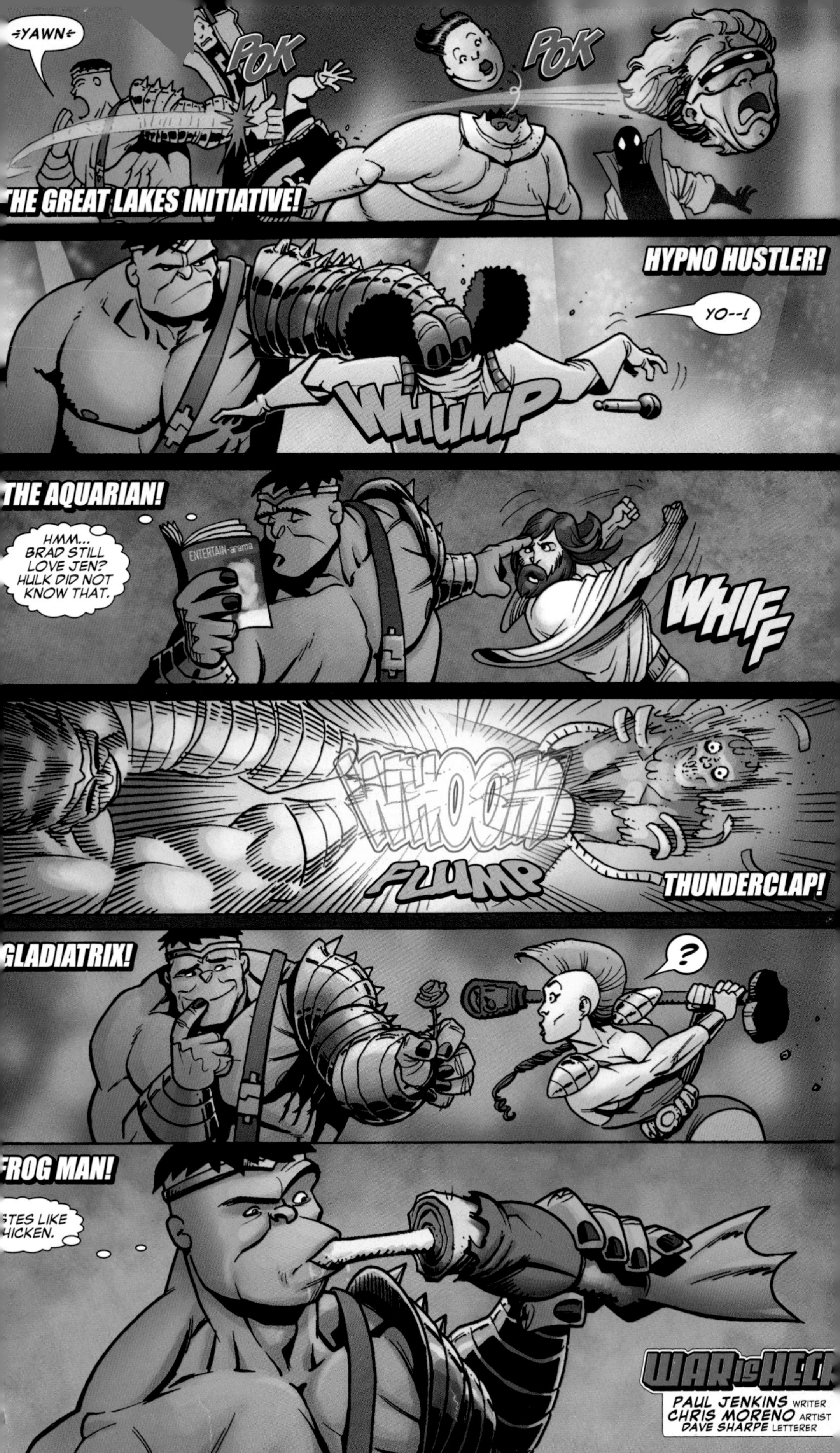

=YAWN=
POK
POK
THE GREAT LAKES INITIATIVE!
HYPNO HUSTLER!
YO--!
WHUMP
THE AQUARIAN!
HMM... BRAD STILL LOVE JEN? HULK DID NOT KNOW THAT.
ENTERTAIN-arama
WHIFF
WHOOM
FLUMP
THUNDERCLAP!
GLADIATRIX!
?
FROG MAN!
STES LIKE HICKEN.
WAR IS HELL
PAUL JENKINS WRITER
CHRIS MORENO ARTIST
DAVE SHARPE LETTERER

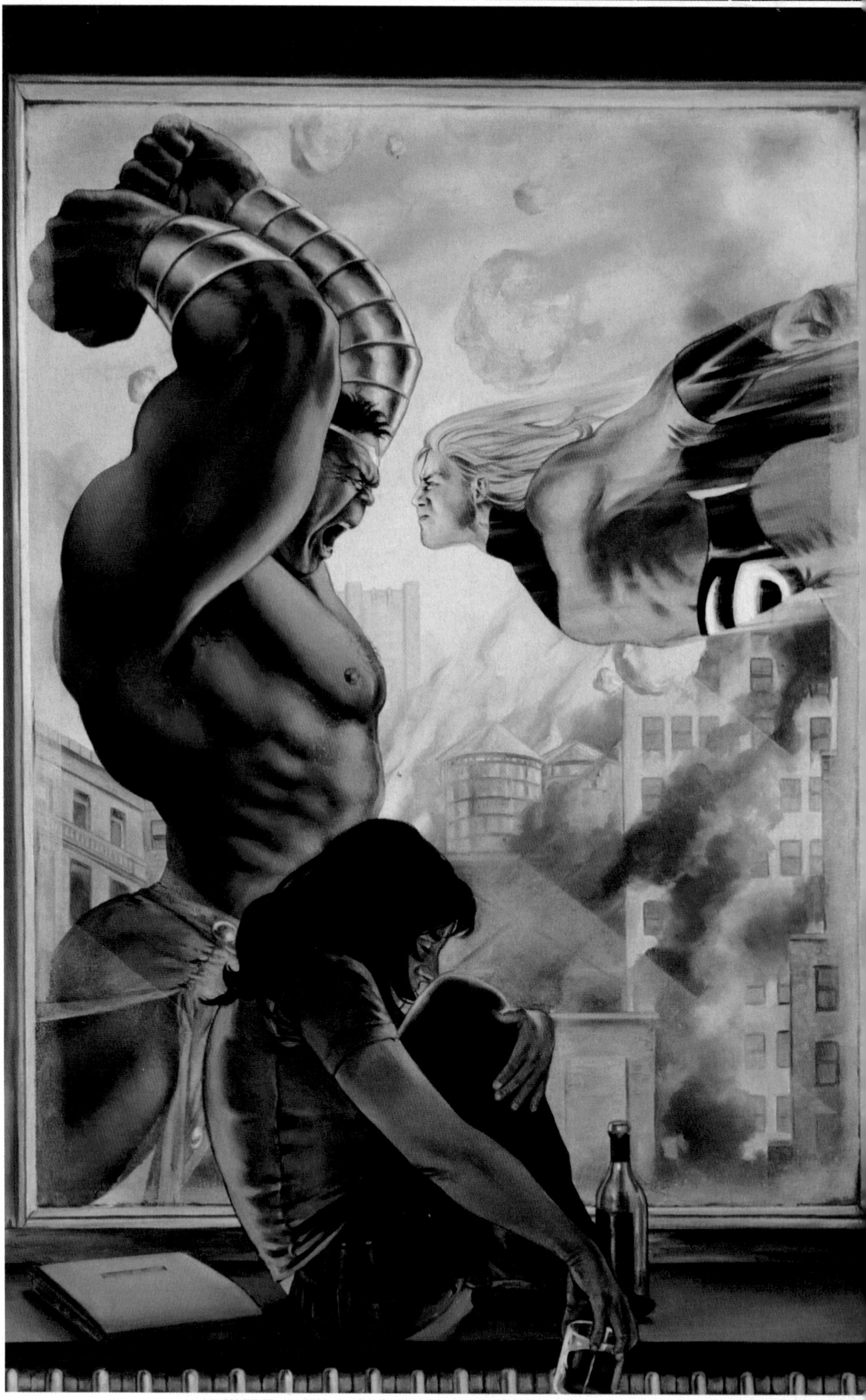

WORLD WAR HULK: FRONT LINE #5

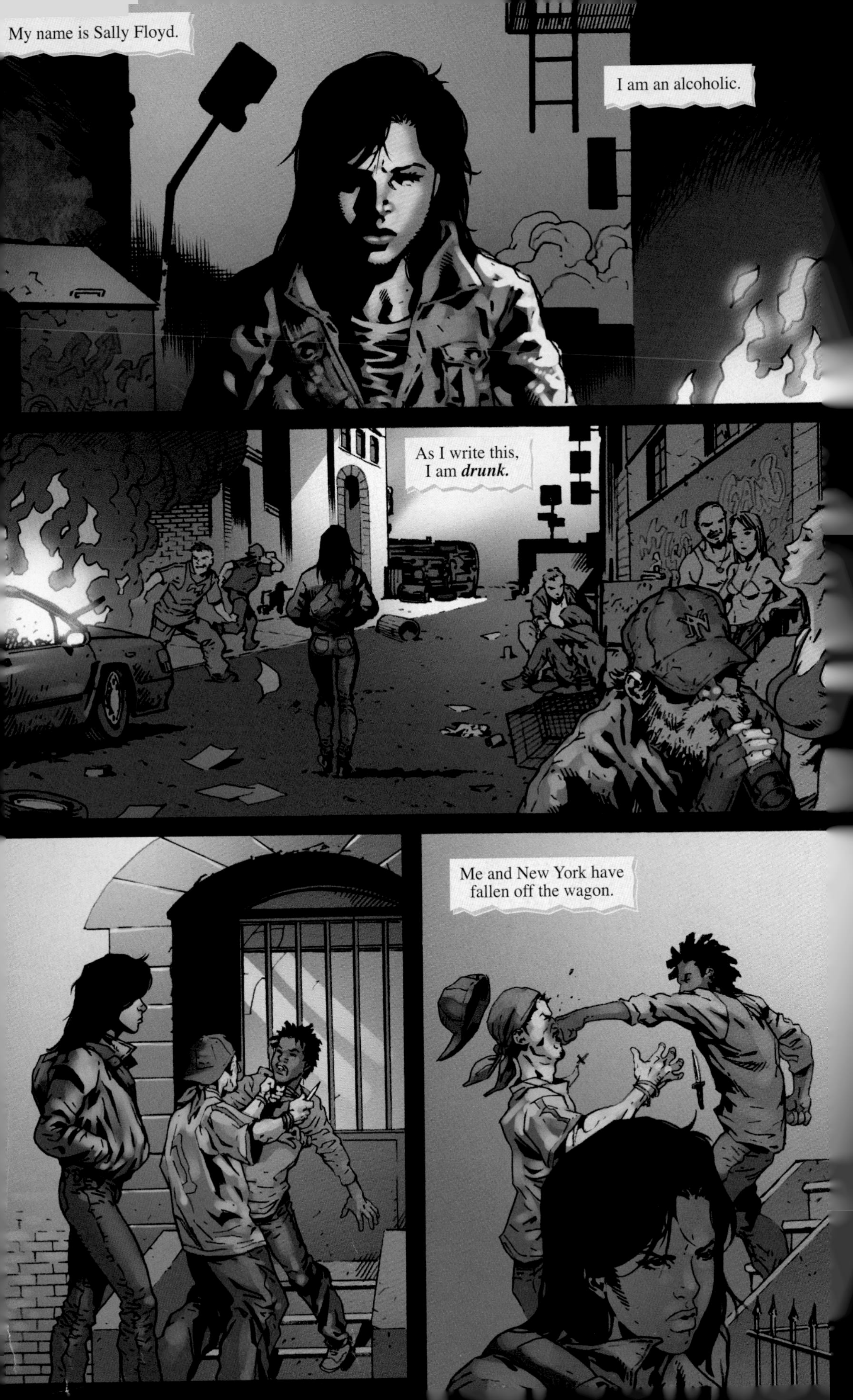
My name is Sally Floyd.
I am an alcoholic.
As I write this, I am ***drunk.***
Me and New York have fallen off the wagon.

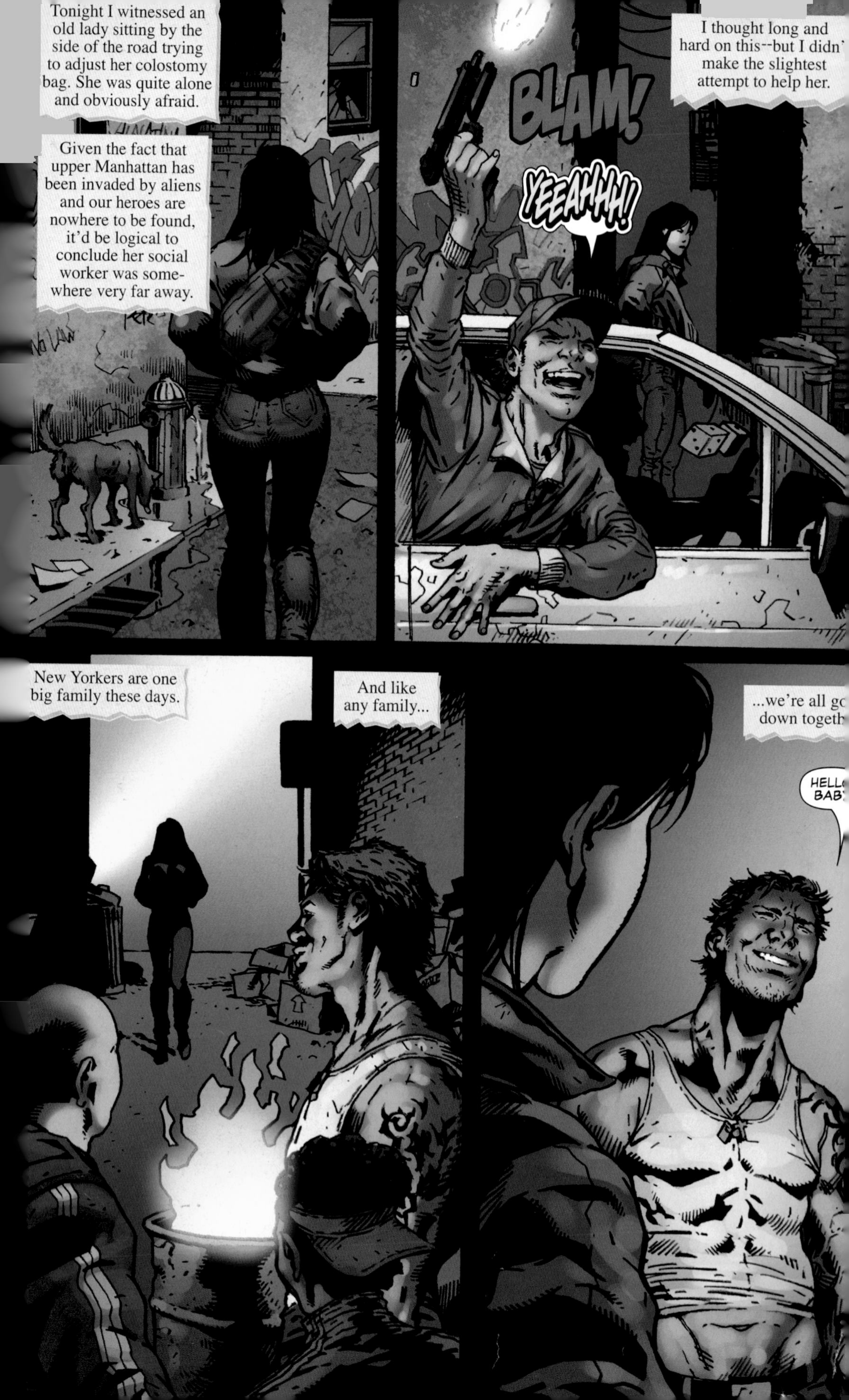
Tonight I witnessed an old lady sitting by the side of the road trying to adjust her colostomy bag. She was quite alone and obviously afraid.
Given the fact that upper Manhattan has been invaded by aliens and our heroes are nowhere to be found, it'd be logical to conclude her social worker was some-where very far away.
BLAM!
YEEAHHH!
I thought long and hard on this--but I didn' make the slightest attempt to help her.
New Yorkers are one big family these days.
And like any family...
...we're all go down togeth

JUS' SO YOU KNOW...I GOT MACE.

HEY... WE'RE COOL, BABY.

RIGHT. AN' I GOT MACE.

THEY CALL ME MUSHROOM, 'CAUSE I'M A FUN GUY.

HOW ABOUT YOU STAY A WHILE... COME DRINK WIT' US, BABY?

'KAY... HOLD ON... I GOTTA GET MY MACE NOW...

JUST STAY RIGHT THERE--

HEY--!

NOW YOU AIN'T LISTENIN' TO ME, LADY. I SAID YOU SHOULD STAY A WHILE AN' THAT MEANS YOU STAY!

YOU NEED TO LEARN SOME RESPECT--

WHACK

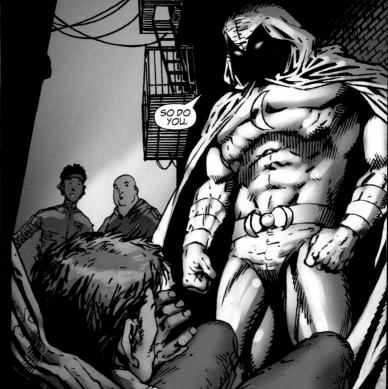

SO DO YOU.

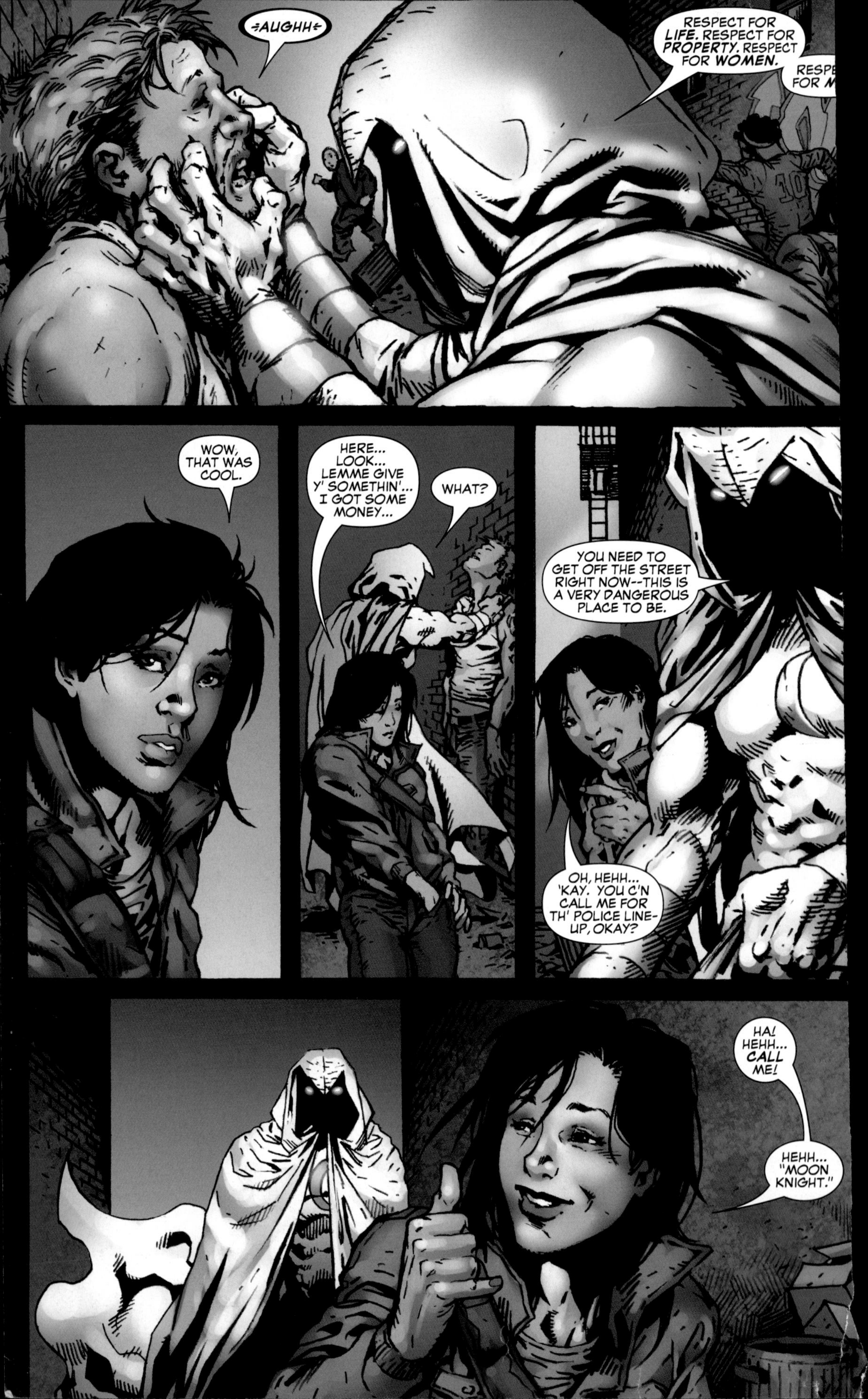

AUGHH
RESPECT FOR LIFE. RESPECT FOR PROPERTY. RESPECT FOR WOMEN.
RESPECT FOR M
WOW, THAT WAS COOL.
HERE... LOOK... LEMME GIVE Y' SOMETHIN'... I GOT SOME MONEY...
WHAT?
YOU NEED TO GET OFF THE STREET RIGHT NOW--THIS IS A VERY DANGEROUS PLACE TO BE.
OH, HEHH... 'KAY. YOU C'N CALL ME FOR TH' POLICE LINE-UP, OKAY?
HA! HEHH... CALL ME!
HEHH... "MOON KNIGHT."

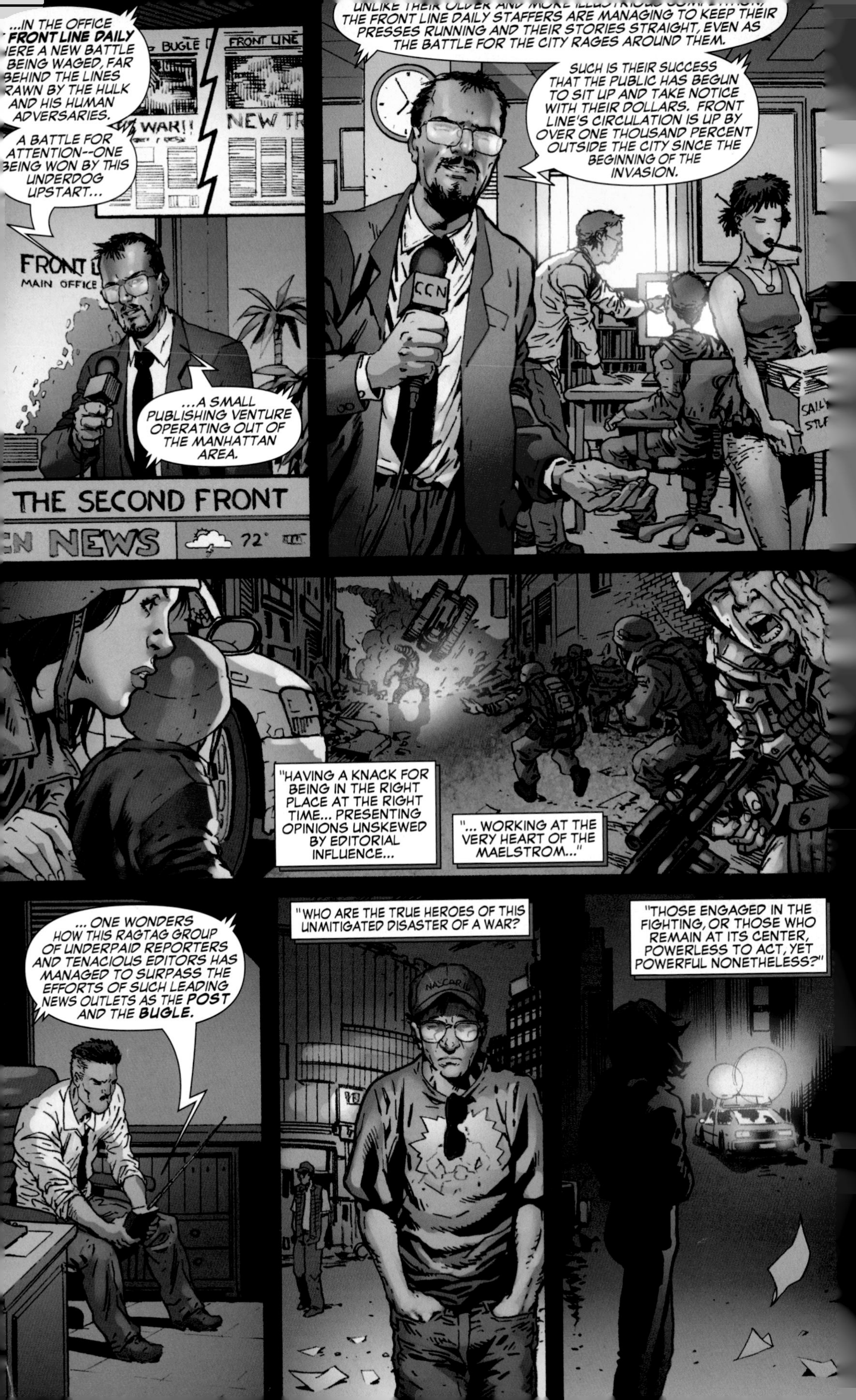

...IN THE OFFICE FRONT LINE DAILY ERE A NEW BATTLE BEING WAGED, FAR BEHIND THE LINES RAWN BY THE HULK AND HIS HUMAN ADVERSARIES.
A BATTLE FOR ATTENTION--ONE BEING WON BY THIS UNDERDOG UPSTART...
BUGLE
FRONT LINE
WAR!!
NEW TR
FRONT L
MAIN OFFICE
...A SMALL PUBLISHING VENTURE OPERATING OUT OF THE MANHATTAN AREA.
THE SECOND FRONT
NEWS
72°
UNLIKE THEIR OLDER AND MORE ILLUSTRIOUS COMPETITION, THE FRONT LINE DAILY STAFFERS ARE MANAGING TO KEEP THEIR PRESSES RUNNING AND THEIR STORIES STRAIGHT, EVEN AS THE BATTLE FOR THE CITY RAGES AROUND THEM.
SUCH IS THEIR SUCCESS THAT THE PUBLIC HAS BEGUN TO SIT UP AND TAKE NOTICE WITH THEIR DOLLARS. FRONT LINE'S CIRCULATION IS UP BY OVER ONE THOUSAND PERCENT OUTSIDE THE CITY SINCE THE BEGINNING OF THE INVASION.
CCN
"HAVING A KNACK FOR BEING IN THE RIGHT PLACE AT THE RIGHT TIME... PRESENTING OPINIONS UNSKEWED BY EDITORIAL INFLUENCE...
"... WORKING AT THE VERY HEART OF THE MAELSTROM..."
... ONE WONDERS HOW THIS RAGTAG GROUP OF UNDERPAID REPORTERS AND TENACIOUS EDITORS HAS MANAGED TO SURPASS THE EFFORTS OF SUCH LEADING NEWS OUTLETS AS THE POST AND THE BUGLE.
"WHO ARE THE TRUE HEROES OF THIS UNMITIGATED DISASTER OF A WAR?
"THOSE ENGAGED IN THE FIGHTING, OR THOSE WHO REMAIN AT ITS CENTER, POWERLESS TO ACT, YET POWERFUL NONETHELESS?"

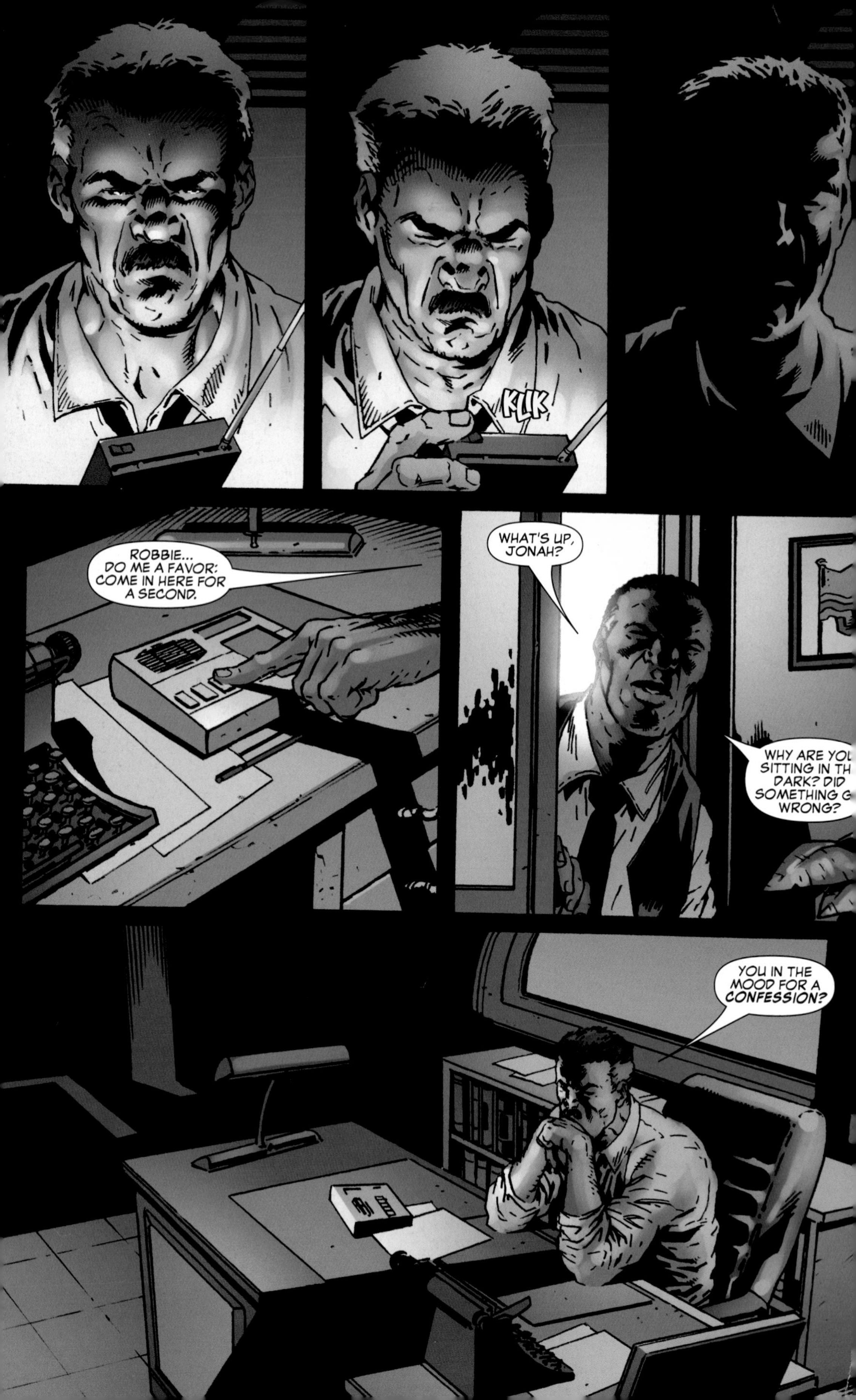
KLIK
ROBBIE... DO ME A FAVOR: COME IN HERE FOR A SECOND.
WHAT'S UP, JONAH?
WHY ARE YOU SITTING IN THE DARK? DID SOMETHING GO WRONG?
YOU IN THE MOOD FOR A CONFESSION?

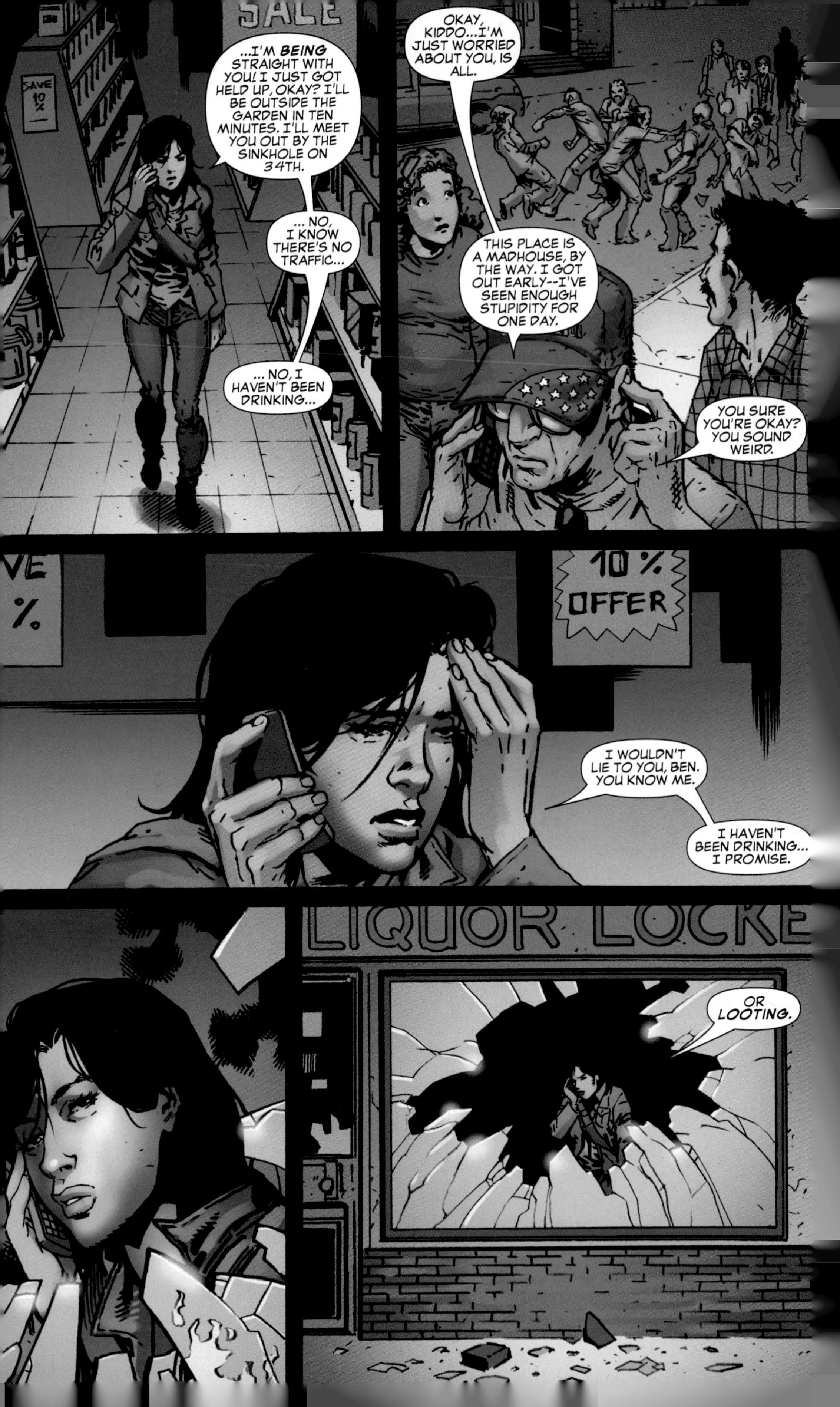
SALE
SAVE 10%
...I'M **BEING** STRAIGHT WITH YOU! I JUST GOT HELD UP, OKAY? I'LL BE OUTSIDE THE GARDEN IN TEN MINUTES. I'LL MEET YOU OUT BY THE SINKHOLE ON 34TH.
... NO, I KNOW THERE'S NO TRAFFIC...
... NO, I HAVEN'T BEEN DRINKING...
OKAY, KIDDO...I'M JUST WORRIED ABOUT YOU, IS ALL.
THIS PLACE IS A MADHOUSE, BY THE WAY. I GOT OUT EARLY--I'VE SEEN ENOUGH STUPIDITY FOR ONE DAY.
YOU SURE YOU'RE OKAY? YOU SOUND WEIRD.
10% OFFER
I WOULDN'T LIE TO YOU, BEN. YOU KNOW ME.
I HAVEN'T BEEN DRINKING... I PROMISE.
LIQUOR LOCKE
OR ***LOOTING.***

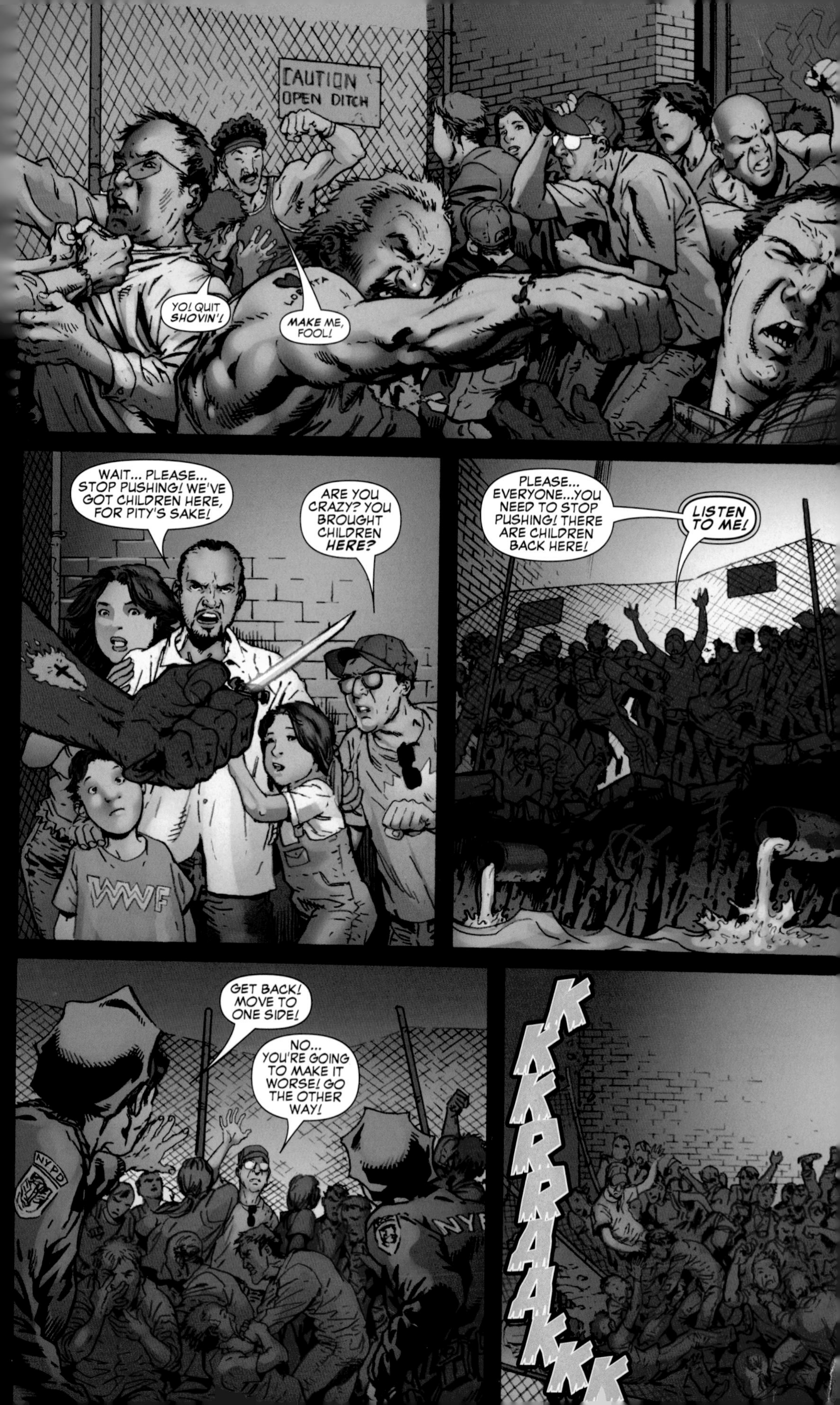
CAUTION
OPEN DITCH
YO! QUIT SHOVIN'!
MAKE ME, FOOL!
WAIT... PLEASE... STOP PUSHING! WE'VE GOT CHILDREN HERE, FOR PITY'S SAKE!
ARE YOU CRAZY? YOU BROUGHT CHILDREN HERE?
WWF
PLEASE... EVERYONE...YOU NEED TO STOP PUSHING! THERE ARE CHILDREN BACK HERE!
LISTEN TO ME!
GET BACK! MOVE TO ONE SIDE!
NO... YOU'RE GOING TO MAKE IT WORSE! GO THE OTHER WAY!
NYPD
KKRRAAKKK

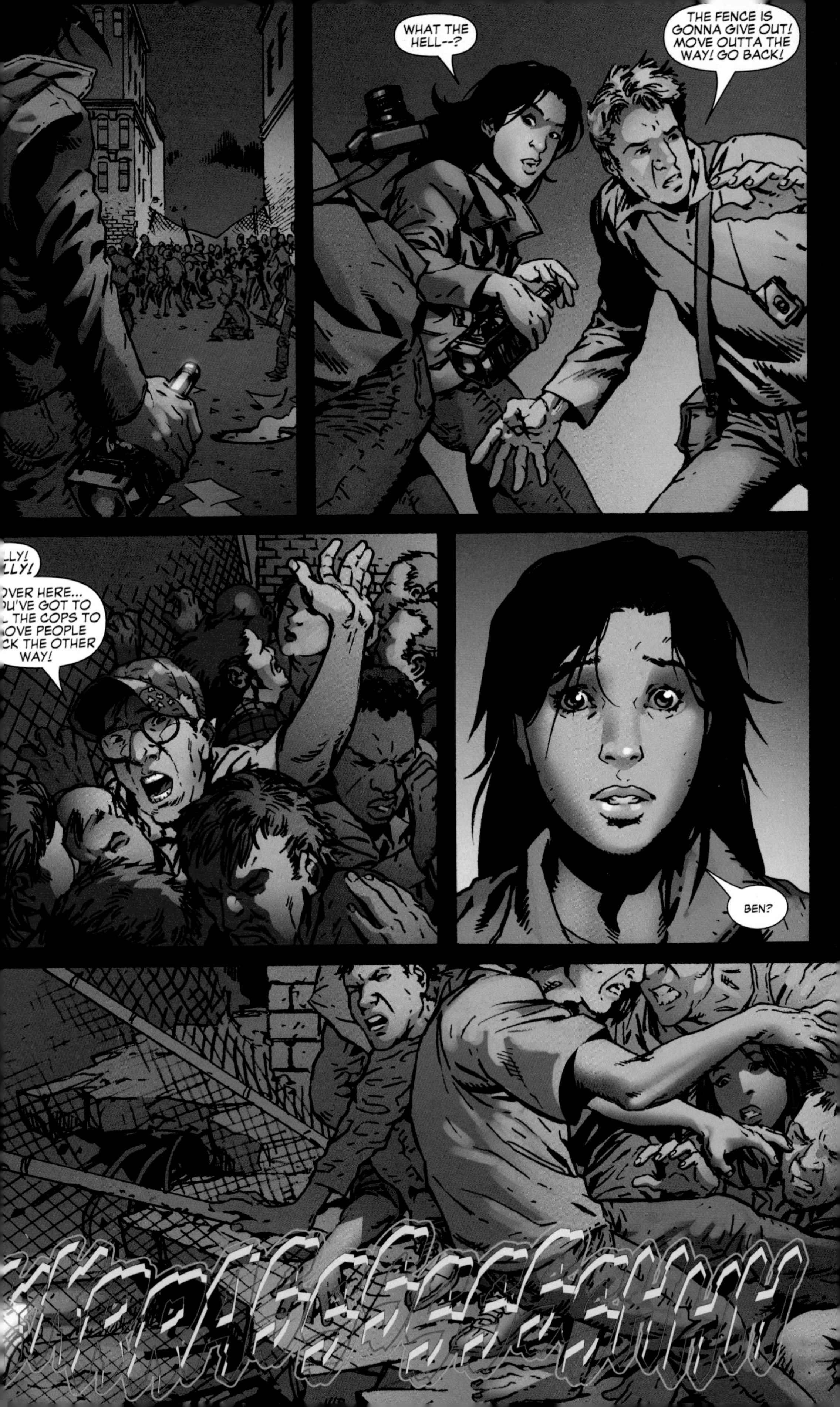
WHAT THE HELL--?
THE FENCE IS GONNA GIVE OUT! MOVE OUTTA THE WAY! GO BACK!
LLY! LLY! OVER HERE... OU'VE GOT TO L THE COPS TO OVE PEOPLE CK THE OTHER WAY!
BEN?

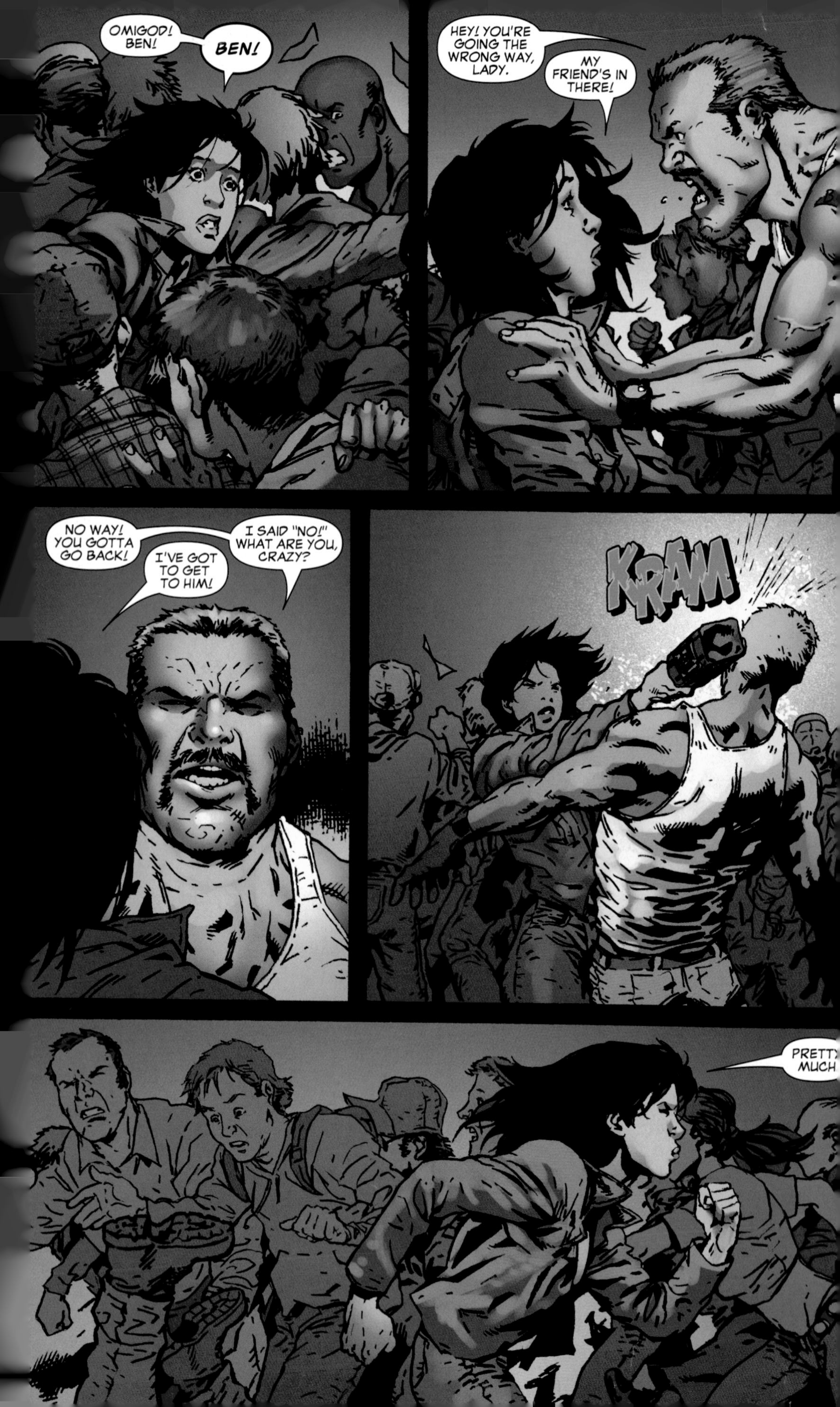
OMIGOD! BEN!
BEN!
HEY! YOU'RE GOING THE WRONG WAY, LADY.
MY FRIEND'S IN THERE!
NO WAY! YOU GOTTA GO BACK!
I'VE GOT TO GET TO HIM!
I SAID "NO!" WHAT ARE YOU, CRAZY?
KRAM
PRETTY MUCH

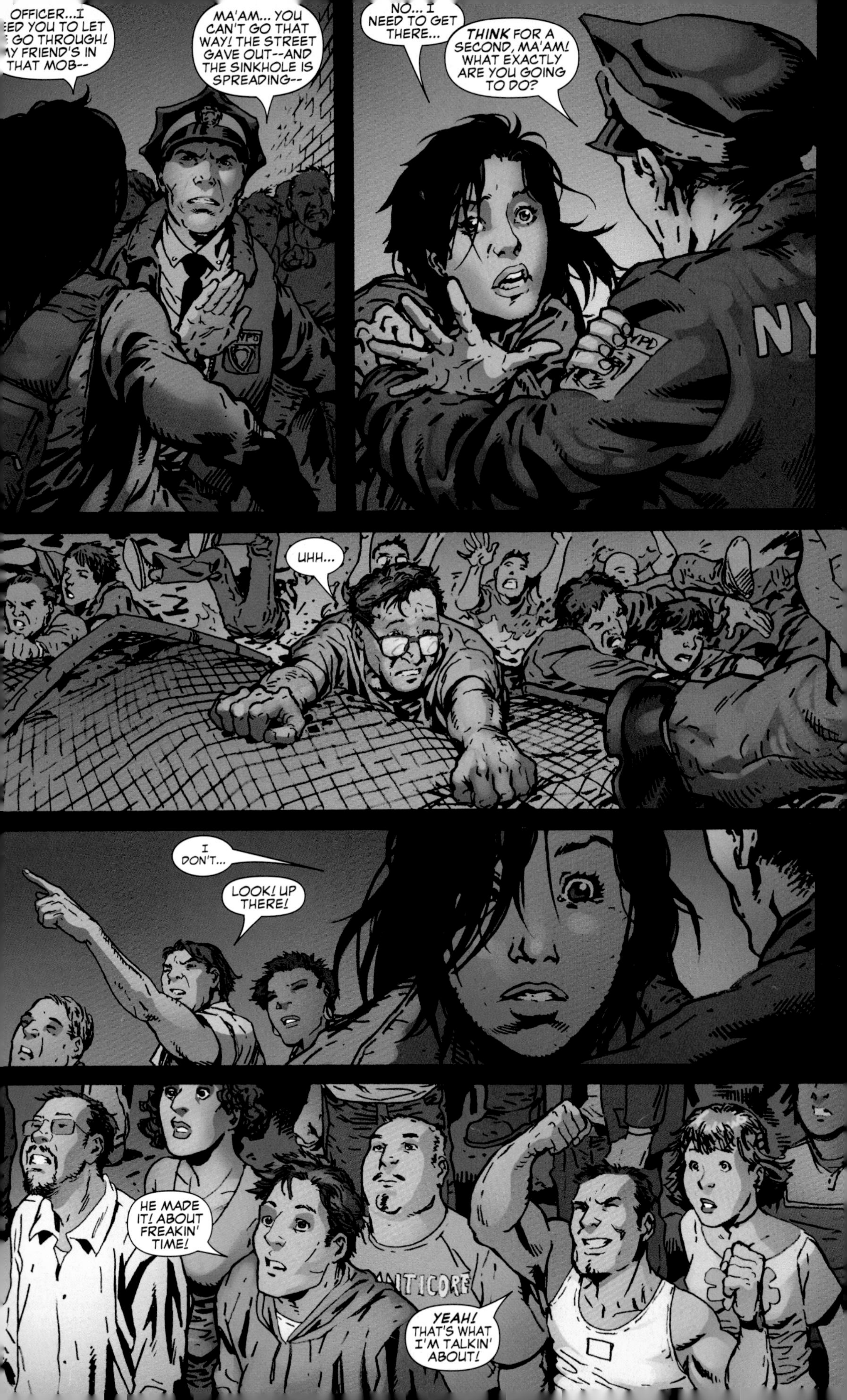
OFFICER...I EED YOU TO LET GO THROUGH! Y FRIEND'S IN THAT MOB--
MA'AM... YOU CAN'T GO THAT WAY! THE STREET GAVE OUT--AND THE SINKHOLE IS SPREADING--
NO... I NEED TO GET THERE...
THINK FOR A SECOND, MA'AM! WHAT EXACTLY ARE YOU GOING TO DO?
NYPD
UHH...
I DON'T...
LOOK! UP THERE!
HE MADE IT! ABOUT FREAKIN' TIME!
YEAH! THAT'S WHAT I'M TALKIN' ABOUT!

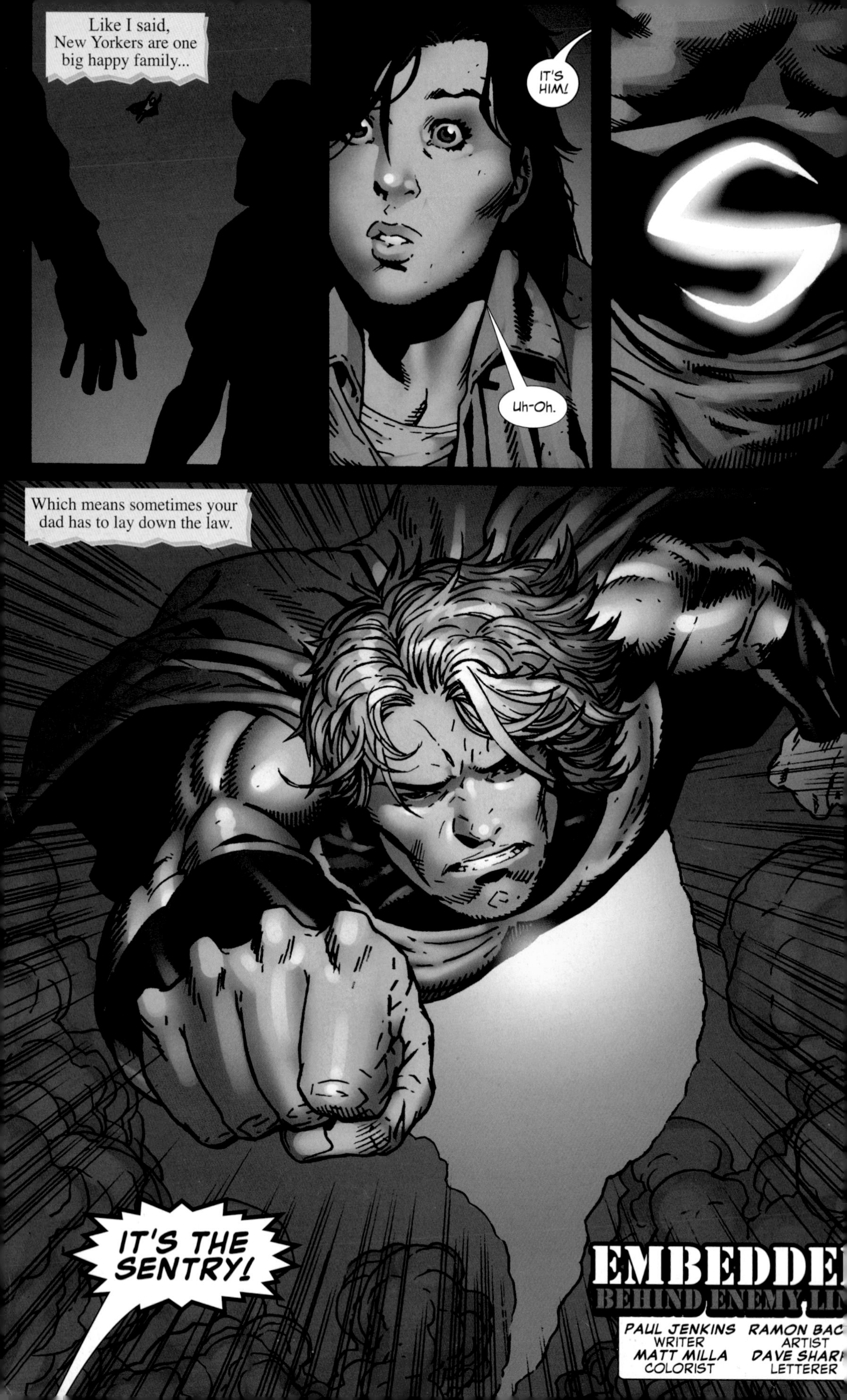
Like I said, New Yorkers are one big happy family...
IT'S HIM!
Uh-Oh.
Which means sometimes your dad has to lay down the law.
IT'S THE SENTRY!
EMBEDDE
BEHIND ENEMY LI
PAUL JENKINS
WRITER
RAMON BAC
ARTIST
MATT MILLA
COLORIST
DAVE SHAR
LETTERER

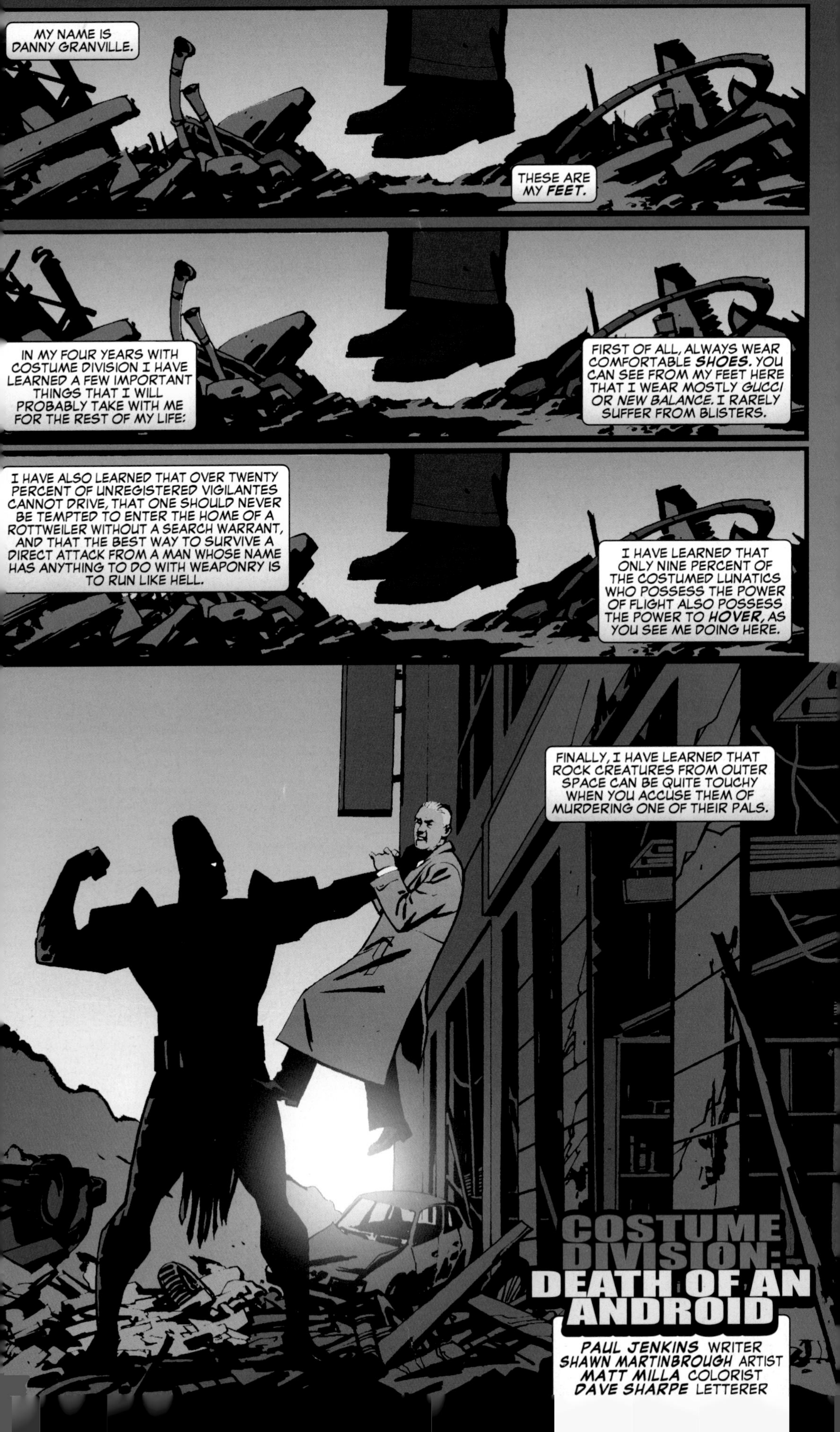

MY NAME IS DANNY GRANVILLE.
THESE ARE MY FEET.
IN MY FOUR YEARS WITH COSTUME DIVISION I HAVE LEARNED A FEW IMPORTANT THINGS THAT I WILL PROBABLY TAKE WITH ME FOR THE REST OF MY LIFE:
FIRST OF ALL, ALWAYS WEAR COMFORTABLE SHOES. YOU CAN SEE FROM MY FEET HERE THAT I WEAR MOSTLY GUCCI OR NEW BALANCE. I RARELY SUFFER FROM BLISTERS.
I HAVE ALSO LEARNED THAT OVER TWENTY PERCENT OF UNREGISTERED VIGILANTES CANNOT DRIVE, THAT ONE SHOULD NEVER BE TEMPTED TO ENTER THE HOME OF A ROTTWEILER WITHOUT A SEARCH WARRANT, AND THAT THE BEST WAY TO SURVIVE A DIRECT ATTACK FROM A MAN WHOSE NAME HAS ANYTHING TO DO WITH WEAPONRY IS TO RUN LIKE HELL.
I HAVE LEARNED THAT ONLY NINE PERCENT OF THE COSTUMED LUNATICS WHO POSSESS THE POWER OF FLIGHT ALSO POSSESS THE POWER TO HOVER, AS YOU SEE ME DOING HERE.
FINALLY, I HAVE LEARNED THAT ROCK CREATURES FROM OUTER SPACE CAN BE QUITE TOUCHY WHEN YOU ACCUSE THEM OF MURDERING ONE OF THEIR PALS.
COSTUME DIVISION:
DEATH OF AN ANDROID
PAUL JENKINS WRITER
SHAWN MARTINBROUGH ARTIST
MATT MILLA COLORIST
DAVE SHARPE LETTERER

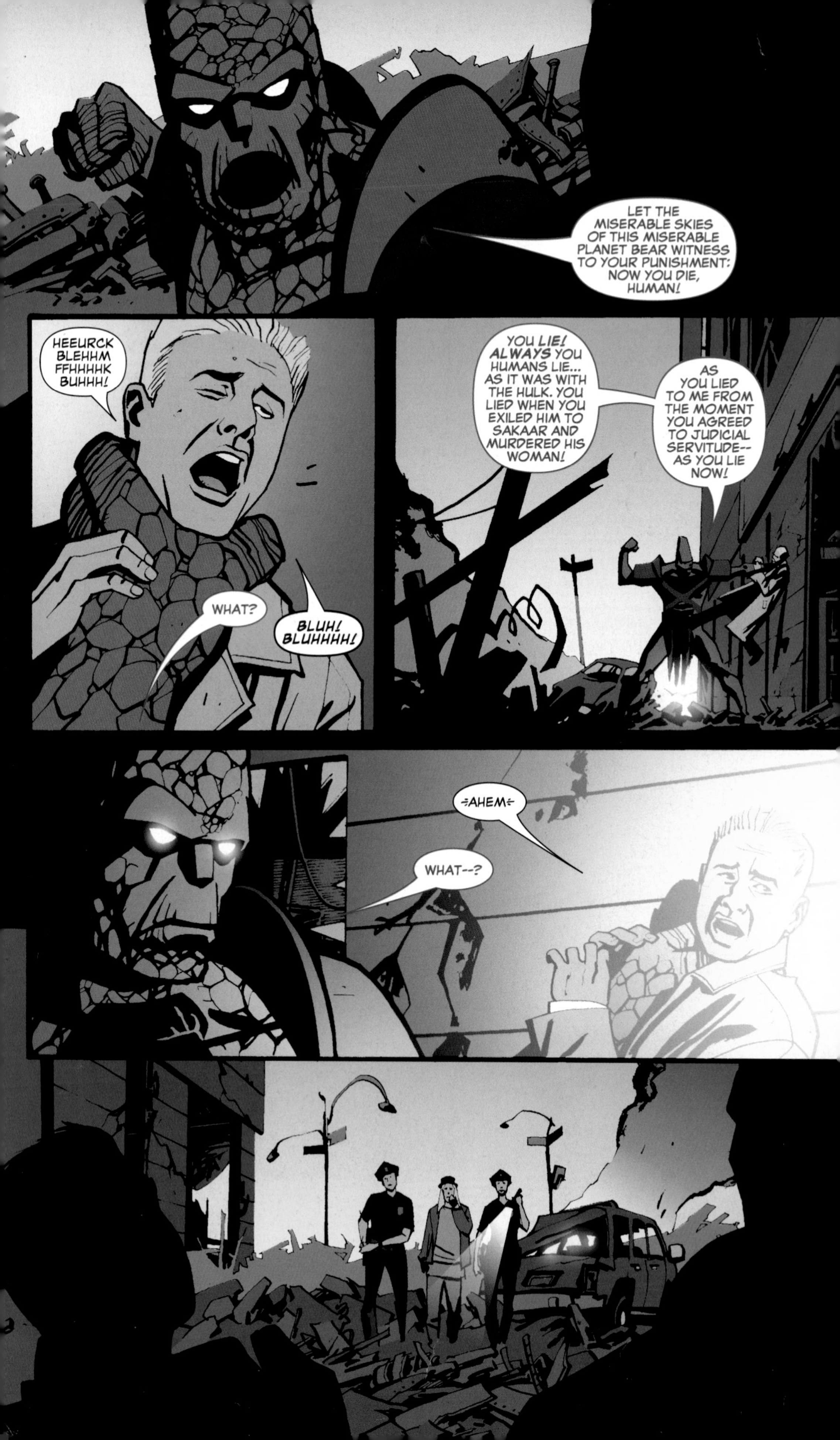
LET THE MISERABLE SKIES OF THIS MISERABLE PLANET BEAR WITNESS TO YOUR PUNISHMENT: NOW YOU DIE, HUMAN!
HEEURCK BLEHHM FFHHHHK BUHHH!
WHAT?
BLUH! BLUHHHH!
YOU LIE! ALWAYS YOU HUMANS LIE... AS IT WAS WITH THE HULK. YOU LIED WHEN YOU EXILED HIM TO SAKAAR AND MURDERED HIS WOMAN!
AS YOU LIED TO ME FROM THE MOMENT YOU AGREED TO JUDICIAL SERVITUDE-- AS YOU LIE NOW!
=AHEM=
WHAT--?

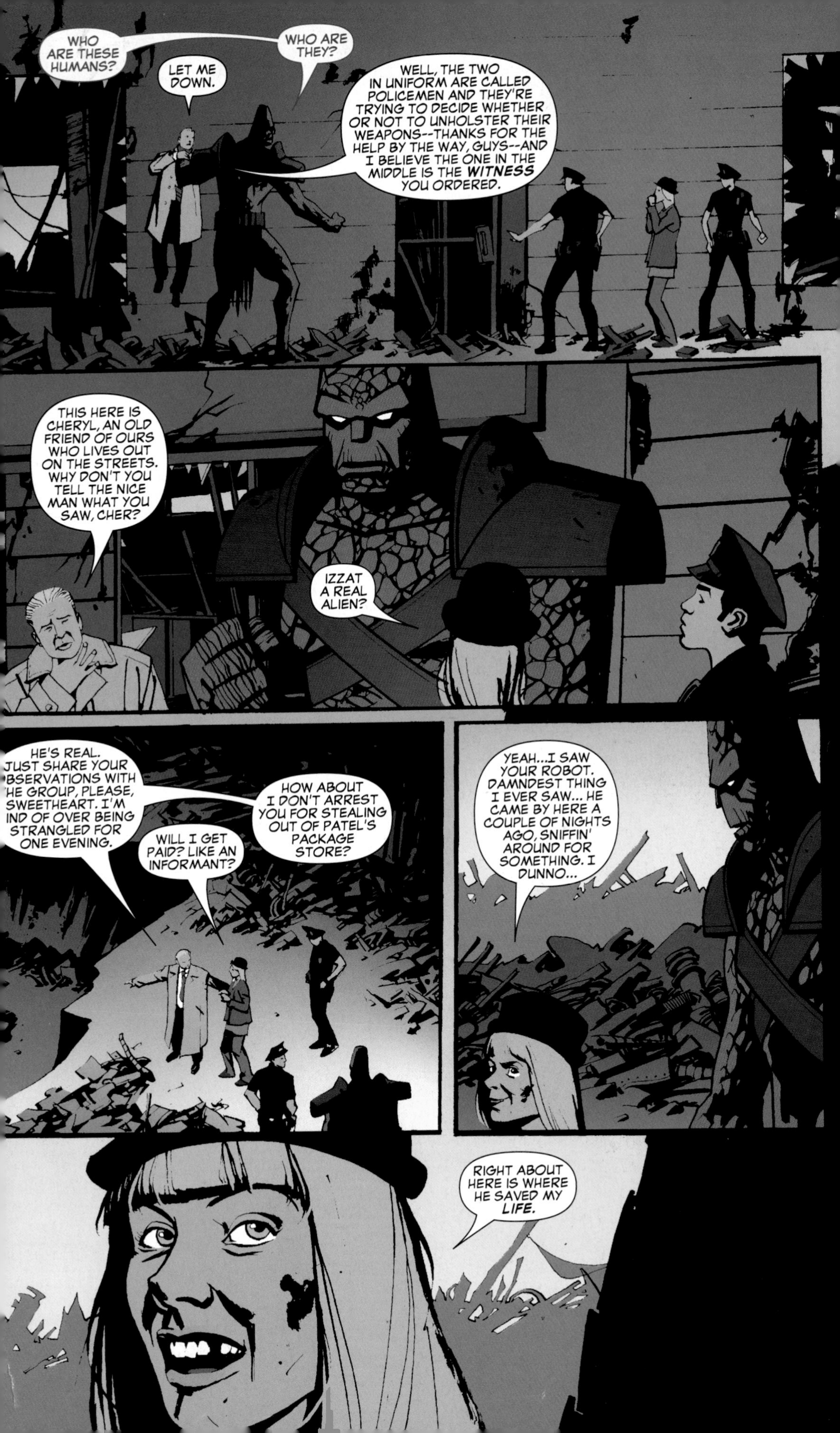
WHO ARE THESE HUMANS?
WHO ARE THEY?
LET ME DOWN.
WELL, THE TWO IN UNIFORM ARE CALLED POLICEMEN AND THEY'RE TRYING TO DECIDE WHETHER OR NOT TO UNHOLSTER THEIR WEAPONS--THANKS FOR THE HELP BY THE WAY, GUYS--AND I BELIEVE THE ONE IN THE MIDDLE IS THE **WITNESS** YOU ORDERED.
THIS HERE IS CHERYL, AN OLD FRIEND OF OURS WHO LIVES OUT ON THE STREETS. WHY DON'T YOU TELL THE NICE MAN WHAT YOU SAW, CHER?
IZZAT A REAL ALIEN?
HE'S REAL. JUST SHARE YOUR BSERVATIONS WITH HE GROUP, PLEASE, SWEETHEART. I'M IND OF OVER BEING STRANGLED FOR ONE EVENING.
WILL I GET PAID? LIKE AN INFORMANT?
HOW ABOUT I DON'T ARREST YOU FOR STEALING OUT OF PATEL'S PACKAGE STORE?
YEAH...I SAW YOUR ROBOT. DAMNDEST THING I EVER SAW... HE CAME BY HERE A COUPLE OF NIGHTS AGO, SNIFFIN' AROUND FOR SOMETHING. I DUNNO...
RIGHT ABOUT HERE IS WHERE HE SAVED MY ***LIFE.***

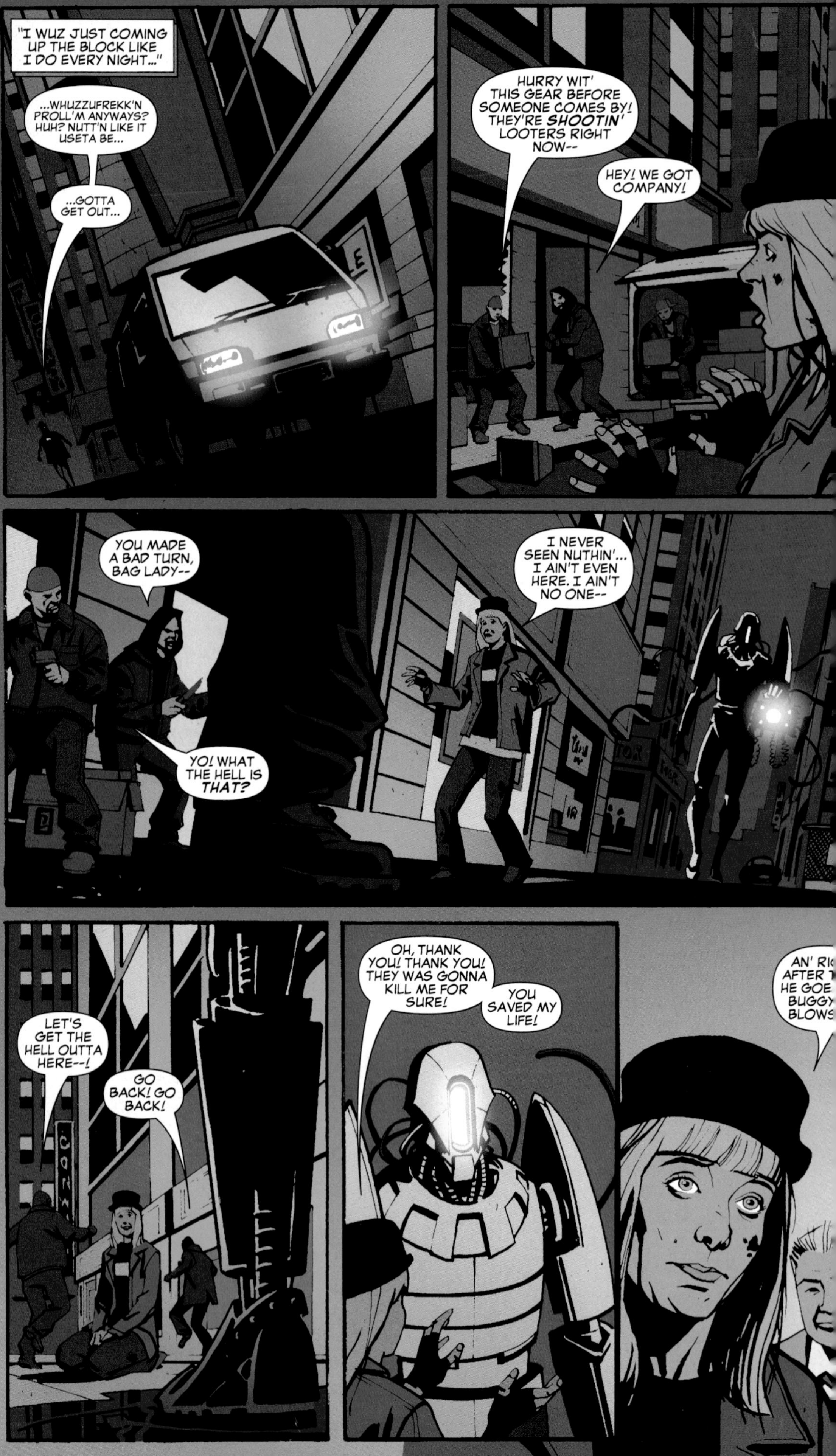
"I WUZ JUST COMING UP THE BLOCK LIKE I DO EVERY NIGHT..."
...WHUZZUFREKK'N PROLL'M ANYWAYS? HUH? NUTT'N LIKE IT USETA BE...
...GOTTA GET OUT...
HURRY WIT' THIS GEAR BEFORE SOMEONE COMES BY! THEY'RE SHOOTIN' LOOTERS RIGHT NOW--
HEY! WE GOT COMPANY!
YOU MADE A BAD TURN, BAG LADY--
YO! WHAT THE HELL IS THAT?
I NEVER SEEN NUTHIN'... I AIN'T EVEN HERE. I AIN'T NO ONE--
LET'S GET THE HELL OUTTA HERE--!
GO BACK! GO BACK!
OH, THANK YOU! THANK YOU! THEY WAS GONNA KILL ME FOR SURE!
YOU SAVED MY LIFE!
AN' RI
AFTER
HE GOE
BUGGY
BLOWS

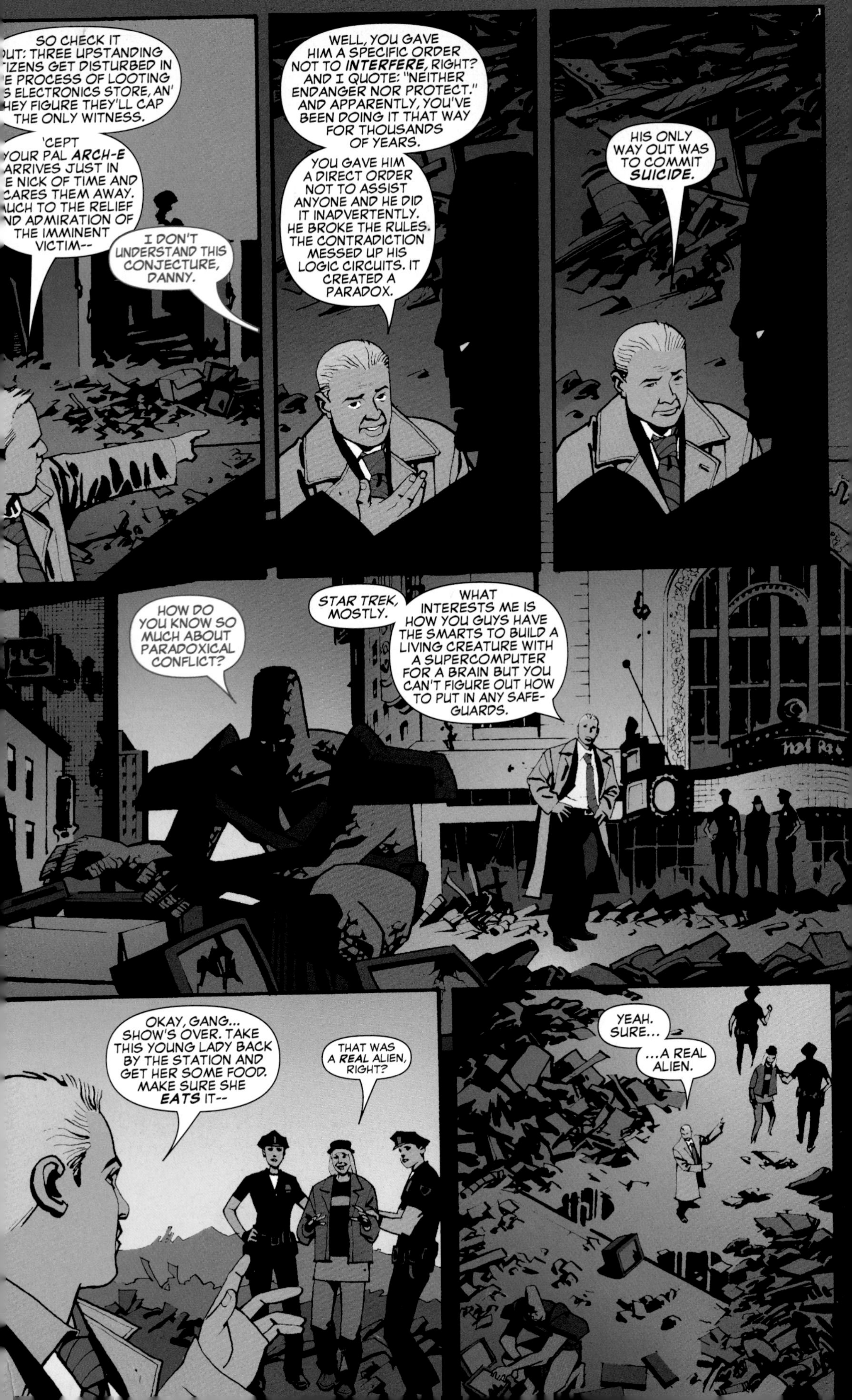
SO CHECK IT OUT: THREE UPSTANDING CITIZENS GET DISTURBED IN THE PROCESS OF LOOTING THIS ELECTRONICS STORE, AN' THEY FIGURE THEY'LL CAP THE ONLY WITNESS.
'CEPT YOUR PAL ARCH-E ARRIVES JUST IN THE NICK OF TIME AND SCARES THEM AWAY. MUCH TO THE RELIEF AND ADMIRATION OF THE IMMINENT VICTIM--
I DON'T UNDERSTAND THIS CONJECTURE, DANNY.
WELL, YOU GAVE HIM A SPECIFIC ORDER NOT TO INTERFERE, RIGHT? AND I QUOTE: "NEITHER ENDANGER NOR PROTECT." AND APPARENTLY, YOU'VE BEEN DOING IT THAT WAY FOR THOUSANDS OF YEARS.
YOU GAVE HIM A DIRECT ORDER NOT TO ASSIST ANYONE AND HE DID IT INADVERTENTLY. HE BROKE THE RULES. THE CONTRADICTION MESSED UP HIS LOGIC CIRCUITS. IT CREATED A PARADOX.
HIS ONLY WAY OUT WAS TO COMMIT SUICIDE.
HOW DO YOU KNOW SO MUCH ABOUT PARADOXICAL CONFLICT?
STAR TREK, MOSTLY.
WHAT INTERESTS ME IS HOW YOU GUYS HAVE THE SMARTS TO BUILD A LIVING CREATURE WITH A SUPERCOMPUTER FOR A BRAIN BUT YOU CAN'T FIGURE OUT HOW TO PUT IN ANY SAFE-GUARDS.
OKAY, GANG... SHOW'S OVER. TAKE THIS YOUNG LADY BACK BY THE STATION AND GET HER SOME FOOD. MAKE SURE SHE EATS IT--
THAT WAS A REAL ALIEN, RIGHT?
YEAH. SURE...
...A REAL ALIEN.

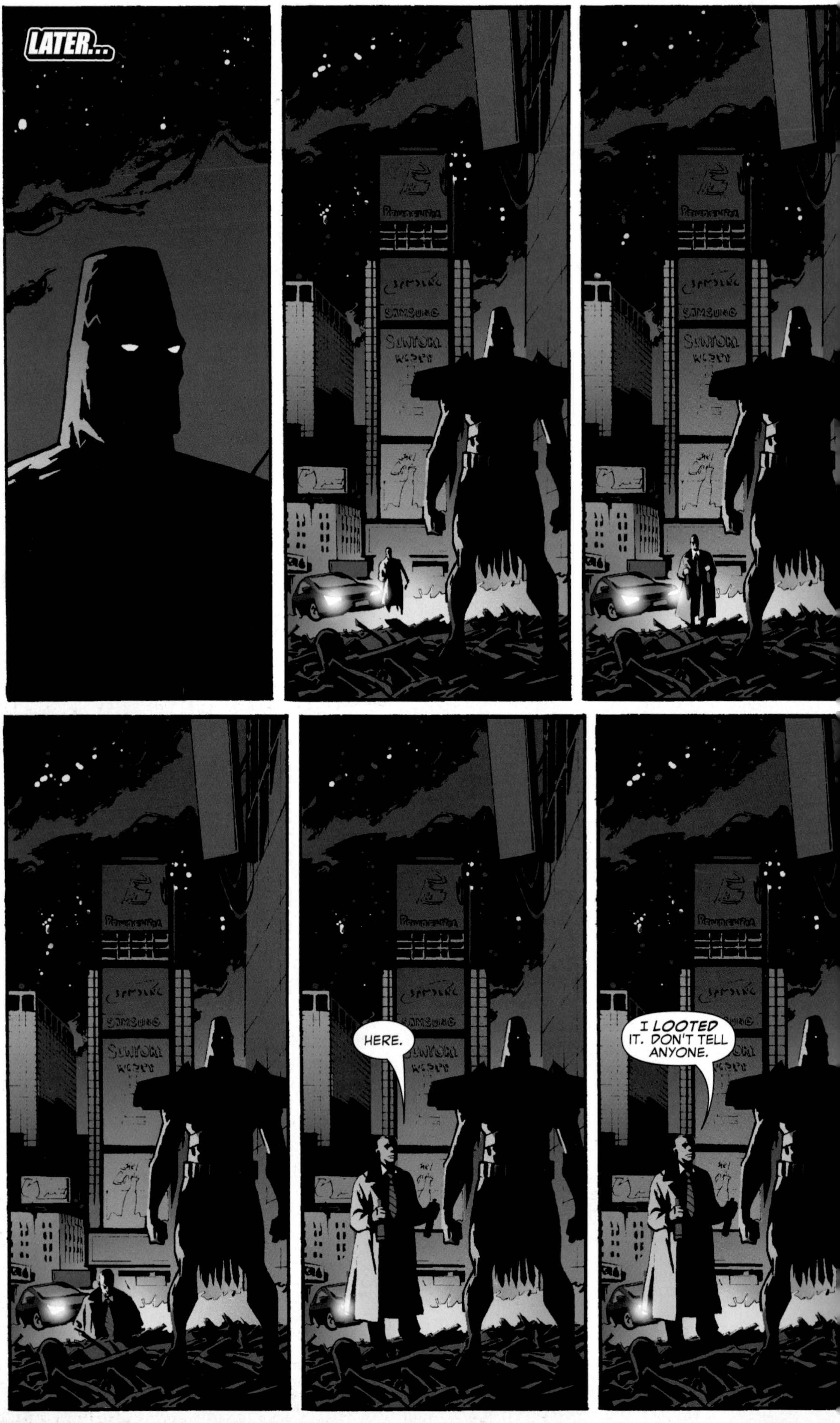
LATER...
HERE.
I LOOTED IT. DON'T TELL ANYONE.

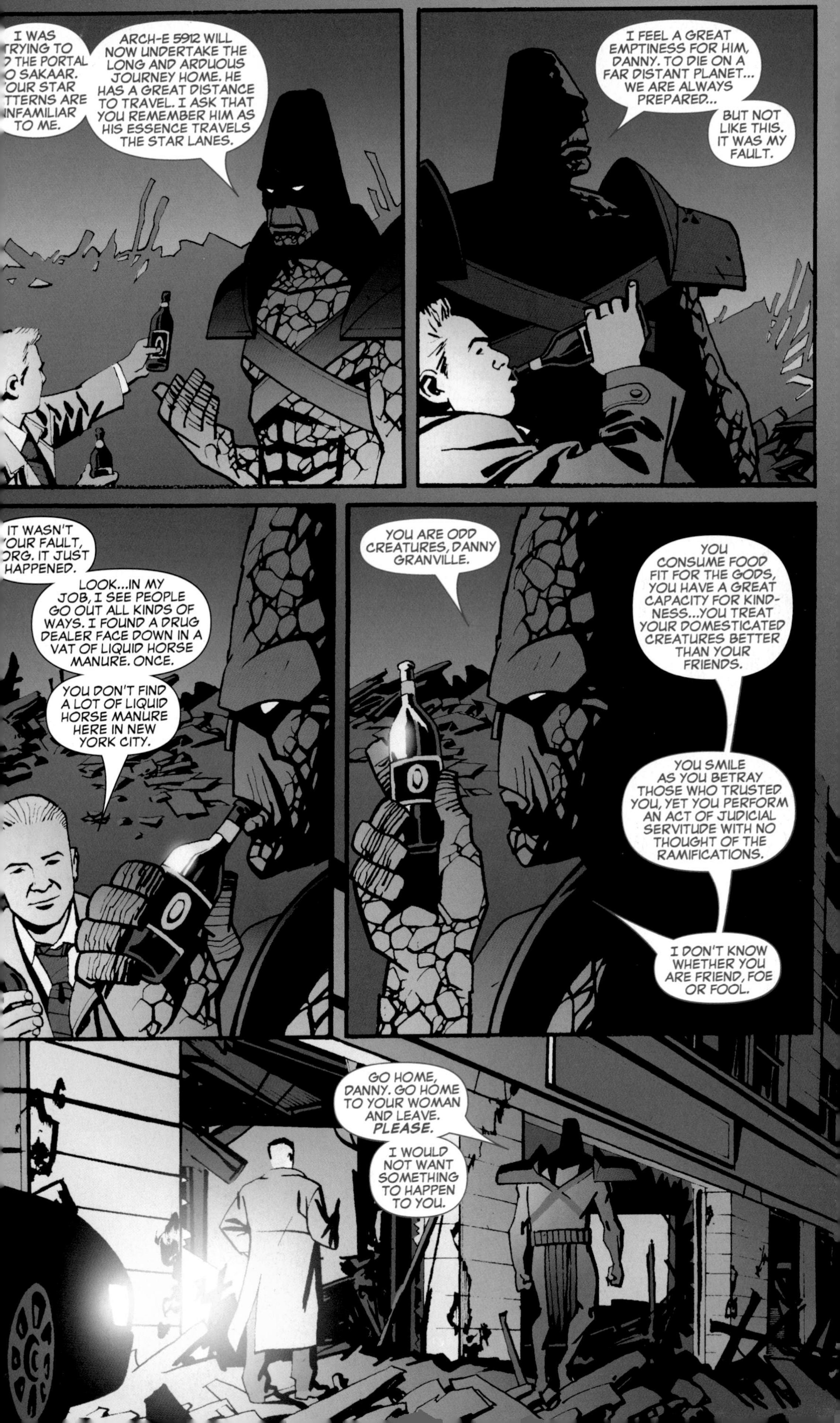
I WAS TRYING TO D THE PORTAL O SAKAAR. OUR STAR TTERNS ARE INFAMILIAR TO ME.
ARCH-E 5912 WILL NOW UNDERTAKE THE LONG AND ARDUOUS JOURNEY HOME. HE HAS A GREAT DISTANCE TO TRAVEL. I ASK THAT YOU REMEMBER HIM AS HIS ESSENCE TRAVELS THE STAR LANES.
I FEEL A GREAT EMPTINESS FOR HIM, DANNY. TO DIE ON A FAR DISTANT PLANET... WE ARE ALWAYS PREPARED...
BUT NOT LIKE THIS. IT WAS MY FAULT.
IT WASN'T OUR FAULT, ORG. IT JUST HAPPENED.
LOOK...IN MY JOB, I SEE PEOPLE GO OUT ALL KINDS OF WAYS. I FOUND A DRUG DEALER FACE DOWN IN A VAT OF LIQUID HORSE MANURE. ONCE.
YOU DON'T FIND A LOT OF LIQUID HORSE MANURE HERE IN NEW YORK CITY.
YOU ARE ODD CREATURES, DANNY GRANVILLE.
YOU CONSUME FOOD FIT FOR THE GODS, YOU HAVE A GREAT CAPACITY FOR KIND-NESS...YOU TREAT YOUR DOMESTICATED CREATURES BETTER THAN YOUR FRIENDS.
YOU SMILE AS YOU BETRAY THOSE WHO TRUSTED YOU, YET YOU PERFORM AN ACT OF JUDICIAL SERVITUDE WITH NO THOUGHT OF THE RAMIFICATIONS.
I DON'T KNOW WHETHER YOU ARE FRIEND, FOE OR FOOL.
GO HOME, DANNY. GO HOME TO YOUR WOMAN AND LEAVE. ***PLEASE.***
I WOULD NOT WANT SOMETHING TO HAPPEN TO YOU.

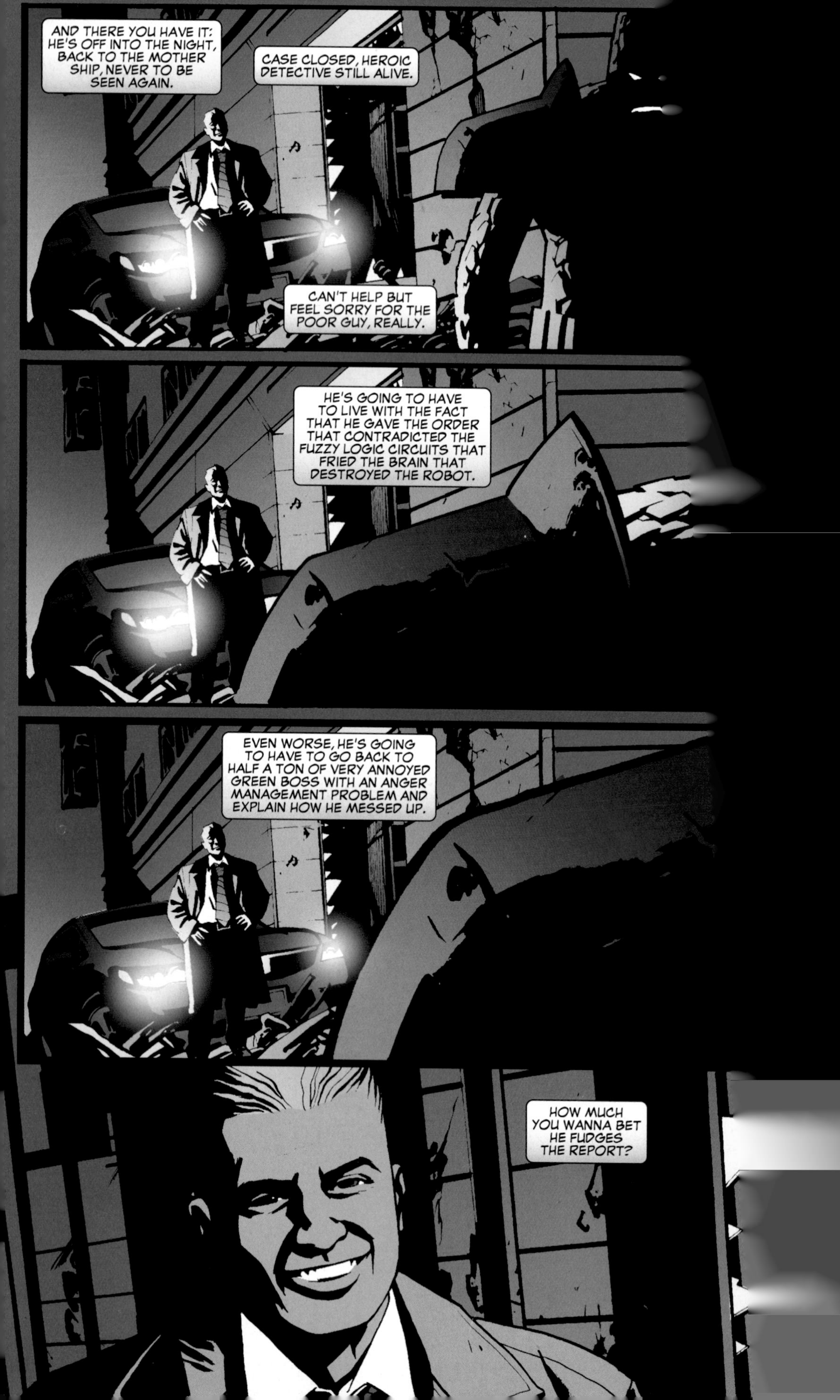
AND THERE YOU HAVE IT: HE'S OFF INTO THE NIGHT, BACK TO THE MOTHER SHIP, NEVER TO BE SEEN AGAIN.
CASE CLOSED, HEROIC DETECTIVE STILL ALIVE.
CAN'T HELP BUT FEEL SORRY FOR THE POOR GUY, REALLY.
HE'S GOING TO HAVE TO LIVE WITH THE FACT THAT HE GAVE THE ORDER THAT CONTRADICTED THE FUZZY LOGIC CIRCUITS THAT FRIED THE BRAIN THAT DESTROYED THE ROBOT.
EVEN WORSE, HE'S GOING TO HAVE TO GO BACK TO HALF A TON OF VERY ANNOYED GREEN BOSS WITH AN ANGER MANAGEMENT PROBLEM AND EXPLAIN HOW HE MESSED UP.
HOW MUCH YOU WANNA BET HE FUDGES THE REPORT?

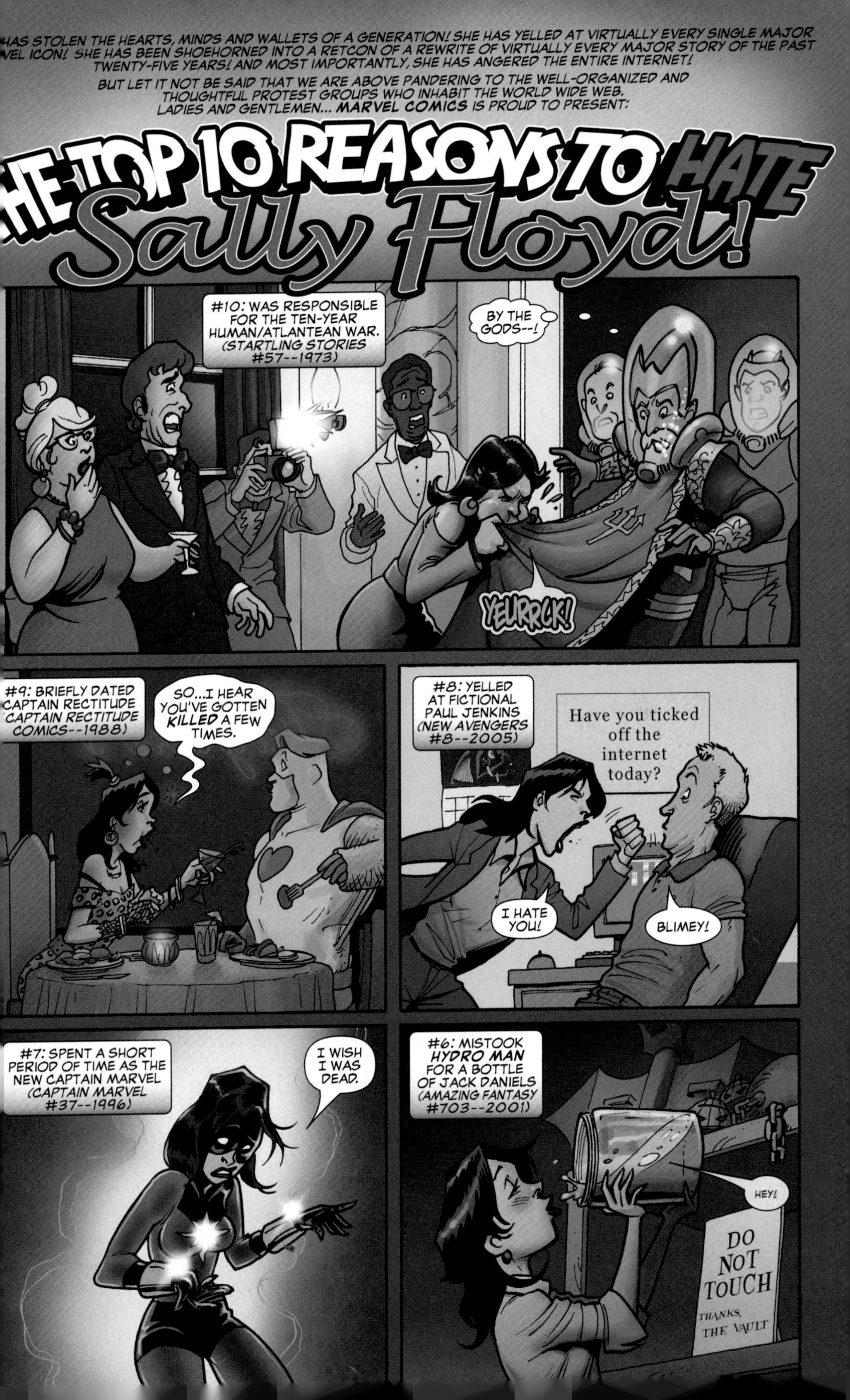
HAS STOLEN THE HEARTS, MINDS AND WALLETS OF A GENERATION! SHE HAS YELLED AT VIRTUALLY EVERY SINGLE MAJOR
VEL ICON! SHE HAS BEEN SHOEHORNED INTO A RETCON OF A REWRITE OF VIRTUALLY EVERY MAJOR STORY OF THE PAST TWENTY-FIVE YEARS! AND MOST IMPORTANTLY, SHE HAS ANGERED THE ENTIRE INTERNET!
BUT LET IT NOT BE SAID THAT WE ARE ABOVE PANDERING TO THE WELL-ORGANIZED AND THOUGHTFUL PROTEST GROUPS WHO INHABIT THE WORLD WIDE WEB. LADIES AND GENTLEMEN... MARVEL COMICS IS PROUD TO PRESENT:
HE TOP 10 REASONS TO HATE Sally Floyd!
#10: WAS RESPONSIBLE FOR THE TEN-YEAR HUMAN/ATLANTEAN WAR. (STARTLING STORIES #57--1973)
BY THE GODS--!
YEURRCK!
#9: BRIEFLY DATED CAPTAIN RECTITUDE (CAPTAIN RECTITUDE COMICS--1988)
SO...I HEAR YOU'VE GOTTEN KILLED A FEW TIMES.
#8: YELLED AT FICTIONAL PAUL JENKINS (NEW AVENGERS #8--2005)
Have you ticked off the internet today?
I HATE YOU!
BLIMEY!
#7: SPENT A SHORT PERIOD OF TIME AS THE NEW CAPTAIN MARVEL (CAPTAIN MARVEL #37--1996)
I WISH I WAS DEAD.
#6: MISTOOK HYDRO MAN FOR A BOTTLE OF JACK DANIELS (AMAZING FANTASY #703--2001)
HEY!
DO NOT TOUCH
THANKS, THE VAULT

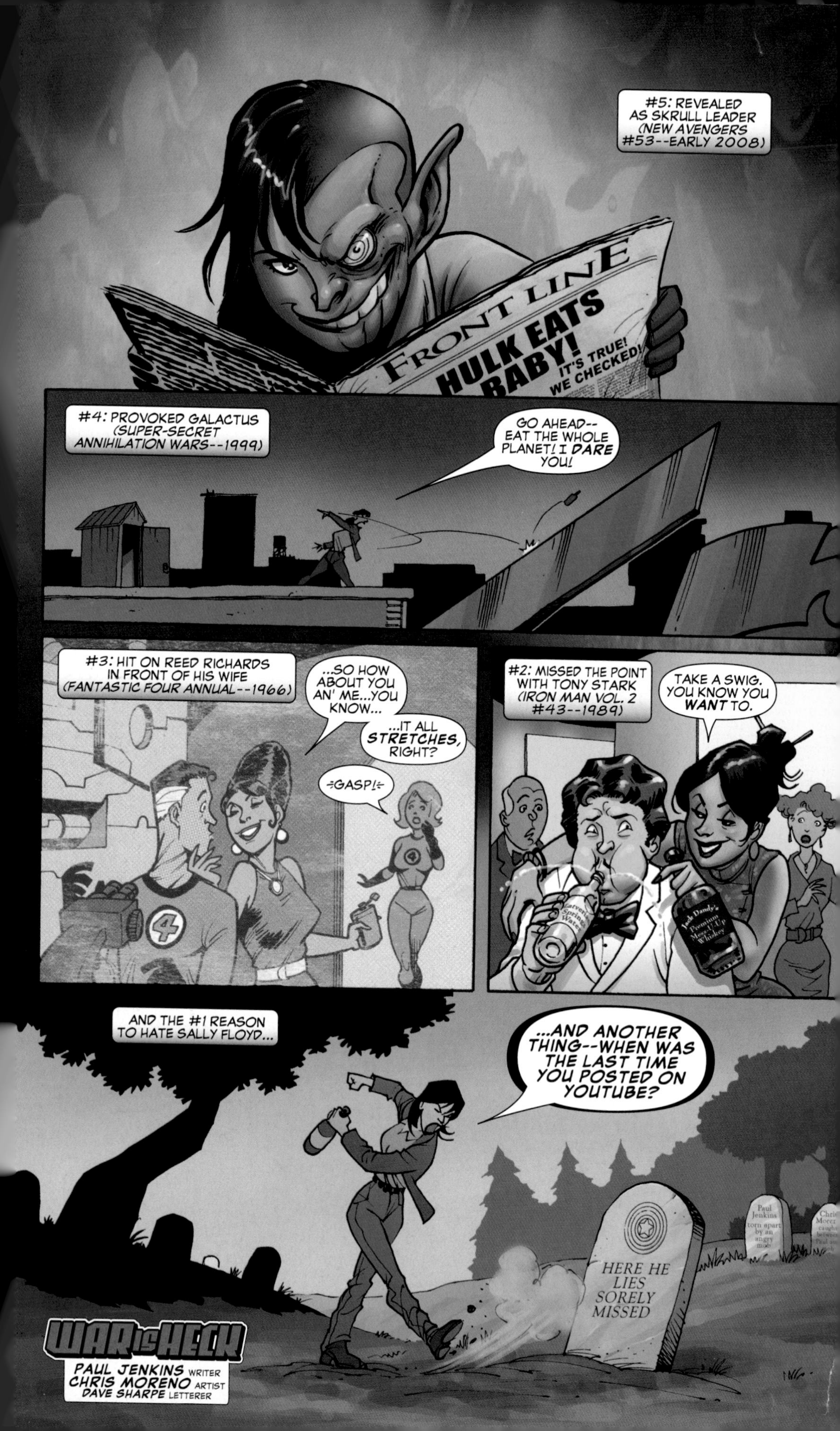
#5: REVEALED AS SKRULL LEADER (NEW AVENGERS #53--EARLY 2008)
FRONT LINE
HULK EATS BABY!
IT'S TRUE! WE CHECKED!
#4: PROVOKED GALACTUS (SUPER-SECRET ANNIHILATION WARS--1999)
GO AHEAD-- EAT THE WHOLE PLANET! I DARE YOU!
#3: HIT ON REED RICHARDS IN FRONT OF HIS WIFE (FANTASTIC FOUR ANNUAL--1966)
...SO HOW ABOUT YOU AN' ME...YOU KNOW...
...IT ALL STRETCHES, RIGHT?
=GASP!=
#2: MISSED THE POINT WITH TONY STARK (IRON MAN VOL. 2 #43--1989)
TAKE A SWIG. YOU KNOW YOU WANT TO.
Jack Dandy's Premium Mess-U-Up Whiskey
AND THE #1 REASON TO HATE SALLY FLOYD...
...AND ANOTHER THING--WHEN WAS THE LAST TIME YOU POSTED ON YOUTUBE?
HERE HE LIES SORELY MISSED
WAR IS HECK
PAUL JENKINS WRITER
CHRIS MORENO ARTIST
DAVE SHARPE LETTERER

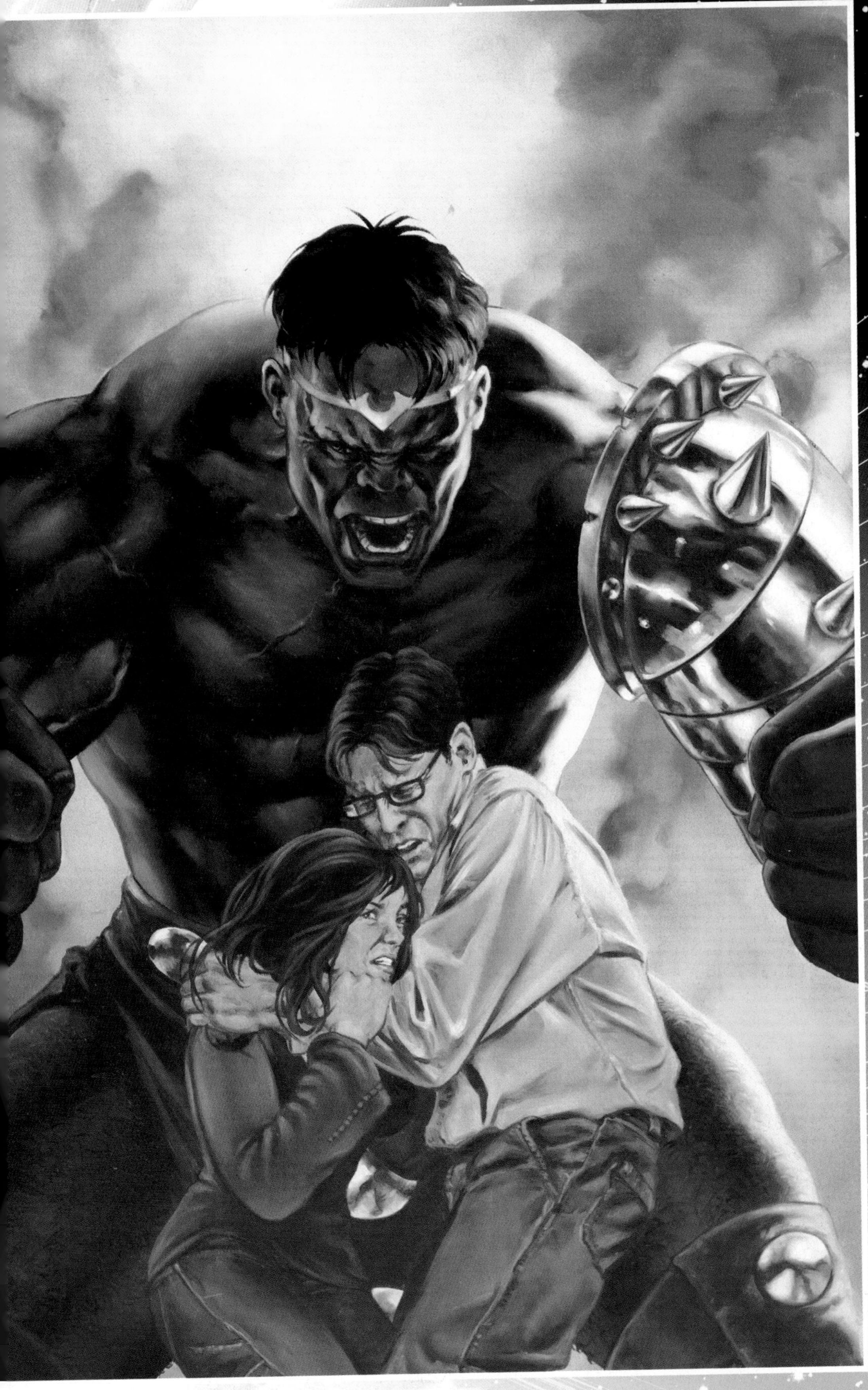

WORLD WAR HULK: FRONT LINE #6

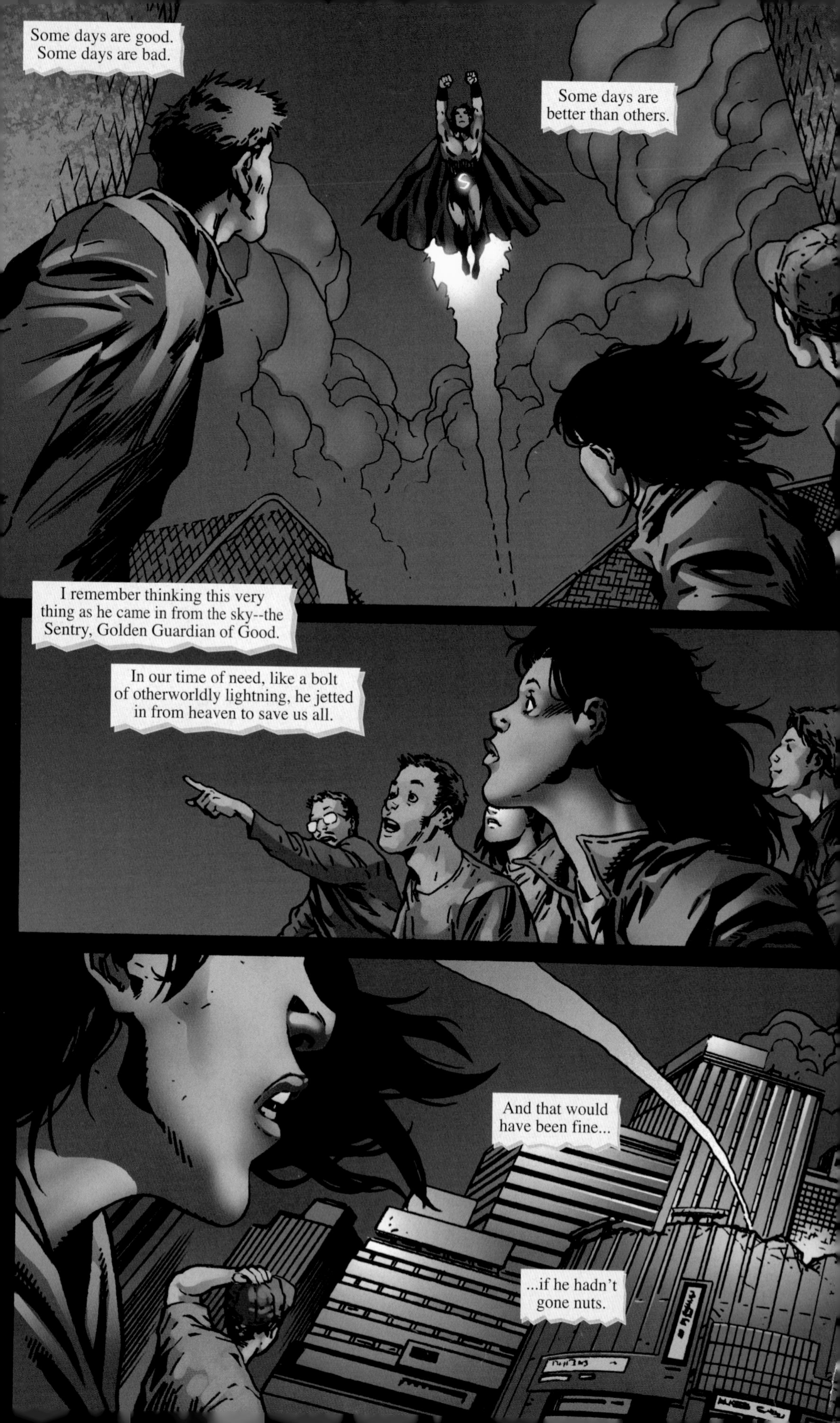
Some days are good. Some days are bad.
Some days are better than others.
I remember thinking this very thing as he came in from the sky--the Sentry, Golden Guardian of Good.
In our time of need, like a bolt of otherworldly lightning, he jetted in from heaven to save us all.
And that would have been fine...
...if he hadn't gone nuts.

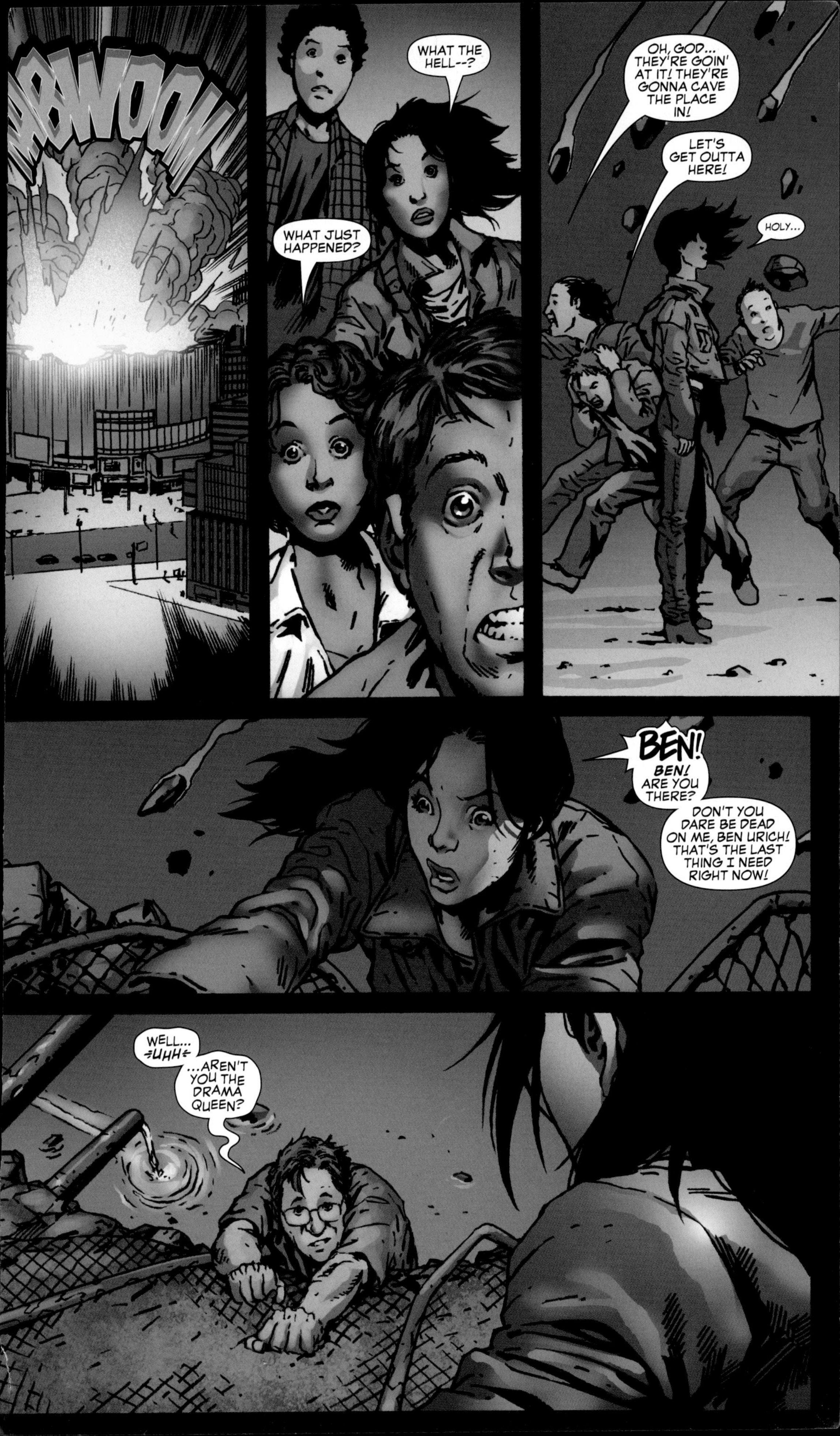
BWOOM
WHAT THE HELL--?
WHAT JUST HAPPENED?
OH, GOD... THEY'RE GOIN' AT IT! THEY'RE GONNA CAVE THE PLACE IN!
LET'S GET OUTTA HERE!
HOLY...
BEN! BEN! ARE YOU THERE?
DON'T YOU DARE BE DEAD ON ME, BEN URICH! THAT'S THE LAST THING I NEED RIGHT NOW!
WELL... UHH ...AREN'T YOU THE DRAMA QUEEN?

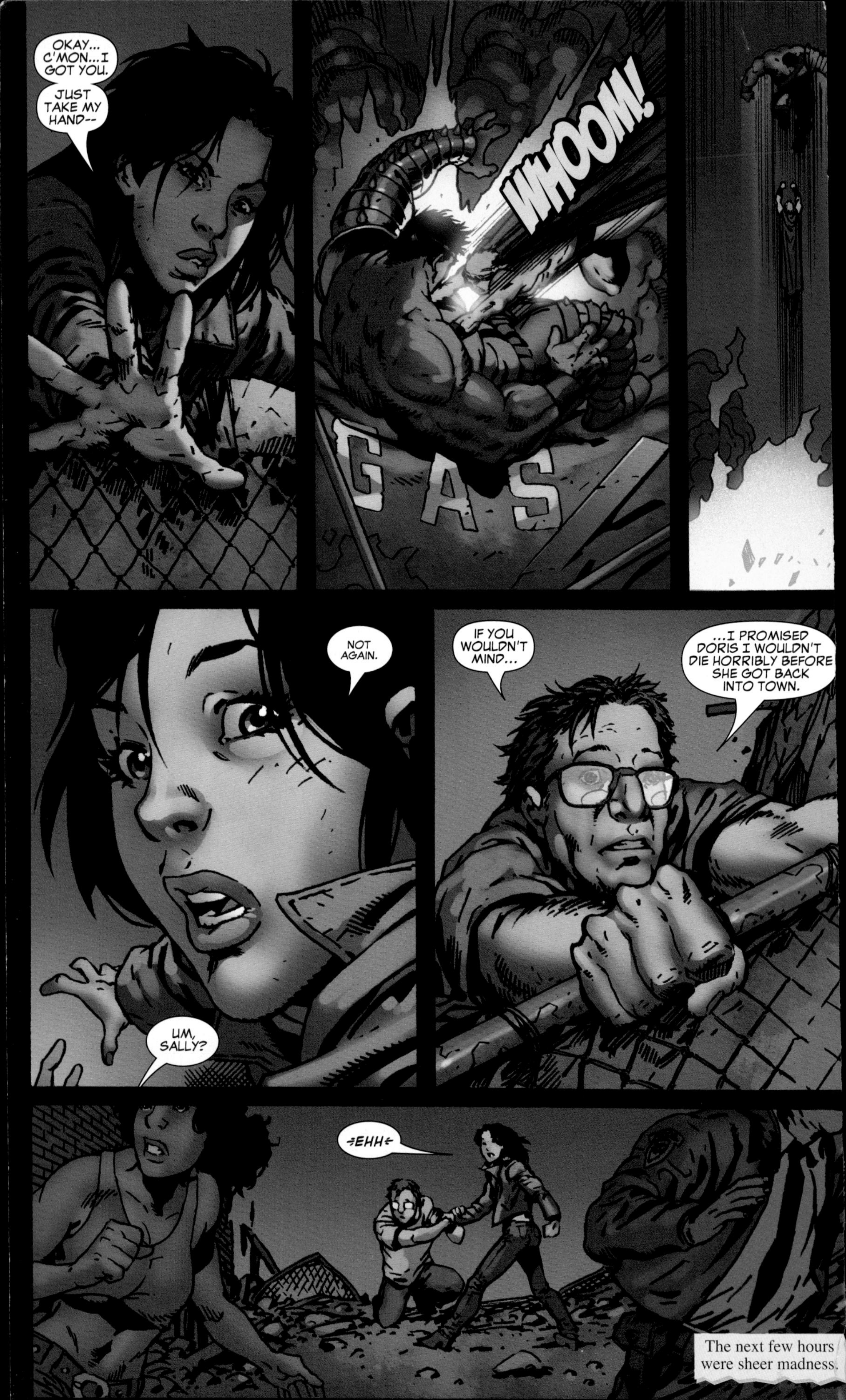
OKAY... C'MON...I GOT YOU.
JUST TAKE MY HAND--
WHOOM!
NOT AGAIN.
UM, SALLY?
IF YOU WOULDN'T MIND...
...I PROMISED DORIS I WOULDN'T DIE HORRIBLY BEFORE SHE GOT BACK INTO TOWN.
EHH
The next few hours were sheer madness.

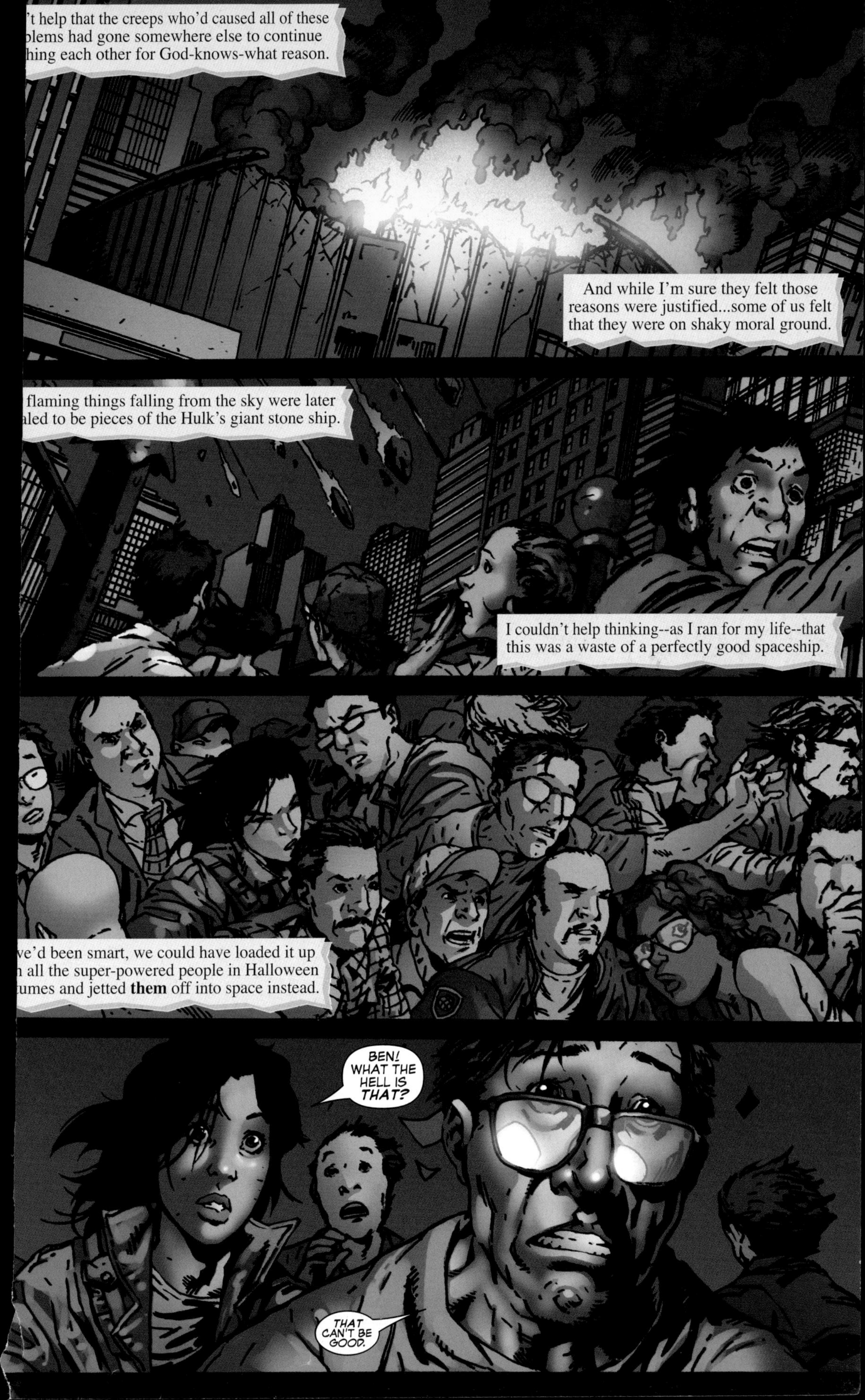
't help that the creeps who'd caused all of these
blems had gone somewhere else to continue
hing each other for God-knows-what reason.
And while I'm sure they felt those reasons were justified...some of us felt that they were on shaky moral ground.
flaming things falling from the sky were later
aled to be pieces of the Hulk's giant stone ship.
I couldn't help thinking--as I ran for my life--that this was a waste of a perfectly good spaceship.
ve'd been smart, we could have loaded it up
n all the super-powered people in Halloween
tumes and jetted **them** off into space instead.
BEN! WHAT THE HELL IS *THAT?*
THAT CAN'T BE GOOD.

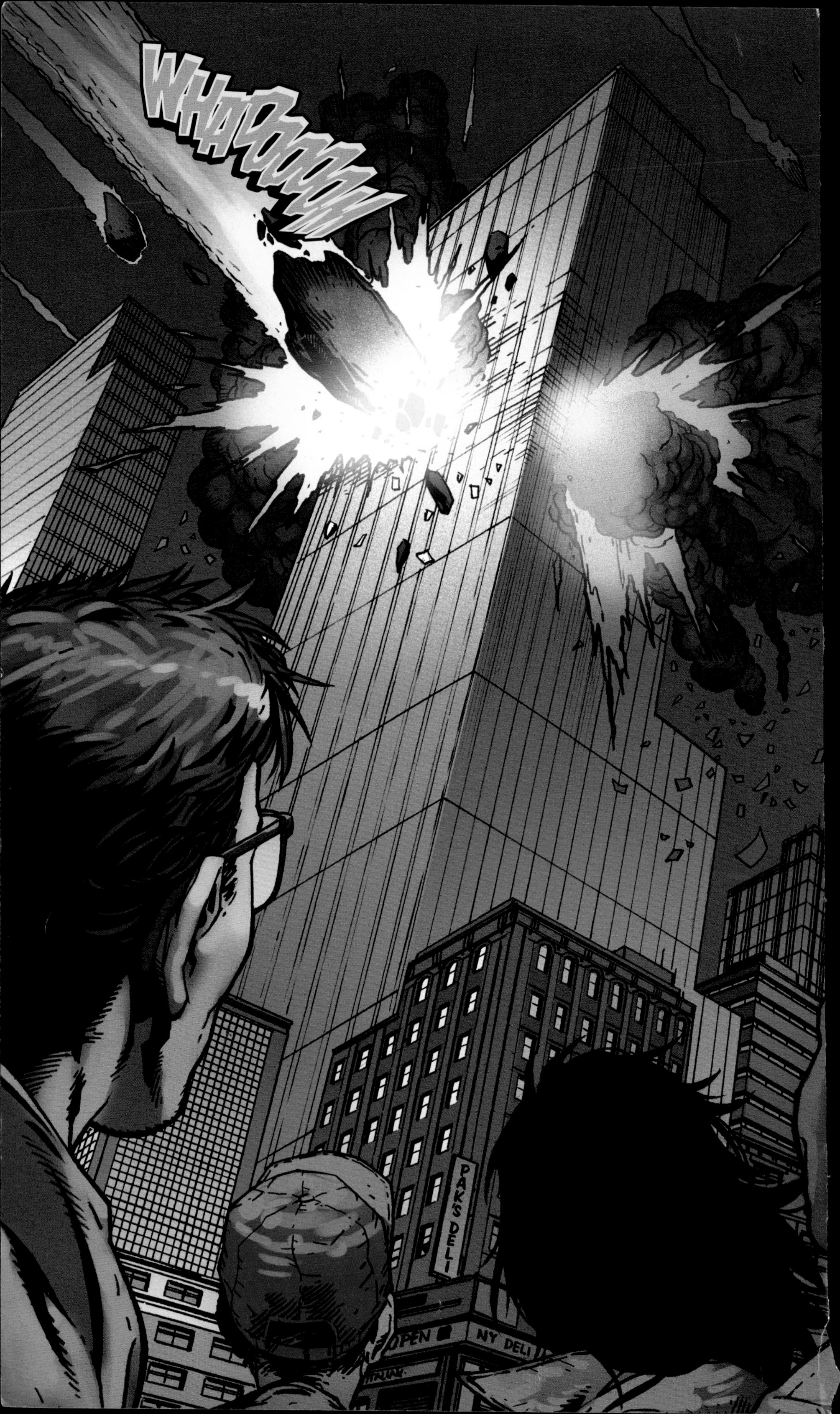
WHADOOOOM
PAK'S DELI
OPEN
NY DELI

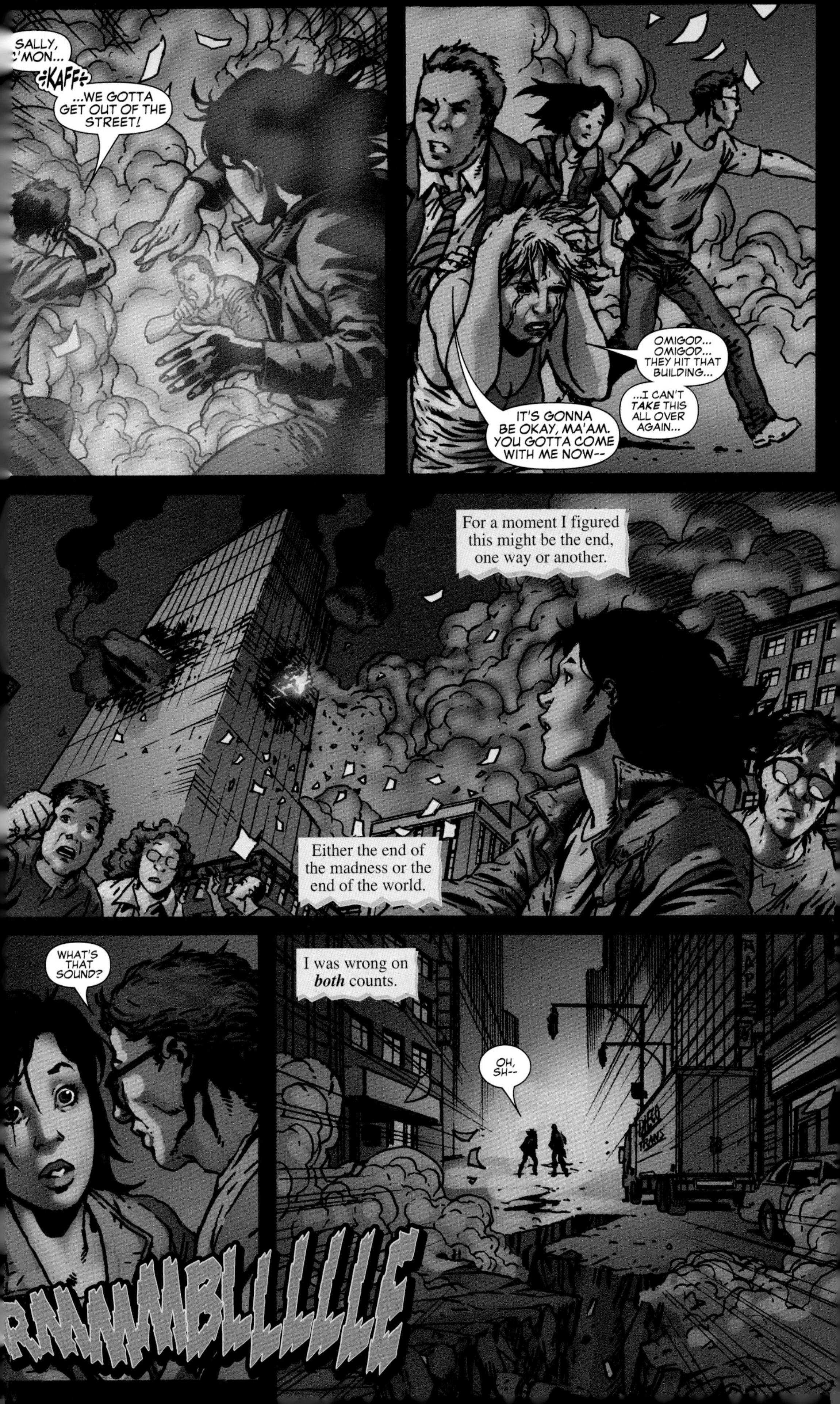
SALLY, C'MON...
KAFF
...WE GOTTA GET OUT OF THE STREET!
OMIGOD... OMIGOD... THEY HIT THAT BUILDING...
...I CAN'T TAKE THIS ALL OVER AGAIN...
IT'S GONNA BE OKAY, MA'AM. YOU GOTTA COME WITH ME NOW--
For a moment I figured this might be the end, one way or another.
Either the end of the madness or the end of the world.
WHAT'S THAT SOUND?
RMMMBLLLLLE
I was wrong on both counts.
OH, SH--

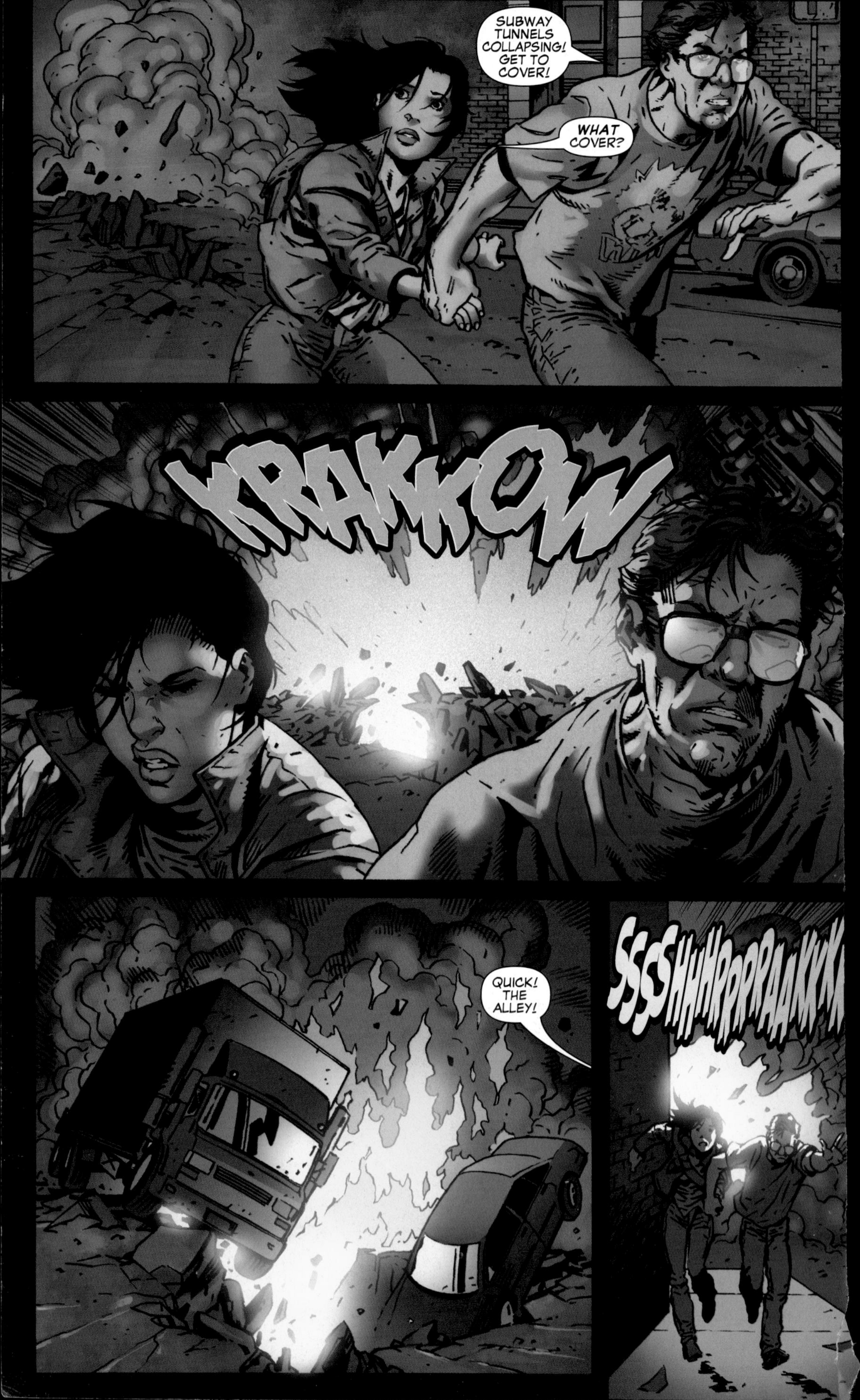
SUBWAY TUNNELS COLLAPSING! GET TO COVER!
WHAT COVER?
KRAKKOW
QUICK! THE ALLEY!
SSSHHHRRRRAAKKKK

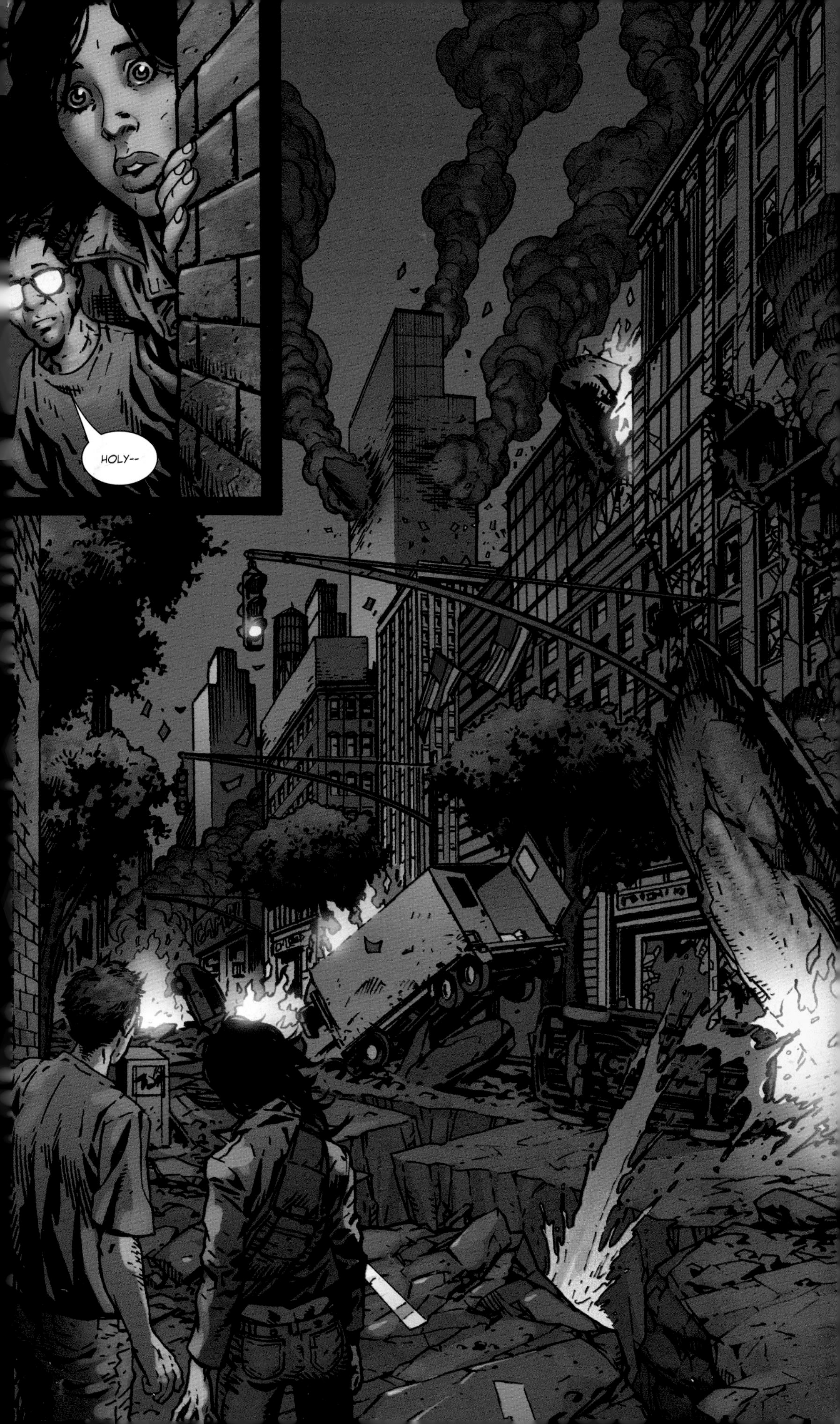
HOLY--

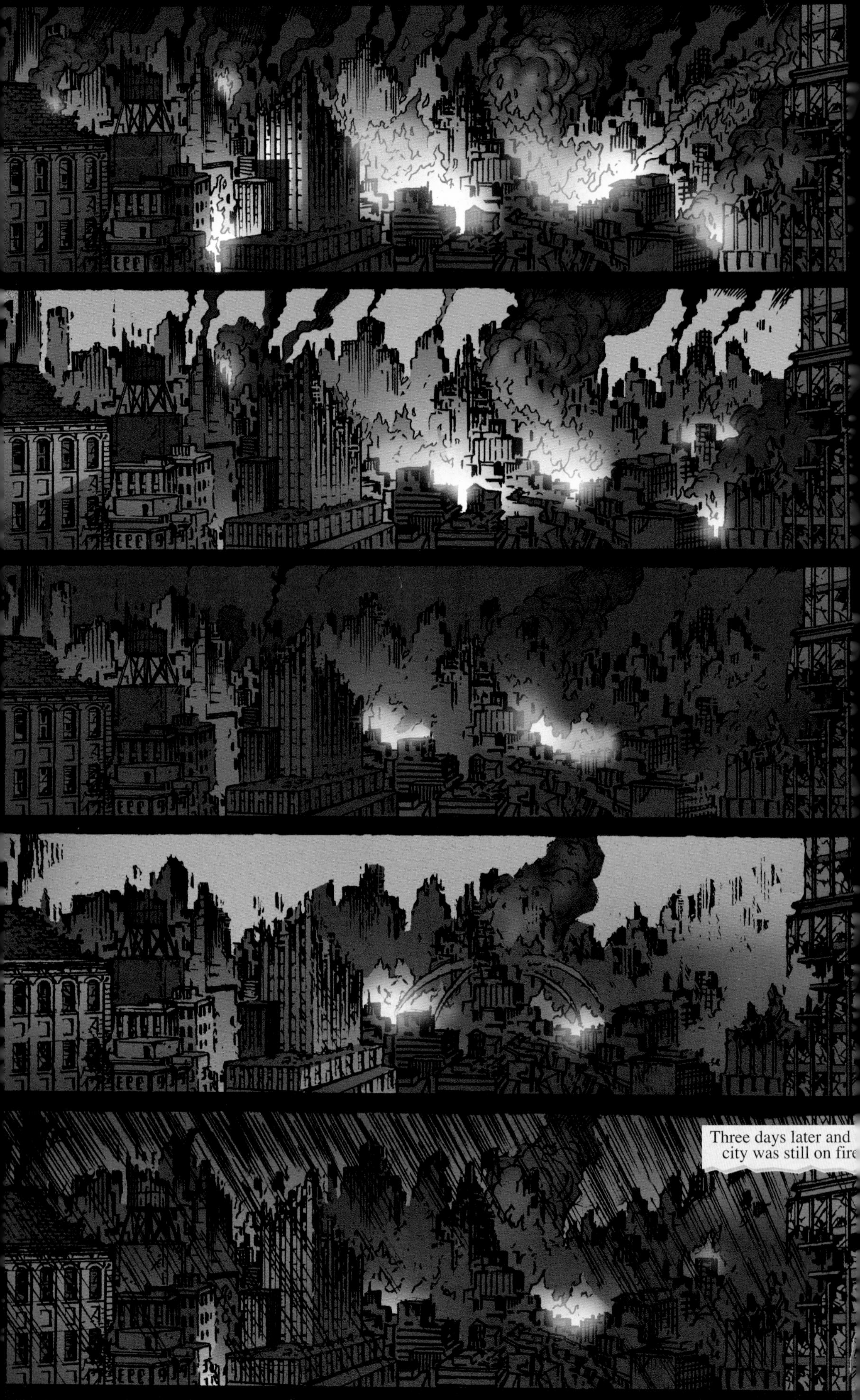
Three days later and
city was still on fire

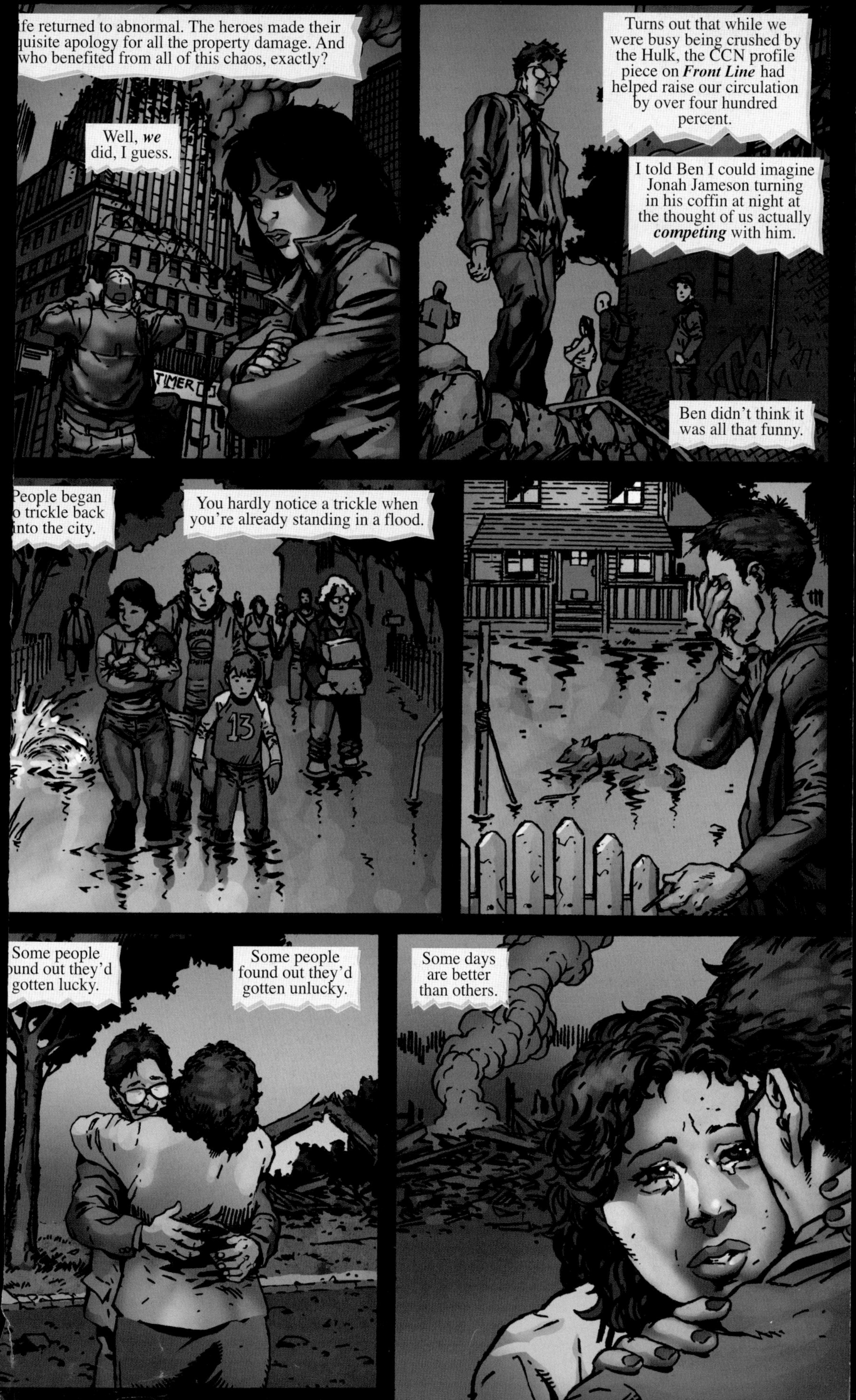
ife returned to abnormal. The heroes made their
quisite apology for all the property damage. And
who benefited from all of this chaos, exactly?
Well, *we* did, I guess.
TIMER
Turns out that while we were busy being crushed by the Hulk, the CCN profile piece on ***Front Line*** had helped raise our circulation by over four hundred percent.
I told Ben I could imagine Jonah Jameson turning in his coffin at night at the thought of us actually ***competing*** with him.
Ben didn't think it was all that funny.
People began
o trickle back
into the city.
You hardly notice a trickle when you're already standing in a flood.
13
Some people
ound out they'd
gotten lucky.
Some people found out they'd gotten unlucky.
Some days are better than others.

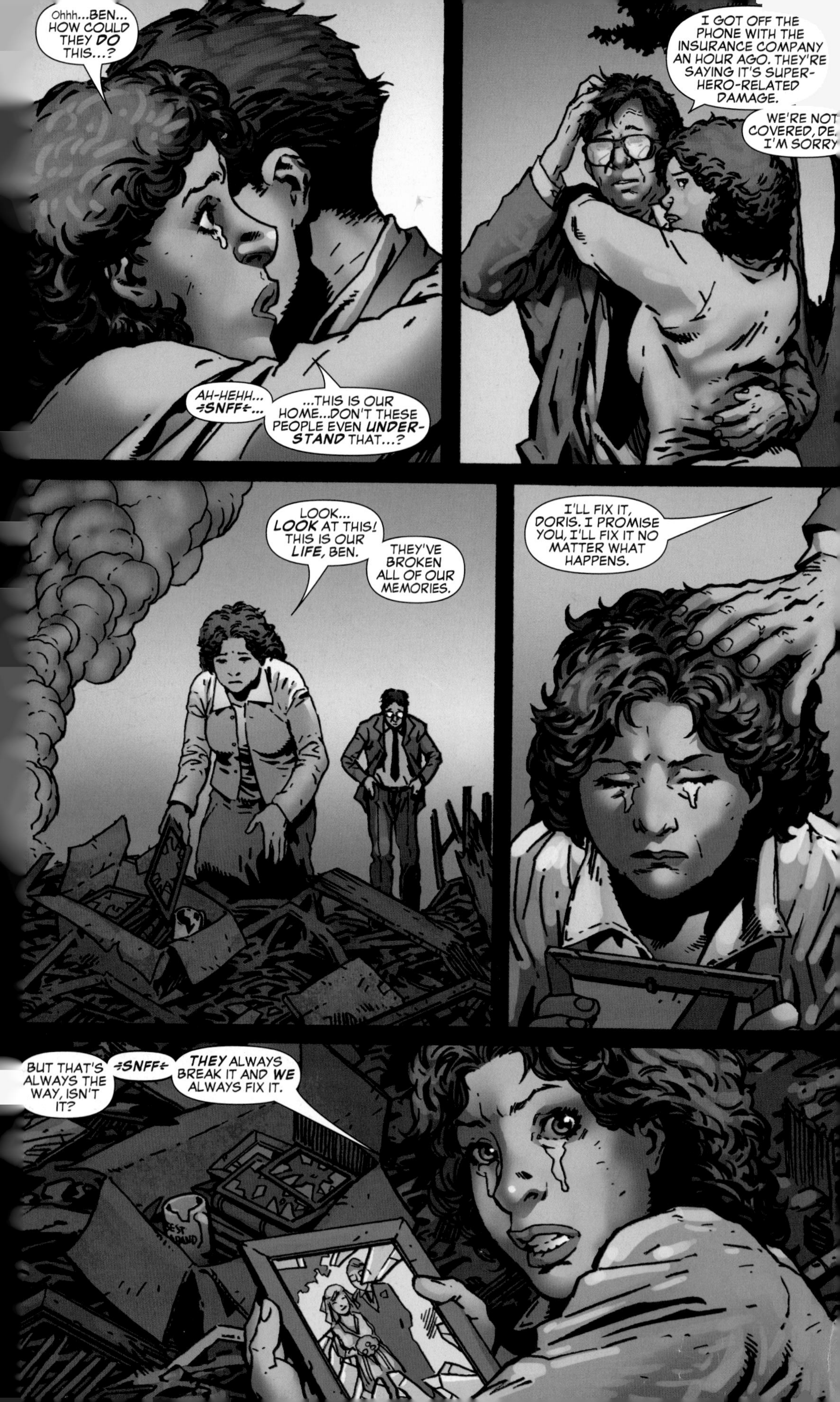
Ohhh...BEN... HOW COULD THEY DO THIS...?
AH-HEHH... SNFF...
...THIS IS OUR HOME...DON'T THESE PEOPLE EVEN UNDERSTAND THAT...?
I GOT OFF THE PHONE WITH THE INSURANCE COMPANY AN HOUR AGO. THEY'RE SAYING IT'S SUPER-HERO-RELATED DAMAGE.
WE'RE NOT COVERED, DE. I'M SORRY
LOOK... LOOK AT THIS! THIS IS OUR LIFE, BEN.
THEY'VE BROKEN ALL OF OUR MEMORIES.
I'LL FIX IT, DORIS. I PROMISE YOU, I'LL FIX IT NO MATTER WHAT HAPPENS.
BUT THAT'S ALWAYS THE WAY, ISN'T IT?
SNFF
THEY ALWAYS BREAK IT AND WE ALWAYS FIX IT.

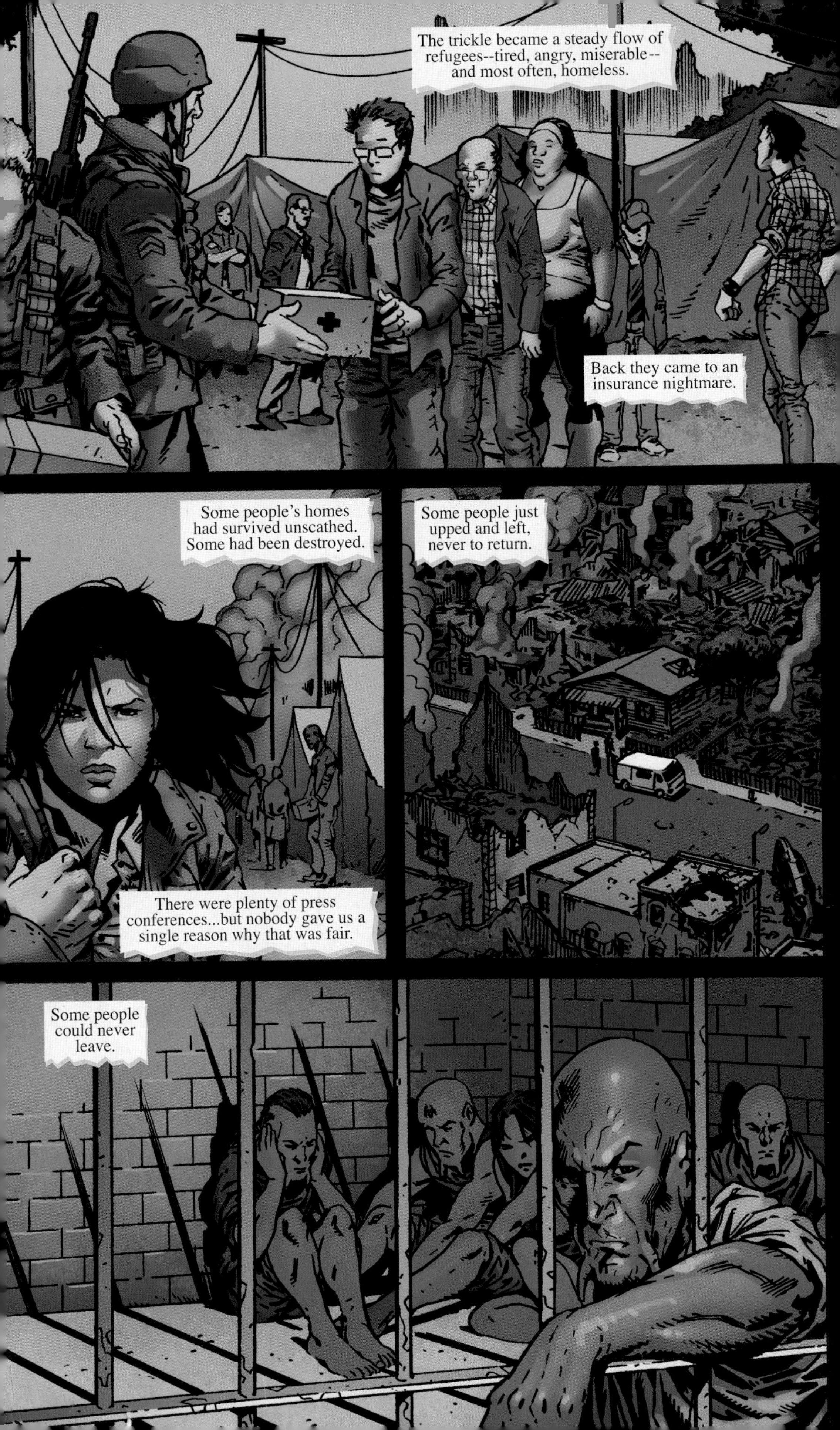
The trickle became a steady flow of refugees--tired, angry, miserable--and most often, homeless.
Back they came to an insurance nightmare.
Some people's homes had survived unscathed. Some had been destroyed.
There were plenty of press conferences...but nobody gave us a single reason why that was fair.
Some people just upped and left, never to return.
Some people could never leave.

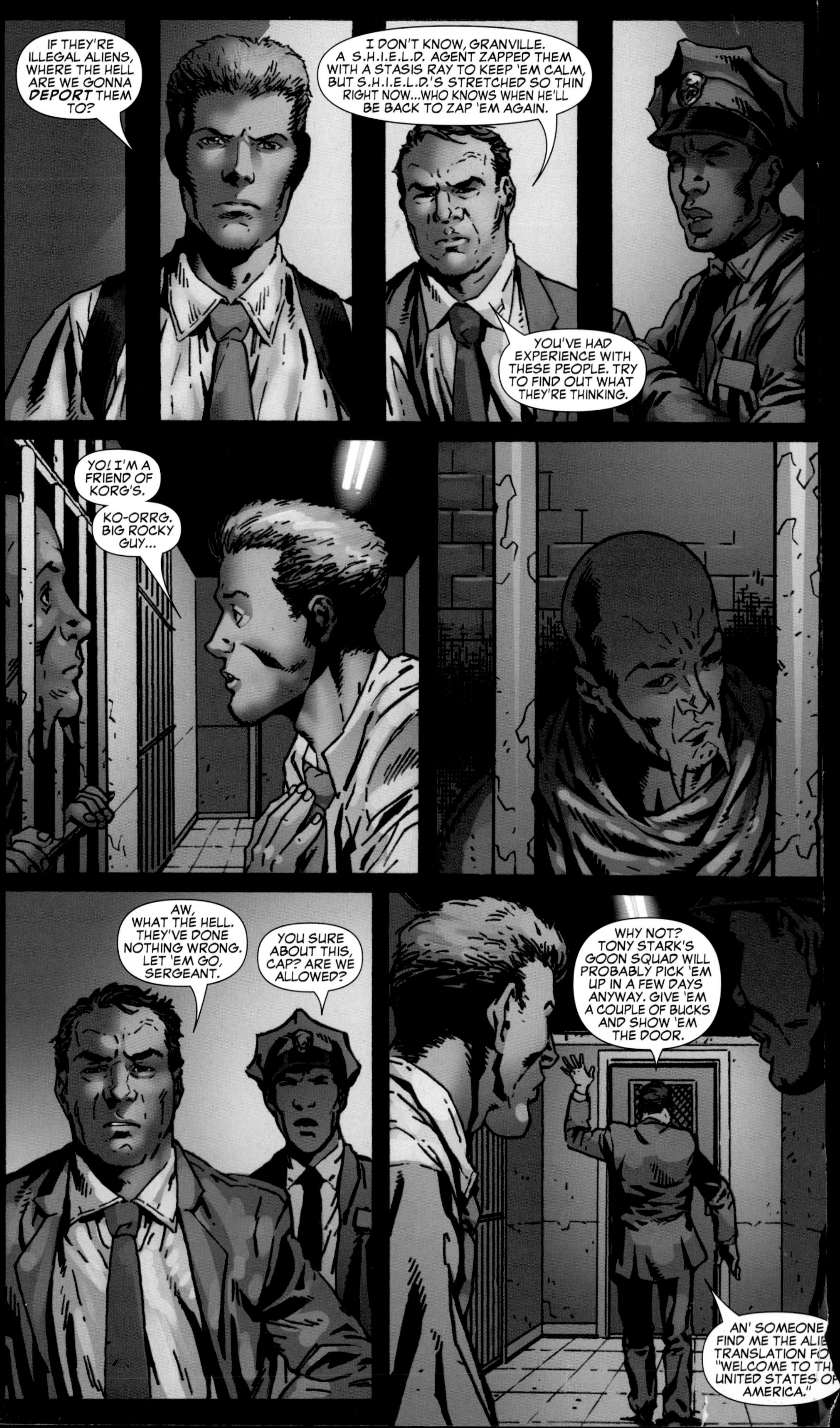
IF THEY'RE ILLEGAL ALIENS, WHERE THE HELL ARE WE GONNA *DEPORT* THEM TO?
I DON'T KNOW, GRANVILLE. A S.H.I.E.L.D. AGENT ZAPPED THEM WITH A STASIS RAY TO KEEP 'EM CALM, BUT S.H.I.E.L.D.'S STRETCHED SO THIN RIGHT NOW...WHO KNOWS WHEN HE'LL BE BACK TO ZAP 'EM AGAIN.
YOU'VE HAD EXPERIENCE WITH THESE PEOPLE. TRY TO FIND OUT WHAT THEY'RE THINKING.
YO! I'M A FRIEND OF KORG'S.
KO-ORRG. BIG ROCKY GUY...
AW, WHAT THE HELL. THEY'VE DONE NOTHING WRONG. LET 'EM GO, SERGEANT.
YOU SURE ABOUT THIS, CAP? ARE WE ALLOWED?
WHY NOT? TONY STARK'S GOON SQUAD WILL PROBABLY PICK 'EM UP IN A FEW DAYS ANYWAY. GIVE 'EM A COUPLE OF BUCKS AND SHOW 'EM THE DOOR.
AN' SOMEONE FIND ME THE ALIE TRANSLATION FO "WELCOME TO TH UNITED STATES O AMERICA."

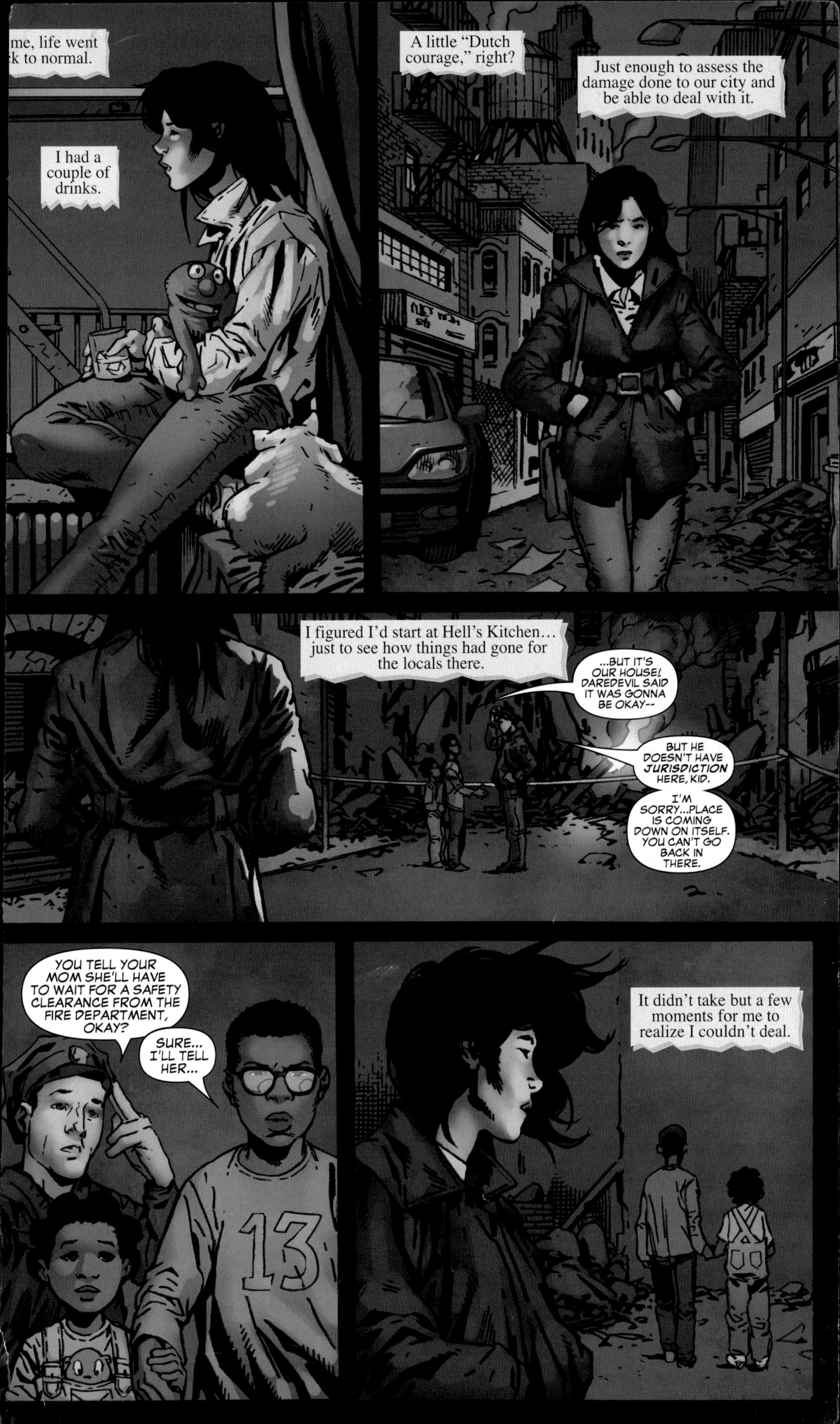

me, life went
k to normal.
I had a couple of drinks.
A little "Dutch courage," right?
Just enough to assess the damage done to our city and be able to deal with it.
I figured I'd start at Hell's Kitchen... just to see how things had gone for the locals there.
...BUT IT'S OUR HOUSE! DAREDEVIL SAID IT WAS GONNA BE OKAY--
BUT HE DOESN'T HAVE JURISDICTION HERE, KID.
I'M SORRY...PLACE IS COMING DOWN ON ITSELF. YOU CAN'T GO BACK IN THERE.
YOU TELL YOUR MOM SHE'LL HAVE TO WAIT FOR A SAFETY CLEARANCE FROM THE FIRE DEPARTMENT, OKAY?
SURE... I'LL TELL HER...
13
It didn't take but a few moments for me to realize I couldn't deal.

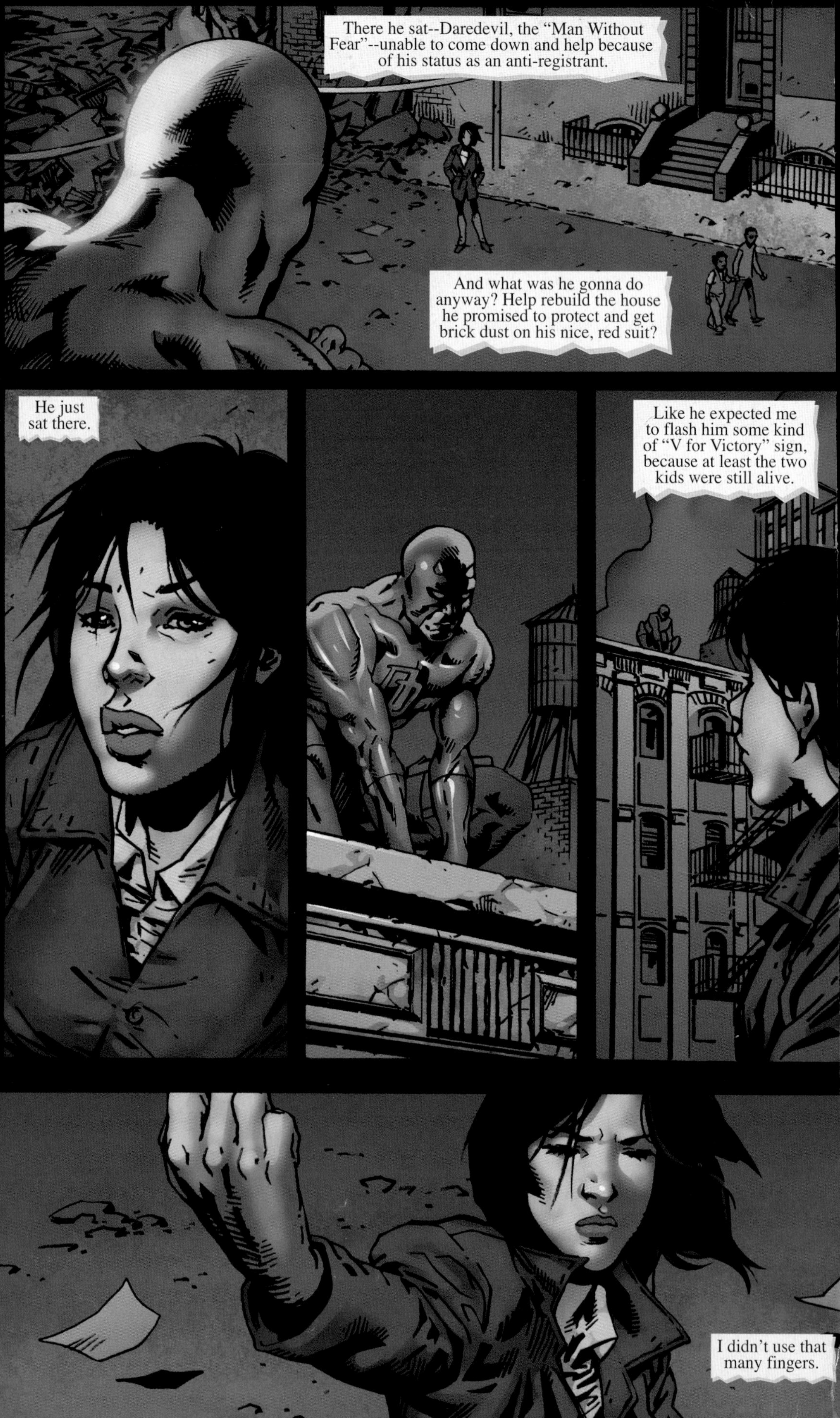
There he sat--Daredevil, the "Man Without Fear"--unable to come down and help because of his status as an anti-registrant.
And what was he gonna do anyway? Help rebuild the house he promised to protect and get brick dust on his nice, red suit?
He just sat there.
Like he expected me to flash him some kind of "V for Victory" sign, because at least the two kids were still alive.
I didn't use that many fingers.

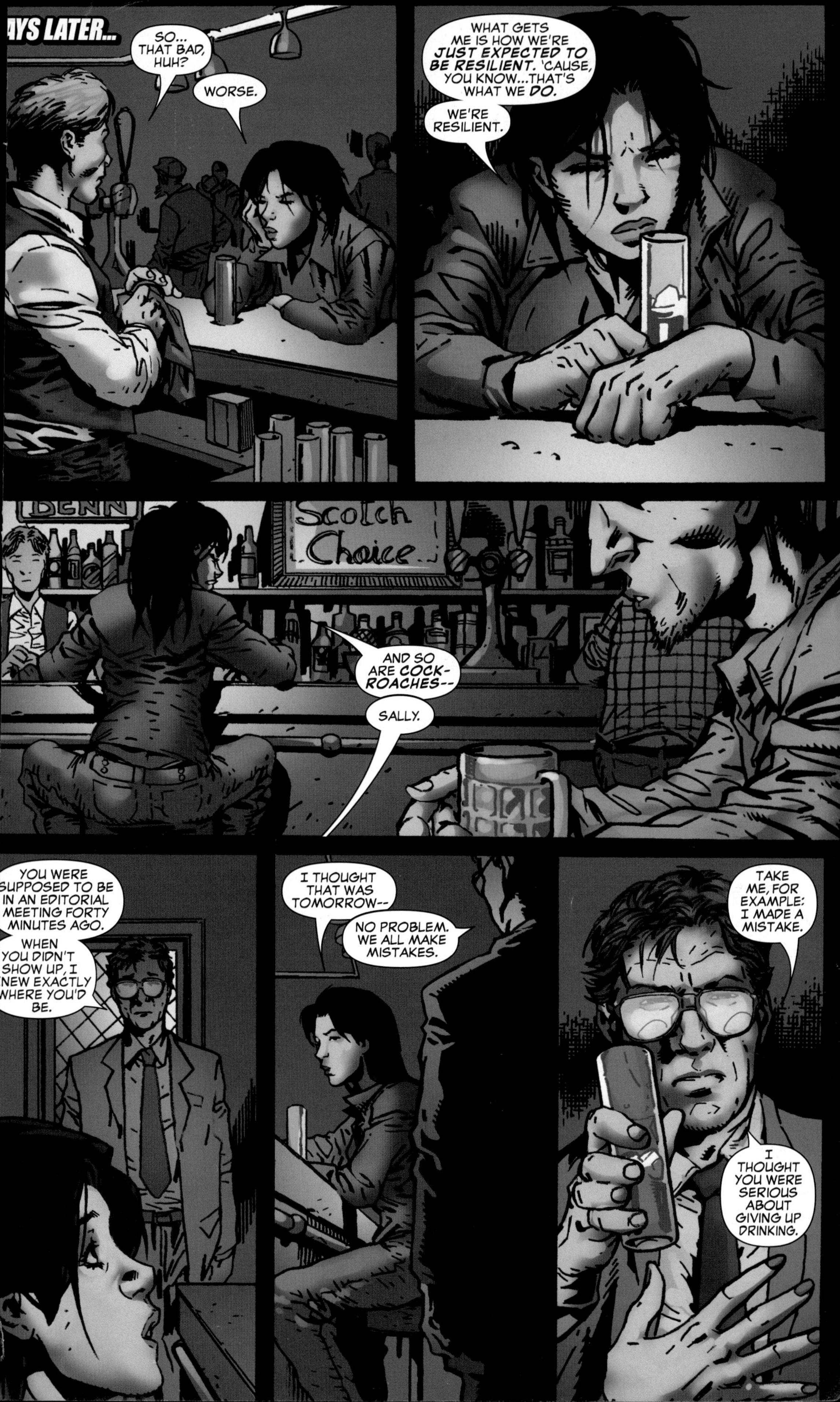
AYS LATER...
SO... THAT BAD, HUH?
WORSE.
WHAT GETS ME IS HOW WE'RE JUST EXPECTED TO BE RESILIENT. 'CAUSE, YOU KNOW...THAT'S WHAT WE DO.
WE'RE RESILIENT.
Scotch Choice
AND SO ARE COCK-ROACHES--
SALLY.
YOU WERE SUPPOSED TO BE IN AN EDITORIAL MEETING FORTY MINUTES AGO.
WHEN YOU DIDN'T SHOW UP, I KNEW EXACTLY WHERE YOU'D BE.
I THOUGHT THAT WAS TOMORROW--
NO PROBLEM. WE ALL MAKE MISTAKES.
TAKE ME, FOR EXAMPLE: I MADE A MISTAKE.
I THOUGHT YOU WERE SERIOUS ABOUT GIVING UP DRINKING.

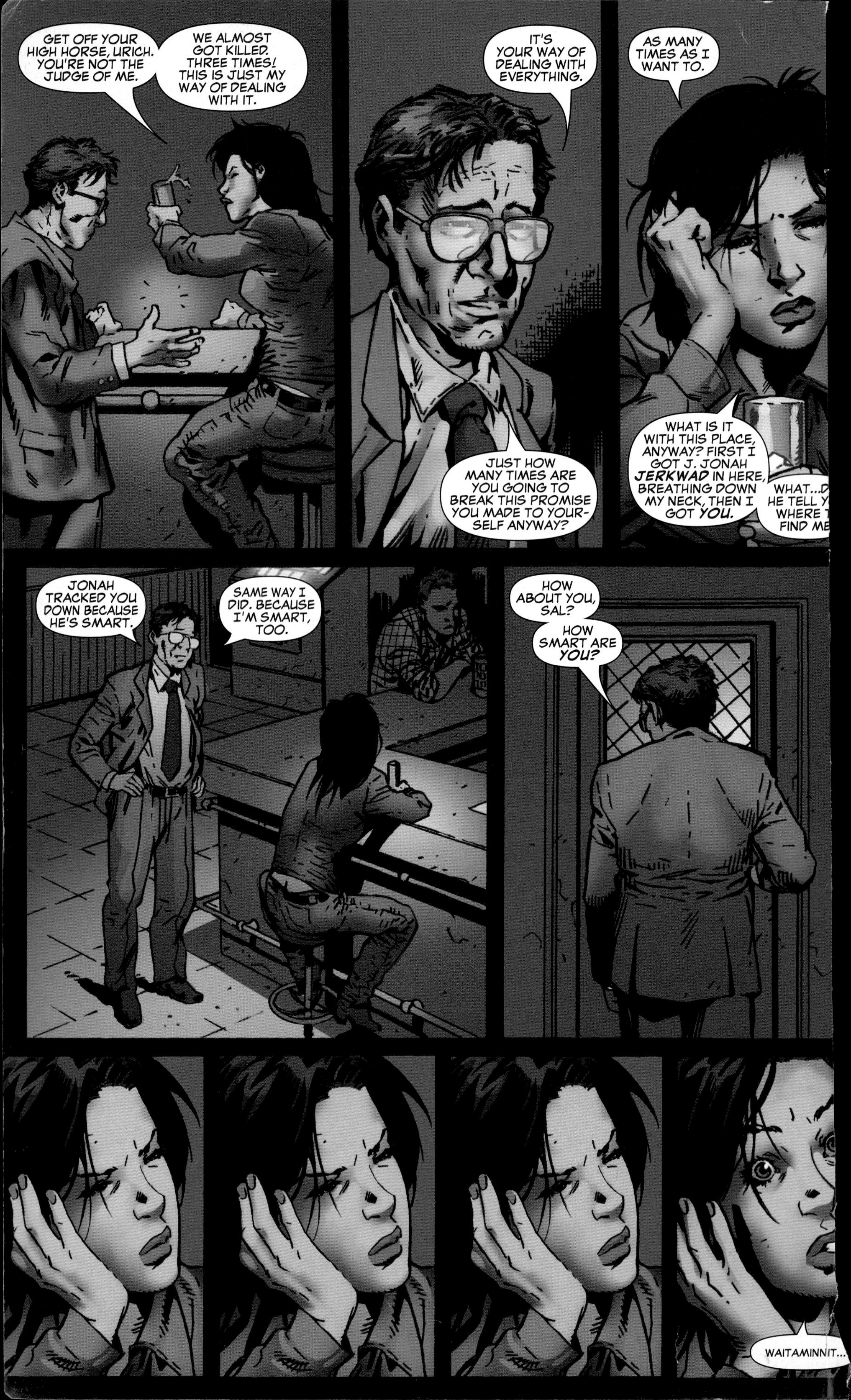
GET OFF YOUR HIGH HORSE, URICH. YOU'RE NOT THE JUDGE OF ME.
WE ALMOST GOT KILLED. THREE TIMES! THIS IS JUST MY WAY OF DEALING WITH IT.
IT'S YOUR WAY OF DEALING WITH EVERYTHING.
JUST HOW MANY TIMES ARE YOU GOING TO BREAK THIS PROMISE YOU MADE TO YOUR-SELF ANYWAY?
AS MANY TIMES AS I WANT TO.
WHAT IS IT WITH THIS PLACE, ANYWAY? FIRST I GOT J. JONAH **JERKWAD** IN HERE, BREATHING DOWN MY NECK, THEN I GOT **YOU.**
WHAT...D HE TELL Y WHERE T FIND ME
JONAH TRACKED YOU DOWN BECAUSE HE'S SMART.
SAME WAY I DID. BECAUSE I'M SMART, TOO.
HOW ABOUT YOU, SAL?
HOW SMART ARE **YOU?**
WAITAMINNIT...

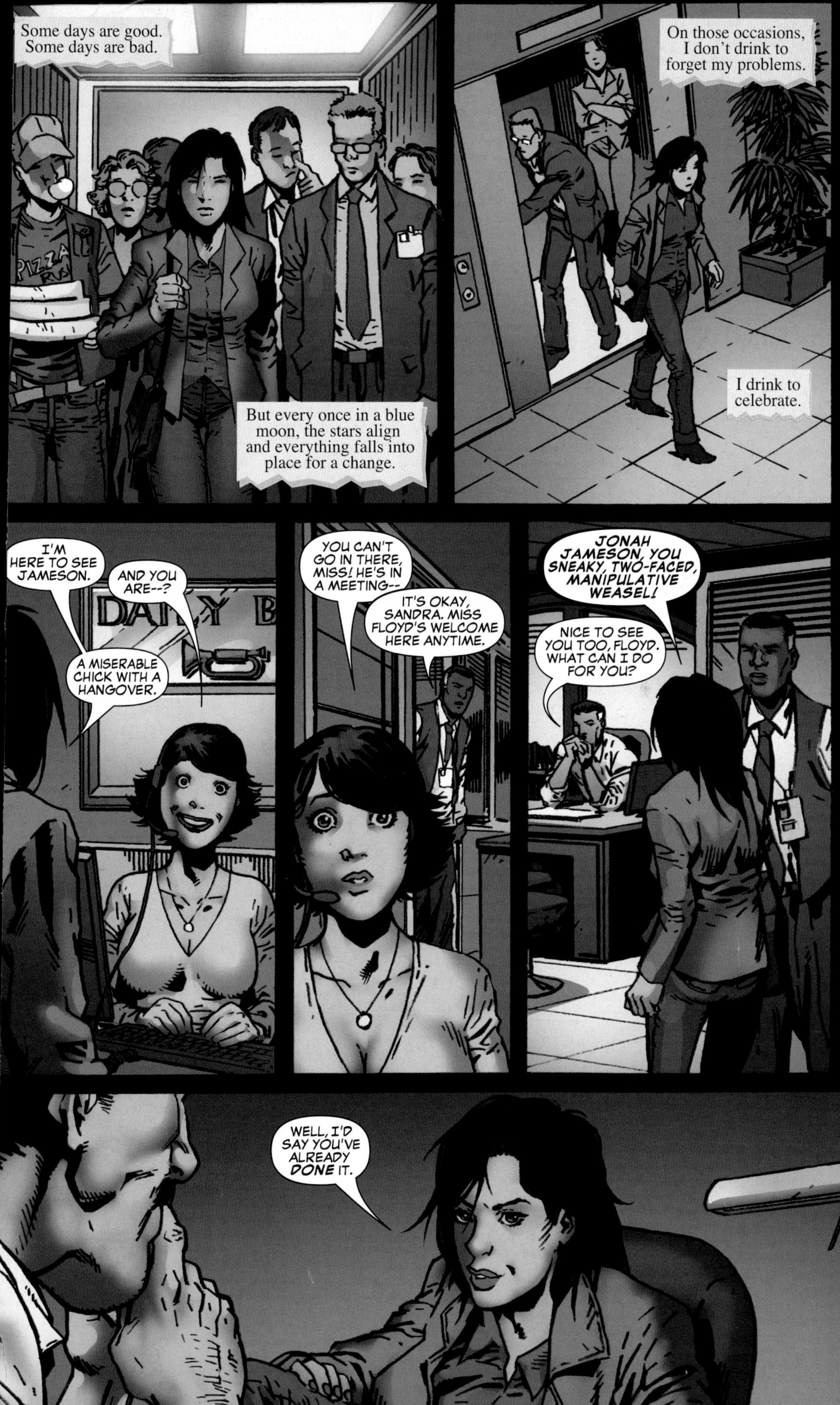
Some days are good. Some days are bad.
But every once in a blue moon, the stars align and everything falls into place for a change.
On those occasions, I don't drink to forget my problems.
I drink to celebrate.
I'M HERE TO SEE JAMESON.
AND YOU ARE--?
A MISERABLE CHICK WITH A HANGOVER.
YOU CAN'T GO IN THERE, MISS! HE'S IN A MEETING--
IT'S OKAY, SANDRA. MISS FLOYD'S WELCOME HERE ANYTIME.
JONAH JAMESON, YOU SNEAKY, TWO-FACED, MANIPULATIVE WEASEL!
NICE TO SEE YOU TOO, FLOYD. WHAT CAN I DO FOR YOU?
WELL, I'D SAY YOU'VE ALREADY DONE IT.

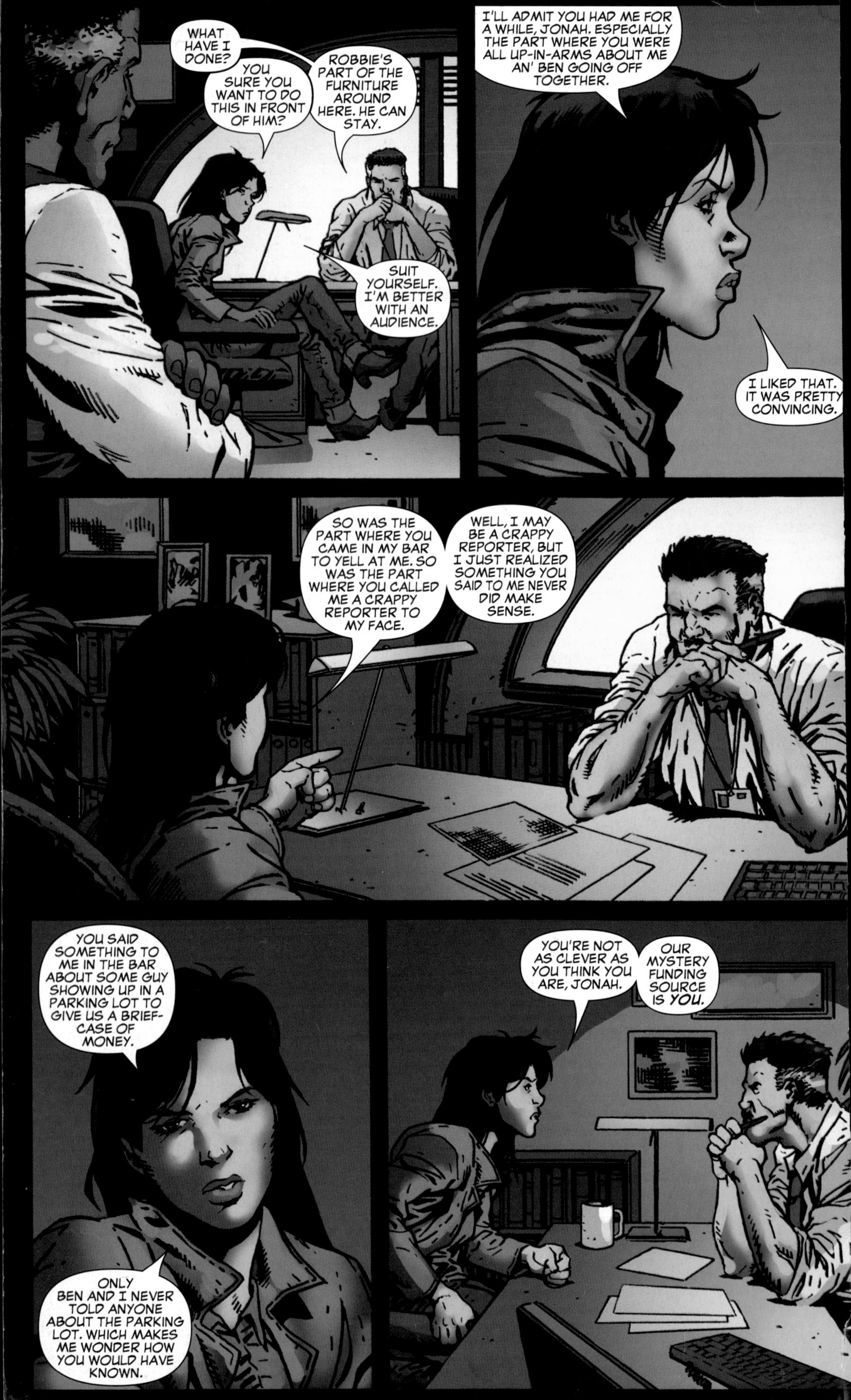
WHAT HAVE I DONE?
YOU SURE YOU WANT TO DO THIS IN FRONT OF HIM?
ROBBIE'S PART OF THE FURNITURE AROUND HERE. HE CAN STAY.
SUIT YOURSELF. I'M BETTER WITH AN AUDIENCE.
I'LL ADMIT YOU HAD ME FOR A WHILE, JONAH. ESPECIALLY THE PART WHERE YOU WERE ALL UP-IN-ARMS ABOUT ME AN' BEN GOING OFF TOGETHER.
I LIKED THAT. IT WAS PRETTY CONVINCING.
SO WAS THE PART WHERE YOU CAME IN MY BAR TO YELL AT ME. SO WAS THE PART WHERE YOU CALLED ME A CRAPPY REPORTER TO MY FACE.
WELL, I MAY BE A CRAPPY REPORTER, BUT I JUST REALIZED SOMETHING YOU SAID TO ME NEVER DID MAKE SENSE.
YOU SAID SOMETHING TO ME IN THE BAR ABOUT SOME GUY SHOWING UP IN A PARKING LOT TO GIVE US A BRIEF-CASE OF MONEY.
ONLY BEN AND I NEVER TOLD ANYONE ABOUT THE PARKING LOT. WHICH MAKES ME WONDER HOW YOU WOULD HAVE KNOWN.
YOU'RE NOT AS CLEVER AS YOU THINK YOU ARE, JONAH.
OUR MYSTERY FUNDING SOURCE IS *YOU*.

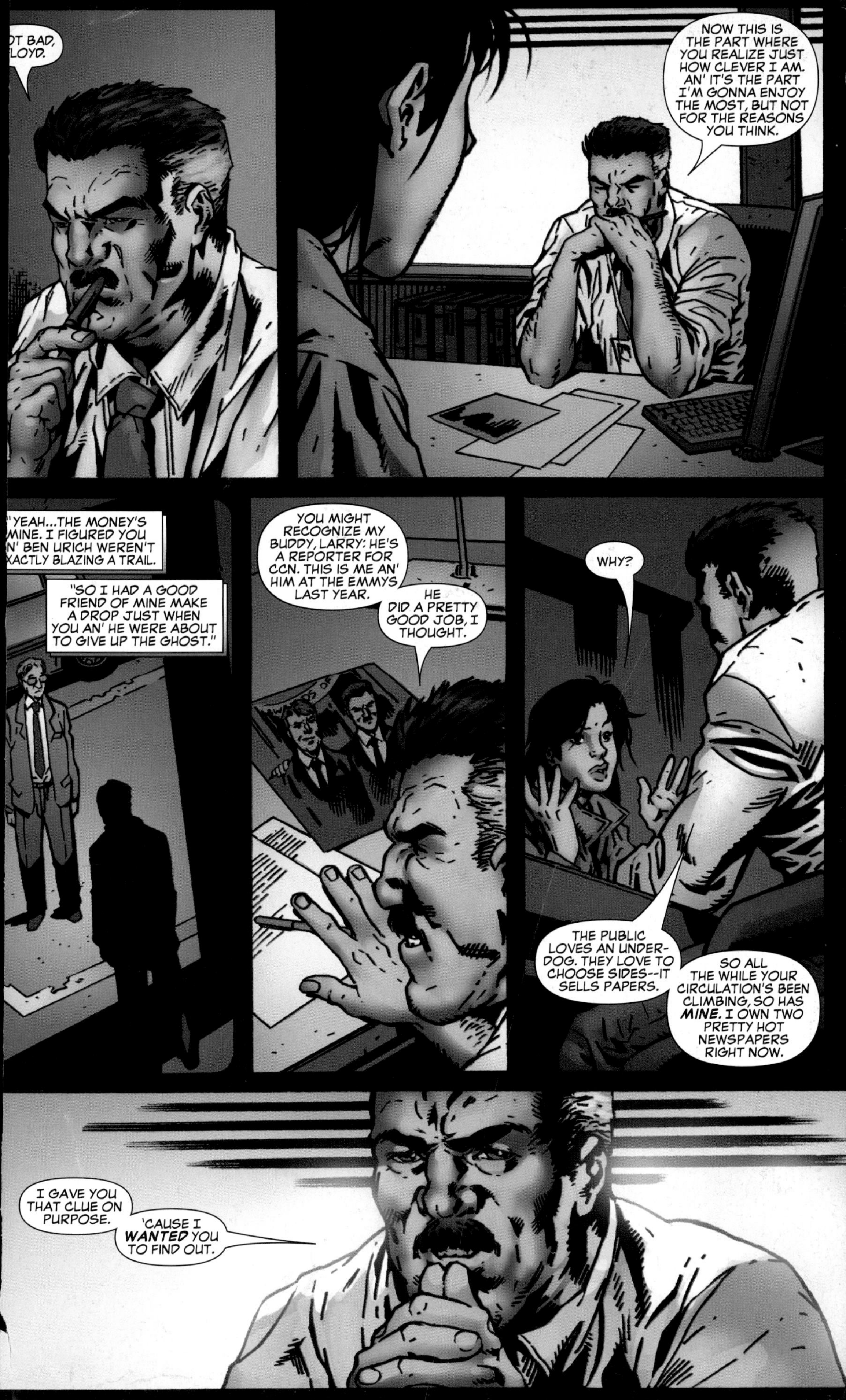
OT BAD, LLOYD.
NOW THIS IS THE PART WHERE YOU REALIZE JUST HOW CLEVER I AM. AN' IT'S THE PART I'M GONNA ENJOY THE MOST, BUT NOT FOR THE REASONS YOU THINK.
"YEAH...THE MONEY'S MINE. I FIGURED YOU AN' BEN URICH WEREN'T EXACTLY BLAZING A TRAIL.
"SO I HAD A GOOD FRIEND OF MINE MAKE A DROP JUST WHEN YOU AN' HE WERE ABOUT TO GIVE UP THE GHOST."
YOU MIGHT RECOGNIZE MY BUDDY, LARRY: HE'S A REPORTER FOR CCN. THIS IS ME AN' HIM AT THE EMMYS LAST YEAR.
HE DID A PRETTY GOOD JOB, I THOUGHT.
WHY?
THE PUBLIC LOVES AN UNDER-DOG. THEY LOVE TO CHOOSE SIDES--IT SELLS PAPERS.
SO ALL THE WHILE YOUR CIRCULATION'S BEEN CLIMBING, SO HAS MINE. I OWN TWO PRETTY HOT NEWSPAPERS RIGHT NOW.
I GAVE YOU THAT CLUE ON PURPOSE.
'CAUSE I WANTED YOU TO FIND OUT.

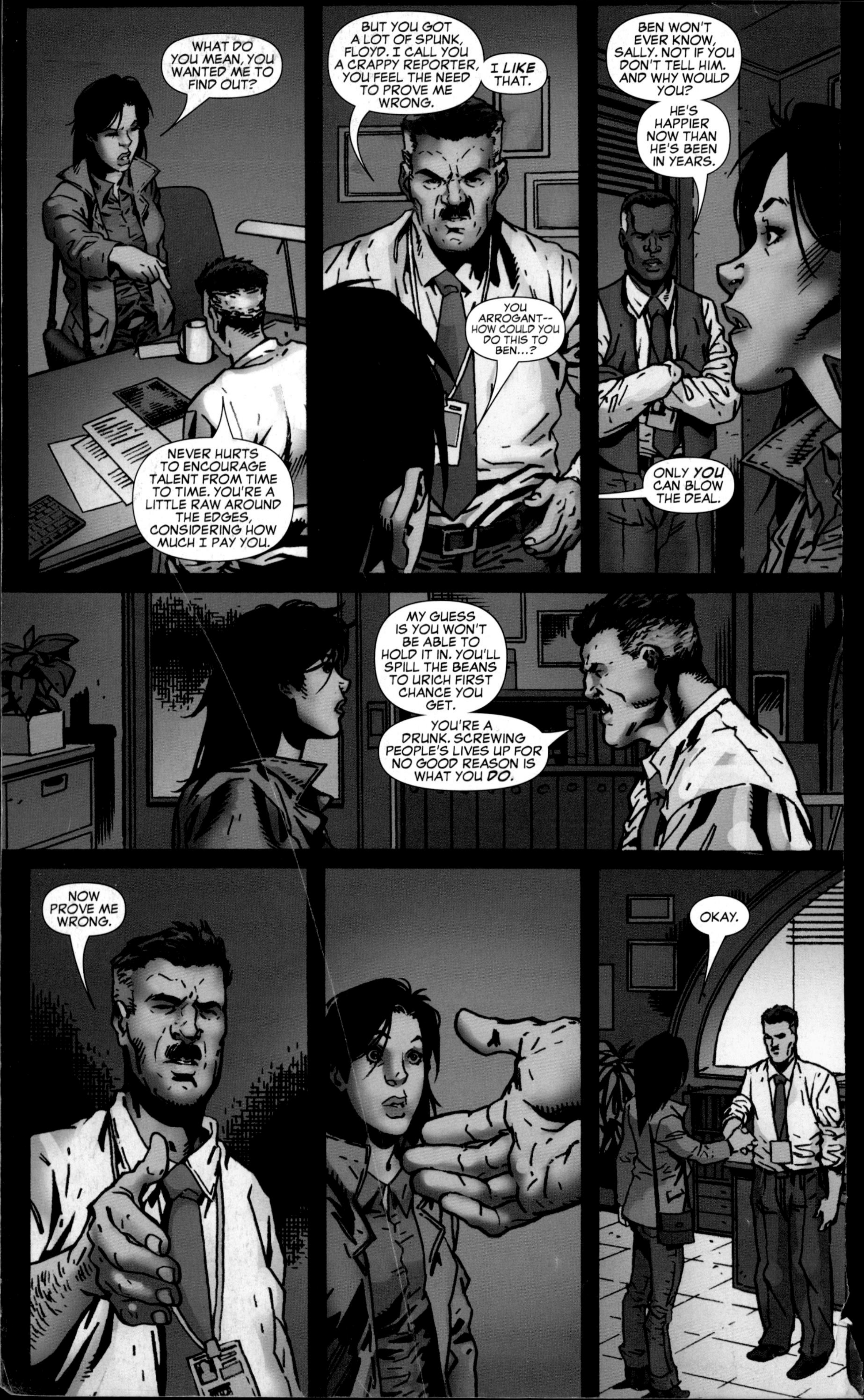
WHAT DO YOU MEAN, YOU WANTED ME TO FIND OUT?
NEVER HURTS TO ENCOURAGE TALENT FROM TIME TO TIME. YOU'RE A LITTLE RAW AROUND THE EDGES, CONSIDERING HOW MUCH I PAY YOU.
BUT YOU GOT A LOT OF SPUNK, FLOYD. I CALL YOU A CRAPPY REPORTER, YOU FEEL THE NEED TO PROVE ME WRONG.
I *LIKE* THAT.
YOU ARROGANT-- HOW COULD YOU DO THIS TO BEN...?
BEN WON'T EVER KNOW, SALLY. NOT IF YOU DON'T TELL HIM. AND WHY WOULD YOU?
HE'S HAPPIER NOW THAN HE'S BEEN IN YEARS.
ONLY *YOU* CAN BLOW THE DEAL.
MY GUESS IS YOU WON'T BE ABLE TO HOLD IT IN. YOU'LL SPILL THE BEANS TO URICH FIRST CHANCE YOU GET.
YOU'RE A DRUNK. SCREWING PEOPLE'S LIVES UP FOR NO GOOD REASON IS WHAT YOU *DO.*
NOW PROVE ME WRONG.
OKAY.

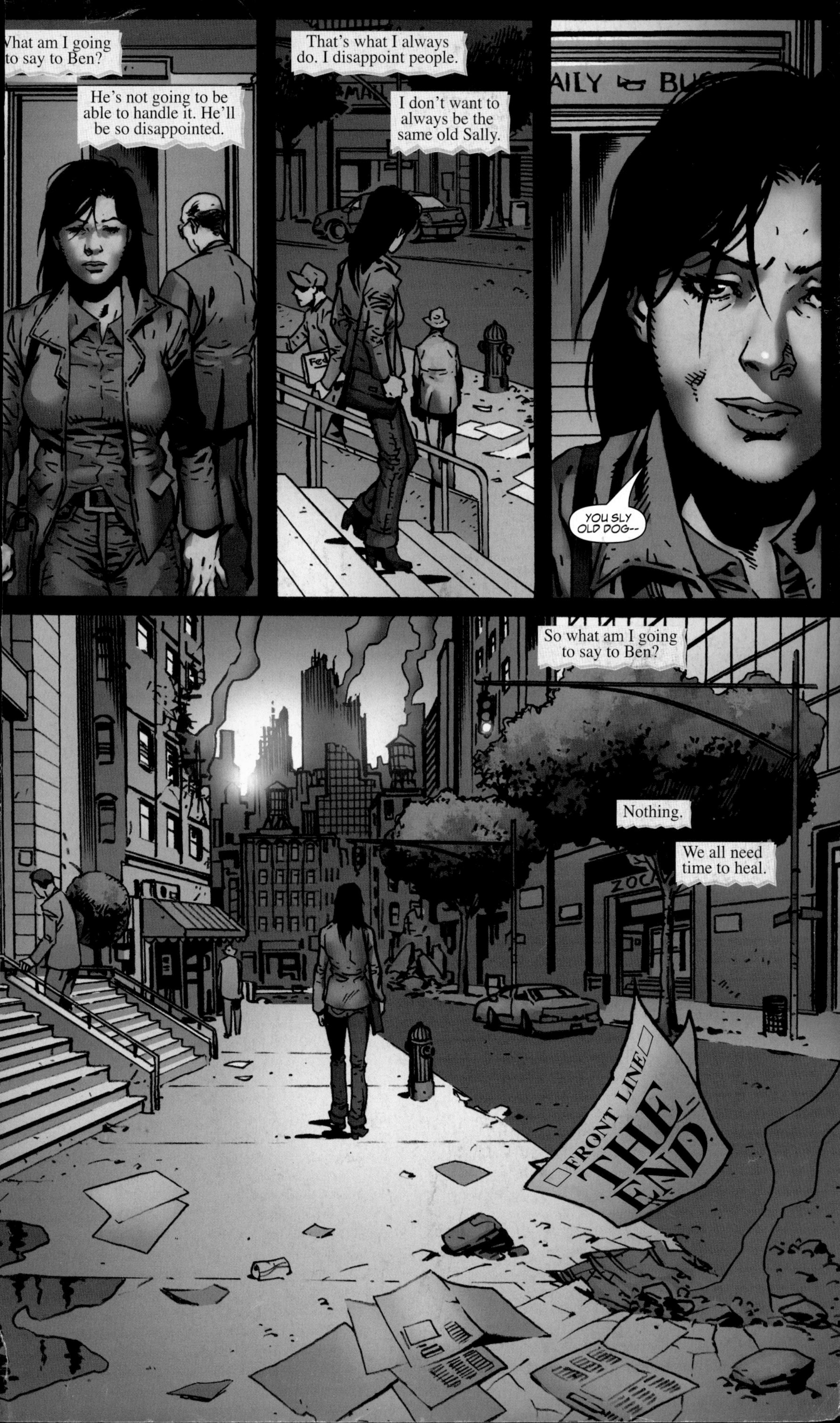
What am I going to say to Ben?
He's not going to be able to handle it. He'll be so disappointed.
That's what I always do. I disappoint people.
I don't want to always be the same old Sally.
YOU SLY OLD DOG--
So what am I going to say to Ben?
Nothing.
We all need time to heal.
FRONT LINE
THE END

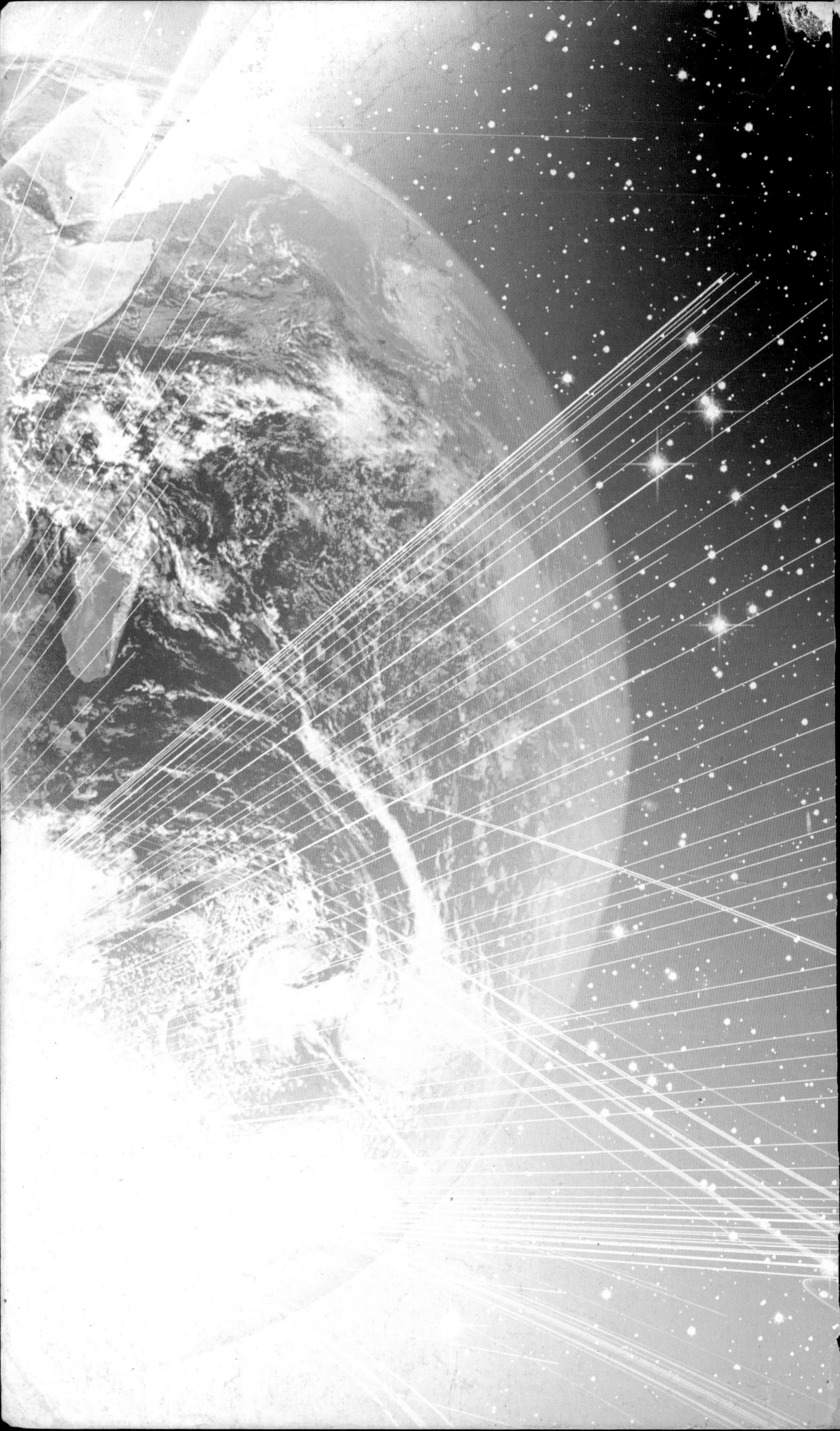